OUR
DAILY
BREAD

OUR
DAILY
BREAD

Timeless Wisdom to
Nourish the Soul

BY
ELISABETH DAY DOUGLAS

BLACK DOG
& LEVENTHAL
PUBLISHERS
NEW YORK

Published by
Black Dog & Leventhal Publishers, Inc.
151 West 19th Street
New York, NY 10011

Distributed by
Workman Publishing Company
708 Broadway
New York, NY 10003

Design by 27.12 Design Ltd., NYC

Manufactured in Hong Kong

ISBN: 1-57912-213-2

g f e d c b a

Library of Congress Cataloging-in-Publication Data

Douglas, Elisabeth Day.
    Our daily bread : timeless wisdom to nourish the soul / by Elisabeth Day Douglas.
       p. cm.
    ISBN 1-57912-213-2
       1. Devotional calendars. I. Title.

BV4810 .D68 2001
242'.2--dc21

                                   2001037667

PART I

Inspiration for Each Day of the Year

PART II

*Words of Wisdom
for the Times of Your Life*

Inspiration for Each Day of the Year

January 1

The least of you will become a thousand,
the smallest a mighty nation:
I am the Lord; in its time I will do this swiftly.
ISAIAH 60:22

Build thee more stately mansions, O my soul,
As the swift seasons roll!
Leave thy low-vaulted past
Let each new temple, nobler than the last,
Shut thee from heaven with a dome more vast,
Till thou at length art free,
Leaving thine outgrown shell by life's unresting sea!
O. W. HOLMES

That daily quarter of an hour, for now forty years or more, I am sure has been one of the greatest sustenances and sources of calm for my life. Of course, such "reading" is hardly reading in the ordinary sense of the word at all. As well could you call the letting a very slowly dissolving lozenge melt imperceptibly in your mouth "eating." Such reading is, of course, meant as directly as possible to feed the heart, to fortify the will—to put these into contact with God—thus, by the book, to get away from the book to the realities it suggests—the longer the better. And above all, perhaps it excludes, by its very object, all criticism, all going off on one's own thoughts as, in any way, antagonistic to the book's thoughts; and this, not by any unreal (and most dangerous) forcing of oneself to swallow, or to "like." What does not attract one's simply humble self, but(on the contrary) by a gentle passing by, by an instinctive ignoring of what does not suit one's soul. This passing by should be without a trace of would—be objective judging; during such reading we are out simply and solely to feed our own poor soul, such as it is hic et nunc. What repels or confuses us now may be the very food of angels; it may even still become the light to our own poor souls in this world's dimness. We must exclude none of such possibilities, the "infant crying for the fight" has nothing to do with more than just humbly finding, and then using, the little light that it requires.

I need not say that I would not restrict you to only one quarter of an hour a day. You might find two such helpful. But I would not exceed the fifteen minutes at any one time; you would sink to ordinary reading, if you did.
~ BARON FRIEDRICH VON HUGEL

January 2

One thing I ask of the Lord,
this is what I seek:
that I may dwell in the house of the lord
all the days of my life,
to gaze upon the beauty of the Lord
and to seek him in his temple.
For in the day of trouble,
he will keep me safe in his dwelling;
he will hide me in the shelter of his tabernacle
and set me high upon a rock.
PSALMS 27:4-5

The grass withers and the flowers fall
but the word of our God stands forever.
ISAIAH 40:8

With grateful hearts the past we own;
The future, all to us unknown,
We to Thy guardian care commit,
And peaceful leave before Thy feet.
P. DODDRIDGE

We are like to Him with whom there is no past or future, with whom a day is as a thousand years, and a thousand years as one day, when we do our work in the great present, leaving both past and future to Him to whom they are ever present, and fearing nothing, because He is in our future as much as He is in our past, as much as, and far more than, we can feel Him to be in our present. Partakers thus of the divine nature, resting in that perfect All-in-all in whom our nature is eternal too, we walk without fear, full of hope and courage and strength to do His will, waiting for the endless good which He is always giving as fast as He can get us able to take it in.

~ GEORGE MACDONALD

January 3

. . . and your strength will equal your days.
DEUTERONOMY 33:25

If as a flower doth spread and die,
Thou would'st extend me to some good,
Before I were by frost's extremity
Nipt in the bud;
The sweetness and the praise were Thine;
But the extension and the room,
Which in Thy garland I should fill, were mine,
At Thy great doom.

For as Thou dost impart Thy grace,
The greater shall our glory be.
The measure of our joys is in this place,
The stuff with Thee.

Let me not languish then, and spend
A life as barren to Thy praise
As is the dust, to that which life doth tend,
But with delays.

All things are busy; only I
Neither bring honey with the bees,
Nor flowers to make that, nor the husbandry
To water these.

I am no link of Thy great chain,
But all my company is a weed,
Lord! place me in Thy concert; give one strain
To my poor reed.
GEORGE HERBERT

He that hath so many causes of joy, and so great, is very much in love with sorrow and peevishness, who loses all these pleasures, and chooses to sit down upon his little handful of thorns. Enjoy the blessings of this day, if God sends them; and the evils of it bear patiently and sweetly: for this day is only ours, we are dead to yesterday, and we are not yet born to the morrow. But if we look abroad, and bring into one day's thoughts the evil of many, certain and uncertain, what will be and what will never be, our load will be as intolerable as it is unreasonable.

~ JEREMY TAYLOR

January 4

If we sin, we are Thine, knowing Thy power: but we will not sin, knowing that we are counted Thine. For to know Thee is perfect righteousness yea, to know Thy power is the root of immortality.
WISDOM OF SOLOMON 15:2-3

Wilt thou forgive that sinn, by which I have wonne
Others to sinn, and made my sinn their dore?
Wilt Thou forgive that sinn which I did shunne
A yeare, or twoe, but wallowed in a score?
. . . Sweare by thy selfe that at my Death thy Sunn
Shall shine as it shines nowe, and heretorfore;
And having done that, thou hast done,
I have noe more.
JOHN DONNE

Without voice and without opening of lips was formed in my soul this word: "Herewith is the fiend overcome.". . . For this sight I laughed mightily, and that made them to laugh that were about me. And their laughing was pleasing to me. I thought I would mine—even Christians had seen as I saw; then should they all have laughed with me. But I saw not Christ laugh. Nevertheless, He is pleased that we laugh in comforting of us, and are joying in God that the fiend is overcome . . . In this our Lord brought to my mind and showed me a part of the fiend's malice and the whole of his weakness; and for that He showed me that His Passion is the overcoming of the fiend. . . . And after this I fell into seriousness and said: "I see, I see three things-game, scorn, and earnest. I see game, that the fiend is overcome. And I see scorn, that God scorns him, and he shall be scorned. And I see earnest, that he is overcome by the Passion of our Lord Jesus Christ, and by His Death that was done full earnestly and with sad travail."

~ LADY JULIAN OF NORWICH

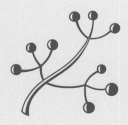

January 5

. . . and to present her to himself as a radiant church, without stain or wrinkle or any other blemish, but holy and blameless.
EPHESIANS 5:27

. . . you also, like living stones, are being built into a spiritual house.
I PETER 2:5

The Doorkeeper

To keep God's door
I am not fit.
I would not ask -for more
Than this
To stand or sit
Upon the threshold of God's House
Out of the reach of sin,
To open wide His door
To those who come,
To welcome Home
His children and His poor:
To wait and watch
The gladness on the face of those
That are within:
Sometimes to catch
A glimpse or trace of those
I love the best, and know
That all I failed to be,
And all I failed to do,
Has not sufficed
To bar them from the
Tree Of Life, the Paradise of God,
The Face of Christ.
JOHN W. TAYLOR

To whatever worlds He carries our souls when they shall pass out of these imprisoning bodies, in those worlds these souls of ours shall find themselves part of the same great Temple; for it belongs not to this earth alone. There can be no end of the universe where God is, to which that growing Temple does not reach, the Temple of a creation to be wrought at last into a perfect utterance of God by a Perfect obedience to God.

~ PHILLIPS BROOKS

January 6

In all ages entering into holy souls, she [Wisdom] maketh them friends of God, and prophets.
WISDOM OF SOLOMON 7:27

Meanwhile with every son and saint of Thine Along the glorious line, Sitting by turns beneath Thy sacred feet

We'll hold communion sweet,
Know them by look and voice, and thank them all
For helping us in thrall,
For words of hope, and bright examples given
To shew through moonless skies that there is light in heaven.

J. KEBLE

In Thee therefore, O Lord God, I place my whole hope and refuge; on Thee I rest my tribulation and anguish; for I find all to be weak and inconstant, whatsoever I behold out of Thee. For many friends cannot profit, nor strong helpers assist, nor prudent counsellors give a profitable answer, nor any precious substance deliver, nor any place, however retired and lonely, give shelter, unless Thou Thyself dost assist, help, strengthen, console, instruct, and guard us. For all things that seem to belong to the attainment of peace and felicity, without Thee, are nothing, and do bring in truth no felicity at all. Thou therefore art the End of all that is good, the Height of life, the Depth of all that can be spoken; and to hope in Thee above all things is the strongest comfort of Thy servants. To Thee therefore do I lift up mine eyes; in Thee, my God, the Father of mercies, do I put my trust. . . . Protect and keep the soul of me the meanest of Thy servants amidst so many dangers of this corruptible life, and by Thy grace accompanying me direct it along the way of peace to its home of everlasting brightness.

~ THOMAS A. KEMPIS

Do not think it wasted time to submit yourself to any influence which may bring upon you any noble feeling.

~ JOHN RUSKIN

January 7

. . . and his incomparably great power for us who believe.
That power is like the working of his mighty strength.
EPHESIANS 1:19

Look up, my soul, with cheerful eye,
See where the great Redeemer stands
Thy glorious Advocate on high,
With precious incense in his hands.

He sweetens every humble groan,
He recommends each broken prayer;
Recline thy hope on him alone,
Whose power and love forbid despair.

ANONYMOUS

A root set in the finest soil, in the best climate, and blessed with all that sun and air and rain can do for it, is not in so sure a way of its growth to perfection, as every man may whose spirit aspires after all that which God ready and infinitely desirous to give him. For the sun meets not the springing bud that stretches towards him with half that certainty, as God, the source of all good, communicates Himself to the soul that longs to partake of Him.

~ WILLIAM LAW

January 8

Therefore, as we have opportunity,
let us do good unto all people. . . .
GALATIANS 6:10

Keep on loving each other as brothers.
HEBREWS 13:1

I ask Thee for a thoughtful love,
Through constant watching wise,
To meet the glad with joyful smiles,
And to wipe the weeping eyes,
And a heart at leisure from itself,
To soothe and sympathize.
A. L. WARING

January 9

In everything that he undertook in the service God's temple and in obedi-
ence to the law and the commands, he sought his God and worked whole-
heartedly. And so he prospered.
2 CHRONICLES 31:21

Then they asked him,
"What must we do to do the works the works God requires?"
JOHN 6:28

Not by your words alone,
But by your actions show
How much from him you have received,
How much to him you owe.
ANONYMOUS

Begin the day by offering it and yourself to God. Look at the day as an
individual thing that begins and ends with completeness in itself; then
take this thing, this day and offer it to God to be a day for His use. . . .
The day at once becomes a unity and life becomes unified. However many
distracting details come into the day, both mind and emotion are dominat-
ed, not by them, but by the sense that you have only one thing to do—
namely, to act in obedience to God with regard to them.
~ GEORGE S. STEWART

January 10

From the rising of the sun to the place where it sets,
the name of the Lord is to be praised.
PSALMS 113:3

Whoever tries to keep his life shall lose it,
and whoever loses his life will preserve it.
LUKE 17:33

O Lord I my best desires fulfil. And help me to resign
Life, health, and comfort, to Thy will,
And make Thy pleasure mine.
WILLIAM COWPER

To love sufferings and afflictions for the love of God is the highest point of most holy charity; for in this there is nothing lovable save the love of God only; there is a great contradiction on the part of our nature; and not only do we forsake all pleasures, but we embrace torments and labours. Our mortal enemy knew well what was the farthest and finest act of love when, having heard from the mouth of God that "Job was a perfect and upright man, one that feareth God, and escheweth evil" he made no account of this in comparison with bearing afflictions, by which he made the last and surest trial of this great servant of God; and to make these afflictions extreme he formed them out of the loss of all his goods, and of all his children, abandonment by all his friends, an arrogant contradiction by his most intimate associates . . . to which he added a collection of almost all human diseases, and particularly a universal, cruel, infectious, and horrible plague. And yet there is the great Job, king of all miserable creatures, seated upon a dunghill as upon the throne of misery, covered with sores, ulcers, and corruption, as with royal robes suitable to the quality of his royalty, with such great abjection and annihilation that, if he had not spoken, it could scarcely have been discovered if Job were a man reduced to a dunghill or the dunghill a corruption in the form of a man. Now, say I, hear the great Job crying out: "Shall we receive good at the hand of God, and shall we not receive evil?"

~ ST. FRANCIS DE SALES

January 11

I will be glad and rejoice in your love;
for you saw my affliction and knew
the anguish of my soul.
PSALMS 31:7

Nay, all by Thee is ordered, chosen, planned
Each drop that fills my daily cup; Thy hand
Prescribes for ills none else can understand.
All, all is known to Thee.
A. L. NEWTON

The remarkable thing about the way in which people talk about God, or about their relation to God, is that it seems to escape them completely that God hears what they are saying. A man says: "At the moment I have not the time or the necessary recollection to think about God, but later on perhaps." Or better still—a young man says, "I am too young now; first of all I will enjoy life-and then." Would it be possible to talk like that if one realized that God heard one?

~ SØREN KIERKEGAARD

January 12

*May the words of my mouth and the meditation of
my heart, be pleasing in your sight,
O Lord, my Rock and my Redeemer.*
PSALMS 19:14

*The thoughts that in our hearts keep place,
Lord, make a holy, heavenly throng,
And steep in innocence and grace
The issue of each guarded tongue.*
T. H. GILL

. . . observe for thyself what place best agrees with thy spirit; whether within doors, or without. Isaac's example in "going out to meditate in the field" will, I believe, best suit with most. Our Lord so much used a solitary garden that even Judas, when he came to betray Him, knew where to find Him: and though He took His disciples thither with Him, yet He was "withdrawn from them" for more secret devotions. . . . So that Christ had His accustomed place, and consequently accustomed duty, and so must we; He hath a place that is solitary, whither He retireth Himself, even from His own disciples, and so must we; His meditations go farther than His words, they affect and pierce His heart and soul, and so must ours. Only there is a wide difference in the object: Christ meditates on the sufferings that our sins had deserved, so that the wrath of His Father passed through all His soul; but we are to meditate on the glory He hath purchased, that the love of the Father, and the joy of the Spirit, may enter at our thoughts, revive our affections, and overflow our souls.

~ RICHARD BAXTER

January 13

*Brothers,
do not slander one another.*
JAMES 4:2

*Get rid of all bitterness, rage and anger,
brawling and slander,
along with every form of malice.*
EPHESIANS 4:31

*If aught good thou canst not say
Of thy brother, foe, or friend,
Take thou, then, the silent way,
lest in word thou shouldst offend.*
ANONYMOUS

Because others are weak, should we be less careful to give them their due? You who complain so much of what others make you suffer, do you think that you cause others no pain? You who are so annoyed at your neighbour's defects, are you perfect? How astonished you would be if those whom you call evil at should make all the comments that they might upon you. But even if the whole world were to bear testimony in your favour, God, who knows all, who has seen all your faults, could confound you with a word; and does it never come into your mind to fear lest He should demand of you why you had not exercised towards your brother a little of that mercy which He, who is your Master, so abundantly bestows on you?

~ FENELON

January 14

I urge, then, first of all, that requests, prayers, intercession and thanksgiving be made for everyone—for kings and all those in authority, that we may live peaceful and quiet lives in all godliness and holiness.
1 TIMOTHY 2:1-2

Oh let my trembling soul be still,
While darkness veils this mortal eye,
And wait thy wise, thy holy will
all is well-since ruled by thee.
ANONYMOUS

If we are really, and always, and equally ready to do whatsoever the King appoints, all the trials and vexations arising from any change in His appointments, great or small, simply do not exist. If He appoints me to work there, shall I lament that I am not to work here? If He appoints me to wait indoors to-day, am I to be annoyed because I am not to work out-of-doors? If I meant to write His messages this morning, shall I grumble because He sends interrupting visitors, rich or poor, to whom I am to speak them, or "show kindness for His sake, or at least obey His command, Be courteous"? If all my members are really at His disposal, why should I be put out if to-day's appointment is some simple work for my hands or errands for my feet, instead of some seemingly more important doing of head or tongue?

~ F. R. HAVERGAL

January 15

Your word is a lamp to my feet and a light for my path.
PSALMS 119:105

Between us and Thyself remove
Whatever hindrances may be,
That so our inmost heart may prove
A holy temple, meet for Thee.
LATIN MASS OF 15TH CENTURY

What is Paradise? All things that are; for all are goodly and Pleasant, and therefore may fitly be called a Paradise. It is said also that Paradise is an outer court Of Heaven. Even, so this world is verily an outer court of the Eternal or of Eternity; and specially is this true of whatever in time, of whatever temporal thing or creature, manifesteth or remindeth us of God or Eternity; for the creatures are a guide and a path unto God and Eternity. Thus this world is an outer court of Eternity, and therefore it may well be called a Paradise, for it is such in truth. And in this Paradise all things are lawful save one tree and the fruits thereof That is to say: Of all things that are, nothing is forbidden and nothing is contrary to God but one thing only: that is self-will, or to will otherwise than as the Eternal Will would have it. For God saith to Adam, that is, to every man, "Whatever thou art, or doest, or leavest undone, or whatever cometh to Pass is all lawful and not forbidden if it be not done from or according to thy will, but for the sake of and according to My Will. But all that is done from thine own will is contrary to the Eternal Will."

It is not that every work which is thus wrought is in itself contrary to the Eternal Will, but in so far as it is wrought from a different will, or otherwise than from the Eternal and Divine Will.

~ THEOLOGIA GERMANICA

January 16

I have fought the good fight, I have finished the race, I have kept the faith. Now there is in store for me the crown of righteousness, which the Lord, the righteous Judge, will give to me on that day—and not only to me, but also to all who have longed for his appearing.
2 TIMOTHY 4:7-8

When sorrow all our heart would ask,
We need not shun our daily task,
And hide ourselves for calm;
The herbs we seek to heal our woe
Familiar by our path way grow,
Our common air is balm.
J. KEBLE

Oh, when we turn away from some duty or some fellow-creature, saying that our hearts are too sick and sore with some great yearning of our own, we may often sever the line on which a divine message was coming to us. We shut out the man, and we shut out the angel who had sent him on to open the door . . . There is a plan working in our lives; and if we keep our hearts quiet and our eyes open, it all works together; and, if we don't, it all fights together, and goes on fighting till it comes right, somehow, some-where.

~ ANNIE KEARY

January 17

I consider that our present sufferings are not comparing
with the glory that will be revealed in us.
ROMANS 8:18

We take with solemn thankfulness Our burden up, nor ask it less,
And count it joy that even we
May suffer, serve, or wait for Thee,
Whose will be done!
J. G. WHITTIER

Now if they ask, Why then did He not appear by means of other and nobler parts of creation, and use some nobler instrument, as the sun, or moon, or stars, or fire, or air, instead of man merely? Let them know that the Lord came not to make a display, but to heal and teach those who were suffering. For the way for one aiming at display would be just to appear and to dazzle the beholders; but for one seeking to heal and teach the way is, not simply to sojourn here, but to give himself to the aid of those in want, and to appear as they who need him can bear it; that he may not, by exceeding the requirements of the sufferers, trouble the very persons that need him, rendering God's appearance useless to them. Now nothing in God's creation had gone astray with regard to their notions of God save man only. Why, neither sun nor moon nor heaven nor the stars nor water nor air had swerved from their order: but knowing their Artificer and Sovereign, the Word, they remain as they were made. But men alone, having rejected what was good, then devised things of nought instead of the truth and have ascribed the honour due to God and their knowledge of Him to demons and men in the shape of stones. With reason, then, since it were unworthy of the Divine Goodness to overlook so grave a matter, while yet men were not able to recognize Him as ordering and guiding the whole, He takes to Himself as an instrument a part of the whole, the human body, and unites Himself with that, in order that since men could not recognize Him in the whole, they should not fail to know Him in the part; and since they could not look up to His invisible power, might be able at any rate, from what resembled themselves, to reason to Him and to contemplate Him.

~ ST. ATHANASIUS

January 18

God is our refuge and strength, an ever-present help in trouble.
Therefore we will not fear, though the earth give way
and the mountains fall into the heart of the sea, though its waters roar and
foam and the mountains quake with their surging.

There is a river whose streams make glad the city of God, the holy place
where the Most High dwells. God is within her, she will not fall; God will
help her at break of day. Nations are in an uproar,
kingdoms fall; he lifts his voice, the earth melts.

PSALMS 46:1-6

Grave on thy heart each past "red-letter day"!
Forget not all the sunshine of the way
By which the Lord hath led thee; answered prayers,
And joys unasked, strange blessings, lifted cares,
Grand promise-echoes! Thus thy life shall be
One record of His love and faithfulness to thee.

F. R. HAVERGAL

What do I love, when I love Thee? Not beauty of bodies, nor the fair harmony of time, nor the brightness of the light so gladsome to our eyes, nor sweet melodies of varied songs, nor the fragrant smell of flowers and ointments and spices, nor manna and honey, nor limbs acceptable to embracements of flesh. None of these I love, when I love my God; and yet I love a kind of light, and melody, and fragrance, and meat, and embracement, when I love my God—the light, melody, fragrance, meat, embracement of my inner man; where there shineth unto my soul what space cannot contain, and there soundeth what time beareth not away, and there smelleth what breath dispenseth not, and there tasteth what eating diminisheth not, and there clingeth what satiety divorceth not. This is it that I love, when I love my God. And what is this? I asked the earth, and it answered me, "I am not He"; and whatsoever things are in it confessed the same. I asked the sea and the deeps, and the living creeping things, and they answered, "We are not thy God; seek above us." I asked the moving air, and the whole air with its inhabitants answered, "Anaximenes was deceived; I am not God." I asked the heavens, sun, moon, stars, and they say "Nor are we the God whom thou seekest." And I replied unto all the things which encompass the door of my flesh, "Ye have told me of my God that ye are not He; tell me something of Him." And they cried out with a loud voice, "He made us." . . . I asked the whole frame of the world about my God; and it answered me, "I am not He, but He made me."

~ ST. AUGUSTINE

January 19

Rejoice always.
1 THESSALONIANS 5:16

For God did not give us a spirit of timidity,
but a spirit of power, of love and of self-discipline.
2 TIMOTHY 1:7

From Thee, My God, My Joy's shall rise,
And run eternal rounds,
Beyond the limits of the skies,
And all created bounds.
ANONYMOUS

We are in 1903 and I am nearly seventy-one years old. I always thought I should love to grow old, and I find it is even more delightful than I thought. It is so delicious to be done with things, and to feel no need any longer to concern myself much about earthly affairs. I seem on the verge of a most delightful journey to a place of unknown joys and pleasures, and things here seem of so little importance compared to things there, that they have lost most of their interest for me. I cannot describe the sort of done-with-the-world feeling I have. It is not that I feel as if I was going to die at all, but simply that the world seems to me nothing but a passageway to the real life beyond; and passage ways are very unimportant places. It is of very little account what sort of things they contain, or how they are furnished. One just hurries through them to get to the place beyond. My wants seem to be gradually narrowing down, my personal wants, I mean, and I often think I could be quite content in the Poor-house! I do not know whether this is piety or old age, or a little of each mixed together, but honestly the world and our life in it does seem of too little account to be worth making the least fuss over, when one has such a magnificent prospect close at hand ahead of one; and I am tremendously content to let one activity after another go, and to await quietly and happily the opening of the door at the end of the passage way, that will let me in to my real abiding place. So you may think of me as happy and contented, surrounded with unnumbered blessings, and delighted to be seventy-one years old.

~ MRS. PEARSALL SMITH

However, as it is written: "no eye has seen, nor ear has heard, no mind has conceived what the God has prepared for those who love him"—but God has revealed it to us by his Spirit.

1 CORINTHIANS 2:9

Send down Thy likeness from above.
And let this my adorning be
Clothe me with wisdom, patience, love,
With lowliness and purity.

JOACHIM LANGE

Great virtues are rare: the occasions for them are very rare; and when they do occur, we are prepared for them, we are excited by the grandeur of the sacrifice, we are supported either by the splendour of the deed in the eyes of the world or by the self complacency that we experience from the performance of an uncommon action. Little things are unforeseen; they return every moment; they come in contact with our pride, our indolence, our haughtiness, our readiness to take offence; they contradict our inclinations perpetually. We would much rather make certain great sacrifices to God, however violent and painful they might be, upon condition that we should be rewarded by liberty to follow our own desires and habits in the detail of life. It is, however, only by fidelity in little things that a true and constant love to God can be distinguished from a passing fervour of spirit.

All great things are only a great number of small things that have been carefully collected together. He who loses nothing will soon grow rich. Besides, let us remember that God looks in our actions only for the motive. The world judges us by appearance; God counts for nothing what is most dazzling to men. What He desires is a pure intention, true docility, and a sincere self-renunciation. All this is exercised more frequently, and in a way that tries us more severely, on common than on great occasions. Sometimes we cling more tenaciously to a trifle than to a great interest. It would give us more pain to relinquish an amusement than to bestow a great sum in charity. We are more easily led away by little things, because we believe them more innocent and imagine that we are less attracted to them; nevertheless, when God deprives us of them, we soon discover, from the pain of deprivation, how excessive and inexcusable was our attachment to them.

~ FENELON

There is no beautifier of complexion, or form, or behaviour, like the wish to scatter joy and not pain around us.

~ RALPH WALDO EMERSON

It is God who arms me with strength
and makes my way perfect.
He makes my feet like the feet of a deer;
he enables me to stand on the heights.

PSALMS 18:32

Thy saints on earth, and those above,
Here join in sweet accord:
One body all in mutual love,

And thou their common Lord.
Yes, thou that body wilt present
Before thy Father's face,
Nor shall a wrinkle or a spot
Its beauteous form disgrace.
ANONYMOUS

Man, by living wholly in submission to the Divine Influence, becomes surrounded with, and creates for himself, internal pleasures infinitely greater than any he can otherwise attain to a state of heavenly Beatitude.

~ J. P. GREAVES

By persisting in a habit of self-denial, we shall, beyond what I can express, increase the inward powers of the mind, and shall produce that cheerfulness and greatness of spirit as will fit us for all good purposes; and shall not have lost pleasure, but changed it; the soul being then filled with its own intrinsic pleasures.

~ HENRY MORE

January 22

Finally, brothers, whatever is true, whatever is noble, whatever is right, whatever is pure, whatever is lovely, whatever is admirable—if anything is excellent or praiseworthy—think about such things.
PHILIPPIANS 4:8

Assisted by his grace,
We still pursue our way;
And hope at last to reach the prize,
Secure in endless day.
ANONYMOUS

It is by doing our duty that we learn to do it. So long as men dispute whether or no a thing is their duty, they get never the nearer. Let them set ever so weakly about doing it, and the face of things alters. They find in themselves strength which they knew not of. Difficulties which it seemed to them they could not get over, disappear. For He accompanies it with the influences of His blessed Spirit, and each performance opens our minds for larger influxes of His grace, and places them in communion with Him.

~ E. B. PUSEY

January 23

As a prisoner for the Lord, then, I urge you to live a life worthy of the calling you have received. Be completely humble and gentle; be patient, bearing with one another in love. Make every effort to keep the unity of the Spirit through the bond of peace.
EPHESIANS 4:1

If thou hast Yesterday thy duty done,
And thereby cleared firm footing for To-day
Whatever clouds make dark To-morrow's sun,
Thou shalt not miss thy solitary way.
J. W. VON GOETHE

O Lord, who art our Guide even unto death, grant us, I pray Thee, grace to follow Thee whithersoever Thou goest. In little daily duties to which Thou callest us, bow down our wills to simple obedience, patience under pain or provocation, strict truthfulness of word and manner, humility, kindness in great acts of duty or perfection, if Thou shouldest call us to them, uplift us to self sacrifice, heroic courage, laying down of life for Thy truth's sake, or for a brother. Amen.

~ CHRITINA G. ROSSETTI

January 24

I will praise the Lord, who counsels me.
PSALMS 16:7

My father, teach us not only thy will, but how to do it. Teach us the best way of doing the best thing, lest we spoil the end by unworthy means.
REV. J.H. JOWETT

Nothing is small or great in God's sight; whatever He wills becomes great to us, however seemingly trifling, and if once the voice of conscience tells us that He requires anything of us, we have no right to measure its importance. On the other hand, whatever He would not have us do, however important we may think it, is as nought to us. How do you know what you may lose by neglecting this duty, which you think so trifling, or the blessing which its faithful performance may bring? Be sure that if you do your very best in that which is laid upon you daily, you will not be left without sufficient help when some weightier occasion arises. Give yourself to Him, trust Him, fix your eye upon Him, listen to His voice, and then go on bravely and cheerfully.

~ JEAN NICOLAS GROU

January 25

*Never be lacking in zeal, but keep your spiritual fervor,
serving the Lord.*
ROMANS 12:11

*Anyone then, who knows the good he ought
to do and doesn't do it, sins.*
JAMES 4:17

*We cannot kindle when we will
The fire that in the heart resides,
The spirit bloweth and is still,*

*In mystery our soul abides:
But tasks in hours of insight willed
Can be through hours of gloom fulfilled.*
MATTHEW ARNOLD

It daily becomes more apparent that God's respect for the freedom of our affections, thoughts, and purposes is complete. It is part of that respect for our freedom that He never forces upon us His own gifts. He offers them, but unless we actively accept them, they remain ineffective as far as we are concerned. Behold, I stand at the door and knock – that is always the relation of God our Redeemer to our souls. He has paid the whole price; He has suffered the atoning Death; yet still He waits till we open the door of our hearts to let in His love which will call our love out. He never breaks down that door. He stands and knocks. And this is true not only of His first demand for admission to the mansion of the soul; it is true also of every room within that mansion. There are many of us who have opened the front door to Him, but have only let Him into the corridors and staircases; all the rooms where we work or amuse ourselves are still closed against Him. There are still greater multitudes who have welcomed Him to some rooms, and hope that He will not ask what goes on behind the doors of others. But sooner or later He asks; and if we do not at once take Him to see, He leaves the room where we were so comfortable with Him, and stands knocking at the closed door. And then we can never again have the joy of His presence in the first room until we open the door at which He is now knocking. We can only have Him with us in the room that we choose for Him, if we really make Him free of all the house.

~ WILLIAM TEMPLE

January 26

Oh, the depth of the riches of the wisdom and knowledge of God! How unsearchable his judgments, and his paths beyond tracing out!
ROMANS 11:33

Dear friends, now we are children of God, and what we will be has not yet been made known.
I JOHN 3:2

No star is ever lost we once have seen,
We always may be what we might have been.
Since Good, though only thought, has life and breath,
God's life—can always be redeemed from death
And evil, in its nature, is decay,
And any hour can blot it all away
The hopes that lost in some far distance seem,
May be the truer life, and this the dream.
A. A. PROCTER

St. Bernard has said, "Man, if thou desire'st a noble and holy life, and unceasingly prayest to God for it, if thou continue constant in this thy desire, it will be granted unto thee without fail, even if only in the day or hour of thy death; and if God should not give it to thee then, thou shalt find it in Him in eternity: of this be assured." Therefore do not relinquish your desire, though it be not fulfilled immediately, or though ye may swerve from your aspirations or even forget them for a time. . . . The love and aspiration which once really existed live forever before God, and in Him ye shall find the fruit thereof that is, to all eternity it shall be better for you than if you had never felt them.

~ J. TAULER

January 27

For this is what the high and lofty One says—he who lives forever, whose name is holy: I live a high and holy place, but also with him who is contrite and lowly in spirit, to revive the spirit of the lowly and to revive the heart of the contrite.

ISAIAH 57:15

Without an end or bound
Thy life lies all outspread in light
Our lives feel Thy life all around,

Making our weakness strong, our darkness bright
Yet is it neither wilderness nor sea,
But the calm gladness of a full eternity.

F. W. FABER

O truth who art Eternity, I And Love who art Truth, I And Eternity who art Love! Thou art my God, to Thee do I sigh night and day. When I first knew Thee, Thou liftedst me up, that I might see there was somewhat for me to see, and that I was not yet such yet as to see. And Thou streaming forth Thy beams of light upon me most strongly, didst beat back the weakness of my sight, and I perceived myself to be far off from Thee in the region of unlikeliness.

~ ST. AUGUSTINE

January 28

Fear the Lord, you his saints,
for those who fear him lack nothing.

PSALMS 34:9

You open your hand and satisfy
the desires of every living thing.

PSALMS 45:16

What Thou shalt to-day provide,
Let me as a child receive
What to-morrow may betide,
Calmly to Thy wisdom leave.
'Tis enough that Thou wilt care;
Why should I the burden bear?

J. NEWTON

Have we found that anxiety about possible consequences increased the clearness of our judgment, made us wiser and braver in meeting the present, and arming ourselves for the future? . . . If we had prayed for this day's bread, and left the next to itself, if we had not huddled our days together, not allotting to each its appointed task, but ever deferring that to the future, and drawing upon the future for its own troubles, which must be met when they come whether we have anticipated them or not, we should have found a simplicity and honesty in our lives, a capacity for work, an enjoyment in it, to which we are now, for the most part, strangers.

~ F. D. MAURICE

January 29

For I am the Lord, your God, who takes hold of your right hand, and says to you, Do not fear; I will help you.
ISAIAH 41:13

Show the wonder of your great love,
you who save by your right hand those who take refuge
in you from their foes.
PSALMS 17:7

I Take Thy hand, and fears grow still
Behold Thy face, and doubts remove
Who would not yield his wavering will
To perfect Truth and boundless Love?
SAMUEL JOHNSON

Do not look forward to the changes and chances of this life in fear rather look to them with full hope that, as they arise, God, Whose you are, will deliver you out of them. He has kept you hitherto, do you but hold fast to His dear hand, and He will lead you safely through all things; and, when you cannot stand, He will bear you in His arms. Do not look forward to what may happen to-morrow; the same everlasting Father who cares for you today, will take care of you to-morrow, and every day. Either He will shield you from suffering, or He will give you unfailing strength to bear it. Be at peace then, and put aside all anxious thoughts and imaginations.

~ ST. FRANCIS DE SALES

January 30

If I rise on the wings of the dawn,
if I settle on the far side of the sea,
even there your hand will guide me,
your right hand will hold me fast.
PSALMS 139:9-10

I Cannot lose Thee I Still in Thee abiding,
The end is clear, how wide soe'er I roam
The Hand that holds the worlds my steps is guiding,
And I must rest at last in Thee, my home.
E. SCUDDER

How can we come to perceive this direct leading of God By a careful looking at home, and abiding within the gates of thy own soul. Therefore, let a man be at home in his own heart, and cease from his restless chase of and search after outward things. If he is thus at home while on earth, he will surely come to see what there is to do at home, what God commands him inwardly without means, and also outwardly by the help of means; and then let him surrender himself, and follow God along whatever path his loving Lord thinks fit to lead him: whether it be to contemplation or action, to usefulness or enjoyment; whether in sorrow or in joy, let him follow on. And if God do not give him thus to feel His hand in all things, let him still simply yield himself up, and go without, for God's sake, out of love, and still press forward.

~ J. TAULER

January 31

. . . in all your ways acknowledge him,
and he will make your paths straight.
PROVERBS 3:6

He makes me lie down in green pastures,
He leads me to still waters. . . .
PSALMS 23:2

IN "Pastures green"? Not always; sometimes He
Who knoweth best, in kindness leadeth me
In weary ways, where heavy shadows be.

So, whether on the hill-tops high and fair
I dwell, or in the sunless valleys, where
The shadows lie, what matter? He is there.
HENRY H. BARRY

The Shepherd knows what pastures are best for his sheep, and they must not question nor doubt, but trustingly follow Him. Perhaps He sees that the best pastures for some of us are to be found in the midst of opposition or of earthly trials. If He leads you there, you may be sure they are green for you, and You will grow and be made strong by feeding there. Perhaps He sees that the best waters for you to walk beside will be raging waves of trouble and Borrow. If this should be the case, He will make them still waters for you, and you must go and lie down beside them, and let them have all their blessed influences upon you.

~ H. W. S.

*Ye have need of patience, that, after ye have done the will of God,
ye might receive the promise.*
HEBREWS 10:36

Let patience have her perfect work.
JAMES 1:4

*Make me patient, kind, and gentle,
Day by day;
Teach me how to live more nearly
As I pray.*
SHARPE'S MAGAZINE

There is a story of a man who prayed earnestly one morning for grace to overcome his besetting sin of impatience. A little later he missed a train by half a minute and spent an hour stamping up and down the station platform in furious vexation. Five minutes before the next train came in he suddenly realized that here had been the answer to his prayer. He had been given an hour to practice the virtue of patience; he had missed the opportunity and wasted the hour. There are also many stories of men who have similarly, missed trains which have been wrecked, and who ascribe their escape to Providence. If they are combining the thought of God as the celestial chess-player with the thought of God as preeminently concerned in their enjoyment of earthly life at the expense of others, there is not much to be said for their point of view. But if they are humbly acknowledging a call to further service on earth before they pass beyond, they are rightly interpreting their escape. In all probability all the events which led up to all these men missing their various trains could be adequately accounted for in terms of the interaction of natural law, human freedom, and divine grace. But at every point within the interaction God sees what are its possibilities for good, and the man who shares His enlightenment and His power and gives himself to make that good come true, has found the meaning of that moment and his 'special providence'. The gates of the future are indeed open, the universe is in the making. But only if made aright can the making stand. . . .

~ LEONARD HODGSON

He defended the cause of the poor and needy, and so all went well.
JEREMIAH 22:16

*Defend the cause of the weak and fatherless,
Maintain the rights of the poor and oppressed.
Rescue the weak and needy;
deliver them from the hand of the wicked.*
PSALMS 82:3-4

*Oh, might we all our lineage prove,
Give and forgive, do good and love;
By soft endearments, in kind strife,
Lightening the load of daily life.*
J. KEBLE

The love of our neighbour is the only door out of the dungeon of self, where we mope and mow, striking sparks, and rubbing phosphorescence out of the walls, and blowing our own breath in our own nostrils, instead of issuing to the fair sunlight of God, the sweet winds of the universe. The man thinks his consciousness is himself; whereas his life consisteth in the inbreathing of God, and the consciousness of the universe of truth. To have himself, to know himself, to enjoy himself, he calls life; whereas, if he would forget himself, tenfold would be his life in God and his neighbours. The region of man's life is a spiritual region. God, his friends, his neighbours, his brothers all, is the wide world in which alone his spirit can find room. Himself is his dungeon. If he feels it not now, he will yet feel it one day-feel it as a living soul would feel being prisoned in a dead body, wrapped in sevenfold cerements, and buried in a stone-ribbed vault within the last ripple of the sound of chanting people in the church above. His life is not in knowing that he lives, but in loving all forms of life. He is made for the All; for God, who is the All, is his life. And the essential joy of his life lies abroad in the liberty of the All. His delights, like those of the Ideal Wisdom, are with the sons of men. His health is in the body of which the Son of Man is the head. The whole region is open to him—nay, he must live in it or perish.

~ GEORGE MACDONALD

February 3

Search me, O God, and know my heart;
Test me and know my anxious thoughts.
See if there is any offensive way in me,
and lead me in the way everlasting.
PSALMS 139:23-24

Wilt thou forgive that sinn where I begunn,
Which is my sinn, though it were done before?
Wilt thou forgive those sinns, through which I runn,
And doe them still, though still I doe deplore?
JOHN DONNE

February 4

Do not let any unwholesome talk
come out of your mouths,
but only what is helpful for building
others up according to their needs,
that it may benefit those who listen.
EPHESIANS 4:29

Set a guard over my mouth,
O Lord; keep watch over the door of my lips.
PSALMS 141:4

What! Never speak one evil work,
Or rash, or idle, or unkind!
Oh, how shall I, most gracious Lord,
This mark of true perfection find?
C. WESLEY

Whosoever would fully and feelingly understand the words of Christ must endeavour to conform his life wholly to the life of Christ. What will it avail thee to dispute profoundly of the Trinity if thou be void of humility and art thereby displeasing to the Trinity? Surely high words do not make a man holy and just; but a virtuous life maketh him dear to God.

~ THOMAS A. KEMPIS

When we remember out temptations to give quick indulgence to disappointment or irritation or unsympathizing weariness . . . and how hard a thing it is from day to day to meet our fellow-men, our neighbors, or even our own households, in all moods, in all discordances between the world without us and the frames within . . . with only kindly feeling finding expression and ungenial feeling at least inwardly imprisoned; we shall be ready to acknowledge that the man who has thus attained is master of himself, and in the graciousness of his power is fashioned upon the style of a Perfect Man.

~ J. H. THOM

February 5

Blessed are they who maintain justice,
who constantly do what is right.
PSALMS 106:3

Obey me, and I will be your God and you will be my people.
Walk in all the ways I command you, that it may go well with you.
JEREMIAH 7:23

Let my heart the cradle be
Of Thy bleak Nativity!
Tossed by wintry tempests wild,
If it rock Thee, Holy Child,
Then, as grows the outer din,
Greater peace shall reign within.
JOHN BANISTER TABB

Ah! wretched sin, what art thou? Thou art nought! For I saw that God is all-thing. I saw not thee. And when I saw that God has made all-thing, I saw thee not. And when I saw that God does all-thing that is done, less and more, I saw thee not. And when I saw our Lord Jesus sit in our soul so worshipfully, and love and like and rule and guard all that He has made, I saw not thee. And thus I am sure that thou art nought; and all those that love thee, and like thee, and follow thee, and wilfully end in thee, I am sure they shall be brought to nought with thee, and endlessly confounded. God shield us all, from thee! Amen, for charity.

~ LADY JULIAN OF NORWICH

February 6

Whoever trusts in the Lord is kept safe.
PROVERBS 29:25

. . . in God I trust; I will not be afraid.
PSALMS 56:11

Enter my heart, O Holy Spirit,
come in blessed mercy and set me free.
Throw open, O Lord, the locked doors of my mind;
cleanse the chambers of my thought for thy dwelling:
light there the fires of thine own holy brightness in new
understandings of truth,
O Holy Spirit, very God, whose presence is liberty,
grant me the perfect freedom
to be thy servant
today, tomorrow, evermore.
ERIC MILNER-WHITE

God has brought us into this time; He, and not ourselves or some dark demon. If we are not fit to cope with that which He has prepared for us, we should have been utterly unfit for any condition that we imagine for ourselves. In this time we are to live and wrestle, and in no other. Let us humbly, tremblingly, manfully look at it, and we shall not wish that the sun could go back its ten degrees, or that we could go back with it. If easy times are departed, it is that the difficult times may make us more in earnest; that they may teach us not to depend upon ourselves. If easy belief is impossible, it is that we may learn what belief is, and in whom it is to be placed.

~ F. D. MAURICE

February 7

Aim for perfection, listen to my appeal, be of one mind, live in peace.
And the God of love and peace will be with you.
2 CORINTHIANS 13:11

And oft, when in my heart was heard
Thy timely mandate, I deferred
The task, in smoother walks to stray;
But thee I now would serve more strictly, if I may.
WILLIAM WORDSWORTH

Pray Him to give you what Scripture calls an honest and good heart, or "a perfect heart"; and, without waiting, begin at once to Obey Him with the best heart you have. Any obedience is better than none. You have to seek His face; obedience is the only way of seeing Him. All your duties are obediences. To do what He bids is to obey Him, and to obey Him is to approach Him. Every act of obedience is an approach—an approach to Him who is not far off, though He seems so, but close behind this visible screen of things which hides Him from us.

~ J. H. NEWMAN

Almighty God, from whom all thoughts of truth and peace proceed, kindle, we pray thee, in the hearts of all men the true love of peace, and guide with thy pure and peaceable wisdom those who take counsel for the nations of the earth; that in tranquility thy kingdom may go forward, till the earth be filled with the knowledge of thy love; through Jesus Christ our Lord.

~ FRANCIS PAGET

He leadeth me beside the still waters.
He restoreth my soul;
He leadeth me in the paths of righteousness
for His name's sake.
PSALMS 23:2-3

Lead me from death
to Life, from falsehood to Truth

Lead me from despair
to Hope, from fear to Trust

Lead me from hate
to Love, from war to Peace

Let Peace fill our heart,
our world, our universe.
SATISH KUMAR, PRAYER FOR PEACE MOVEMENT

. . . He will guide us in a sure path, though it be a rough one: though shadows hang upon it, yet He will be with us. He will bring us home at last. Through much trial it may be, and weariness, in much fear and fainting of heart, in much sadness and loneliness, in griefs that the world never knows, and under burdens that the nearest never suspect. Yet He will suffice for all. By His eye or by His voice He will guide us, if we be docile and gentle; by His staff and by His rod, if we wander or are wilful: any how, and by all means, He will bring us to His rest.

~ H. E. MANNING

If you believe, you will receive whatever you ask for in prayer.
MATTHEW 21:22

Everything is possible for him who believes.
MARK 9:23

Now, God be prais'd, that to believing souls
Gives light in darkness, comfort in despair!
WILLIAM SHAKESPEARE,

Five years ago I came to believe in Christ's teaching, and my life suddenly changed; I ceased to desire what I had previously desired, and began to desire what I formerly did not want . . . The direction of my life and my desires became different, and good and evil changed places. . . .

I, like that thief on the cross, have believed Christ's teaching and been saved. And this is no far-fetched comparison, but the closest expression of the condition of spiritual despair and horror at the problem of life and death in which I lived formerly, and of the condition of peace and happiness in which I am now. I, like the thief, knew that I had lived and was living badly. . . . I, like the thief, knew that I was unhappy and suffering . . . I, like the thief to the cross, was nailed by some force to that life of suffering and evil. And as, after the meaningless sufferings and evils of life, the thief awaited the terrible darkness of death, so did I await the same thing.

In all this I was exactly like the thief, but the difference was that the thief was already dying, while I was still living. The thief might believe that his salvation lay there beyond the grave, but I could not be satisfied with that, because besides a life beyond the grave life still awaited me here. But I did not understand that life. It seemed to me terrible. And suddenly I heard the words of Christ and understood them, and life and death ceased to seem to me evil, and instead of despair I experienced happiness and the joy of life undisturbed by death.

~ LEO TOLSTOY

February 10

Blest are the humble souls that wait
With sweet submission to His will;
Harmonious all their passions move,
And in the midst of storms are still.
P. DODDRIDGE

O give us patience and steadfastness in adversity, strengthen our weakness, comfort us in trouble and distress, help us to fight; grant unto us that in true obedience and contentation of mind we may give over our own wills unto thee our Father in all things, according to the example of they beloved Son, that in adversity we grudge not, but offer up ourselves unto thee without contradiction . . . O give us a willing and cheerful mind, that we may gladly suffer and bear all things for thy sake.

~ BISHOP MILES COVERDALE

February 11

Then his disciples said to each other,
"Could someone have brought him food?"

"My food," said Jesus,
"is to do the will of him who sent me and to finish his work."
JOHN 4:33-34

I have finished the work which Thou gavest me to do.
JOHN 17:4

He who God's will has borne and done,
And his own restless longings tilled;
What else he does, or has foregone,
His mission he has well fulfilled.
ANONYMOUS

He told me that God always gave us light in our doubts when we had no other design but to please Him and to act for His love.

That our sanctification did not depend upon changing our works, but in doing that for God's sake which commonly we do for our own. That it was lamentable to see how many people mistook the means for the end, addicting themselves to certain works, which they performed very imperfectly, by reason of their human or selfish regards.

That the most excellent method which he had found of going to God was that of doing our common business without any view of pleasing men, and (as far as we are capable) purely for the love of God. . . . That his view of prayer was nothing else but a sense of the Presence of God, his soul being at that time insensible to everything but Divine Love. That when the appointed times of prayers were passed, he found no difference, because he still continued with God, praising and blessing Him with all his might, so that he passed his life in continual joy; yet hoped that God would give him somewhat to suffer, when he should have grown stronger. . . . That we ought not to be weary of doing little things for the love of God, for He regards not the greatness of the work, but the love with which it is performed. . . . "The time of business," said he, "does not with me differ from the time of prayer, and in the noise and clatter of my kitchen, while several persons are at the same time calling for different things, I possess God in as great tranquility as if I were upon my knees at the Blessed Sacrament."

~ BROTHER LAWRENCE

February 12

. . . the benefit you reap leads to holiness, and the result is eternal life.
ROMANS 6:22

All this is for your benefit, so that the grace that is reaching more and more people may cause thanksgiving to overflow to the glory of God.
2 CORINTHIANS 4:15

For even the purest delight may pall,
And power must fail, and the pride must fall,
And the love of the dearest friends grow small—
But the glory of the Lord is all in all.
R. D. BLACKMORE

We are full of inconsistencies, and so is all around us. But those inconsistencies are the mark of the passage from the lower consistency of unconscious animal life to the higher consistency of spiritual life . . . Yet we ought never to be satisfied with inconsistency. We must struggle forward toward a rational and effectual unity. The conditions of that unity are, the Gospel tells us, to be found only in Christ the Son of God. . . . There is but one perfect unity, and that is in the heavens: yet it came down from the heavens that we might be raised into fellowship with it. Daily taking up the cross and following Jesus the Christ as Lord, daily turning and becoming as little children in the Sonship of the Heavenly Father, are the means by which it is attained. So with all our inconsistencies and weaknesses and sins we are kept in the one Way, the one Truth, and the one Life; and each step that we take brings us nearer to the one Father above.

~ F. J. A. HORT

February 13

Yet not as I will, but as you will.
MATTHEW 26:39

. . . your kingdom come, your will be done,
on earth as it is in heaven.
MATTHEW 6:10

To have, each day, the thing I wish,
Lord, that seems best to me;
But not to have the thing I wish, Lord, that seems best to Thee.
Most truly, then, Thy will is done, When mine O Lord, is crossed,
'Tis good to see my plans o'erthrown, My ways in Thine all lost.
H. BONAR

Do everyday or two something for no other reason than that you would rather not do it, so that when the hour of dire need draws nigh, it may find you not unnerved and untrained to stand the test. . . .

~ WILLIAM JAMES

Dare to look up to God, and say, "Make use of me for the future as Thou wilt. I am of the same mind; I am one with Thee. I refuse nothing which seems good to Thee. Lead me whither Thou wilt, clothe me in whatever dress Thou wilt. Is it Thy will that I should be in a public or a private condition, dwell here, or be banished, be poor or rich? Under all these circumstances, I will testify unto Thee before men."

~ EPICTETUS

February 14

Cast your cares on the Lord and he will sustain you;
PSALMS 55:22

I would like you to be free from concern.
1 CORINTHIANS 7:32

O LORD, how happy should we be
If we could cast our care on Thee,
If we from self could rest;
And feel at heart that One above,
In perfect wisdom, perfect love,
Is working for the best.
J. ANSTICE

Cast all thy care on God. See that all thy cares be such as thou canst cast on God, and then hold none back. Never brood over thyself; never stop short in thyself; but cast thy whole self, even this very care which distresseth thee, upon God. Be not anxious about little things, if thou wouldst learn to trust God with thine all. Act upon faith in little things; commit thy daily cares and anxieties to Him; and He will strengthen thy faith for any greater trials. Rather, give thy whole self into God's hands and so trust Him to take care of thee in all lesser things, as being His, for His own sake, whose thou art.

~ E. B. PUSEY

February 15

*Finally, all of you, live in harmony with one another,
be sympathetic, love as brothers . . .*
1 PETER 3:8

How good and pleasant it is when brothers live together in unity!
PSALMS 133:1

> Come, children, let us go
> We travel hand in hand
> Each in his brother finds his joy
> In this wild stranger land.
> The strong be quick to raise
> The weaker when they fall
> Let love and peace and patience bloom
> In ready help for all.
> G. TERSTEEGEN

There is only one way of following Jesus and of worshipping God, and that is to be reconciled with our brethren. If we come to hear the word of God and receive the sacrament without first being reconciled with our neighbours, we shall come to our own damnation. In the sight of God we are murderers. Therefore "go thy way, first be reconciled with thy brother, and then come and offer thy gift." This is a hard way, but it is the way Jesus requires if we are to follow Him. It is a way which brings much personal humiliation and insult, but it is indeed the way to Him, our crucified Brother, and therefore a way of grace abounding. In Jesus the service of God and the service of the least of the brethren were one. He went His way and became reconciled with His brother and offered Himself as the one true sacrifice to His Father.

We are still living in the age of grace, for each of us still has a brother, we are still "with him in the way." The court of judgement lies ahead, and there is still a chance for us to be reconciled with our brother and pay our debt to him. The hour is coming when we shall meet the judge face to face, and then it will be too late. We shall then receive our sentence and be made to pay the last farthing. But do we realize that at this point our brother comes to us in the guise not of law, but of grace? It is grace that we are allowed to find favour with our brother, and pay our debt to him; it is grace that we are allowed to become reconciled with him. In our brother we find grace before the seat of judgement.

Only He can speak thus to us, who as our Brother has Himself become our grace, our atonement, our deliverance from judgement. The humanity of the Son of God empowers us to find favour with our brother. May the disciples of Jesus think upon this grace aright!

~ DIETRICH BONHOEFFER

February 16

*. . . to love the Lord your God and to serve
him with all your heart and with all your soul . . .*
DEUTERONOMY 11:13

And you, my son Solomon,
acknowledge the God of your father,
and serve him with wholehearted devotion and
with a willing mind . . .
1 CHRONICLES 28:9

My spirit bare before Thee stands;
I bring no gift, I ask no sign,
I come to Thee with empty hands,
the surer to be filled from Thine.
DORA GREENWELL

Little things come daily, hourly, within our reach, and they are not less calculated to set forward our growth in holiness, than are the greater occasions which occur but rarely. Moreover, fidelity in trifles, and an earnest seeking to please God in little matters, is a test of real devotion and love. Let your aim be to please our dear Lord perfectly in little things, and to attain a spirit of childlike simplicity and dependence. In proportion as self-love and self-confidence are weakened, and our will bowed to that of God, so will hindrances disappear, the internal troubles and contests which harassed the soul vanish, and it will be filled with peace and tranquility.

~ JEAN NICOLAS GROU

February 17

Blessed is the man who perseveres under trial,
because when he has stood the test,
he will receive the crown of life that God
has promised to those who love him.
JAMES 1:12

In the bitter waves of woe,
Beaten and tossed about
By the sullen winds that blow
From the desolate shores of doubt,
Where the anchors that faith has cast
Are dragging in the gale,
I am quietly holding fast
To the things that cannot fail.
WASHINGTON GLADDEN

In the darkest hour through which a human soul can pass, whatever else is doubtful, this at least is certain. If there be no God and no future state, yet, even then, it is better to be generous than selfish, better to be chaste than licentious, better to be true than false better to be brave than to be a coward. Blessed beyond all earthly blessedness is the man who, in the tempestuous darkness of the soul, has dared to hold fast to these venerable landmarks. Thrice blessed is he, who, when all is drear and cheerless within and without, when his teachers terrify him, and his friends shrink from him, has obstinately clung to moral good. Thrice blessed, because his night shall pass into clear, bright day.

~ F. W. ROBERTSON

---

*In this you greatly rejoice, though now for a little while you may have had
to suffer grief in all kinds of trials. These have come so that your faith— of
greater worth than gold . . . may be proved genuine and may result in praise,
glory and honor when Jesus Christ is revealed.*

1 PETER 1:6-7

*O Thou our reminder of Christ crucified,
Living Bread the life of us for whom he died,
Lend this life to me then: feed and feast my mind,
There be thou the sweetness man was meant to find.*

*Bring the tender tale true of The Pelican;
Bathe me, Jesus Lord, in what thy bosom ran—
Blood that but one drop of has the world to win
All the world forgiveness of its world of sin.*

*Jesu, whom I look at shrouded here below,
I beseech thee send me what I thirst for so,
Some day to gaze on thee face to face in light,
And be blest forever with thy glory's sight.*

ST. THOMAS AQUINAS

There is no moment at which God does not present Himself under the
guise of some suffering, some consolation, or some duty. All that occurs
within us, around us, and by our means covers and hides His divine
action. His action is there, most really and certainly present, but in an
invisible manner, the result of which is that we are always being taken by
surprise and that we only recognize His action after it has passed away.
Could we pierce the veil, and were we vigilant and attentive, God would
reveal Himself continuously to us and we should rejoice in His action in
everything that happened to us.

~ J. P. DE CAUSSADE

---

*Teach me to do your will, for you are my God;
may your good Spirit lead me on level ground.*

PSALMS 143:10

*Do not merely listen to the word and so deceive yourselves.
Do what it says.
Anyone who listens to the word but does not do what it says
is like a man who looks at his face in a mirror
and after looking at himself, goes away and
immediately forgets what he looks like.
But the man who looks intently into the perfect law
that gives freedom, and continues to do this,
not forgetting what he has heard, but doing it
—he will be blessed in what he does.*

JAMES 1:22

Cheered by the presence of God, I will do at each moment, without anxiety, according to the strength which He shall give me, the work that His

Providence assigns me. I will leave the rest without concern; it is not my affair. I ought to consider the duty to which I am called each day, as the work that God has given me to do, and to apply myself to it in a manner worthy of His glory, that is to say, with exactness and in peace. I must neglect nothing; I must be violent about nothing.

~ FENELON

It is thy duty oftentimes to do what thou wouldst not; thy duty, too, to leave undone what thou wouldst do.

~ THOMAS A. KEMPIS

February 20

Therefore let us stop passing judgement on one another. Instead, make up your mind not to put any stumbling block or obstacle in your brother's way.
ROMANS 14:13

To keep God's door
I am not fit.
I would not ask for more
Than this—To stand or sit
Upon the threshold of God's House . . .
To wait and watch
The gladness on the face of those
That are within:
Sometimes to catch
A glimpse or trace of those
I love the best, and know
That all I failed to do,
Has not sufficed
To bar them from the Tree
Of Life, the Paradise of God,
The Face of Christ.
JOHN W. TAYLOR

A vexation arises, and our expressions of impatience hinder others from taking it patiently. Disappointment, ailment, or even weather depresses us; and our look or tone of depression hinders others from maintaining a cheerful and thankful spirit. We say an unkind thing and another is hindered in learning the holy lesson of charity that thinketh no evil. We say a provoking thing, and our sister or brother is hindered in that day's effort to be meek. How sadly, too, we may hinder without word or act! For wrong feeling is more infectious than wrong doing; especially the various phases of ill temper—gloominess, touchiness, discontent, irritability—do we not know how catching these are?

~ F. R. HAVERGAL

February 21

Which of you, if his son asks for bread, will give him a stone? Or if he asks for a fish, will give him a snake? If you, then, though you are evil, know how to give good gifts to your children, how much more will your Father in heaven give good gifts to those who ask him!
MATHEW 7:9-11

For His great love has compassed
Our nature, and our need
We know not; but He knoweth,
And He will bless indeed.
Therefore, O heavenly Father,
Give what is best to me
And take the wants unanswered,
As offerings made to Thee.
ANONYMOUS

Whatsoever we ask which is not for our good, He will keep it back from us. And surely in this there is no less of love than in the granting what we desire as we ought. Will not the same love which prompts you to give a good, prompt you to keep back an evil, thing? If, in our blindness, not knowing what to ask, we pray for things which would turn in our hands to sorrow and death, will not our Father, out of His very love, deny us? How awful would be our lot, if our wishes should straightway pass into realities; if we were endowed with a power to bring about all that we desire; if the inclinations of our will were followed by fulfillment of our hasty wishes, and sudden longings were always granted. One day we shall bless Him, not more for what He has granted than for what He has denied.

~ H. E. MANNING

February 22

And when you pray, do not be like the hypocrites, for they love to pray standing in the synagogues and on the street corners to be seen by men. . . . But when you pray, go into your room, close the door and pray to your Father, who is unseen. Then your Father, who sees what is done in secret, will reward you.
MATTHEW 6:5-6

We breathe our secret wish,
The importunate longing which no man may see;
We ask it humbly, or, more restful still,
We leave it all to Thee.
SUSAN COOLIDGE

People would like to applaud sermons, and there are sermons which are quite adequately appraised by such a welcome. Applause is a relief to one's feelings and, like any other discharge of feeling, it helps men to remain after an appeal what they were before it. But any serious presentation of truth asks for silence that it may be considered; and Jesus could not then, and He can seldom now, enjoy that privilege of silence. Men want what stirs their blood; and thus in His Church He still rides on amongst the excited feelings of a crowd who, by their shoutings, show that they have not stopped to understand.

~ W. M. MACGREGOR

February 23

Yet do not turn away from the Lord,
but serve the Lord with all your heart.
SAMUEL 12:20

Be strong and take heart, all you who hope in the Lord.
PSALMS 31:24

I am glad to think
I am not bound to make the world go right;
But only to discover and to do,
With cheerful heart, the work that God appoints.
I will trust in Him,
That He can hold His own; and I will take
His will, above the work He sendeth me,
To be my chiefest good.
J. INGELOW

No felt evil or defect becomes divine until it is inevitable; and only when resistance to it is exhausted and hope has fled, does surrender cease to be premature. The hardness of our task lies here; that we have to strive against the grievous things of life, while hope remains, as if they were evil; and then, when the stroke has fallen, to accept them from the hand of God, and doubt not they are good. But to the loving, trusting heart all things are possible; and even this instant change, from overstrained will to sorrowful repose, from fullest resistance to complete surrender, is realized without convulsion.

~ JAMES MARTINEAU

February 24

Make every effort to live in peace
with all men and to be holy.
HEBREWS 12:14

I have told you these things,
so that in me you may have peace.
JOHN 16:33

O Thou, the primal fount of life and peace,
Who shedd'st Thy breathing quiet all around,
In me command that pain and conflict cease,
And turn to music every jarring sound.
J. STERLING

Accustom yourself to unreasonableness and injustice. Abide in peace in the presence of God, who sees all these evils more clearly than you do, and who permits them. Be content with doing with calmness the little which depends upon yourself, and let all else be to you as if it were not.

~ FENELON

It is rare when injustice, or slights patiently borne, do not leave the heart at the close of the day filled with marvelous joy and peace.

~ ANONYMOUS

February 25

But now this is what the Lord says—he who created you, O Jacob,
he who formed you, O Israel: "Fear not, for I have redeemed you;
I have summoned you by name; you are mine."
ISAIAH 43:1

Thou art as much His care as if beside
Nor man nor angel lived in heaven or earth;
Thus sunbeams pour alike their glorious tide,
To light up worlds, or wake an insect's mirth.

J. KEBLE

God beholds thee individually, whoever thou art. "He calls thee by thy name." He sees thee, and understands thee. He knows what is in thee, all thy own peculiar feelings and thoughts, thy dispositions and likings, thy strength and thy weakness. He views thee in thy day of rejoicing and thy day of sorrow. He sympathizes in thy hopes and in thy temptations; He interests himself in all thy anxieties and thy remembrances, in all the risings and fallings of thy spirit. He compasses thee round, and bears thee in His arms; He takes thee up and sets thee down. Thou dost not love thyself better than He loves thee. Thou canst not shrink from pain more than He dislikes thy bearing it; and if He puts it on thee, it is as thou wilt put it on thyself, if thou art wise, for a greater good afterwards.

~ JOHN HENRY NEWMAN

February 26

And everyone who calls on the name of the Lord will be saved.

ACTS 2:21

The Lord is near to all who call on him . . .

PSALMS 145:18

I love the Lord, for he heard my voice;
he heard my cry for mercy.
Because he turned his ear to me,
I will call on him as long as I live.

PSALMS 116:1-2

Take courage, and turn your troubles, which are without remedy, into material for spiritual progress. Often turn to our Lord, who is watching you, poor frail little being as you are, amid your labours and distractions. He sends you help, and blesses your affliction. This thought should enable you to bear your troubles patiently and gently, for love of Him who only allows you to be tried for your own good. Raise your heart continually to God, seek His aid, and let the foundation stone of your consolation be your happiness in being His. All vexations and annoyances will be comparatively unimportant while you know that you have such a Friend, such a Stay, such a Refuge. May God be ever in your heart.

~ ST. FRANCIS DE SALES

February 27

But blessed is the man who trusts in the Lord,
whose confidence is in him.

JEREMIAH 17:27

Trust in the Lord and do good;
dwell in the land and enjoy safe pasture.

PSALMS 37:3

Build a little fence of trust
Around to-day;
Fill the space with loving work,
And therein stay;
Look not through the sheltering bars
Upon to-morrow,
God will help thee bear what comes,
Of joy or sorrow,

MARY FRANCES BUTTS

Let us bow our souls and say, "Behold the handmaid of the Lord!" Let us
lift up our hearts and ask, "Lord, what wouldst thou have me to do?"
Then light from the opened heaven shall stream on our daily task, revealing the grains of gold, where yesterday all seemed dust; a hand shall sustain us and our daily burden, so that, smiling at yesterday's fears, we shall
say, "This is easy, this is light"; every "lion in the way," as we come up to
it, shall be seen chained, and leave open the gates of the Palace Beautiful;
and to us, even to us, feeble and fluctuating as we are, ministries shall be
assigned, and through our hands blessings shall be conveyed in which the
spirits of just men made perfect might delight.

~ ELIZABETH CHARLES

February 28

Dear friends, let us love one another, for love comes from God. Everyone
who loves has been born of God and knows God.

1 JOHN 4:7

I will tell you the truth, whatever you did for one of the least
of these brothers of mine, you did for me.

MATTHEW 26:40

Then next, to love our brethren that were made
Of that self mould, and that self Maker's hand . . .
That we, and to the same again shall fade,
Where they shall have like heritage of land,
However here on higher steps we stand;
Which also were with self-same price redeemed
That we, however of us light esteemed.

And were they not, yet since that loving Lord
Commanded us to love them for His sake,
Even for His sake, and for His sacred word,
Which in His last bequest He to us spake,
We should them love, and with their needs partake;
Knowing that whatso'er to them we give,
We give to Him by whom we all do live.

EDMUND SPENSER

Oh blessed Lord, who hast commanded us to love one another, grant us
grace that having received thine undeserved bounty, we may love everyone
in thee and for thee. We implore thy clemency for all; but especially for the
friends whom thy love has given to us. Love thou them, O thou fountain
of love, and make them to love thee with all their heart, that they may
will, and speak, and do those things only which are pleasing to thee.

~ ST. ANSELM

February 29

But for you who revere my name, the sun of righteousness will rise with healing in its wings.
MALACHI 4:2

Heal me, O Lord, and I will be healed.
JEREMIAH 17:14

We tell Thee of our care,
Of the sore burden, pressing day by day,
And in the light and pity of Thy face,
The burden melts away.
SUSAN COOLIDGE

Let the healing grace of your love, O Lord, so transform me that I may play my part in the transfiguration of the world from a place of suffering, death and corruption to a realm of infinite light, joy and love. Make me so obedient to your Spirit that my life may become a living prayer, and a witness to your unfailing presence.

~ MARTIN ISRAEL

Give me strength to be the first to tender the healing word and the renewal of friendship, that the bonds of amity and the flow of charity may be strengthened for the good of the brethren and the furthering of thine eternal, loving purpose.

~ CECIL HUNT

Never again will they hunger; never again will they thirst.
REVELATIONS 7:16

Every good and perfect gift is from above . . .
JAMES 1:17

One there lives whose guardian eye
Guides our earthly destiny;
One there lives, who, Lord of all,
Keeps His children lest they fall
Pass we, then, in love and praise
Trusting Him through all our days,
Free from doubt and faithless sorrow,—
God provideth for the morrow.

R. HEBER

It has been well said that no man ever sank under the burden of the day. It is when to-morrow's burden is added to the burden of today that the weight is more than a man can bear. Never load yourselves so, my friends. If you find yourselves so loaded, at least remember this: it is your own doing, not God's. He begs you to leave the future to Him, and mind the present.

~ GEORGE MACDONALD

And over all these virtues put on love,
which binds them all together in perfect unity.
COLOSSIANS 3:14

This is the message you heard from the beginning:
We should love one another.
1 JOHN 3:11

So to the calmly gathered thought
The innermost of life is taught,
The mystery, dimly understood,
That love of God is love of good;
That to be saved is only this—
Salvation from our selfishness.

J. G. WHITTER

The Spirit of Love, wherever it is, is its own blessing and happiness, because it is the truth and reality of God in the soul; and therefore is in the same joy of life, and is the same good to itself everywhere and on every occasion. Would you know the blessing of all blessings? It is this God of Love dwelling in your soul, and killing every root of bitterness, which is the pain and torment of every earthly, selfish love. For all wants are satisfied, all disorders of nature are removed, no life is any longer a burden, every day is a day of peace, everything you meet becomes a help to you, because everything you see or do is all done in the sweet, gentle element of Love.

~ WILLIAM LAW

Why, you do not even know what will happen tomorrow. . . . you ought to say, "If it is the Lord's will, we will live and do this or that."
JAMES 4:14

I will hasten and not delay to obey your commands.
PSALMS 119:60

"Lie still, be strong, today: but, Lord, tomorrow,
What of tomorrow, Lord?
Shall there be rest from toil, be truce from sorrow,
Be living green upon the sward,
Now but a barren grave to me, Be joy for sorrow?"

'Did I not die for thee?
Do I not live for thee? Leave me tomorrow.'
CHRISTINA G. ROSSETTI

Alas! How much of my life is lavished away! Oh the intricacies, windings, wanderings, turnings, tergiversations, of my deceitful youth! I have lived in the midst of a crooked generation, and with them have turned aside unto crooked ways. High time it is now for me to make straight paths for my feet, and to redeem what is past by amending what is present and to come. Flux, flux (in the German tongue, quick, quick) was a motto of Bishop Jewel's, presaging the approach of his death. May I make good use thereof; make haste, make haste, God knows how little time is left me, and may I be a good husband to improve the short remnant thereof.

~ THOMAS FULLER

To him who overcomes, I will give the right to sit with me on my throne, just as I overcame and sat down with my Father on his throne.
REVELATIONS 3:21

Though temptations now attend thee,
And thou tread'st the thorny road,
His right hand shall still defend thee,
Soon he'll bring thee home to Go
Full deliverance
Thou shalt have in heaven above.
ANONYMOUS

Though every good man is not so logically subtile as to be able by fit mediums to demonstrate his own immortality, yet he sees it in a higher light: his soul, being purged and enlightened by true sanctity, is more capable of those divine irradiations, whereby it feels itself in conjunction with God. It knows that God will never forsake His own life which He hath quickened in it; He will never deny those ardent desires of a blissful fruition of Himself, which the lively sense of His own goodness hath excited within it: those breathings and gaspings after an eternal participation of Him are but the energy of His own breath within us; if He had had any mind to destroy it, He would never have shown it such things as He hath done.

~ DR. JOHN SMITH

And so after waiting patiently,
Abraham received what was promised.
HEBREWS 6:15

This is our God; we waited for him and he saved us. This is the Lord,
we waited for him, let us rejoice and be glad in his salvation.
ISAIAH 25:9

Now, Lord, what wait I for
On Thee alone
My hope is all rested,—
Lord, seal me Thine own!
Only Thine own to be,
Only to live to Thee.
Thine, with each day begun,
Thine, with each set of sun,
Thine, till my work is done.
ANNA WARNER

We always used to think it was one of the elementary rights of man that he should be able to plan his life in advance, both private life and professional. That is a thing of the past. The pressure of events is forcing us to give up "being anxious for the morrow." But it makes all the difference in the world whether we accept this willingly and in faith (which is what the Sermon on the Mount means) or under compulsion. For most people not to plan for the future means to live irresponsibly and frivolously, to live just for the moment, while some few continue to dream of better times to come. But we cannot take either of these courses. We are still left with only the narrow way, a way often hardly to be found, of living every day as if it were our last, yet in faith and responsibility living as though a splendid future still lay before us. "Houses and fields and vineyards shall yet again be bought in this land," cries Jeremiah as the Holy City is about to be destroyed, a striking contrast to his previous prophecies of woe. It is a divine sign and pledge of better things to come, just when all seems blackest. Thinking and acting for the sake of the coming generation, but taking each day as it comes without fear and anxiety that is the spirit in which we are being forced to live in practice. It is not easy to be brave and hold out, but it is imperative.

~ DIETRICH BONHOEFFER

The Lord is my rock, my fortress and my deliverer;
my God is my rock, in whom I take refuge.
PSALMS 18:2

. . . like streams of water in the desert and
the shadow of a great rock in a thirsty land.
ISAIAH 32:2

Leave God to order all thy ways,
And hope in Him, whate'er betide.
Thou 'lt find Him in the evil days

Thy all-sufficient strength and guide;
Who trusts in God's unchanging love,
Builds on the rock that nought can move.
G. NEUMARCK

Be Thou, O Rock of Ages, nigh!
So shall each murmuring thought be gone;
And grief and fear and care shall fly,
As clouds before the mid-day sun.
C.WESLEY

Our whole trouble in our lot in this world rises from the disagreement of our mind therewith. Let the mind be brought to the lot, and the whole tumult is instantly hushed; let it be kept in that disposition, and the man shall stand at ease, in his affliction, like a rock unmoved with waters beating upon it.

~ T. BOSTON

March 7

There are different kinds of working,
but the same God works all of them in all men.
1 CORINTHIANS 12:6

I form the light and create darkness,
I make prosperity and create
disaster; I, the Lord, do all these things.
ISAIAH 45:7

"All is of God that is, and is to be;
And God is good." Let this suffice us still,
Resting in childlike trust upon His will,
Who moves to His great ends, unthwarted by the ill.
J. G. WHITTIER

This, then, is of faith, that everything, the very least, or what seemed to us great, every change in the seasons, everything which touches us in mind, body, or estate, whether brought about through this outward sense-less nature, or by the will of man, good or bad, is overruled to each of us by the all-holy and all-loving will of God. Whatever befalls us, however it befalls us, we must receive as the will of God. If it befalls us through man's negligence, or ill-will, or anger, still it is, in every the least circumstance, to us the will of God. For if the least thing could happen to us without God's permission, it would be something out of God's control. God's providence or His love would not be what they are. Almighty God Himself would not be the same God; not the God whom we believe, adore, and love.

~ E. B. PUSEY

Now make confession to the Lord,
the God of your fathers, and do his will.
EZRA 10:11

Let us not become weary in doing good,
for at the proper time we will reap
a harvest if we do not give up.
Therefore as we have opportunity,
let us do good . . .
GALATIANS 6:9-10

The task Thy wisdom hath assigned,
Oh, let me cheerfully fulfil;
In all my works Thy presence find,
And prove Thine acceptable will.
C. WESLEY

It cannot be thought that God sends events to a living soul in order that
the soul may be simply passive under the events. If God sends you an
event, it must have a meaning; it must be a sign to you that you are to do
something, to brace yourself up to some action or to some state of feeling.
All that God sends to a human spirit must be significant. God has sent us
His Word. We know that He designs us not simply to hear it, but to
embrace it with a living faith and a loving obedience. We are to meditate
upon it, to apply it to our consciences, mould our character and conduct
in conformity to it. Now the same God who has sent us His Word equally
sends us the daily occurrences of life, the chief difference being that,
whereas the Word has a general voice for all, in which each is to find his
own case represented, the occurrences are charged with a more specific
message to individuals. Now there is many a man who says, "I will conform myself to the general indication of God's will made to me by His
Word"; comparatively few who say, "I will conform myself to the special
indications of God's will made to me by His Providence." But why so few?
Does not God come home to us more closely, more searchingly, more personally by His Providence than even by His Word? Does not His finger
rest upon each of us more particularly in the government of affairs than
even in revelation? And why are we to imagine, as many seem to imagine,
that no other events but such as are afflictive and calamitous have a voice
for us? Why not every event? Why is not the ordinary intercourse of life to
be regarded as furnishing in God's design and intention opportunities of
either doing or receiving good?

~ EDWARD MEYRICK GOULBURN

. . . and you are to rejoice before the
Lord your God in everything you put your hand to.
DEUTERONOMY 12:18

. . . sing psalms, hymns and spiritual songs
with gratitude in your hearts to God.
COLOSSIANS 3:16

. . . Blessed be thy holy Name,
O Lord, my God!
Forever blessed by thy holy Name,
For that I am made
The work of thy hands,
Curiously wrought
By thy divine Wisdom,
Enriched
By thy Goodness,
Being more thine
Than I am mine own.
O Lord!

THOMAS TRAHERNE

If any one would tell you the shortest, surest way to all happiness and all perfection, he must tell you to make it a rule to yourself to thank and praise God for everything that happens to you. For it is certain that what-ever seeming calamity happens to you, if you thank and praise God for it, you turn it into a blessing. Could you, therefore, work miracles, you could not do more for yourself than by this thankful spirit; for it heals with a word speaking, and turns all that it touches into happiness.

~ WILLIAM LAW

March 10

God is our refuge and strength, an ever-present help in trouble.
Therefore we will not fear, though the earth give way
and the mountains fall into the heart of the of the sea,
though its waters roar and foam
and the mountains quake with their surging.

PSALMS 46:1-3

"Do not be afraid . . . I am with you and will rescue you,"
declares the Lord.

JEREMIAH 1:8

When through the deep waters I call thee to go,
The rivers of sorrow shall not overflow;
For I will be with thee thy troubles to bless,
And sanctity to thee thy deepest distress.

ANONYMOUS

Good Lord, give me the grace, in all my fear and agony, to have recourse to that great fear and wonderful agony that thou, my sweet Saviour, hadst at the Mount of Olivet before thy most bitter passion, and in the meditation thereof, to conceive ghostly comfort and consolation profitable for my soul.

~ ST. THOMAS MORE

Turn it as thou wilt, thou must give thyself to suffer what is appointed thee. But if we did that, God would bear us up at all times in all our sor-rows and troubles, and God would lay His shoulder under our burdens, and help us to bear them. For if, with a cheerful courage we submitted ourselves to God, no suffering would be unbearable.

~ TAULER

Cast your cares on the Lord and
he will sustain you; he will never let the righteous fall.
PSALMS 55:22

Still raise for good the supplicating voice,
But leave to heav'n the measure and the choice,
Safe in His power, whose eyes discern afar
The secret ambush of a specious pray'r.
Implore His aid, in His decisions rest,
Secure whate'er He gives, He gives the best.
SAMUEL JOHNSON

The circumstances of her life she could not alter, but she took them to the Lord, and handed them over into His management; and then she believed that He took it, and she left all the responsibility and the worry and anxiety with Him. As often as the anxieties returned she took them back; and the result was that, although the circumstances remained unchanged, her soul was kept in perfect peace in the midst of them. And the secret she found so effectual in her outward affairs, she found to be still more effectual in her inward ones which were in truth even more utterly unmanageable. She abandoned her whole self to the Lord, with all that she was and all that she had; and, believing that He took that which she had committed to Him, she ceased fret and worry, and her life became all sunshine in the gladness of belonging to Him.

~ H. W. S.

"The Lord bless you and keep you;
the Lord make his face shine upon you
and be gracious to you;
the Lord turn his face toward you and give you peace."
NUMBERS 6:24-26

Jesus, My Lord, I look to thee;
Where else can helpless sinners go?
Thy boundless love shall set me free
From all my wretchedness and woe.
ANONYMOUS

I am serene because I know thou lovest me. Because thou lovest me, naught can move me from my peace. Because thou lovest me, I am as one to whom all good has come.

~ GAELIC PRAYER

There is a faith in God, and a clear perception of His will and designs, and providence, and glory, which gives to its possessor a confidence and patience and sweet composure, under every varied and troubling aspect of events, such as no man can realize who has not felt its influences in his own heart.

~ SAMUEL D. ROBBINS

March 13

Your beauty should not come from outward adornment . . . Instead, it should be that of your inner self, the unfading beauty of a gentle and quiet spirit, which is of great worth in God's sight.
1 PETER 3:3-4

As some rare perfume in a vase of clay
Pervades it with a fragrance not its own,
So, when Thou dwellest in a mortal soul,
All Heaven's own sweetness seems around it thrown.
H. B. STOWE

The truth of a thing, then, is the blossom of it, the thing it is made for, the topmost stone set on with rejoicing; truth in a man's imagination is the power to recognize this truth of a thing; and wherever, in anything that God has made, in the glory of it, be it sky or flower or human face, we see the glory of God, there a true imagination is beholding a truth of God.

~ GEORGE MACDONALD

Some glances of real beauty may be seen in their faces, who dwell in true meekness. There is a harmony in the sound of that voice to which Divine love gives utterance, and some appearance of right order in their temper and conduct whose passions are regulated.

~ JOHN WOOLMAN

March 14

I call on you, O God, for you will answer me,
give ear to me and hear my prayer.
PSALMS 17:6

Pour out your hearts to him,
for God is our refuge.
PSALMS 62:8

Sure the Lord thus far has brought me,
By his watchful tender care;
Sure, 'tis he himself has taught me
How to seek his face by prayer:
After so much mercy past,
Will he give me up at last?
ANONYMOUS

Trouble and perplexity drive us to prayer, and prayer driveth away trouble and perplexity.

~ P. MELANCHTHON

Lord, I know not what I ought to ask of Thee; Thou only knowest what we need; Thou lovest me better than I know how to love myself. O Father! give to Thy child that which he himself knows not how to ask. I dare not ask either for crosses or consolations; I simply present myself before Thee; I open my heart to Thee. Behold my needs which I know not myself; see, and do according to Thy tender mercy. Smite, or heal; depress me, or raise me up; I adore all Thy purposes without knowing them; I am silent; I offer myself in sacrifice; I yield myself to Thee; I would have no other desire than to accomplish Thy will. Teach me to pray; pray Thyself in me.

~ FENELON

March 15

Answer me, O Lord, out of the goodness of your love;
in your great mercy turn to me.
PSALMS 69:16

May your unfailing love be my comfort . . .
PSALMS 119:76

Love divine has seen and counted
Every tear it caused to fall;
And the storm which Love appointed
Was its choicest gift of all.
ANONYMOUS

It is indeed natural to us to wish and to plan, and it is merciful in the Lord to disappoint our plans, and to cross our wishes. For we cannot be safe, much less happy, but in proportion as we are weaned from our own wills, and made simply desirous of being directed by His guidance. This truth (when we are enlightened by His Word) is sufficiently familiar to the judgement; but we seldom learn to reduce it into practice without being trained a while in the school of disappointment. The schemes we form look so plausible and convenient that when they are broken we are ready to say, "What a pity!" We try again, and with no better success; we are grieved, and perhaps angry, and plan another, and so on; at length, in a course of time, experience and observation begin to convince us that we are not more able than we are worthy to choose aright for ourselves. Then the Lord's invitation to cast our cares upon Him, and His promise to take care of us, appear valuable; and when we have done planning, His plan in our favour gradually opens, and He does more and better for us than we could either ask or think. . . .We judge of things by their present appearance, but the Lord sees them in their consequences; if we could do so likewise, we should be perfectly of His mind; but as we cannot, it is an unspeakable mercy that He will manage for us, whether we are pleased with His management or not . . . .

~ JOHN NEWTON

March 16

So whether you eat or drink or whatever you do,
do it all for the glory of God.
1 CORINTHIANS 11:31

How happy is he born and taught
That serveth not another's will;
Whose armour is his honest thought,
And simple truth his utmost skill!

Whose passions not his masters are;

Whose soul is still prepared for death,
Untied unto the world by care
Of public fame or private breath.

Who envies none that chance doth raise,
Nor vice; who never understood
How deepest wounds are given by praise;
Nor rules of state, but rules of good.

Who hath his life from rumours freed;
Whose conscience is his strong retreat;
Whose state can neither flatterers feed,
Nor ruin make oppressors great;

Who God doth late and early pray
More of His grace than gifts to lend;
And entertains the harmless day
With a religious book or friend;

This man is freed from servile bands
Of hope to rise or fear to fall:
Lord of himself, though not of lands,
And having nothing, yet has all.
SIR HENRY WOTTON

There is no action so slight nor so mean but it may be done to a great purpose, and ennobled therefore; nor is any purpose so great but that slight actions may help it, and may be done so as to help it much, most especially, that chief of all purposes— the pleasing of God.

~ JOHN RUSKIN

March 17

But as for you, continue in what you have learned and have become convinced of, because you know from whom you learned it . . .
2 TIMOTHY 3:14

For the ear tests words as the tongue tastes food. Let us discern for ourselves what is right; let us learn together what is good.
JOB 34:3-4

What have I learnt where'er I've been,
From all I've heard, from all I've seen?
What know I more that's worth the knowing?
What have I done that's worth the doing?
What have I sought that I should shun?
What duties have I left undone?
PYTHAGORAS

What refuge, then, in self-education; when a man feels himself powerless in the gripe of some unseen and inevitable power, and knows not whether it be chance, or necessity, or a devouring fiend? . . . There is but one escape, one chink through which we may see light, one rock on which our feet may find standing-place, even in the abyss: and that is the belief, intuitive, inspired, due neither to reasoning nor to study, that the billows are God's billows; and that though we go down to Hell, He is there also; the belief that not we, but He, is educating us; that these seemingly fantastic and incoherent miseries . . . have in His mind a spiritual coherence, an organic unity and purpose (though we see it not); that sorrows do not come singly, only because He is making short work with our spirits.

~ CHARLES KINGSLEY

Our fallibility and the shortness of our knowledge should make us peaceable and gentle. Because I may be mistaken, I must not be dogmatical and confident, peremptory and imperious. I will not break the certain laws of charity for a doubtful doctrine of uncertain truth.

Religion begins in knowledge, proceeds in practice, and ends in happiness.

~ BENJAMIN WHICHCOTE

March 18

How good and pleasant it is when brothers live together in unity!
PSALMS 133:1

*Carry each other's burdens,
and in this way you will fulfill the law of Christ.*
GALATIANS 6:2

*Make us of one heart and mind;
Courteous, pitiful, and kind;
Lowly, meek, in thought and word,
Altogether like our Lord.*
C. WESLEY

And I offer also for all those whom I have in any way grieved, vexed, oppressed, and scandalized, by word or deed, knowingly or unknowingly; that thou mayest equally forgive us all our sins, and all or offences against each other. Take away, O Lord, from our hearts all suspiciousness, indignation, anger and contention, and whatever is calculated to wound charity, and to lessen brotherly love.

~ THOMAS A. KEMPIS

Kindly words, sympathizing attentions, watchfulness against wounding men's sensitiveness—these cost very little, but they are priceless in their value.

~ F. W. ROBERTSON

March 19

*. . . if we are faithless, he will remain faithful,
for he cannot disown himself.*
2 TIMOTHY 2:13

. . . that we might be justified by faith.
GALATIANS 3:24

*Tis faith that conquers earth and hell
By a celestial power;*

This is the grace that shall prevail
In the decisive hour.
ANONYMOUS

O Lord Jesus Christ, only-begotten Son of thy eternal Father, thou hast said with thy most pure lips: "Without me ye can do nothing." O Lord, my Lord, with faith I embrace in my heart and soul the words spoken by thee; help me, a sinner, to accomplish the task begun for thine own sake by me, in the name of the Father and of the Son and of the Holy Ghost.

~ PRAYER, EASTERN ORTHODOX CHURCH

Lord, I believe thou art the way, the truth and the life. Make me so to walk with thee that by thee I may come to the Father; make my faith strong to believe all that thou hast revealed, for thou art the very truth. Give me thy life that I may say, "I live, yet not I, but Christ liveth in me": by thy divine omnipotence direct and strengthen my faith . . .

~ S. C. HUGHSON

March 20

"Worship the Lord your God, and serve him only."
MATTHEW 4:10

My Father, I abandon myself to you. Do with me as you will.
Whatever you may do with me, I thank you.
I am prepared for anything, I accept everything.
Provided your will is fulfilled in me and in all
creatures I ask for nothing more my God.
I place my soul in your hands.
I give it to you, my God,
with all the love of my heart
because I love you.
And for me it is a necessity of love,
this gift of myself,
this placing of myself in your hands
without reserve
in boundless confidence
because you are my Father.
CHARLES DE FOUCAULD

Desire only the will of God; seek Him alone, and you will find peace.

~ FENELON

I've been a great deal happier since I have given up thinking about what is easy and pleasant, and being discontented because I couldn't have my own will. Our life is determined for us; and it makes the mind very free when we give up wishing, and only think of bearing what is laid upon us, and doing what is given us to do.

~ GEORGE ELIOT

March 21

. . . for your Father knows what you need before you ask him.
MATTHEW 6:8

. . . you heavenly Father knows that you need them.
But seek first his kingdom . . . and all these things
will be given to you . . .
MATTHEW 6:32-33

All as God wills, who wisely heeds
To give or to withhold;
And knoweth more of all my needs
Than all my prayers have told.
J. G. WHITTIER

Doth He not know what is best for us, and what conduceth most unto His own glory? So is it to live in the exercise of faith that if God calls us unto any of those things which are peculiarly dreadful unto our natures, He will give us such supplies of spiritual strength and patience as shall enable us to undergo them, if not with ease and joy, yet with peace and quietness beyond our expectation. Multitudes have had experience that those things which at a distance have had an aspect of overwhelming dread, have been far from unsupportable in their approach, when strength has been received from above to encounter with them. And moreover it is in this case required that we be frequent and steady in comparing these things with those which are eternal, both as unto the misery which we are freed from and that blessedness which is prepared for us.

~ JOHN OWEN

March 22

"Well done, good and faithful servant! You have been faithful with a few
things; I will put you in charge of many things."
MATTHEW 25:21

Dear friend, you are faithful in what you are doing . . .
3 JOHN 5

In all the little things of life,
Thyself, Lord, may I see;
In little and in great alike
Reveal Thy love to me.
H. BONAR

There is another very safe and simple way of escape when the dull mood begins to gather round one, and that is to, turn as promptly and as strenu-ously as one can to whatever work one can at the moment do. If the ener-gy, the clearness, the power of intention, is flagging in us, if we cannot do our best work, still let us do what we can-for we can always do something; if not high work, then low work; if not vivid and spiritual work, then the plain, needful drudgery.

When it is dull and cold and weary weather with us, when the light is hid-den, and the mists are thick, and the sleet begins to fall, still we may get on with the work which can be done as well in the dark days as in the bright; work which otherwise will have to be hurried through in the sun-shine, taking up its happiest and most fruitful hours. When we seem poorest and least spiritual, when the glow of thankfulness seems to have died quite away, at least we can go on with the comparatively featureless bits of work, the business letters, the mechanism of life, the tasks which may be almost as well done then as ever. And not only, as men have found and said in every age, is the activity itself a safeguard for the time, but also very often, I think, the plainer work is the best way of getting back into the light and warmth that are needed for the higher.

~ FRANCIS PAGET

March 23

I can do everything through him who gives me strength.
PHILLIPPIANS 4:13

Strive thou with studious care to find
Some good thy hands may do;
Some way to serve and bless mankind,
Console the heart, relieve the mind,
And open comforts new.
ANONYMOUS

Grant us grace, our Father, to do our work this day as workmen who need not be ashamed. Give us the spirit of diligence and honest enquiry in our quest for the truth, the spirit of charity in all our dealings with our fellows, and the spirit of gaiety, courage, and a quiet mind in facing all tasks and responsibilities.

~ REINHOLD NIEBUHR

And give me, good Lord, an humble, lowly, quiet, peaceable, patient, charitable, kind and filial and tender mind, every shade, in fact, of charity, with all my words and all my works, and all my thoughts, to have a taste of thy holy blessed Spirit.

~ ST. THOMAS MORE

March 24

Find rest, O my soul, in God alone.
PSALMS 62:5

I will lie down and sleep in peace, for you alone,
O Lord, make me dwell in safety.
PSALMS 4:8

He lay with quiet heart in the stern asleep:
Waking, commanded both the winds and sea.
Christ, though this weary body slumber deep,
Grant that my heart may keep its watch with thee.
O Lamb of God that carried all our sin,
Guard thou my sleep against the enemy.
ALCUIN OF YORK

We sleep in peace in the arms of God, when we yield ourselves up to His providence, in a delightful consciousness of His tender mercies; no more restless uncertainties, no more anxious desires, no more impatience at the place we are in; for it is God who has put us there, and who holds us in His arms. Can we be unsafe where He has placed us?

~ FENELON

One evening when Luther saw a little bird perched on a tree, to roost there for the night, he said, "This little bird has had its supper, and now it is getting ready to go to sleep here, quite secure and content, never troubling itself what its food will be, or where its lodging on the morrow. Like David, it 'abides under the shadow of the Almighty.' It sits on its little twig content, and lets God take care."

~ ANONYMOUS

March 25

I will listen to what God the Lord will say;
he promises peace to his people . . .
PSALMS 85:8

There is a voice, "a still, small voice" of love,
Heard from above;
But not amidst the din of earthly sounds,
Which here confounds;
By those withdrawn apart it best is heard,
And peace, sweet peace, breathes in each gentle word.
ANONYMOUS

Speak, Lord, for thy servant heareth. Grant us ears to hear, eyes to see, wills to obey, hearts to love; then declare what thou wilt, reveal what thou wilt, command what thou wilt, demand what thou wilt—Amen.

~ CHRISTINA G. ROSSETTI

O Lord Jesus Christ, Thou Word and Revelation of the Eternal Father, come, we pray Thee, take possession of our hearts, and reign where thou hast right to reign. So fill our minds with the thought and our imaginations with the picture of Thy love, that there may be in us no room for any desire that is discordant with Thy holy will. Cleanse us, we pray Thee, from all that may make us deaf to Thy call or slow to obey it, Who, with the Father and the Holy Spirit, art one God, blessed forever.

~ WILLIAM TEMPLE

March 26

Think how you have instructed many, how you have strengthened
feeble hands. Your words have supported those who stumbled;
you have strengthened faltering knees.
JOB 4:3-4

May I reach
That purest heaven, be to other souls
The cup of strength in some great agony,
Enkindle generous ardour, feed pure love,
Be the sweet presence of a good diffused,
And in diffusion ever more intense!
So shall I join the choir invisible
Whose music is the gladness of the world.
GEORGE ELIOT

Hence we perceive that the true motive for our striving to set ourselves free is to manifest our freedom by resigning it through an act to be renewed every moment, ever resuming and ever resigning it; to the end that our service may be entire, that the service of the hands may likewise be the service of the will; even as the Apostle, being free from all, made himself servant to all. This is the accomplishment of the great Christian paradox, "Whosoever will be great, let him be a minister; and whosoever will be chief, let him be a servant."

~ J. C. AND AUGUSTUS HARE

O Lord give me strength to refrain from the unkind silence that is born of hardness of heart; the unkind silence that clouds the serenity of understanding and is the enemy of peace. Give me strength to be the first to tender the healing word and the renewal of friendship, that the bonds of amity and the flow of charity may be strengthened for the good of the brethren and the furthering of thine eternal, loving purpose.

~ CECIL HUNT

March 27

. . . if we love one another,
God lives in us and his love is made complete in us.
1 JOHN 4:12

God is love.
Whoever lives in love lives in God,
and God in him.
1 JOHN 4:16

O Love, how cheering is Thy ray!
All pain before Thy presence flies;
Care, anguish, sorrow, melt away,
Where'er Thy healing beams arise.
0 Father, nothing may I see,
Nothing desire, or seek, but Thee.
P. GERHARDT

The Spirit of Love must work the works, and speak the tones, of Love. It cannot exist and give no sign, or a false sign. It cannot be a spirit of Love, and mantle into irritable and selfish impatience. It cannot be a spirit of Love, and at the same time make self the prominent object. It cannot rejoice to lend itself to the happiness of others, and at the same time be seeking its own. It cannot be generous, and envious. It cannot be sympathizing, and unseemly; self-forgetful, and vain-glorious. It cannot delight in the rectitude and purity of other hearts, as the spiritual elements of their peace, and yet unnecessarily suspect them.

~ J. H. THOM

March 28

Sing praises to the Lord, enthroned in Zion.
PSALMS 9:11

*I will give thanks to the Lord because of his righteousness
and will sing praise to the name of the Lord Most High.*
PSALMS 7:17

*For blessings of the fruitful season,
For work and rest, for friends and home,
For the great gifts of thought and reason,
To praise and bless Thee, Lord, we come.*

*Yes, and for weeping and for wailing,
For bitter hail and blighting frost,
For high hopes on the low earth trailing,
For sweet joys missed, for pure aims crossed.*
E. SCUDDER

Almighty God, Father of all mercies, we thine unworthy servants do give
thee most humble and hearty thanks for all thy goodness and loving-kindness to us, and to all men; We bless thee for our creation, preservation and
all the blessings of this life; but above all, for thine inestimable love in the
redemption of the world by our Lord Jesus Christ; for the means of grace,
and for the hope of glory. And, we beseech thee, give us that due sense of
all thy mercies, that our hearts may be unfeignedly thankful, and that we
shew forth thy praise, not only with our lips, but in our lives . . .
~ BOOK OF COMMON PRAYER

March 29

I will fear no evil, for you are with me . . .
PSALMS 23:4

The Lord shall preserve you from all harm . . .
PSALMS 122:7

*No coward soul is mine,
No trembler in the world's storm-troubled sphere:
I see Heaven's glories shine,
And faith shines equal, arming me from fear.*
EMILY BRONTE

Be like the promontory, against which the waves continually break; but it
stands firm, and tames the fury of the water around it. Unhappy am I,
because this has happened to me? Not so, but happy am I, though this has
happened to me, because I continue free from pain, neither crushed by the
present, nor fearing the future. Will then this which has happened prevent
thee from being just, magnanimous, temperate, prudent, secure against
inconsiderate opinions and falsehood? Remember, too, on every occasion
which leads thee to vexation to apply this principle: that this is not a misfortune, but that to bear it nobly is good fortune.
~ MARCUS ANTONINUS

March 30

You guide me with your counsel, and afterward you will take me into glory.
PSALMS 73:24

You will be secure, because there is hope;
you will look about you and take your rest in safety.
JOB 11:18

Lord, through this hour
Be Thou our Guide,
So by Thy power
No foot shall slide.
WESTMINSTER CHIMES

Go forth to meet the solemnities and to conquer the trials of existence, believing in a Shepherd of your souls. Then faith in Him will support you in duty, and duty firmly done will strengthen faith; till at last, when all is over here, and the noise and strife of the earthly battle fades upon your dying ear, and you hear, instead thereof, the deep and musical sound of the ocean of eternity, and see the lights of heaven shining on its waters still and fair in their radiant rest, your faith will raise the song of conquest, and in its retrospect of the life which has ended, and its forward stance upon the life to come, take up the poetic inspiration of the Hebrew king, "Surely goodness and mercy have followed me all the days Of my life, and I will dwell in the house of the Lord forever."

~ STOPFORD A. BROOKE

March 31

For you will have a covenant with the stones of the field,
and the wild animals will be at peace with you.
JOB 6:23

All your strength is in your union.
All your danger is in discord;
Therefore be at peace henceforward,
And as brothers live together.
HENRY WADSWORTH LONGFELLOW

All creatures are living in the hand of God; the senses only perceive the action of the creature, but faith sees the divine action in everything; faith believes that Jesus Christ is alive in everything and operates throughout the whole extent of the centuries; faith believes that the shortest moment and the tiniest atom contain a portion of His hidden life and His mysterious actio. . . If we had faith, we should welcome all creatures; we should, as it were, caress them interiorly for contributing so favourably to our perfection when applied by the hand of God.

~ J. P. DE CAUSSADE

April 1

"I have loved you with an everlasting love."
JEREMIAH 31:3

For God so loved the world that
he gave his one and only Son . . .
JOHN 3:16

That Love is all there is,
Is all we know of Love;
It is enough, the freight should be
Proportioned to the groove.
EMILY DICKINSON

To know that Love alone was the beginning of nature and creature, that
nothing but Love encompasses the whole universe of things, that the gov-
erning Hand that overrules all, the watchful Eye that sees through all, is
nothing but omnipotent and omniscient Love, using an infinity of wisdom, to save every misguided creature from the miserable works of his
own hands, and make happiness and glory the perpetual inheritance of all
the creation, is a reflection that must be quite ravishing to every intelli-
gent creature that is sensible of it.

~ WILLIAM LAW

April 2

Don't you know that you yourselves are God's temple
and that God's Spirit lives in you?
1 CORINTHIANS 3:16

Oh thou who camest from above,
The pure celestial fire to impart,
Kindle a flame of sacred love
On the mean altar of my heart.

There let it for thy glory burn
With inextinguishable blaze,
And trembling to its source return
In humble prayer, and fervent praise.
CHARLES WESLEY

We have our treasure in earthen vessels, but thou, O Holy Spirit, when
thou livest in a man, thou livest in what is infinitely lower. Thou Spirit of
Holiness, thou livest in the midst of impurity and corruption; thou Spirit
of Wisdom, thou livest in the midst of folly; thou Spirit of Truth, thou
livest in one who is himself deluded. Oh, continue to dwell there, thou
who dost not seek a desirable dwelling place, for thou wouldst seek there
in vain, thou Creator and Redeemer, to make a dwelling for thyself; oh,
continue to dwell there, that one day thou mayst finally be pleased by the
dwelling which thou didst thyself prepare in my heart, foolish, deceiving,
and impure as it is.

~ SØREN KIERKEGAARD

But as for you, the Lord your God has not permitted you to do so.
DEUTERONOMY 18:20

LORD, for the erring thought
Not into evil wrought;
Lord, for the wicked will
Betrayed and baffled still
For the heart from itself kept,
Our Thanksgiving accept.
W. D. HOWELLS

What an amazing, what a blessed disproportion between the evil we do, and the evil we are capable of doing, and seem sometimes on the very verge of doing! If my soul has grown tares, when it was full of the seeds of nightshade, how happy ought I to be! And that the tares have not wholly strangled the wheat, what a wonder it is! We ought to thank God daily for the sins we have not committed.

~ F. W. FABER

We give thanks often with a tearful, doubtful voice, for our spiritual mercies positive; but what an almost infinite field there is for mercies negative! We cannot even imagine all that God has suffered us not to do, not to be.

~ F. R. HAVERGAL

You are surprised at your imperfections—why? I should infer from that, that your self-knowledge is small. Surely, you might rather be astonished that you do not fall into more frequent and more grievous faults, and thank God for His upholding grace.

~ JEAN NICOLAS GROU

How many are your works, O Lord! In wisdom you made them all; the earth is full of your creatures. There is the sea, vast and spacious, teeming with creatures beyond number— living things both large and small.
PSALMS 104:24-25

All things bright and beautiful,
All creatures great and small,
All things wise and wonderful,
The Lord God made them all.
CECIL F. ALEXANDER

We cannot in any better manner glorify the Lord and Creator of the universe than that in all things, how small soever they appear to our naked eyes, but which have yet received the gift of life and power of increase, we contemplate the display of his omnificence and perfections with the utmost admiration.

~ ANTON VAN LEEUWENHOEK

What inexpressible joy for me, to look up through the apple blossom and the fluttering leaves, and to see God's love there; to listen to the thrush that has built his nest among them, and to feel God's love, who cares for the birds, in every note that swells his little throat; to look beyond to the bright blue depths of the sky, and feel they are a canopy of blessing—the roof of the house of my Father; that if clouds pass over it, it is the unchangeable light they veil; that, even when the day itself passes, I shall see that the night itself only unveils new worlds of light; and to know that if I could unwrap fold after fold of God's universe, I should only unfold more and more blessing, and see deeper and deeper into the love which is at the heart of all.

~ ELIZABETH CHARLES

April 5

Yet I reserve seven thousand in Israel—all whose knees have not bowed down to Baal and all whose mouths have not kissed him.
1 KINGS 19:18

Back then, complainer; loathe thy life no more,
Nor deem thyself upon a desert shore,
Because the rocks the nearer prospect close.
Yet in fallen Israel are there hearts and eyes
That day by day in prayer like thine arise:
Thou know'st them not, but their Creator knows.
J. KEBLE

Every life is a profession of faith and exercises an inevitable and silent propaganda. As far as lies in its power, it tends to transform the universe and humanity into its own image. Thus we all have a cure of souls. Every man is a center of perpetual radiation like a luminous body; he is, as it were, a beacon which entices a ship upon the rocks if it does not guide it into port. Every man is a priest, even involuntarily; his conduct is an unspoken sermon, which is for ever preaching to others—but there are priests of Baal, of Moloch, and of all the false gods. Such is the high importance of example. Thence comes the terrible responsibility which weighs upon us all. An evil example is a spiritual poison: it is the proclamation of a sacrilegious faith, of an impure God. Sin would be an evil only for him who commits it, were it not a crime towards the weak brethren, whom it corrupts. Therefore it has been said: "It were better for a man not to have been born than to offend one of these little ones."

~ HENRI-FREDERIC AMIEL

April 6

We are hard pressed on every side,
but not crushed; perplexed,
but not in despair; persecuted, but not abandoned;
struck down, but not destroyed.
2 CORINTHIANS 4:8-9

Therefore do not lose heart . . .
2 CORINTHIANS 4:16

Discouraged in the work of life,
Disheartened by its load,
Shamed by its failures or its fears,
I sink beside the road;
But let me only think of Thee,
And then new heart springs up in me.

S. LONGFELLOW

O my God, thou art very near, in my heart and about my way; yet often thou dost seem very far off and my soul fainteth for looking after thee: thou dost lead me through dark places and withdrawest thyself from me. In the desolate time, when I feel perplexed and forsaken, I would think upon the cross of my Savior and his dreadful cry, that my faith may hold fast in his faith and that despair may not seize me. Help me to remember the days of vision and sure confidence, guide me to stay my soul in the revelations of thyself which thou hast given me in time past through all thy prophets and servants, and bring me out of the valley of the dark shade once more into the light of thy presence, through Jesus Christ our Lord.

~ W. R. MATTHEWS

April 7

"I am willing . . ."
MATTHEW 8:3

. . . be transformed by the renewing of your mind.
Then you will be able to test and approve what
God's will is—his good, pleasing and perfect will.
ROMANS 12:2

Thou knowest what is best
And who but Thee, O God, hath power to know?
In Thy great will my trusting heart shall rest;
Beneath that will my humble head shall bow.

T. C. UPHAM

Let no riches make me ever forget myself, no poverty make me to forget thee: let no hope or fear, no pleasure or pain, no accident without, no weakness within, hinder or discompose my duty, or turn me from the ways of thy commandments . . .

~ JEREMY TAYLOR

Suffer me never to think that I have knowledge enough to need no teaching, wisdom enough to need no correction, talents enough to need no grace, goodness enough to need no progress, humility enough to need no repentance, devotion enough to need no quickening, strength sufficient without thy Spirit; lest, standing still, I fall back for evermore.

~ ERIC MILNER-WHITE

April 8

"I am the good shepherd.
The good shepherd lays down his life for the sheep."
JOHN 10:11

The Lord is my shepherd, I shall not want.
PSALMS 23:1

The King of love my shepherd is,
Whose goodness faileth never;
I nothing lack if I am his,
And he is mine forever.
SIR HENRY WILLIAMS BAKER

Who is it that is your shepherd? The Lord! Oh, my friends, what a wonderful announcement! The Lord God of heaven and earth, the almighty Creator of all things, He who holds the universe in His hand as though it were a very little thing, He is your shepherd, and has charged Himself with the care and keeping of you, as a shepherd is charged with the care and keeping of his sheep. If your hearts could really take in this thought, you would never have a fear or a care again; for with such a shepherd, how could it be possible for you ever to want any good thing?

~ H. W. S.

April 9

When tempted, no one should say,
"God is tempting me." For God cannot be tempted by evil,
nor does he tempt anyone; but each one is tempted when,
by his own evil desire, he is dragged away and enticed.
JAMES 1:13-14

One more temptation;
the straight road to Accra.
Lord, keep my feet steady on the pedals
even on the straight road to Accra.

Lord,
I sing hallelujah
when the ride is ended
for you brought the truck and the people
in safety
through the hustle and bustle of Accra.

Lord, all is mercy,
because
"Jesus is mine."
Hallelujah. Amen.
BY A YOUNG GHANAIAN CHRISTIAN

O Christ, guide and strengthen all who are tempted in this hour.
~ UNITED SOCIETY FOR
THE PROPAGATION OF THE GOSPEL

Christian life means a walking; it goes by steps. There is a straight fence run for us between right and wrong. There is no sitting on that fence. No; only walking, one side or other. You can hardly look across without stepping through.

~ R.W. BARBOUR

Blessed Lord, who wast tempted in all things like as we are, have mercy upon our frailty. Out of weakness give us strength. Grant to us thy fear, that we may fear thee only. Support us in time of temptation. Embolden us in the time of danger. Help us to do thy work with good courage, and to continue thy faithful soldiers and servant unto our life's end; through Jesus Christ our Lord.

~ BISHOP BROOKE FOSS WESTCOTT

April 10

What good is it, my brothers,
if a man claims to have faith but has no deeds?
JAMES 2:14

Who is wise and understanding among you? Let him show it by his good
life, by deeds done in the humility that comes from wisdom.
JAMES 3:13

Teach me, my God and King,
In all things Thee to see,
And what I do in anything,
To do it as for Thee.
GEORGE HERBERT

Both the spiritual and the bodily powers of a man increase and become perfected and strengthened by their exercise. By exercising your hand in writing, sewing, or knitting you will accustom it to such work; by frequently exercising yourself in composition you will learn to write easily and well; by exercising yourself in doing good works or in conquering your passions and temptations, you will in time learn to do good works easily and with delight: and with the help of God's all-active grace you will easily learn to conquer your passions. But if you cease writing, sewing, knitting, or if you only do so seldom, you will write, sew, and knit badly. If you do not exercise yourself in composition, or do so very seldom, if you live in the material cares of life only, it will probably become difficult for you to connect a few words together, especially upon spiritual subjects; the work set you will seem to you like an Egyptian labor. If you cease praying, or pray seldom, prayer will be oppressive to you. If you do not fight against your passions, or only do so seldom and feebly, you will find it very difficult to fight against them; they will give you no rest, and your life will be poisoned by them, if you do not learn how to conquer these evil inward enemies that settle in your heart. Therefore labor and activity are indispensable for all. Life without activity is not life, but something monstrous—a sort of phantom of life. This is why it is the duty of every man to fight continually and persistently against the slothfulness of the flesh. God preserve every Christian from indulging it! "They that are Christ's have crucified the flesh with the affections and lusts." "Unto every one that hath shall be given, and he shall have abundance; but from him that hath not shall be taken away even that which he hath."

~ FATHER JOHN SERGIEFF

April 11

. . . make every effort to be found spotless,
blameless and at peace with him.
2 PETER 3:14

Thy Sinless mind in us reveal,
Thy spirit's plenitude impart!
Till all my spotless life shall tell
The abundance of a loving heart.
C. WESLEY

Almighty God, from whom all thoughts of truth and peace proceed:
Kindle, we pray thee, in the hearts of all men the true love of peace; and
guide with thy pure and peaceable wisdom those who take counsel for the
nations of the earth; that in tranquility thy kingdom may go forward,
till the earth is filled with the knowledge of thy love; through Jesus
Christ our Lord.

~ BISHOP FRANCIS PAGET

Even the smallest discontent of conscience may render turbid the whole
temper of the mind; but only produce the effort that restores its peace, and
over the whole atmosphere a breath of unexpected purity is spread; doubt
and irritability pass as clouds away; the withered sympathies of earth and
home open their leaves and live; and through the clearest blue the deep is
seen of the heaven where God resides.

~ JAMES MARTINEAU

April 12

Aim for perfection, listen to my appeal,
be of one mind, live in peace.
2 CORINTHIANS 13:11

Whoever loves God must also love his brother.
1 JOHN 4:21

Cure thy children's warring madness,
Bend our pride to thy control;
Shame our wanton selfish gladness,
Rich in goods and poor in soul.
Lest we miss thy Kingdom's goal.
Lest we miss the Kingdom's goal.
HARRY EMERSON FOSDICK

It requires far more of the constraining love of Christ to love our cousins
and neighbors as members of the heavenly family, than to feel the heart
warm to our suffering brethren in Tuscany or Madeira. To love the whole
Church is one thing; to love—that is, to delight in the graces and veil the
defects—of the person who misunderstood me and opposed my plans yesterday, whose peculiar infirmities grate on my most sensitive feelings, or
whose natural faults are precisely those from which my natural character
most revolts, is quite another.

~ ELIZABETH CHARLES

Lord, you return gladly and lovingly to lift up the one who offends you and I do not turn to raise up and honor the one who angers me.

~ ST. JOHN OF THE CROSS

April 13

No, in all these things we are more than conquerors
through him who loved us.
ROMANS 8:37

O Jesu, king most wonderful,
Thou conqueror renowned,
Thou sweetness most ineffable,
In whom all joys are found!

When once thou visitest the heart,
Then truth egins to shine;
Then earthly vanities depart;
Then kindles love divine.
LATIN, 11TH CENTURY

Ye are brothers! Ye are men!
And we conquer but to save.
THOMAS CAMPBELL

If a man, by putting on Christ's life, can get nothing more than he Hath already, and serve no end, what good will it do him' This life is not chosen in order to serve any end, or to get anything by it, but for the love of its nobleness, and because God loveth and esteemeth it so greatly. And who-ever saith that he hath had enough of it, and may now lay it aside, hath never tasted nor known it; for he who hath truly felt or tasted it can never give it up again. And he who hath put on the life of Christ with the intent to win or deserve ought thereby, hath taken it up as an hireling and not for love, and is altogether without it. For he who doth not take it up for love, hath none of it at all; he may dream indeed that he hath put it on, but he is deceived. Christ did not lead such a life as His for the sake of reward, but out of love; and love maketh such a life light and taketh away all its hardships, so that it becometh sweet and is gladly endured. But to him who hath not put it on from love but, as he dreameth, for the sake of reward, It is utterly bitter and a weariness, and he would fain be quit of it. And it is a sure token of an hireling that he wisheth his work were at an end. But he who truly loveth it is not offended at its toil nor suffering, nor the length of time it lasteth.

~ THEOLOGIA GERMANICA

April 14

. . . having nothing, and yet possessing everything.
2 CORINTHIANS 6:10

Blessed is the man who finds wisdom,
the man who gains
understanding, for she is more profitable than silver and
yields better returns than gold.
PROVERBS 3:13-14

So shall my undivided life
To Thee, my God, be given
And all this earthly course below
Be one dear path to heaven.

H. BONAR

If I build my felicity upon my estate or reputation, I am happy so long as the tyrant or the railer will give me leave to be so. But when my concernment takes up no more room or compass than myself, then so long as I know where to breathe and to exist, I know also where to be happy: for I know I may be so in my own breast, in the court of my own conscience; where, if I can but prevail with myself to be innocent, I need bribe neither judge nor officer to be pronounced so. The pleasure of the religious man is an easy and a portable pleasure, such a one as he carries about in his bosom without alarming either the eye or envy of the world. A man putting all his pleasures into this one is like a traveler's putting all his goods into one jewel; the value is the same, and the convenience greater.

There is nothing that can raise a man to that generous absoluteness of condition as neither to cringe, to fawn, or to defend meanly, but that which gives him that happiness within himself for which men depend upon others. For surely I need salute no great man's threshold, sneak to none of his friends or servants, to speak a good word for me to my conscience. It is a noble and a sure defiance of a great malice, backed with a great interest; which yet can have no advantage of a man but from his own expectations of something that is without himself. But if I can make my duty my delight; if I can feast and please and caress my mind with the pleasures of worthy speculations or virtuous practices; let greatness and malice vex and abridge me if they can: my pleasures are as free as my will; no more to be controlled than my choice or the unlimited range of my thoughts and my desires.

~ ROBERT SOUTH

April 15

And we know that in all things God works
for the good of those who love him, who have been
called according to his purpose.

ROMANS 8:28

You intended to harm me,
but God intended it for good . . .

GENESIS 50:20

Do all the good you can,
By all the means you can,
In all the ways you can,
In all the places you can,
At all the times you can,
To all the people you can,
As long as ever you can.

JOHN WESLEY

To those who know themselves, all things work together for good, and all things seem to be, as they are to them, good. The goods which God gives seem "very good," and God Himself in them, because they know that they deserve them not. The evils which God allows and overrules seem also "very good," because they see in them His loving hand, put forth to heal them of what shuts out God from the soul. They love God intensely, in that He is so good to them in each, and every, the least good, because it is more than they deserve: how much more in the greatest! They love God for every, and each, the very greatest of what seem evils, knowing them to be, from His love, real goods. For He by whom "all the hairs of our head are numbered," and who "knoweth whereof we are made," directs everything which befalls us in life, in perfect wisdom and love, to the well-being of our souls.

~ E. B. PUSEY

April 16

The same Lord is Lord of all and richly blesses all who call on him, for, "Everyone who calls on the name of the Lord will be saved."
ROMANS 10:12-13

The one who calls you is faithful and he will do it.
1 THESSALONIANS 5:24

Be still, my soul!—the Lord is on thy side
Bear patiently the cross of grief and pain
Leave to thy God to order and provide,—
In every change He faithful will remain.
HYMNS FROM THE LAND OF LUTHER

It was no relief from temporal evils that the Apostle promised. . . . No, the mercy of God might send them to the stake, or the lions; it was still His mercy, if it but kept them "unspotted from the world." It might expose them to insult, calumny, and wrong; they received it still as mercy, if it "established them in every good word and work." O brethren! how many of you are content with such faithfulness as this on the part of your heavenly Father? Is this, indeed, the tone and tenor of your prayers?

~ WILLIAM ARCHER BUTLER

April 17

You will keep in perfect peace him whose mind is steadfast, because he trusts in you.
ISAIAH 26:3

. . . and trust in the Lord.
PSALMS 4:5

Just to let thy Father do
What He will;
just to know that He is true,
And be still;
Just to trust Him, this is all!
Then the day will surely be
Peaceful, whatsoe'er befall,
Bright and blessed, calm and free.
F. R. HAVERGAL

Another branch of blessedness is a power of reposing ourselves and our concerns upon the Lord's faithfulness and care, and may be considered in two respects: a reliance upon Him that He will surely provide for us, guide us, protect us, be our help in trouble, our shield in danger, so that, however poor, weak, and defenceless in ourselves, we may rejoice in His all-sufficiency as our own; and further, in consequence of this, a peaceful, humble submission to His will under all events which, upon their first impression, are contrary to our own views and desires. Surely, in a world like this, where every thing is uncertain, where we are exposed to trials on every hand, and know not but a single hour may bring forth something painful, yea dreadful, to our natural sensations, there can be no blessedness but so far as we are thus enabled to entrust and resign all to the direction and faithfulness of the Lord our Shepherd. For want of more of this spirit multitudes of professing Christians perplex and wound themselves and dishonor their high calling by continual anxieties, alarms, and complaints. They think nothing safe under the Lord's keeping unless their own eye is likewise upon it, and are seldom satisfied with any of His dispensations: for though He gratify their desires in nine instances, a refusal in the tenth spoils the relish of all, and they show the truths of the Gospel can afford them little comfort, if self is crossed. But blessed is the man who trusteth in the Lord, and whose hope the Lord is. He shall not be afraid of evil tidings: he shall be kept in perfect peace, though the earth be moved, and the mountains cast into the midst of the sea.

~ JOHN NEWTON

April 18

Let everything that has breath praise the Lord.
PSALMS 150:6

I praise you because I am fearfully and wonderfully made;
your works are wonderful . . .
PSALMS 139:14

What asks our Father of His children save
Justice and mercy and humility,
A reasonable service of good deeds,
Pure living, tenderness to human needs,
Reverence, and trust, and prayer for light to see
The Master's footprints in our daily ways?
No knotted scourge, nor sacrificial knife,
But the calm beauty of an ordered life
Whose every breathing is unworded praise.
J.G. WHITTIER

As long as rivers shall run down to the sea, or shadows touch the mountain slopes, or stars graze in the vault of heaven, so long shall your honor, your name, your praises endure.

~ VIRGIL

Take away, O Lord, the veil of my heart while I read the scriptures. Blessed art thou, O Lord: O teach me thy statures! Give me a word, O Word of the Father: touch my heart: enlighten the understandings of my heart: open my lips and fill them with thy praise.

~ BISHOP LANCELOT ANDREWES

April 19

*The gracious hand of our God
is on everyone who looks to him . . .*
EZRA 8:22

My times are in your hands; deliver me from my enemies . . .
PSALMS 31:15

*Today, beneath Thy chastening eye,
I crave alone for peace and rest
Submissive in Thy hand to lie,
And feel that it is best.*
J. G. WHITTIER

Be still and cool in thy own mind and spirit from thy own thoughts, and then thou wilt feel the principle of God, to turn thy mind to the Lord God, from whom life comes; whereby thou mayest receive His strength, and power to allay all blustering storms and tempests. That is it which works up into patience, into innocency, into soberness, into stillness, into stayed-ness, into quietness, up to God with His power. . . . Therefore be still awhile from thy own thoughts, searching, seeking, desires, and imaginations, and be stayed in the principle of God in thee, that it may raise thy mind up to God, and stay it upon God; and thou wilt find strength from Him, and find Him to be a God at hand, a present help in the time of trouble and need.

~ GEORGE FOX

April 20

. . . we also rejoice in our sufferings, because we know that suffering produces perseverance; perseverance, character; and character, hope.
ROMANS 5:3-4

It was good for me to be afflicted so that I might learn your decrees.
PSALMS 119:71

*The path of sorrow, and that path alone,
Leads to the land where sorrow is unknown.
No traveller e'er reached that bless'd abode,
Who found not thorns and briars in his road.*
ANONYMOUS

Lord, teach me the art of patience whilst I am well, and give me the use of it when I am sick. In that day either lighten my burden or strengthen my back. Make me, who so often in my health have discovered my weakness presuming on my own strength, to be strong in my sickness when I solely rely on thy assistance.

~ THOMAS FULLER

If we consider how much men can suffer if they list, and how much they do suffer for greater and little causes, and that no causes are greater than the proper causes of patience in sickness (that is, necessity and religion) we cannot, without huge shame to our nature, to our persons, and to our manners, complain of this tax and impost of nature. . . .

Sickness is the more tolerable, because it cures very many evils, and takes away the sense of all the cross fortunes, which amaze the spirits of some men, and transport them certainly beyond all the limits of patience. Here all losses and disgraces, domestic cares and public evils, the apprehensions of pity and a sociable calamity, the fears of want and the troubles of ambition, lie down and rest upon the sick man's pillow. . . .

~ JEREMY TAYLOR

April 21

*Whoever has my commands and obeys them,
he is the one who loves me.*
JOHN 14:21

I love you, O Lord, my strength.
PSALMS 18:1

*Blest be Thy love, dear Lord,
That taught us this sweet way,
Only to love Thee for Thyself,
And for that love obey.*
J. AUSTIN

O Lord, who hast taught us that all our doings without love are nothing worth; Send thy Holy Spirit, and pour into our hearts that most excellent gift of love, the very bond of peace and of all virtues, without which whosoever liveth is counted dead before thee: Grant this for thine only Son Jesus Christ's sake.

~ BOOK OF COMMON PRAYER

God is Infinite; and to love the boundless, reaching on from grace to grace, adding charity to faith, and rising upwards ever to see the Ideal still above us, and to die with it unattained, aiming insatiably to be perfect even as the Father is perfect—that is to love God.

~ F. W. ROBERTSON

April 22

The Lord has done great things for us, and we are filled with joy.
PSALMS 126:3

Come and share your master's happiness!
MATTHEW 25:23

*Joy to the world! the Lord is come;
Let earth receive her King.
Let ev'ry heart prepare Him room,
An heav'n and nature sing.*
ISAAC WATTS

As for that which is beyond your strength, be absolutely certain that our Lord loves you, devotedly and individually: loves you just as you are. How often that conviction is lacking even in those souls who are most devoted to God! They make repeated efforts to love Him, they experience the joy of loving, and yet how little they know, how little they realize, that God loves them incomparably more than they will ever know how to love Him. Think only of this and say to yourself, "I am loved by God more than I can either conceive or understand." Let this fill all your soul and all your prayers and never leave you. You will soon see that this is the way to find God. It contains the whole of St. John's teaching: "As for us, we have believed in the love which God has for us. . . ." Accustom yourself to the wonderful thought that God loves you with a tenderness, a generosity, and an intimacy which surpasses all your dreams. Give yourself up with joy to a loving confidence in God and have courage to believe firmly that God's action towards you is a masterpiece of partiality and love. Rest tranquilly in this abiding conviction.

~ HENRI DE TOURVILLE

April 23

Better a little with the fear of the Lord,
great wealth with turmoil.
PROVERBS 15:16

One man pretends to be rich, yet has nothing;
another pretends to be poor, yet has great wealth.
PROVERBS 13:7

. . . I asked for riches that I might be happy;
I was given poverty that I might be wise.
I asked for power that I might have the praise of men;
I was given weakness that I might feel the need of God
I asked for all things that I might enjoy life;
I was given life that I might enjoy all things.
. . . Almost despite myself my unspoken prayers were answered;
I am, among all men, most richly blessed.
PRAYER OF AN UNKNOWN CONFEDERATE SOLDIER

My friends, do you remember that old Scythian custom, when the head of a house died? How he was dressed in his finest dress, and set in his chariot, and carried about to his friends' houses; and each of them placed him at his table's head, and all feasted in his presence? Suppose it were offered to you in plain words, as it is offered to you in dire facts, that you should gain this Scythian honour, gradually, while you yet thought yourself alive. Suppose the offer were this: You shall die slowly; your blood shall daily grow cold, your flesh petrify, your heart beat at last only as a rusted group of iron valves. Your life shall fade from you, and sink through the earth into the ice of Caina; but, day by day, your body shall be dressed more gaily, and set in higher chariots, and have more orders on its breast— crowns on its head, if you will. Men shall bow before it, stare and shout round it, crowd after it up and down the streets; build palaces for it, feast with it at their tables' heads all the night long; your soul shall stay enough within it to know what they do, and feel the weight of the golden dress on its shoulders, and the furrow of the crown-edge on the skull—no more. Would you take the offer, verbally made by the death angel? Would the meanest among us take it, think you? Yet practically and verily we grasp at it, every one of us, in a measure; many of us grasp at it in its fullness of horror. Every man accepts it who desires to advance in life without knowing what life is; who means only that he is to get more horses, and more footmen, and more fortune, and more public honor, and—not more personal soul. He only is advancing in life whose heart is getting softer, whose blood warmer, whose brain quicker, whose spirit is entering into living peace.

~ JOHN RUSKIN

April 24

Carry each other's burdens,
and in this way you will fulfill the law of Christ.
GALATIANS 6:2

"I tell you the truth, whatever you did for one of the least of these brothers
of mine, you did for me."
MATTHEW 25:40

Is thy cruse of comfort wasting?
Rise and share it with another,
And through all the years of famine,
It shall serve thee and thy brother.
Is thy burden hard and heavy?
Do thy steps drag heavily?
Help to bear thy brother's burden
God will bear both it and thee.
ELIZABETH CHARLES

However perplexed you may at any hour become about some question of truth, one refuge and resource is always at hand: you can do something for some one besides yourself. When your own burden is heaviest, you can always lighten a little some other burden. At the times when you cannot see God, there is still open to you this sacred possibility, to show God; for it is the love and kindness of human hearts through which the divine reality comes home to men, whether they name it or not. Let this thought, then, stay with you; there may be times when you cannot find help, but there is no time when you cannot give help.

~ GEORGE S. MERRIAM

April 25

Train a child in the way he should go,
and when he is old he will not turn from it.
PROVERBS 22:6

But I have stilled and quieted my soul;
like a weaned child with its mother,
like a weaned child is my soul within me.
PSALMS 131:2

When I was a child,
I talked like a child,
I thought like a child,
I reasoned like a child.
When I became a man,
I put childish ways behind me.
1 CORINTHIANS 13:11

"What does God do all day?" once asked a little boy. One could wish that more grown-up people would ask so very real a question. Unfortunately most of us are not even boys in religious intelligence, but only very unthinking babes. It no more occurs to us that God is engaged in any particular work in the world than it occurs to a little child that its father does anything except be its father. Its father may be a cabinet minister absorbed in the nation's work or an inventor deep in schemes for the world's good; but to this master-egoist he is father and nothing more. Childhood, whether in the physical or in the moral world, is the great self-centered period of life; and a personal God who satisfies personal ends is all that for a long time many a Christian understands.

But as clearly as there comes to the growing child a knowledge of his father's part in the world, and a sense of what real life means, there must come to every Christian, whose growth is true, some richer sense of the meaning of Christianity and a larger view of Christ's purpose for mankind.

~ HENRY DRUMMOND

For as children tremble and fear everything in the blind darkness, so we in the light sometimes fear what is no more to be feared than the things children in the dark hold in terror and imagine will come true.

~ LUCRETIUS

April 26

You need to persevere so that when you have done the will of God,
you will receive what he has promised.
HEBREWS 10:36

With the Lord a day is like a thousand years, and a thousand years are
like a day. The Lord is not slow in keeping his promise . . .
1 PETER 3:8-9

Lord! who Thy thousand years dost wait
To work the thousandth part
Of Thy vast plan, for us create
With zeal a patient heart.
J. H. NEWMAN

I believe that if we could only see beforehand what it is that our heavenly Father means us to be—the soul beauty and perfection and glory, the glorious and lovely spiritual body that this soul is to dwell in through all eternity—if we could have a glimpse of this, we should not grudge all the trouble and pains He is taking with us now, to bring us up to that ideal, which is His thought of us. We know that it is God's way to work slowly, so we must not be surprised if He takes a great many years of discipline to turn a mortal being into an Immortal, glorious angel.

~ ANNIE KEARY

His time is forever, everywhere his place.

~ ABRAHAM COWLEY

The strongest of all warriors are these two—Time and Patience.

~ LEO TOLSTOY

---

*Therefore each of you must put off falsehood and speak truthfully to his
neighbor, for we are all members of one body.*
EPHESIANS 4:25

Appear I always what I am?
And am I what I am pretending?
Know I what way my course is bending?
And sound my word and thought the same?
ANONYMOUS

Wisdom without honesty is mere craft and cozenage. And therefore the
reputation of honesty must first be gotten; which cannot be but by living
well. A good life is a main argument.

Truth is man's proper good and the only immortal thing was given to our
mortality to use. No good Christian or ethnic, if he be honest, can miss it; no
statesman or patriot should. For without truth all the actions of mankind are
craft, malice, or what you will rather than wisdom. Homer says he hates him
worse than hell mouth that utters one thing with his tongue and keeps another
in his breast. Which high expression was grounded on divine reason; for a lying
mouth is a stinking pit, and murders with the contagion it venteth. Beside,
nothing is lasting that is feigned; it will have another face than it had, ere long.
As Euripides said, "No lie ever grows old."

~ BEN JONSON

I must speak the truth, and nothing but the truth.
. . . An honest man's word is as good as his bond.

~ MIGUEL DE CERVANTES

Almighty God, bestow upon us the meaning of words, the light of understanding, the nobility of diction and the faith of the true nature. And grant
that what we believe we may also speak.

~ ST. HILARY

Great peace have they who love your law . . .
PSALMS 119:165

I am a man of peace.
PSALMS 120:6

Drop thy still dews of quietness,
Till all our strivings cease;
Take from our souls the strain and stress,
And let our ordered lives confess
The beauty of thy peace.
J. G. WHITTIER

Every morning compose your soul for a tranquil day, and all through it be
careful often to recall your resolution, and bring yourself back to it, so to
say. If something discomposes you, do not be upset, or troubled; but having discovered the fact, humble yourself gently before God, and try to
bring your mind into a quiet attitude. Say to yourself, "Well, I have made a

false step; now I must go more carefully and watchfully." Do this each time, however frequently you fall. When you are at peace use it profitably, making constant acts of meekness, and seeking to be calm even in the most trifling things. Above all, do not be discouraged; be patient; wait; strive to attain a calm, gentle spirit.

~ ST. FRANCIS DE SALES

April 29

"Father, I have sinned against heaven and against you.
I am no longer worthy to be called your son."
LUKE 15:21

Bad I am, but yet thy child.
Father, be thou reconciled.
Spare thou me, since I see
With thy might that thou art mild.

I have life left with me still
And thy purpose to fulfil;
Yea a debt to pay thee yet;
Help me, sir, and so I will . . .
GERARD MANLEY HOPKINS

Jesus did love a man who was able, sometimes, to be reckless. He did not care for the rulers as a class, but when one of them forgot his dignity, and ran after a peasant teacher and fell on the road at His feet, we read that "Jesus, seeing him, loved him." He did not choose for His disciples discreet and futile persons, but a man whose temper was not always under control, and whose tongue was rough when he was roused, and another who might have been a saint, but his fife got twisted and he betrayed his Lord. He saw a widow flinging into the treasury all that she had, which no doubt was a very foolish action, but it stirred His heart with gladness to see somebody venturing herself simply upon God. He wanted life in men, energy, impulse; for about them He held the conviction that, even though they may have fallen to be last, it is in them by His grace to be first, true saints, the splendor and light of His kingdom.

~ W. M. MACGREGOR

April 30

Tell the Israelites to move on.
EXODUS 14:15

"No one who puts his hand to the plow and looks back is fit for
service in the kingdom of God."
LUKE 9:62

Be trustful, be steadfast, whatever betide thee,
Only one thing do thou ask of the Lord,
Grace to go forward wherever He guide thee,
Simply believing the truth of His word.
ANONYMOUS

The hearts and minds of the Apostles are filled with the thought and the love of Him who had redeemed them and in whom they had found their true life, and with the work which they were to do in His service, for His glory, for the spreading of His Kingdom. This too was one of the greatest and most blessed among the truths which Luther was especially ordained to reproclaim—that we are not to spend our days in watching our own vices, in gazing at our own sins, in stirring and raking up all the mud of our past lives; but to lift our thoughts from our own corrupt nature to Him who put on that nature in order to deliver it from corruption, and to fix our contemplations and our affections on Him who came to clothe us in His perfect righteousness, and through whom and in whom, if we are united to Him by a living faith, we too become righteous. Thus, like the Apostle, we are to forget that which is behind, and to keep our eyes bent on the prize of our high calling, to which we are to press onward, and which we may attain, in Christ Jesus.

~ AUGUSTUS AND J. C. HARE

Be joyful always; pray continually;
give thanks in all circumstances . . .
1 THESSALONIANS 5:16-18

All the days of the oppressed are wretched,
but the cheerful heart has a continual feast.
PROVERBS 15:15

Thrice blest will all our blessings be,
When we can look through them to Thee;
When each glad heart its tribute pays
Of love and gratitude and praise.
M. J. COTTERILL

Most high, almighty, good Lord God, to Thee belong praise, glory, honour, and All blessings! Praised be my Lord God with all His creatures; and specially our brother the sun, who brings us the day, and who brings us the light; fair is he, and shining with a very great splendour: O Lord, to us he signifies Thee!

Praised be my Lord for our sister the moon, and for the stars, the which He has set clear and lovely in heaven.

Praised be my Lord for our brother the wind, and for air and cloud, calms and all weather, by the which Thou upholdest in life all creatures.

Praised be my Lord for our sister water, who is very serviceable unto us, and humble, and precious, and clean.

Praised be my Lord for our brother fire, through whom Thou givest us light in the darkness; and he is bright, and pleasant, and very mighty, and strong.

Praised be my Lord for our mother the earth, the which doth sustain and keep us, and bringeth forth divers fruits, and flowers of many colours, and grass.

Praised be my Lord for all those who pardon one another for His loves sake, and who endure weakness and tribulation; blessed are they who peaceably shall endure, for Thou, O most Highest, shalt give them a crown.

Praised be my Lord for our sister, the death of the body, from whom no man escapeth. Woe to him who dieth in mortal sin! Blessed are they who are found walking by Thy most holy will, for the second death shall have no power to do them harm.

Praise ye, and bless ye the Lord, and give thanks unto Him, and serve Him with great humility.

~ ST. FRANCIS OF ASSISI

Make it your ambition to lead a quiet life . . .
1 THESSALONIANS 4:11

. . . that we may live peaceful and quiet lives
in all godliness and holiness.
1 TIMOTHY 2:2

Give me my scallop shell of quiet,
My staff of faith to walk upon,
My scrip of joy, immortal diet,
My bottle of salvation,
my gown of glory, hope's true gage
And thus I'll take my pilgrimage.
SIR WALTER RALEIGH

All beneficent and creative power gathers itself together in silence, ere it issues out in might. Force itself indeed is naturally silent and only makes itself heard, if at all, when it strikes upon obstructions to bear them away as it returns to equilibrium again. The very hurricane that roars over land and ocean flits noiselessly through spaces where nothing meets it. The blessed sunshine says nothing as it warms the vernal earth, tempts out the tender grass, and decks the field and forest in their glory. Silence came before creation, and the heavens were spread without a word. Christ was born at dead of night; and though there has been no power like His, "He did not strive nor cry, neither was His voice heard in the streets."

Nowhere can you find any beautiful work, any noble design, any durable endeavour, that was not matured in long and patient silence ere it spake out in its accomplishment. There it is that we accumulate the inward power which we distribute and spend in action, put the smallest duty before us in dignified and holy aspects, and reduce the severest hardships beneath the foot of our self-denial. There it is that the soul, enlarging all its dimensions at once, acquires a greater and more vigorous being, and gathers up its collective forces to bear down upon the piecemeal difficulties of life and scatter them to dust. There alone can we enter into that spirit of self-abandonment by which we take up the cross of duty, however heavy, with feet however worn and bleeding they may be. And thither shall we return again, only into higher peace and more triumphant power, when the labour is over and the victory won, and we are called by death into God's loftiest watchtower of contemplation.

~ JAMES MARTINEAU

May 3

The Lord is good, a refuge in times of trouble.
He cares for those who trust in him . . .
NAHUM 1:7

Jesus my Lord,
Come to me,
Comfort me, console me.
Visit the hearts
In strange lands
Yearning for you.
Visit the dying and those
who have died without you.
Jesus, my Lord,
Visit also those
Who persecute you.
Lord Jesus, you are my light
In the darkness.
You are my warmth

In the cold.
You are my happiness
In sorrow . . .
ANONYMOUS

But let such remember that God loves them better than they love them-selves; that He desires their salvation more earnestly than they desire it, that He has given them unfailing means of salvation, if they will but use such means. What more need they save faith and trust? Their overween-ing fearfulness comes of self—from measuring God by their own poor standard, rather than themselves by His boundless greatness. They have not looked chiefly at His Glory, His Will, His Love, but at themselves. Let them look higher, and fear will yield to love; peace will come to their souls, and Eternity will cease to dismay them. It must do more—it must become a source of abiding rest and joy. Hear. St. Paul telling us that "our light affliction, which is but for a moment, worketh for us a far more exceeding and eternal weight of glory!" Will not this thought carry you over many waves of this troublesome life, through many heartaches, and wearinesses, and sorrows?

~ JEAN NICOLAS GROU

May 4

Fight the good fight of the faith.
1 TIMOTHY 6:12

You armed me with strength for battle,
you made my adversaries bow at my feet.
PSALMS 18:39

Thus strong in the Redeemer's strength,
Sin, death, and hell we trample down,
Fight the good fight, and win at length,
Through mercy, an eternal crown.
ANONYMOUS

Go face the fire at sea, or the cholera in your friend's house, or the burglar in your own, or what danger lies in the way of duty, knowing you are guarded by the cherubim of Destiny.

~ RALPH WALDO EMERSON

The snares of the enemy will be so known to thee and discerned, the way of help so manifest and easy, that their strength will be broken, and the poor entangled bird will fly away singing, from the nets and entanglements of the fowler; and praises will spring up, and great love in thy heart to the Forgiver and Redeemer.

~ I. PENINGTON

May 5

You are all sons of the light and sons of the day.
1 THESSALONIANS 5:5

Blessed are those who have learned to acclaim you,
who walk in the light of your presence, O Lord.
PSALMS 89:15

Teach me thy love to know;
That this new light, which now I see,
May both the work and workman show:
Then by a sunne-beam I will climbe to thee.
GEORGE HERBERT

To walk in the light means that we confess our sins without reserve. Sometimes we do not really confess our sins when we think we are doing so: we rather admit our sins than confess them, and we seek in all possible ways to explain, to extenuate, and to excuse them. . . . We think of the evil nature we have inherited, of the bias in our constitution to this or that attractive vice, of the defects of our education, of the violence of temptation, of the compulsion of circumstances; we do not deny what we have done—we cannot—but we mitigate it by every possible plea. This is not walking in the light. In all such self-excusing there is a large element of voluntary self-deception which keeps the life in the dark. To walk in the light requires us to accept our responsibilities without reserve, to own our sin that we may be able to disown it, and not to own it with such qualifications and reserves as amount to saying in the long run, It was indeed I who did it, but after all it is not I who should bear the blame. A man who makes it his business not to confess his sin, but to understand it and explain it, no matter how philosophical he may seem, is walking in darkness, and the truth is not in him. . . . Finally, to walk in the light means that when we confess our sins to God we do not keep a secret hold of them in our hearts. Where there is something hidden in the heart, hidden from God and from man, the darkness is as deep and dreadful as it can be. The desire to keep such a secret hold of sin is itself a sin to be confessed, to be declared in its exceeding sinfulness, to be unreservedly renounced . . . . The man who has a guilty secret in his life is a lonely man. There can be no cordial Christian overflow from his heart to the hearts of others, nor from theirs to his. And he is a man doomed to bear in his loneliness the uneffaced stain of his sin. The cleansing virtue of the atonement cannot reach him where he dwells by himself in the dark.
~ JAMES DENNEY

May 6

If anyone says, "I love God," yet hates his brother, he is a liar.
For anyone who does not love his brother, whom he has seen, cannot love
God, whom he has not seen.
1 JOHN 4:20-21

Be devoted to one another in brotherly love.
Honor one another above yourselves.
ROMANS 12:10

Swiftly arose and spread around me the peace and
knowledge that pass all the argument of the earth,
And I know that the hand of God is the promise of my own,
And I know that the spirit of God is the brother of my own,
And that all the men ever born are also brothers . . .
WALT WHITMAN

You have not fulfilled every duty, unless you have fulfilled that of being pleasant.

~ CHARLES BUXTON

A heart unloving among kindred has no love towards God's saints and angels. If we have a cold heart towards a servant or a friend, why should we wonder if we have no fervour towards God? If we are cold in our private prayers, we should be earthly and dull in the most devout religious order; if we cannot bear the vexations of a companion, how should we bear the contradiction of sinners? if a little pain overcomes us, how could we endure a cross? if we have no tender, cheerful, affectionate love to those with whom our daily hours are spent, how should we feel the pulse and ardour of love to the unknown and the evil, the ungrateful and repulsive?

~ H. E. MANNING

May 7

. . . rejoice that your names are written in heaven.
LUKE 10:20

He determines the number of the stars and calls them each by name.
PSALMS 147:4

O Hidden Life, vibrant in every atom,
O Hidden Light, shining in every creature,
O Hidden Love, embracing all in Oneness,
May each who feels himself as one with Thee
Know he is therefore one with every other.
ANNIE BESANT

Blessed be you, harsh matter, barren soil, stubborn rock: you who yield only to violence, you who force us to work if we would eat. Blessed be you, perilous matter, violent sea, untamable passion: you who unless we fetter you will devour us. Blessed be you, mighty matter, irresistible march of evolution, reality ever new-born; you who, by constantly shattering our mental categories, force us to go ever further and further in our pursuit of the truth. Blessed be you, universal matter, unmeasurable time, boundless ether, triple abyss of stars and atoms and generations: you who by overflowing and dissolving our narrow standards of measurement reveal to us the dimensions of God . . .

~ TEILHARD DE CHARDIN, SJ

May 8

He . . . must work,
doing something useful with his own hands . . .
EPHESIANS 4:28

"Why have you been standing here
all day long doing nothing?"
MATTHEW 20:6

Let us, then, be up and doing,
With a heart for any fate;
Still achieving, still pursuing,
Learn to labor and to wait.
HENRY WADSWORTH LONGFELLOW

The day returns and brings us the petty round of irritation concerns and duties. Help us to play the man, help us to perform them with laughter and kind faces. Let cheerfulness abound with industry. Give us to go blithely on our business all this day, bring us to our resting beds weary and content and undishonoured, and grant us in the end the gift of sleep.

~ ROBERT LOUIS STEVENSON

Eternal Father of my soul, let my first thought today be of thee, let my first impulse be to worship thee, let my first speech be thy name, let my first action be to kneel before thee in prayer.

~ JOHN BAILLIE

O God, grant that I may do and suffer all things this day for the glory of thy name.

~ A PRAYER USED BY THE CURE D'ARS

May 9

My son, do not despise the Lord's discipline and
do not resent his rebuke,
because the Lord disciplines those he loves,
as a father the son he delights in.
PROVERBS 3:11-12

The Lord gave and the Lord has taken away;
may the name of the Lord be praised.
JOB 1:21

What Thou hast given, Thou canst take,
And when Thou wilt new gifts can make.
All flows from Thee alone;
When Thou didst give it, it was Thine;
When Thou retook'st it, 'twas not mine.
Thy will in all be done.
JOHN AUSTIN

We are ready to praise when all shines fair; but when life is overcast, when all things seem to be against us, when we are in fear for some cherished happiness, or in the depths of sorrow, or in the solitude of a life which has no visible support, or in a season of sickness, and with the shadow of death approaching—then to praise God; then to say, "This fear, loneliness, affliction, pain, and trembling awe are as sure token of love, as life, health, joy, and the gifts of home:" "The Lord gave, and the Lord hath taken away"; on either side it is He, and all is love alike; "blessed be the name of the Lord"—this is the true sacrifice of praise. What can come amiss to a soul which is so in accord with God? What can make so much as one jarring tone in all its harmony? In all the changes of this fitful life, it ever dwells in praise.

~ H. E. MANNING

When I am afraid, I will trust in you.
PSALMS 56:3

Though he slay me,
yet will I hope in him . . .
JOB 13:15

"My times are in thy hand,"
My God, I wish them there;
My life, my friends, my soul, I leave
Entirely to your care.
ANONYMOUS

Father in Heaven, when the thought of Thee wakes in our hearts, let it not awaken like a frightened bird that flies about in dismay, but like a child waking from its sleep with a heavenly smile.

~ SØREN KIERKEGAARD

THE SERVANT: Lord, what wilt Thou teach me?

ETERNAL WISDOM: I will teach thee to die and will teach thee to live. I will teach thee to receive Me lovingly, and will teach thee to praise Me lovingly. Behold, this is what properly belongs to thee.

THE SERVANT: Eternal Wisdom, if I had the power to fulfil my wishes, I know not whether, in this temporal state, I ought to wish anything else, as to doctrine, than how to die to myself and all the world, how to live wholly for Thee. But Lord, dost Thou mean a spiritual dying or a bodily dying?

ETERNAL WISDOM: I mean both one and the other.

THE SERVANT: What need have I, Lord, of being taught how to die bodily? Surely it teaches itself when it comes.

ETERNAL WISDOM: He who puts his teaching off till then, will find it too late.

~ "THE BLESSED HENRY SUSO"

Do good to your servant
according to your word, O Lord.
PSALMS 119:65

Whoever wants to become great among
you must be your servant . . .
MATTHEW 20:26

Make us worthy, Lord,
To serve our fellow-men
Throughout the world who live and die
In poverty and hunger.

> *Give them, through our hands*
> *this day their daily bread,*
> *And by our understanding love,*
> *Give peace and joy.*
> MOTHER TERESA

So long as we love we serve; so long as we are loved by others, I would almost say that we are indispensable; and no man is useless while he has a friend.

~ ROBERT LOUIS STEVENSON

If we do not lay out ourselves in the service of mankind, whom should we serve?

~ ABIGAIL ADAMS

Lord, thou hast made us citizens of a fair city and inheritors of a valiant freedom. Grant that thy spirit may invest our mightiest endeavors and our humblest toil. Nourish in us the fruits of the Spirit that the splendour of London may shine forth in the world, to thy honour and glory and the welfare of the brethren.

~ A PRAYER FOR LONDON, CECIL HUNT

May 12

> *God is our refuge and strength,*
> *an ever-present help in trouble.*
> *Therefore we will not fear, though the earth give way*
> *and the mountains fall into the heart of the sea,*
> *though its waters roar and foam*
> *and the mountains quake with their surging.*
> PSALMS 46:1-3

> *Fix'd on this ground will I remain,*
> *Though my heart fail, and flesh decay;*
> *This anchor shall my soul sustain,*
> *When earth's foundations melt away:*
> *Mercy's full power I then shall prove,*
> *Lov'd with an everlasting love.*
> ANONYMOUS

Give us grace and strength to forbear and to persevere. . . . Give us courage and gaiety and the quiet mind, spare to us our friends, soften to us our enemies.

~ ROBERT LOUIS STEVENSON

Thou art never at any time nearer to the God than when under tribulation; which He permits for the purification and beautifying of thy soul.

~ M. MOLINOS

The Lord's goodness surrounds us at every moment. I walk through it almost with difficulty, as though through thick grass and flowers.

~ R.W. BARBOUR

May 13

Blessed is the man whom God corrects,
So do not despise the discipline of the Almighty.
For he wounds, but he also binds up;
he injures, but his hands also heal.
JOB 5:17-18

O Jerusalem, wash the evil from your heart and be saved.
JEREMIAH 4:14

. . . Yet I argue not
Against Heaven's hand or will, nor bate a jot
of heart or hope; but still bear up and steer
Right onward.
JOHN MILTON

Only the individual conscience, and He who is greater than the conscience, can tell where worldliness prevails. Each heart must answer for
itself, and at its own risk. That our souls are committed to our own
keeping, at our own peril, in a world so mixed as this, is the last reason
we should slumber over the charge, or betray the trust. If only that outlet
to the Infinite is kept open, the inner bond with eternal life preserved,
while not one movement of this world's business is interfered with, nor
one pulse-beat of its happiness repressed, with all natural associations dear
and cherished, with all human sympathies fresh and warm, we shall yet
be near to the kingdom of heaven, within the order of the Kosmos of
God-in the world, but not of the world-not taken out of it, but kept from
its evil.

~ J. H. THOM

May 14

For the Lord takes delight in his people;
he crowns the humble with salvation.
PSALMS 149:4

Put on therefore . . . kindness,
humbleness of mind, meekness, long-suffering.
COLOSSIANS 3:12

Meekness, humility, and love,
Did through thy conduct shine;
Oh may my whole deportment prove
A copy, Lord, of thine.
ANONYMOUS

How much the more thou knowest, and how much the better thou under-
standest, so much the more grievously shalt thou therefore be judged,
unless thy life be also more holy. Be not therefore extolled in thine own
mind for any art or science, but rather let the knowledge given thee make
thee more humble and cautious. If thou thinkest that thou knowest much,
know also that there be many things more which thou knowest not.

All perfection in this life hath some imperfection mixed with it; and no

knowledge of ours is without some darkness. An humble knowledge of thyself is a surer way to God than a deep search after learning. Yet learning is not to be blamed, nor the mere knowledge of anything whatsoever to be disliked, it being good in itself, and ordained of God; but a good conscience and a virtuous life is always to be preferred before it . . . . Truly at the day of judgement we shall not be examined on what we have read, but what we have done; not how well we have spoken, but how religiously we have lived.

~ THOMAS A. KEMPIS

May 15

"Come to me, all you who are weary and burdened,
and I will give you rest. Take my yoke upon you and learn from me,
for I am gentle and humble in heart, and you will find rest for your souls.
For my yoke is easy and my burden is light."
MATTHEW 11:28-30

Let us not seek out of thee what we can
only find in thee, O Lord.
Peace and rest and joy and bliss,
which abide only in thine abiding joy.
Lift up our souls above the weary round of
harassing thoughts to thy eternal presence.
that we may breathe freely,
there repose in thy love,
there be at rest from all things that weary us:
and thence return, arrayed in thy peace,
to do and to bear
whatsoever shall best please thee,
O blessed Lord.
E. B. PUSEY

There are two deep principles in Nature in apparent contradiction—one, the aspiration after perfection; the other, the longing after repose. In the harmony of these lies the rest of the soul of man. There have been times when we have experienced this. Then the winds have been hushed, and the throb and tumult of the passions have been blotted out of our bosoms. That was a moment when we were in harmony with all around, reconciled to ourselves and to our God; when we sympathized with all that was pure, and that was beautiful, all that was lovely.

~ F. W. ROBERTSON

May 16

Finally, be strong in the Lord and in his mighty power. . . .
Stand firm then, with the belt of truth buckled around your waist,
with the breastplate of righteousness in place, and with your feet with the
readiness that comes from the gospel of peace.
EPHESIANS 6:10, 14-15

I can do all things, and can bear
All sufferings, if my Lord be near;
Sweet pleasures mingle with the pains,
While his left hand my head sustains.
ANONYMOUS

We know that in the moral, as in the physical order, nature abhors a
vacancy. Consciously or unconsciously, as the years go by, all men more
and more submit their lives to some allegiance; with whatever uncertainty
and changefulness, some one motive, or group of motives, grows stronger
and stronger in them; they tend, at least, to bring every thought into cap-
tivity to some one obedience. For better or for worse, things which seemed
difficult or impossible a few years ago will come almost naturally to a man
a few years hence; he will have got accustomed to take a certain course, to
obey certain impulses or principles wherever they appear. We may indeed
distinguish three states in which a man may be. He may be yielding his
heart more and more to the love of self, in whatsoever way of pride, or
avarice, or lust, or sloth. Or he may be yielding his heart more and more
to the love of God, falteringly, it may be, with many struggles and failures,
but still really getting to love God more, to move more readily and more
loyally to do God's will wherever he sees it. Or, thirdly, he may be like the
man of whom our Lord spoke. He may, by God's grace, have cast out an
evil spirit from his heart; he may have broken away from the mastery ot
some bad passion, some tyrannous hunger or hatred; and he may be hesi-
tating, keeping his heart swept, clear and empty; his will may be poised, as
it were, between the one love and the other. Ah! but that can only be for a
very little while. That balance never lasts; one way or the other the will
must incline; one service or the other must be chosen, and that soon.

~ FRANCIS PAGET

May 17

Be devoted to one another in brotherly love.
Honor one another above yourselves.
ROMANS 12:10

. . . love your neighbor as yourself.
MATTHEW 19:19

Can I see another's woe,
And not be in sorrow too?
Can I see another's grief,
And not seek for kind relief?
WILLIAM BLAKE

What is meant by our neighbour we cannot doubt; it is every one with
whom, we are brought into contact. First of all, he is literally our neighbour who is next to us in our own family and household; husband to wife,
wife to husband, parent to child, brother to sister, master to servant, servant to master. Then it is he who is close to us in our own neighbour-
hood, in our own town, in our own parish, in our own street. With these
all true charity begins. To love and be kind to these is the very beginning
of all true religion. But, besides these, as our Lord teaches, it is every one
who is thrown across our path by the changes and chances of life; he or

she, whosoever it be, whom we have any means of helping—the unfortunate stranger whom we may meet in traveling, the deserted friend whom no one else cares to look after.

~ A. P. STANLEY

May 18

Whoever does not love does not know God, for God is love.
I JOHN 4. 8

And all must love the human form,
In heathen, turk, or jew;
Where Mercy, Love, & Pity dwell
There God is dwelling too.
WILLIAM BLAKE

Oh, how many times we can most of us remember when we would gladly have made any compromise with our consciences, would gladly have made the most costly sacrifices to God, if He would only have excused us from this duty of loving, of which our nature seemed utterly incapable. It is far easier to feel kindly, to act kindly, toward those with whom we are seldom brought into contact, whose tempers and prejudices do not rub against ours, whose interests do not clash with ours, than to keep up an habitual, steady, self-sacrificing love towards those whose weaknesses and faults are always forcing themselves upon us, and are stirring up our own. A man may pass good muster as a philanthropist who makes but a poor master to his servants, or father to his children.

~ E. D. MAURICE

May 19

"Be still, and know that I am God . . . ."
PSALMS 46:10

Trust in him at all times, O people;
pour out your hearts to him,
for God is our refuge.
PSALMS 62:8

Jesus, with thy word complying,
Firm our faith and hope shall be;
On thy faithfulness relying,
We will seek our rest in thee.
ANONYMOUS

"Rest in the Lord, wait patiently for Him." In Hebrew, "be silent to God, and let Him mould thee." Keep still, and He will mould thee to the right shape.

~ MARTIN LUTHER

Let the blessing of Saint Peter's Master be . . . upon all that are lovers of virtue, and dare trust in his Providence, and be quiet and go a-angling.

~ IZAAK WALTON

Silence never shows itself to so great an advantage as when it is made the reply to calumny and defamation, provided that we give no occasion for them. We might produce an example of it in the behavior of One in whom it appeared in all its majesty, and One whose silence, as well as His person, was altogether divine. When one considers this subject only in its sublimity, this great instance could not but occur to me; and since I only make use of it to show the highest example of it, I hope I do not offend in it. To forbear replying to an unjust reproach, and overlook it with a generous or, if possible, with an entire neglect of it, is one of the most heroic acts of a great mind; and (I must confess) when I reflect upon the behavior of some of the greatest men in antiquity, I do not so much admire them that they deserved the praise of the whole age they lived in, as because they contemned the envy and detraction of it.

~ JOSEPH ADDISON

May 20

Consider the blameless, observe the upright;
there is a future for the man of peace.
PSALMS 37:37

The mind of sinful man is death,
but the mind controlled by the
Spirit is life and peace.
ROMANS 8:23

Calm soul of all things! make it mine
To feel, amid the city's jar,
That there abides a peace of thine,
Man did not make, and cannot mar.
MATTHEW ARNOLD

Remember that when with thine understanding thou goest forth to find God, in order to rest in Him, thou must place neither limit nor comparison with thy weak and narrow imagination. For He is infinite beyond all comparison; He is through all and in all, and in Him are all things. Himself thou wilt find within thy soul, wherever thou shalt seek Him in truth, that is, in order to, find thyself. For His delight is to be with us, the children of men, to make us worthy of Him, though He hath no need of us. In meditation do not be so tied down to certain points that thou wilt meditate on them alone; but wherever thou shalt find rest, there stop and taste the Lord, at whatever step He shall will to communicate Himself to thee. Though thou leave what thou hadst laid down, have no scruple; for the whole end of these exercises is to taste the Lord; yet with intent not to make this the chief end; but rather to love His works the more, with purpose to imitate Him as far as we can. And having found the end, we need be no longer anxious as to the means laid down to attain it. One of the hindrances to true peace and quietness is the anxiety and thought we give to such works, binding the spirit and dragging it after one thing or another; in this way insisting that God should lead it by the path we wish, and forcing it to walk along the road of our own imagining; unconsciously caring more to do our own will in this case than the will of our Lord; and this is nothing else but to seek God by flying from Him and to wish to please Him without doing His will. If thou desire really to advance in this path, and to reach the desired end, have no other purpose, no other wish, than to find God; and wheresoever He wills to manifest Himself to thee, there

quit all else and go no farther till thou have leave. Forget all other things and rest thee in the Lord.

~ LORENZO SCUPOLI

May 21

For this God is our God for ever and ever;
he will be our guide even to the end.
PSALMS 48:14

Let the beloved of the Lord rest secure in him;
for he shields him all day long,
and the one the Lord loves rests between his shoulders.
DEUTERONOMY 33:12

"Unnumber'd years of bliss
I to my sheep will give;
And while my throne unshaken stands
Shall all my chosen live."

Enough, my gracious Lord,
Let faith triumphant cry;
My heart can on this promise live,
Can with this promise die.
ANONYMOUS

I have seemed to see a need of everything God gives me, and want nothing that He denies me. There is no dispensation, though afflictive, but either in it, or after it, I find that I could not be without it. Whether it be taken from or not given me, sooner or later God quiets me in Himself without it. I cast all my concerns on the Lord, and live securely on the care and wisdom of my heavenly Father. My ways, you know, are, in a sense, hedged up with thorns, and grow darker and darker daily; but yet I distrust not my good God in the least, and live more quietly in the absence of all by faith, than I should do, I am persuaded, if I possessed them.

~ ANONYMOUS

May 22

But the Lord said to Samuel, "Do not consider his appearance or his
height, for I have rejected him. The Lord does not look at the things man
looks at. Man looks at the outward appearance,
but the Lord looks at the heart."
I SAMUEL 16:14

The heart should have fed upon the truth, as insects on a leaf, till it be
tinged with the color, and show its food in every . . . minutest fiber.
SAMUEL TAYLOR COLERIDGE

Do you habitually thus unlock your hearts and subject your thoughts to Almighty God? Are you living in this conviction of His Presence? And have you this special witness that that Presence is really set up within you unto your salvation, namely, that you live in the sense of it? Do you believe, and act on the belief, that His light penetrates and shines through your heart, as the sun's beams through a room? You know how things look when the sun's beams are on it—the very air then appears full of impurities which, before it came out, were not seen. So it is with our souls. We are full of stains and corruptions, we see them not, they are like the air before the sun shines; but though we see them not, God sees them: He pervades us as the sunbeam. Our souls, in His view, are fall of things which offend, things which must be repented of forgiven, and put away. He, in the words of the Psalmist, "has set our misdeeds before Him, our secret sins in the light of His countenance." This is most true, though it be not at all welcome doctrine to many. We cannot hide ourselves from Him; and our wisdom, as our duty, lies in embracing this truth, acquiescing in it, and acting upon it. Let us then beg Him to teach us the Mystery of His Presence in us, that, by acknowledging it, we may thereby possess it fruitfully. Let us confess it in faith, that we may possess it unto justification. Let us so own it as to set Him before us in everything. "I have set God always before me," says the Psalmist, "for He is on my right hand, therefore I shall not fall." Let us in all circumstances thus regard Him. Whether we have sinned, let us not dare keep from Him, but, with the prodigal son, rise up and go to Him. Or, if we are conscious of nothing, still let us not boast in ourselves or justify ourselves, but feel that "He who judgeth us is the Lord". . . . Let us have no secret apart from Him.

~ JOHN HENRY CARDINAL NEWMAN

May 23

*Resentment kills a fool,
and envy slays the simple.*
JOB 5:2

*But as for me, my feet had almost slipped;
I had nearly lost my foothold.
For I envied the arrogant when
I saw the prosperity of the wicked.*
PSALMS 73:2-3

*Love thyself last: cherish those hearts that hate thee;
Corruption wins not more than honesty.
Still in thy right hand carry gentle peace,
To silence envious tongues: be just, and fear not.*
WILLIAM SHAKESPEARE

Clemens has his head full of imaginary piety. He is often proposing to himself what he would do if he had a great estate. He would outdo all charitable men that are gone before him, he would retire from the world, he would have no equipage, he would allow himself only necessaries, that widows and orphans, the sick and distressed, might find relief out of his estate. He tells you that all other way of spending an estate is folly and madness. Now, Clemens has at present a moderate estate, which he spends upon himself in the same vanities and indulgences as other people do. He might live upon one-third of his fortune and make the rest the support of the poor; but he does nothing of all this that is in his power, but pleases himself with what he would do if his power was greater. Come to thy senses, Clemens. Do not talk what thou wouldst do if thou wast an angel, but consider what thou canst do as thou art a man. Make the best use of thy present state, do now as thou thinkest thou wouldst do with a great estate, be sparing, deny thyself, abstain from all vanities, that the

poor may be better maintained, and then thou art as charitable as thou canst be in any estate. Remember the poor widow's mite.

~ WILLIAM LAW

May 24

Blessed is the man who perseveres under trial, because when he has stood the test, he will receivethe crown of life that God has promised those who love him.
JAMES 1:12

I cannot say,
Beneath the pressure of life's cares to-day,
I joy in these;
But I can say
That I had rather walk this rugged way,
If Him it please.
S. G. BROWNING

The proper and natural effect, and in the absence of all disturbing and intercepting forces, the certain and inevitable accompaniment of peace (or reconcilement) with God is our own inward peace, a calm and quiet temper of mind. . . . The chameleon darkens in the shade of him who bends over it to ascertain its colours. In like manner, but with yet greater caution, ought we to think respecting a tranquil habit of inward life, considered as a spiritual sense, as the medial organ in and by which our peace with God, and the lively working of His grace in our spirit, are perceived by us. This peace which we have with God in Christ, is inviolable; but because the sense and persuasion of it may be interrupted, the soul that is truly at peace with God may for a time be disquieted in itself, through weakness of faith, or the strength of temptation, or the darkness of desertion, losing sight of that grace, that love and light of God's countenance, on which its tranquillity and joy depend.

But when these eclipses are over, the soul is revived with new consolation, as the face of the earth is renewed and made to smile with the return of the sun in the spring; and this ought always to uphold Christians in the saddest times, namely, that the grace and love of God towards them depend, not on their sense, nor upon anything in them, but is stiff in itself, incapable of the smallest alteration.

~ SAMUEL TAYLOR COLERIDGE

May 25

Going a little farther, he fell with his face to the ground and prayed, "My Father, if it be possible, may this cup be taken from me. Yet not as I will, but as you will."
MATTHEW 26:39

O Lord my God, do Thou Thy holy will,—
I will lie still.
I will not stir, lest I forsake Thine arm,
And break the charm

Which lulls me, clinging to my Father's breast,
In perfect rest.

J. KEBLE

Saturday, in the morning. I have this day solemnly renewed my baptismal covenant and self-dedication, which I renewed when I was received into the communion of the church. I have been before God; and have given myself, all that I am and have to God, so that I am not in any respect my own. I can claim no right in myself, no right in this understanding, this will, these affections that are in me; neither have I any right to this body or any of its members; no right to this tongue, these hands nor feet; no right to these senses, these eyes, these ears, this smell or taste. I have given myself clear away. . . . This I have done. And I pray God, for the sake of Christ, to look upon it as a self-dedication; and to receive me now as entirely His own, and deal with me in all respects as such; whether He afflicts me or prospers me, or whatever He pleases to do with me, who am His. Now henceforth I am not to act in any respect as my own. I shall act as my own, if I ever make use of any of my powers to anything that is not to the glory of God, or do not make the glorifying of Him my whole and entire business; if I murmur in the least at afflictions; if I grieve at the prosperity of others; if I am any way uncharitable; if I am angry because of injuries; if I revenge my own cause; if I do anything purely to please myself, or avoid anything for the sake of my ease, or omit anything because it is great self-denial; if I trust to myself; if I take any of the praise of any good that I do, or rather God does by me; or if I am in any way proud.

~ JONATHAN EDWARDS

May 26

Moses also said, "You will know that it was the Lord when he gives you meat to eat in the evening and all the bread you want in the morning, because he has heard your grumbling against him. Who are we? You are not grumbling against us, but against the Lord."

EXODUS 16:8

Without murmur, uncomplaining,
In His hand,
Leave whatever things thou canst not
Understand.

K. R. HAGENBACH

Jesus hath now many lovers of the heavenly kingdom, but few bearers of His Cross. He hath many desirous of consolation, but few of tribulation. He findeth many companions of His table, but few of His abstinence. All desire to rejoice with Him, few are willing to endure anything for Him, or with Him. Many follow Jesus unto the breaking of bread, but few to the drinking of the cup of His Passion. Many reverence His miracles, few follow the ignominy of His Cross. Many love Jesus so long as no adversities befall them, many praise and bless Him so long as they receive any consolations from Him; but if Jesus hide Himself and leave them but a little while, they fall either into complaining or into too much dejection of mind.

But they who love Jesus for the sake of Jesus, and not for some special comfort of their own, bless Him in all tribulations and anguish of heart as well as in the state of highest comfort. Yea, although He should never be

willing to give them comfort, they notwithstanding would ever praise Him, and wish to be always giving thanks.

O how powerful is the pure love of Jesus, which is mixed with no self-interest or self-love! Are not all those to be called mercenary who are ever seeking consolations? Do they not show themselves to be rather lovers of themselves than of Christ, who are always thinking of their own profit and advantage? Where shall one be found who is willing to serve God for nought?

. . . If thou bear the Cross cheerfully, it will bear thee, and lead thee to the desired end, namely, where there shall be an end of suffering, though here there shall not be. If thou bear it unwillingly, thou makest for thyself a burden and increasest thy load, and yet notwithstanding thou must bear it. If thou cast away one cross, without doubt thou shalt find another, and that perhaps a more heavy one.

~ THOMAS A. KEMPIS

May 27

Whoever can be trusted with very little can also be trusted with much, and whoever is dishonest with very little will also be dishonest with much.

LUKE 16:10

That best portion of a good man's life,
little, nameless, unremembered acts
Of kindness and of love.

WILLIAM WORDSWORTH

No lofty reasonings about God and about His relations to us and ours will do away with the obstinate fact that if we love Him really, and not in our reveries alone, we must love our neighbor too, really, and not in theory alone. It is no use at all to see (as who can fail to see?) that He is in all things and persons and consequently is to be found and loved in them and they in Him, unless our belief flows over into action and in the practical affairs of daily life we do thus see Him and them too and do act upon what we see. Few things are more disconcerting than the oft recurring phenomenon of high ideals and fine and subtle speculations upon the nature of God and of the spiritual life—much devotion too, and even aus-terity—in combination with an almost total insensibility to the duty of charity to others. In such persons one is sometimes bewildered to find a sort of contempt for this realized charity, as if it were an inferior, elemen-tary, unintelligent kind of thing. Or perhaps, by a remarkable obliquity of judgment, they will consider that their superior perceptions somehow absolve them from deference to this Commandment, or at least from any-thing so coarse as putting it into vulgar practice. But though one may be a competent art critic without having ever handled a brush or a chisel, and may legitimately pass judgment upon a book which one could not have written oneself, in the life of the soul there are no such privileges: knowl-edge there is no knowledge at all unless it is also and equally action, and if it is not that, then it is worse than ignorance.

~ R. H. J. STEUART

The Lord is the everlasting God,
The creator of the ends of the earth.
He will not grow tired or weary,
and his understanding no one can fathom.
He gives strength to the weary and increases the power of the weak.
Even youths grow tired and weary,
and young men stumble and fall;
but those who hope in the Lord will renew their strength.
They will soar on wings like eagles,
they will run and not grow weary,
they will walk and not be faint.

ISAIAH 40:28-31

Give us grace and strength to forbear and to persevere . . .
Give us courage and gaiety and the quiet mind,
Spare to us our friends,
Soften to us our enemies.
ROBERT LOUIS STEVENSON

Go forth to meet the solemnities and to conquer the trials of existence,
believing in a Shepherd of your souls. Then faith in Him will support you
in duty, and duty finely done will strengthen faith; till at last, when all is
over here, and the noise and strife of the earthly battle fades upon your
dying ear, and you hear, instead thereof, the deep and musical sound of the
ocean of eternity, and see the lights of heaven shining on its waters still
and fair in their radiant rest, your faith will raise the song of conquest,
and in its retrospect of the life which has ended, and its forward glance
upon the life to come, take up the poetic inspiration of the Hebrew king,
"Surely goodness and mercy have followed me all the days of my life, and I
will dwell in the house of the Lord forever."

~ STOPFORD A. BROOKE

We do not want you to become lazy, but to imitate those who through faith
and patience inherit what has been promised.
HEBREWS 6:12

There is most joy in virtue when 'tis hardest won.
LUCAN

Burn from my brain and from my breast
Sloth, and the cowardice that clings,
And stiffness and the soul's arrest:
And feed my brain with better things.
GILBERT KEITH CHESTERTON

May 30

Where you die, I will die.
RUTH 1:17

Very rarely will anyone die for a righteous man, though for a good man someone might possibly dare to die. But God demonstrates his own love for us in this: While we were still sinners, Christ died for us.
ROMANS 5:7-8

Though Love repine, and Reason chafe,
There came a voice without reply,—
'Tis man's perdition to be safe,
When for the truth he ought to die.
RALPH WALDO EMERSON

But we must not disguise from ourselves that God's dealings with this world are still a very difficult problem. After reading the Old Testament we have no right to think that what perplexed the chosen people for so many centuries, will all be plain to us even with the New Testament to guide us. There is a great deal of shallow optimism which "heals too slightly" the wounds which experience inflicts upon Faith and Hope. It is useless to say, "God's in His heaven; All's right with the world," when many things are obviously all wrong in the world . . . This world exists for the realization in time of God's eternal purposes. Some of these are bound up with individual lives, for God intended each one of us to do and to be something; others have a far wider scope, and require far more time for their fulfilment. The manifold evils in the world are allowed to exist because only through them can the greater good be brought into activity. This greater good is not any external achievement, but the love and heroism and self-sacrifice which the great conflict calls into play. We must try to return to the dauntless spirit of the early Christians. . . . And let us remember, when we are inclined to be disheartened, that the private soldier is a poor judge of the fortunes of a great battle.

~ W. R. INGE

May 31

. . . for he is our God and we are the people of his pasture,
the flock under his care.
PSALMS 95:7

He makes me lie down in green pastures.
PSALMS 23:2

I can hear these violets chorus
To the sky's benediction above;
And we all are together lying
On the bosom of Infinite Love.

Oh, the peace at the heart of Nature!
Oh, the light that is not of day!
Why seek it afar forever,
When it cannot be lifted away?
W. C. GANNETT

"He maketh me to lie down in green pastures, he leadeth me beside the still waters"—the very beauty of this picture may serve only to hide from us the depths of its meaning. We seem to see the shepherd walking before his flock through fields decked out with green and gold and all the glory of a generous God, coming at last to the silent pool with the reflection of the sky sleeping in its heart, and it seems as though it were for the glory of the summer and the sleeping beauty of the pool that the sheep followed the shepherd. And indeed it is for that reason that many do seek the Good Shepherd. They think of religion not as a necessity but as a luxury, not as life but as a kind of addition to life which it is very nice to have but which we could quite well do without. But it is not for the green and gold of summer fields that the sheep seeks to find them, but because they are good to eat. It is not for the sleeping beauty in the heart of silent waters that the flock follows on to find them, but because they are good to drink. It is not luxury that they ask of the shepherd, it is the bare necessities. And we cannot make too sure of this: that religion, communion with God, is not luxury, but a necessity for the soul. We must have God.

The Good Shepherd intensifies to the point of torture the hunger of the soul until it becomes a passion in man to make the world in which he lives as beautiful and as good as he perceives that it is meant to be; He intensifies the hunger to the point of torture that He may satisfy it by the gift of communion with Himself and the moral power that springs from that communion.

~ G. A. STUDDERT KENNEDY

Even the sparrow has found a home,
and the swallow a nest for herself,
where she may have her young—a place near your altar.
PSALMS 84:3

Our birth is but a sleep and forgetting:
The soul that rises with us, our life's star,
Hath had elsewhere its setting,
And cometh from afar:
Not in entire forgetfulness,
And not in utter nakedness,
But trailing clouds of glory do we come
From God, who is our home . . . .
WILLIAM WORDSWORTH

Almighty Father, Son and Holy Ghost, eternal ever blessed gracious God; to me the least of Saints, to me allow that I may keep a door in paradise. That I may keep the smallest door, the furthest, the darkest, coldest door, the door that is least used, the stiffest door. If so it be but in thine house, O God, if so be that I may see thy glory even afar, and hear thy voice O God, and know that I am with thee O God.

~ ST. COLUMBA

Then God said,
"Let us make men in our image, in our likeness . . ."
GENESIS 1:26

Then every tempting form of sin,
Shamed in Thy presence, disappears,
And all the glowing, raptured soul
The likeness it contemplates wears.
P. DODDRIDGE

Consider that all which appears beautiful outwardly, is solely derived from the invisible Spirit which is the source of that external beauty, and say joyfully, 'Behold, these are streamlets from the uncreated Fountain; behold, these are drops from the infinite Ocean of all good! Oh! how does my inmost heart rejoice at the thought of that eternal, infinite Beauty, which is the source and origin of all created beauty!

~ LORENZO SCUPOLI

I believe that no Divine truth can truly dwell in any heart, without an external testimony in manner, bearing, and appearance, that must reach the witness within the heart of the beholder, and bear an unmistakable, though silent, evidence to the eternal principle from which it emanates.

~ M. A. SCHIMMELPENNINCK

June 3

A cheerful heart is good medicine,
but a crushed spirit dries up the bones.
PROVERBS 17:22

Paradise itself were dim
And joyless, if not shared with him!
THOMAS MOORE

Holy Ghost, dispel our sadness,
Pierce the cloud of sinful night;
Come, thou source of joy and gladness,
Breathe thy life, and shed thy light.
ANONYMOUS

He will weave no longer a spotted life of shreds and patches, but he will live with a divine unity. He will cease from what is base and frivolous in his life, and be content with all places, and with any service he can render. He will calmly front the morrow, in the negligency of that trust which carries God with it, and so hath already the whole future in the bottom of the heart.

~ RALPH WALDO EMERSON

He who believes in God is not careful for the morrow, but labors joyfully and with a great heart. "For He giveth His beloved, as in sleep." They must work and watch, yet never be careful or anxious, but commit all to Him, and live in serene tranquility; with a quiet heart, as one who sleeps safely and quietly.

~ MARTIN LUTHER

June 4

God is not unjust; he will not forget your work and the love you
have shown him as you have helped his people and continue to
help them. We want each of you to show this same diligence to the very end,
in order to make your hope sure. We do not want
you to become lazy, but to imitate those who through faith and patience
inherit what has been promised.
HEBREWS 6:10-12

Say not, 'Twas all in vain,
The anguish and the darkness and the strife;
Love thrown upon the waters comes again
In quenchless yearnings for a nobler life.
ANNA SHIPTON

To whatever world death introduce you, the best conceivable preparation for it is to labor for the highest good of the world in which you live. Be the change which death brings what it may, he who has spent his life in trying to make this world better can never be unprepared for another. If heaven is for the pure and holy, if that which makes men good is that which best qualifies for heaven, what better discipline in goodness can we conceive for a human spirit . . . than to live and labor for a brother's welfare? To find our deepest joy, not in the delights of sense, nor in the gratification of per-

sonal ambition, nor even in the serene pursuits of culture and science—
nay, not even in seeking the safety of our own souls, but in striving for the
highest good of those who are dear to our Father in heaven, and the moral
and spiritual redemption of that world for which the Son of God lived and
died—say, can a nobler school of goodness be discovered than this? Where
shall love and sympathy and beneficence find ampler training, or patience,
courage, dauntless devotion, nobler opportunities of exercise, than in the
war with evil? . . . Live in this, find your dearest work here, let love to
God and man be the animating principle of your being; and then, let death
come when it may, and carry you where it will, you will not be unprepared
for it . . . for you cannot in God's universe go where love and truth and
self-devotion are things of naught, or where a soul, filled with undying
faith in the progress and identifying its own happiness with the final triumph of goodness, shall find itself forsaken.

~ JOHN CAIRD

June 5

*. . . and that you may love the Lord your God,
listen to his voice and hold fast to him.*
DEUTERONOMY 30:20

"Speak, Lord, for your servant is listening."
1 SAMUEL 3:9

*I have just hung up; why did he telephone?
I don't know . . . Oh! I get it . . .
I talked a lot and listened very little.*

*Forgive me, Lord, it was a monologue and not a dialogue.
I explained my idea and did not get his;
Since I didn't listen, I learned nothing,
Since I didn't listen, I didn't help,
Since I didn't listen, we didn't communicate.*

*Forgive me, Lord, for we were connected,
and now we are cut off.*
MICHEL QUOIST

O my God how does it happen in this poor old world that thou art so
great and yet nobody finds thee, that thou callest so loudly and yet nobody
hears thee, that thou art so near and yet nobody feels thee, that thou
givest thyself to everybody and yet nobody knows thy name? Men flee
from thee and say they cannot find thee; they turn their backs and say
they cannot see thee; they stop their ears and say they cannot hear thee.

~ HANS DENCK

June 6

*And in him you too are being built together
to become a dwelling in which
God lives by his Spirit.*
EPHESIANS 2:22

Don't you know that you yourselves are God's temple
and that God's Spirit lives in you?
1 CORINTHIANS 3:16

None the place ordained refuseth,
They are one, and they are all,
Living stones, the Builder chooseth
For the courses of his wall.
JEAN INGELOW

The Lord showed me, so that I did see clearly, that he did not dwell in these temples which men had commanded and set up, but in people's hearts . . . his people were his temple, and he dwelt in them.

~ GEORGE FOX

Slowly, through all the universe, that temple of God is being built. Wherever, in any world, a soul, by free-willed obedience, catches the fire of God's likeness, it is set into the growing walls, a living stone. When, in your hard fight, in your tiresome drudgery, or in your terrible temptation, you catch the purpose of your being, and give yourself to God, and so give Him the chance to give Himself to you, your life, a living stone, is taken up and set into that growing wall. . . . Wherever souls are being tried and ripened, in whatever commonplace and homely ways—there God is hewing out the pillars for His temple.

~ PHILLIPS BROOKS

June 7

The people walking in darkness have seen a great light;
on those living in the land of the shadow of death a light has dawned.
ISAIAH 9:2

Blessed are those who have learned to acclaim you,
who walk in the light of your presence, O Lord.
PSALMS 89:15

O God, who broughtest me from the rest of last night
Unto the joyous light of this day,
Be thou bringing me from the new light of this day
Unto the guiding light of eternity.
Oh! from the new light of this day
Unto the guiding light of eternity.
CARMINA GADELICA

Stay with me, and then I shall begin to shine as thou shinest: so to shine as to be a light to others. The light, O Jesus, will be all from thee. None of it will be mine. No merit to me. It will be thou who shinest through me upon others. O let me thus praise thee, in the way which thou dost love best, by shining on all those around me. Give light to them as well as to me; light them with me, through me. Teach me to show forth thy praise, thy truth, thy will. Make me preach thee without preaching—not by words, but by my example and by the catching force, the sympathetic influence, of what I do—by my visible resemblance to thy saints, and the evident fulness of the love which my heart bears to thee.

~ JOHN HENRY CARDINAL NEWMAN

Our Father in heaven, I thank thee that thou hast led me into the light. I thank thee for sending the Savior to call me from death to life. I confess that I was dead in sin before I heard his call, but when I heard him, like Lazarus, I arose . . . Give me strength, O Father, to break the bonds; give me courage to live a new life in thee; give me faith, to believe that with thy help I cannot fail. And this I ask in the Savior's name who has taught me to come to thee.

~ PRAYER FROM TAIWAN

June 8

"Let the little children come to me, and do not hinder them, for the kingdom of God belongs to such as these."
LUKE 18:16

"For he who is least among you all—he is the greatest."
LUKE 9:48

He prayeth best who loveth best
All things both great and small;
For the dear God who loveth us,
He made and loveth all.
SAMUEL TAYLOR COLERIDGE

In small proportions we just beauties see,
And in short measures life may perfect be.
BEN JOHNSON

Practice yourself, for heaven's sake, in little things; and thence proceed to greater.

~ EPICTETUS

O Lord, you have made us very small, and we bring our years to an end like a tale that is told; help us to remember that beyond our brief day is the eternity of your love.

~ REINHOLD NIEBUHR

Love's secret is to be always doing things for God, and not to mind because they are such very little ones.

~ F. W. FABER

June 9

An angry man stirs up dissension,
and a hot-tempered one commits many sins.
PROVERBS 29:22

Everyone should be quick to listen,
slow to speak and slow to become angry, for man's anger
does not bring about the righteous life that God desires.
JAMES 1:19-20

Purge from our hearts the stains so deep and foul,
Of wrath and pride and care;

Send Thine own holy calm upon the soul,
And bid it settle there!
ANONYMOUS

Let this truth be present to thee in the excitement of anger—that to be moved by passion is not manly, but that mildness and gentleness, as they are more agreeable to human nature, so also are they more manly. . . . For in the same degree in which a man's mind is nearer to freedom from all passion, in the same degree also is it nearer to strength.

~ MARCUS ANTONINUS

Anger is a short madness.

~ HORACE

Anger is a weed, hate is the tree.

~ ST. AUGUSTINE

June 10

You, O lord, keep my lamp burning;
my god turns my darkness into light.
PSALMS 18:28

Let him who walks in the dark, who has no light,
trust in the name of the Lord and rely on his God.
ISAIAH 50:10

When we in darkness walk,
Nor feel the heavenly flame,
Then is the time to trust our God,
And rest upon His name.
A. M. TOPLADY

There is hardly a man or woman in the world who has not got some corner of self into which he or she fears to venture with a light. The reasons for this may be various, as various as the individual souls. Nevertheless, in spite of the variety of reasons, the fact is universal. For the most part we hardly know our own reasons. It is an instinct, one of the quick instincts of corrupt nature. We prophesy to ourselves that, if we penetrate into that corner of self, something will have to be done which either our laziness or our immortification would shrink from doing. If we enter that sanctuary, some charm of easy devotion or smooth living will be broken. We shall find ourselves face to face with something unpleasant, something which will perhaps constrain us to all the trouble and annoyance of a complete interior revolution, or else leave us very uncomfortable in conscience. . . . So we leave this corner of self curtained off, locked up like a room in a house with disagreeable associations attached to it, unvisited like a lumber closet where we are conscious that disorder and dirt are accumulating, which we have not just now the vigor to grapple with. But do we think that God cannot enter there except by our unlocking the door? Or see anything when He is there, unless we hold Him a light? . . . We know how His eye rests upon us incessantly, and takes us all in, and searches us out, and as it were burns us up with His holy gaze. His perfections environ us with the most awful nearness, flooding us with insupportable light. . . . to be straightforward with God is neither an easy nor a common grace. O with what unutterable faith must we believe in our own falsehood, when we can feel it to be anything like a shelter in the presence of the all-seeing God!

~ FREDERICK WILLIAM FABER

June 11

When I called, you answered me;
you made me bold and stouthearted.
PSALMS 138:3

"Ask and it will be given to you . . ."
LUKE 11:9

Lord, one thing we want,
More holiness grant;
For more of thy mind and thy image we pant
While onward we move
To Canaan above,
Come, fill us with holiness, fill us with love.
ANONYMOUS

. . . Everywhere, O Truth, dost Thou give audience to all who ask counsel of Thee, and at once answerest all, though on manifold matters they ask Thy counsel. Clearly dost Thou answer, though all do not clearly hear. All consult Thee on what they will, though they hear not always what they will. . . . Too late loved I Thee, O Thou Beauty of ancient days, yet ever new! too late I loved Thee! And behold Thou wert within, and I abroad, and there I searched for Thee; deformed as I was, running after those beauties which Thou hast made. Thou wert with me, but I was not with Thee.

~ ST. AUGUSTINE

It is faith's work to claim and challenge loving-kindness out of all the roughest strokes of God.

~ S. RUTHERFORD

June 12

I have fought the good fight, I have finished the race,
I have kept the faith. Now there is in store for me the crown
of righteousness, which the Lord, the righteous Judge,
will award to me on that day . . .
2 TIMOTHY 4:7-8

Servant of God, well done, well hast thou fought
The better fight, who single hast maintained
Against revolted multitudes the cause
Of truth, in word mightier than they in arms.
JOHN MILTON

We listened to a man whom we felt to be, with all his heart and soul and strength, striving against whatever was mean and unmanly and unright-eous in our little world. It was not the cold clear voice of one giving advice and warning from serene heights to those who were struggling and sinning below, but the warm living voice of one who was fighting for us and by our sides, and calling on us to help him and ourselves and one another. And so, wearily and little by little, but surely and steadily on the whole, was brought home to the young boy, for the first time, the meaning of his life; that it was no fool's or sluggard's paradise into which he had wandered by chance, but a battle-field ordained from of old, where there are no spectators, but the youngest must take his side, and the stakes are life and death.

~ THOMAS HUGHES

June 13

Your word is a lamp to my feet and a light for my path.
PSALMS 119:105

But if we walk in the light, as he is in the light,
we have fellowship with one another . . .
1 JOHN 1:7

Lead, kindly Light, amid the encircling gloom;
Lead thou me on!
The night is dark, and I am far from home;
Lead thou me on!
Keep thou my feet: I do not ask to see
The distant scene; one step enough for me.
JOHN HENRY CARDINAL NEWMAN

Thus out of small beginnings greater things have been produced by His hand that made all things of nothing, and give being too all things that are; and, as one small candle may light a thousand, so the light here kindled hath shone unto many, yea in some sort to our whole nation.

~ WILLIAM BRADFORD

. . . Then fold the arms of thy faith, and wait in quietness until light goes up in the darkness. Fold the arms of thy Faith, I say, but not of thy Action: bethink thee of something that thou oughtest to do, and go and do it, if it be but the sweeping of a room, or the preparing of a meal, or a visit to a friend; heed not thy feelings: do thy work.

~ GEORGE MACDONALD

June 14

On the day the Lord gives you relief from suffering
and turmoil and cruel bondage . . .
ISAIAH 14:3

Stilled now be every anxious care
See God's great goodness everywhere
Leave all to Him in perfect rest:
He will do all things for the best.
ANONYMOUS

O Lord, support us all the day long, until the shadows lengthen and the evening comes, and the busy world is hushed, and the fever of life is over, and our work is done. Then in thy mercy grant us a safe lodging, and a holy rest, and peace at the last.

~ JOHN HENRY CARDINAL NEWMAN

O Lord, who art as the Shadow of a great Rock in a weary land, who beholdest Thy weak creatures weary of labor, weary of pleasure, weary of hope deferred, weary of self; in Thine abundant compassion, and unutterable tenderness, bring us, I pray Thee, unto Thy rest. Amen.

~ CHRISTINA G. ROSSETTI

Thou hast made us for Thyself, O Lord; and our heart is restless until it rests in Thee.

~ ST. AUGUSTINE

June 15

"Therefore, whoever humbles himself like this child is the greatest in the kingdom of heaven."
MATTHEW 18:4

The fear of the Lord teaches a man wisdom,
and humility comes before honor.
PROVERBS 15:33

The only wisdom we can hope to acquire
Is the wisdom of humility: humility is endless.
T. S. ELIOT

" . . . there's nothing so becomes a man
As modest stillness and humility . . . "
WILLIAM SHAKESPEARE

Humility, that is lowliness or self-abasement, is an inward bowing down or prostrating of the heart and of the conscience before God's transcendent worth. Righteousness demands and orders this, and through charity a loving heart cannot leave it undone. . . . For to pay homage to God by every outward and inward act, this is the first and dearest work of humility, the most savory among those of charity, and the most meet among those of righteousness. The loving and humble heart cannot pay homage enough either to God or to His noble manhood, nor can it abase itself as much as it would. And that is why a humble man thinks that his worship of God and his lowly service are always failing short. And he is meek, reverencing Holy Church and the sacraments. And he is discreet in food and drink, in speech, in the answers which he makes to everybody; and in his behavior, dress, and lowly service he is without hypocrisy and without pretence. And he is humble in his devotions, both outwardly and inwardly, before God and before all men, so that none is offended because of him. And so he overcomes and casts out pride, which is the source and origin of all other sins. By humility the snares of the devil, and of sin, and of the world are broken, and man is set in order and established in the very condition of virtue. And heaven is opened to him, and God stoops to hear his prayers, and he is fulfilled with grace. And Christ, that strong rock, is his foundation. Whosoever therefore grounds his virtue in humility, he shall never err.

~ JOHN OF RUYSBROECK

June 16

Great and marvelous are your deeds, Lord God Almighty.
Just and true are your ways, King of the ages.
REVELATIONS 15:3-4

WE would not meager gifts down-call
When Thou dost yearn to yield us all
But for this life, this little hour,
Ask all Thy love and care and power.
J. INGELOW

God so loveth us that He would make all things channels to us and mes-
sengers of His love. Do for His sake deeds of love, and He will give thee
His love. Still thyself, thy own cares, thy own thoughts for Him, and He
will speak to thy heart. Ask for Himself, and He will give thee Himself.
Truly, a secret hidden thing is the love of God, known only to them who
seek it, and to them also secret, for what man can have of it here is how
slight a foretaste of that endless ocean of His love.

~ E. B. PUSEY

June 17

The righteous will flourish like a palm tree,
they will grow like a cedar of Lebanon . . .
PSALMS 92:12

"See how the lilies of the field grow, they do not labor or spin."
MATTHEW 6:28

A creed is a rod,
And a crown is of night;
But this thing is God,
To be man with thy might,
To grow straight in the strength of thy spirit, and
to live out thy life as the light.
ALGERNON CHARLES SWINBURNE

Interpose no barrier to His mighty lifegiving power, working in you all the
good pleasure of His will. Yield yourself up utterly to His sweet control.
Put your growing into His hands as completely as you have put all your
other affairs. Suffer Him to manage it as He will. Do not concern yourself
about it, nor even think of it. Trust Him absolutely and always. Accept
each moment's dispensation as it comes to you from His dear hands, as
being the needed sunshine or dew for that moment's growth. Say a continual "yes" to your Father's will.

~ H. W. S.

Thine own self-will and anxiety, thy hurry and labor, disturb thy peace
and prevent Me from working in thee. Look at the little flowers, in the
serene summer days; they quietly open their petals, and the sun shines
into them with his gentle influences. So will I do for thee, if thou wilt
yield thyself to Me.

~ G. TERSTEEGEN

"And do not set your heart on what you will eat or drink;
do not worry about it."
LUKE 12:29

If that is how God clothes the grass of the field, which is here today and
tomorrow is thrown into the fire, will he not much more clothe you,
O you of little faith?
MATTHEW 6:30

They do not toil:
Content with their allotted task
They do but grow; they do not ask
A richer lot, a higher sphere,
But in their loveliness appear,
And grow, and smile, and do their best,
And unto God they leave the rest.
MARIANNE FARNINGHAM

As to those things which it still remains to say or do, we win think of those in their proper time, and God will provide for all; sufficient unto the day is the evil thereof; will not tomorrow and the next day bring with them their peculiar graces? Let us then think only of the present and follow the order of God, let us leave the past to His mercy, the future to Providence, striving peaceably an the time and without anxiety, first of all for salvation; and for the rest, let us leave its success entirely to God, casting on His parental bosom all our vain anxieties. . . . Let us then often say by a simple reflection of confidence and surrender, that can do more for us and better remedy all our ills than our own most anxious cares: "O Lord, while I do not wish to neglect anything of what Thou ordainest for me, for the good of my soul or my body, I hope that in due time and place Thou wilt grant me the thought, the movement, and the facility to undertake and carry out such and such things which come so often and at such inappropriate times to present themselves to my spirit. I give them all up to Thee with their various outcomes, in the intention of occupying myself more freely with Thee, of waiting patiently and with complete resignation for everything to happen at the will of Thy wise Providence." . . . Happy the persons who, in order to become more recollected in God and more disposed to prayer, are able to banish constantly all this waste of the spirit, retaining only what is in the strictest sense necessary for the present which so soon passes, and for the future which will not be what one imagines and perhaps will never come.

~ J. P. DE CAUSSADE

The Lord watches over you— the Lord is your shade at your right hand.
PSALMS 121:5

Under Thy wings, my God, I rest,
Under Thy shadow safety lie;
By Thy own strength in peace possessed,
While dreaded evils pass me by.
A. L. WARING

Almighty God, our heavenly Father, without whose help labor is useless, without whose light search is vain, invigorate my studies and direct my enquiries, that I may by due diligence and right discernment establish myself and others in thy holy Faith. Take not, O Lord, thy Holy Spirit from me, let not evil thoughts have dominion in my mind. Let me not linger in ignorance and doubt, but enlighten and support me for the sake of Jesus Christ our Lord. Amen.

~ SAMUEL JOHNSON

Neither go back in fear and misgiving to the past, nor in anxiety and forecasting to the future; but lie quiet under His hand, having no will but His.

~ H. E. MANNING

Let God do with me what He will, anything He will; whatever it be, it will be either heaven itself or some beginning of it.

~ WILLIAM MOUNTFORD

June 20

The eternal God is your refuge . . . .
DEUTRONOMY 33:27

Godhead here in hiding, whom I do adore
Masked by these bare shadows' shape and nothing more,
See, Lord, at thy service low lies here a heart
Lost, all lost in wonder at the God thou art.
ST. THOMAS AQUINAS

In time of trouble go not out of yourself to seek for aid; for the whole benefit of trial consists in silence, patience, rest, and resignation. In this condition divine strength is found for the hard warfare, because God Himself fights for the soul.

~ M. MOLINOS

In vain will you let your mind run out after help in times of trouble; it is like putting to sea in a storm. Sit still, and feel after your principles; and, if you find none that furnish you with somewhat of a stay and prop, and which point you to quietness and silent submission, depend upon it you have never yet learned Truth from the Spirit of Truth, whatever notions thereof you may have picked up from this and the other description of it.

~ M. A. KELTY

June 21

I have strayed like a lost sheep . . . .
PSALMS 119:176

"Father, I thank you that you have heard me . . . ."
JOHN 11:41

I love in solitude to shed
The penitential tear;
And all his promises to plead,

When none but God is near.
I love to think on mercies past,
And future good implore;
And all my cares and sorrows cast
On him whom I adore.
ANONYMOUS

Though this patient, meek resignation is to be exercised with regard to all outward things and occurrences of life, yet it chiefly respects our own inward state, the troubles, perplexities, weaknesses, and disorders of our own souls. And to stand turned to a patient, meek, humble resignation to God, when your own impatience, wrath, pride, and irresignation attack yourself, is a higher and more beneficial performance of this duty, than when you stand turned to meekness and patience, when attacked by the pride, or wrath, or disorderly passions of other people.

~ WILLIAM LAW

June 22

. . . weeping may remain for a night,
but rejoicing comes in the morning.
PSALMS 30:5

I can do all things, and can bear
All sufferings, if my Lord be near;
Sweet pleasures mingle with the pains,
While his left hand my head sustains.
ANONYMOUS

Everything which happens, either happens in such wise that thou art formed by nature to bear it, or that thou art not formed, by nature to bear it. If then, it happens to thee in such way that thou art formed by nature to bear it, do not complain, but bear it as thou art formed by nature to bear it. But, if it happens in such wise that thou art not able to bear it, do not complain; for it will perish after it has consumed thee. Remember, however, that thou art formed by nature to bear everything, with respect to which it depends on thy own opinion to make it endurable and tolerable, by thinking that it is either thy interest or thy duty to do this.

~ MARCUS ANTONINUS

June 23

Why are you downcast, O my soul?
Why so disturbed within me?
Put your hope in God,
for I will yet praise him, my savior and my God.
PSALMS 42:11

I Praise Thee while my days go on;
I love Thee while my days go on:
Through dark and dearth, through fire and frost,
With emptied arms and treasure lost,
I thank Thee while my days go on.
ELIZABETH BARRETT BROWNING

Beware of letting your care degenerate into anxiety and unrest; tossed as you are amid the winds and waves of sundry troubles, keep your eyes fixed on the Lord, and say, "Oh, my God, I look to Thee alone; be Thou my guide, my pilot"; and then be comforted. When the shore is gained, who will heed the toil and the storm? And we shall steer safely through every storm, so long as our heart is right, our intention fervent, our courage steadfast, and our trust fixed on God. If at times we are somewhat stunned by the tempest, never fear; let us take breath, and go on afresh. Do not be disconcerted by the fits of vexation and uneasiness which are sometimes produced by the multiplicity of your domestic worries. No indeed, dearest child, all these are but opportunities of strengthening yourself in the loving, forbearing graces which our dear Lord sets before us.

~ ST. FRANCIS DE SALES

June 24

"This is the way; walk in it."
ISAIAH 30:21

O Jesus
Be the canoe that holds me in the sea of life.
Be the steer that keeps me straight.
Be the outrigger that supports me in times of great temptation.
Let thy spirit be my sail that carries me through each day.
Keep my body strong,
so that I may paddle steadfastly on,
in the long voyage of life.
A NEW HEBRIDEAN PRAYER

Most of us die of something; of disease, accident, old age. But occasionally there appears in our midst a man who resolves to die for something, like Winkelried when he gathered the spears of the Austrians into his breast at the battle of Sempach. This dying for something, instead of waiting to die of something, as most of us do, this deliberate dying for something deemed worthy of it, is the strongest form of self-affirmation I know of. The power and vitality of it are tremendous, and the stamp that it leaves on the world is indelible. The Christian religion is an example of it.

~ L. P. JACKS

June 25

"I desire to do your will,
O my God; your law is in my heart."
PSALMS 40:8

God wills us free, man wills us slaves,
I will as God wills, God's will be done.
DANIEL BLISS

We mustn't be in a hurry to fix and choose our own lot; we must wait to be guided. We are led on, like the little children, by a way that we know not. It is a vain thought to flee from the work that God appoints us, for the sake of finding a greater blessing to our own souls; as if we could choose for ourselves where we shall find the fullness of the Divine

Presence, instead of seeking it where alone it is to be found, in
loving obedience.

~ GEORGE ELIOT

Everywhere and at all times it is in thy power piously to acquiesce in thy
present condition, and to behave justly to those who are about thee.

~ MARCUS ANTONINUS

June 26

*There is not a righteous man on earth
who does what is right and never sins.*
ECCLESIASTES 7:20

*For thou lovest all the things that are,
And abhorrest nothing which thou hast made:
For never wouldst thou have made anything if thou hadst hated it.
And how could anything have endured,
If it had not been thy Will?
Or been preserved, if not called by Thee?
But thou sparest all:
For they are thine,
O Lord, Thou lover of souls.*
WISDOM OF SOLOMON 11:24-26

When they sin against you—for there is no one who does not sin—and
you become angry with them and give them over to the enemy, who takes
them captive to his own land, far away or near; and if they have a change
of heart in the land where they are held captive, and repent and plead with
you in the land of their conquerors and say, "We have sinned, we have
done wrong, we have acted wickedly"; and if they turn back to you with
all their heart and soul in the land of their enemies who took them captive, and pray to you toward the land you gave their fathers, toward the
city you have chosen and the temple I have built for your Name; then
from heaven, your dwelling place, hear their prayer and their plea, and
uphold thier cause. And forgive your people, who have sinned against you;
forgive all the offenses they have committed against you, and cause their
conquerors to show them mercy; . . .

~ 1 KINGS 8:46-51

June 27

*Create in me a pure heart,
O God, and renew a steadfast spirit within me.*
PSALMS 51:10

*Think what Spirit dwells within thee;
Think what Father's smiles are thine;
Think that Jesus died to win thee:
Child of heaven, canst thou repine?*
ANONYMOUS

When you close your doors, and make darkness within, remember never
to say that you are alone, for you are not alone; nay, God is within, and

your genius is within. And what need have they of light to see what you
are doing?

~ EPICTETUS

Then does a good man become the tabernacle of God, wherein the divine
Shechinah does rest, and which the divine glory fills, when the frame of
his mind and life is wholly according to that idea and pattern which he
receives from the mount.

~ DR. JOHN SMITH

June 28

. . . doing what is right and just and fair:
for giving prudence to the simple . . .
PROVERBS 1:3-4

The Lord protects the simple-hearted . . .
PSALMS 116:6

'Tis the gift to be simple,
'Tis the gift to be free,
'Tis the gift to come down
Where we ought to be.
SHAKER SONG

This deliverance of the soul from all useless and selfish and unquiet cares,
brings to it an unspeakable peace and freedom; this is true simplicity. This
state of entire resignation and perpetual acquiescence produces true liberty; and this liberty brings perfect simplicity. The soul which knows no self-
seeking, no interested ends, is thoroughly candid; it goes straight forward
without hindrance; its path opens daily more and more to 'perfect day', in
proportion as its self-renunciation and its self-forgetfulness increase; and
its peace, amid whatever troubles beset it, will be as boundless as the
depths of the sea.

~ FENELON

June 29

The Lord is the strength and my shield;
my heart trusts in him, and I am helped.
My heart leaps for joy and
I will give thanks to him in song.
PSALMS 28:7

No coward soul is mine,
No trembler in the world's storm-troubled sphere:
I see Heaven's glories shine,
And faith shines equal, arming me from fear.

O God within my breast,
Almighty, ever-present Deity!
Life—that in me has rest,
As I—undying Life—have power in Thee!
EMILY BRONTE

The humblest citizen of all the land, when clad in the armor of a righteous cause, is stronger than all the hosts of Error.

~ WILLIAM JENNINGS BRYAN

Oh, be at least able to say in that day, Lord, I am no hero. I have been
careless, cowardly, sometimes all but mutinous. Punishment I have
deserved, I deny it not. But a traitor I have never been; a deserter I have
never been. I have tried to fight on Thy side in Thy battle against evil. I
have tried to do the duty which lay nearest me; and to leave whatever
Thou didst commit to my charge a little better than I found it. I have not
been good, but I have at least tried to be good. Take the will for the deed,
good Lord. Strike not my unworthy name off the roll-call of the noble and
victorious army, which is the blessed company of all, faithful people; and
let me, too, be found written in the Book of Life; even though I stand the
lowest and last upon its list. Amen.

~ C. KINGSLEY

June 30

*But for you who revere my name, the sun of righteousness
will rise with healing in its wings. And you will go out and
leap like calves released from the stall.*
MALACHI 4:2

If my immortal Savior lives,
Then my eternal life is sure;
His word a firm foundation gives,
Here let me build, and rest secure.

Here, O my soul, thy trust repose;
If Jesus is for ever mine,
Not death itself, that last of foes,
Shall break a union so divine.
ANONYMOUS

Fondly do we hope, fervently do we pray, that this mighty scourge of war
may speedily pass away. Yet, if God wills that it continue until all the
wealth piled by the bondsman's two hundred and fifty years of unrequited
toil shall be sunk, and until every drop of blood drawn with the lash shall
be paid by another drawn with the sword, as was said three thousand
years ago, so still it must be said, "The judgments of the Lord are true and
righteous altogether." With malice toward none, with charity for all, with
firmness in the right as God gives us to see the right, let us strive on to
finish the work we are in, to bind up the nation's wounds, to care for him
who shall have borne the battle and for his widow and his orphan, to do
all which may achieve and cherish a just and lasting peace among ourselves and with all nations.

~ ABRAHAM LINCOLN

. . . and in the morning you will see the glory of the Lord.
EXODUS 16:7

But I cry to you for help, O Lord;
in the morning my prayer comes before you.
PSALMS 88:13

Every day is a fresh beginning,
Every morn is the world made new.
You who are weary of sorrow and sinning,
Here is a beautiful hope for you;
A hope for me and a hope for you.
SUSAN COLLIDGE

Be patient with every one, but above all with yourself. I mean, do not be disturbed because of your imperfections, and always rise up bravely from a fall. I am glad that you make a daily new beginning; there is no better means of progress in the spiritual life than to be continually beginning afresh, and never to think that we have done enough.

~ ST. FRANCIS DE SALES

Because perseverance is so difficult, even when supported by the grace of God, thence is the value of new beginnings. For new beginnings are the life of perseverance.

~ E. B. PUSEY

I will instruct you and teach you in the way you should go;
I will counsel you and watch over you.
PSALM 32:8

Oh, keep thy conscience sensitive;
No inward token miss;
And go where grace entices thee;
Perfection lies in this.
F. W. FABER

Every man is represented as having a kind of court and tribunal in his own breast; where he tries himself and all his actions, and conscience, under one notion or another, sustains all parts in this trial. The court is called the court of a man's conscience, and the bar at which the sinner stands impleaded is called the bar of conscience. Conscience also is the accuser, and it is the record and the register of our crimes, in which the memory of them is preserved; and it is the witness which gives testimony for or against us; hence are those expressions of the testimony of our consciences, and that a man's own conscience is to him, instead of a thousand witnesses. And it is likewise the judge which declares the law, and what we ought or ought not to have done, in such or such a case, and accordingly passes sentence upon us by acquitting or condemning us . . . . Hence we should reverence our consciences and stand in awe of them, and have a great regard to their testimony and verdict. For conscience is a domestic judge, and kind of a familiar god; and therefore next to the

supreme Majesty of heaven and earth, every man should be afraid to offend his own reason and conscience which, whenever we knowingly do amiss, will beat us with many stripes and handle us more severely than the greatest enemy we have in the world . . . . The most sensual man that ever was in the world never felt his heart touched with so delicious and lasting a pleasure as that is which springs from a clear conscience and a mind fully satisfied with his own actions.

This makes all calm and serene within, when there is nothing but clouds and darkness about him.

~ JOHN TILLOTSON

July 3

He himself will redeem Israel from all their sins.

PSALMS 130:8

This is the month, and this the happy morn,
Wherein the Son of Heav'n's eternal King,
Of wedded maid and virgin mother born,
Our great redemption from above did bring;
For so the holy sages once did sing,
That He our deadly forfeit should release,
And with His Father work us a perpetual peace.

JOHN MILTON

When you wake, or as soon as you are dressed, offer up your whole self to God, soul and body, thoughts and purposes and desires, to be for that day what He wills. Think of the occasions of the sin likely to befall you, and go, as a child, to your Father which is in heaven, and tell Him in childlike, simple words, your trials—in some such simple words as these—"Thou knowest, good Lord, that I am tempted to" —(then name the temptations to it ,and the ways in which you sin, as well as you know them). But, good Lord, for love of Thee, I would this day keep wholly from all (naming the sin) and be very (naming the opposite grace). I will not, by Thy grace, do one (N.) act, or speak one (N.) word, or give one (N.) look, or harbor one (N.) thought in my soul. If Thou allow any of these temptations to come upon me this day, I desire to think, speak, and do only what Thou willest. Lord, without Thee I can do nothing; with Thee I can do all.

~ E. B. PUSEY

July 4

Remember,
O Lord, your great mercy and love,
for they are from old.
PSALMS 25:6

Faith of our fathers! holy faith!
We will be true to thee till death.

F. W. FABER

Be not so much discouraged in the sight of what is yet to be done, as comforted in His good-will towards thee. 'Tis true, He hath chastened thee with rods and sore afflictions; but did He ever take away His loving kindness from thee? or did His faithfulness ever fail in the sorest, blackest, thickest, darkest night that ever befell thee?

~ I. PENINGTON

We call Him the "God of our fathers"; and we feel that there is some sta-bility at center, while we can tell our cares to One listening at our right hand, by whom theirs are remembered and removed.

~ JAMES MARTINEAU

July 5

---

*A bruised reed he will not break,
and a smoldering wick he will not snuff out.*
PSALMS 42:3

*Dear God, be good to me;
The sea is so wide,
And my boat is so small.*
BRETON FISHERMEN'S PRAYER

Blessed are all thy saints, O God and King, who have traveled over the tempestuous sea of this mortal life, and have made the harbor of peace and felicity. Watch over us who are still in our dangerous voyage; and remember such as lie exposed to the rough storms of trouble and tempta-tions. Frail is our vessel, and the ocean is wide; but as in thy mercy thou hast set our course, so steer the vessel of our life toward the everlasting shore of peace, and bring us at length to the quiet haven of our heart's desire, where thou, O our God, are blessed, and livest and reignest for ever and ever.

~ ST. AUGUSTINE

July 6

---

*"The gracious hand of our God is on everyone who looks to him, but his
great anger is against all who forsake him."*
EZRA 8:22

*I do not ask my cross to understand,
My ways to see;
Better in darkness just to feel Thy hand,
And follow Thee.*
ADELAIDE A. PROCTER

Being thus arrived in a good harbor, and brought safe to land, they fell upon their knees and the God of Heaven who had brought them over the vast and furious ocean, and delivered them from all the perils and miseries thereof, again to set their feet on the firm and stable earth, their proper element.

~ WILLIAM BRADFORD

O Lord, if only my will may remain right and firm towards Thee, do with me whatsoever it shall please Thee. For it cannot be anything but good, whatsoever Thou shalt do with me. If it be Thy will I should be in dark-ness, be Thou blessed; and, if it be Thy will I should be in light, be Thou

again blessed. If Thou vouchsafe to comfort me, be Thou blessed; and, if
Thou wilt have me afflicted, be Thou equally blessed. O Lord I for
Thy sake I will cheerfully suffer whatever shall come on me with
Thy permission.

~ THOMAS A. KEMPIS

July 7

The Lord is my light and my salvation—
whom shall I fear?
The Lord is the stronghold of my life—
of whom shall I be afraid?
PSALMS 27:1

. . . let us be self-controlled, putting on faith and love as a breastplate,
and the hope of salvation as a helmet.
1 THESSALONIANS 5:8

My Father! see
I trust the faithfulness displayed of old,
I trust the love that never can grow cold—
I trust in Thee.
CHRISTIAN INTELLIGENCER

He will complete the work begun
He will his own defend;
Will give me strength my course to run,
And, love me to the end.
ANONYMOUS

Whatsoever befalleth thee, receive it not from the hand of any creature,
but from Him alone, and render back all to Him, seeking in all things
His pleasure and honor, the purifying and subduing of thyself. What can
harm thee, when all must first touch God, within whom thou hast
enclosed thyself?

~ R. LEIGHTON

How God rejoices over a soul, which, surrounded on all sides by suffering
and misery, does that upon earth which the angels do in heaven; namely,
loves, adores, and praises God!

~ G. TERSTEEGEN

July 8

"Speak up for those who cannot speak for themselves,
for the rights of all who are destitute.
Speak up and judge fairly;
defend the rights of the poor and needy."
PROVERBS 31:8-9

Be kind and compassionate to one another,
forgiving each other,
just as in Christ God forgave you.
EPHESIANS 4:32

If I can stop one Heart from breaking
I shall not live in vain
If I can ease one Life the Aching
Or cool one pain
Or help one fainting Robin
Unto his Nest again
I shall not live in Vain.
EMILY DICKENSON

We may, if we choose, make the worst of one another. Every one has his weak points; every one has his faults; we may make the worst of these; we may fix our attention constantly upon these. But we may also make the best of one another. We may forgive, even as we hope to be forgiven. We may put ourselves in the place of others, and ask what we should wish to be done to us, and thought of us, were we in their place. By loving whatever is lovable in those around us, love will flow back from them to us, and life will become a pleasure instead of a pain; and earth will become like heaven; and we shall become not unworthy followers of Him whose name is Love.

~ A. P. STANLEY

July 9

Bear with each other and forgive whatever grievances you may have against one another. Forgive as the Lord forgave you.
COLOSSIANS 3:13

Such mercy He by His most holy rede
Unto us taught, and to approve it true,
Ensampled it by His most righteous deed,
Showing us mercy (miserable crew!)
That we the like should to the wretches show,
And love our brethren; thereby to approve
How much Himself that loved us we love.
EDMUND SPENSER

The human value is not the ultimate, but only the penultimate value; the last, the highest value is God the Father. He alone is the cause and the measure of all things, cause and measure of all valuations, cause and measure of all love
. . . Because this Father loves men—no matter whether they are good or bad-and because we prove ourselves His children precisely by showing that same love, are we to love men. My relation to men has therefore its ultimate roots in a transcendental fact, namely in that fundamental relation of love in which God includes men, all men. Man is a mystery. He is the culmination-point of an eternal love which issues from God; a point in the actuality of the world where, as nowhere else, the love of God bums. That is the reason why man is worth loving: not by reason of what he is in himself or for himself, but by reason of what he is for God; or in the language of theology: not for a natural but for a supernatural reason. I shall never reach man by starting from the earth; I must first reach to heaven to find man through God. The flood stream of the love of man passes through the heart of God. I must first have God before I can have man. God is the way to man . . . .

~ KARL ADAM

July 10

Do you seek a man skilled in his work?
PROVERBS 22:29

He . . . must work, doing something useful with his own hands . . .
EPHESIANS 4:28

. . . May he bless all who build the bridge,
and keep them faithful and safe in their work.

May the peoples of this city be united and godfearing,
happy and prosperous,
preserving the good heritage of the past,
and building the future on foundations of
righteousness and love.
G. A.

Human felicity is produced not so much by great pieces of good fortune
that seldom happen, as by little advantages that occur every day.
   When men are employed, they are best contented; for on the days they
worked they were good-natured and cheerful, and, with the consciousness
of having done a good day's work, they spent the evening jollily; but on
our idle days they were mutinous and quarrelsome.
~ BENJAMIN FRANKLIN

July 11

Better a dry crust with peace and quiet,
than a house full
of feasting with strife.
PROVERBS 17:1

Ah, dearest Jesus, holy Child,
Make thee a bed, soft, undefiled,
Within my heart, that it may be
A quiet chamber kept for thee.
MARTIN LUTHER

Calm Soul of all things! make it mine
To feel, amid the city's jar,
That there bides a peace of thine,
Man did not make, and can not mar.
MATTHEW ARNOLD

What physic, what chiurgery, what wealth, favor, authority can relieve,
bear out, assuage, or expel a troubled conscience? A quiet mind cureth all.
~ ROBERT BURTON

"Be strong and courageous. Do not be afraid or terrified because of them, for the Lord your God goes with you; he will never leave you nor forsake you."
DEUTERONOMY 31:6

Stay with me, God. The night is dark,
The night is cold: my little spark
Of courage dies. The night is long;
Be with me, God, and make me strong.
ANONYMOUS SOLDIER

Though I sympathize, I do not share in the least the feeling of being disheartened and cast down. It is not things of this sort that depress me, or ever will. The contrary things, praise, openings, the feeling of the greatness of my work, and my inability in relation to it, these things oppress and cast me down; but little hindrances, and closing up of accustomed or expected avenues, and the presence of difficulties to be overcome—I'm not going to be cast down by trifles such as these.

~ JAMES HINTON

His God instructs him and teaches him the right way.
ISAIAH 28:26

Wherever He may guide me,
No want shall turn me back
My Shepherd is beside me,
And nothing can I lack.
His wisdom ever waketh,
His sight is never dim—
He knows the way He taketh,
And I will walk with Him.
A. L. WARING

Lord, I thank you for teaching me how to live in the present moment. In this way I enjoy each simple task as I do it without thinking that I must hurry on to the next thing. I do what I am doing with all my ability and all my concentration. My mind is no longer divided, and life is more peaceful. Thank you for teaching me how to do this, and please help me how to show others the way to learn to trust you more completely and to do everything which has to be done at your time and your speed.

~ MICHAEL HOLLINGS AND ETTA GULLICK

Command those who are rich in this present world not to be arrogant nor to put their hope in wealth, which is so uncertain, but to put their hope in God, who richly provides us with everything for our enjoyment.
1 TIMOTHY 6:17

Do not conform any longer to the pattern of this world,
but be transformed by the renewing of your mind.
ROMANS 12:2

Almighty God, unto whom all hearts are open,
all desires known, and from whom no secrets are hid;
Cleanse the thoughts of our hearts
by the inspiration of thy Holy Spirit,
that we may perfectly love thee,
and worthily magnify thy holy Name.
THE BOOK OF COMMON PRAYER

O Lord, our Savior, who hast warned us that thou wilt require much of those to whom much is given; grant that we whose lot is cast in so goodly a heritage may strive together the more abundantly by prayer, by almsgiving, by fasting, and by every other appointed means, to extend to others what we so richly enjoy; and as we have entered into the labors of other men, so to labor that in their turn other men may enter into ours to the fulfillment of thy holy will, and our own everlasting salvation; through Jesus Christ our Lord.

~ ST. AUGUSTINE

July 15

"Now you have been pleased to bless the house of your servant,
that it may continue forever in your sight;
for you, O Lord, have blessed it,
and it will be blessed forever."
1 CHRONICLES 17:27

May the love of the Lord Jesus draw us to himself;
May the power of the Lord Jesus strengthen us in his service;
May the joy of the Lord Jesus fill our souls.
May the blessing of the God almighty, the Father, the Son,
and the Holy Ghost,
be amongst you and remain with you always.
WILLIAM TEMPLE

"God bless us every one!" said Tiny Tim, the last of all.

~ CHARLES DICKENS

May God, the Lord, bless us with all heavenly benediction, and make us pure and holy in his sight. May the riches of his glory abound in us. May He instruct us with the word of truth, inform us with the Gospel of salvation, and enrich us with his love, Through Jesus Christ, our Lord.

~ GELASIAN SACRAMENTARY

The blessing of the Lord rest and remain upon all his people, in every land, of every tongue; the Lord meet in mercy all that seek him; the Lord comfort all who suffer and mourn; the Lord comfort all who suffer and mourn; the Lord hasten his coming, and give us, his people, the blessing of peace.

~ BISHOP HANDLEY MOULE

*Then my head will be exalted above the enemies who surround me;
at his tabernacle will I sacrifice with shouts of joy;
I will sing and make music to the Lord.*
PSALMS 27:6

*You are holy, Lord, the only God,
and your deeds are wonderful.
You are strong.
You are great.
You are the Most High,
You are almighty.
You, holy Father, are
King of heaven and earth.*

*. . . You are our faith,
Our great consolation.
You are our eternal life,
Great and wonderful Lord,
God almighty,
Merciful Savior.*
ST. FRANCIS OF ASSISI

We who in a mystery represent the Cherubim and sing the thrice-holy hymn to the life-giving Trinity: Let us lay aside the cares of this world; for now we are to receive the King of all who comes accompanied by unseen hosts of angels, Alleluia, alleluia, alleluia.
~ LITURGY OF ST. JOHN CHRYSOSTOM

*For great is your love toward me;
you have delivered me from the depths of the grave.*
PSALMS 86:13

*BELIEV'ST thou in eternal things?
Thou knowest, in thy inmost heart,
Thou art not clay; thy soul hath wings,
And what thou seest is but part.
Make this thy med'cine for the smart
Of every day's distress; be dumb,
In each new loss thou truly art
Tasting the power of things that come.*
T. W. PARSONS

"No man ever saw God and lived"; and yet I shall not live till I see God; and when I have seen Him I shall never die. What have I ever seen in this world that hath been truly the same thing that it seemed to me? I have seen marble buildings, and a chip, a crust, a plaster, a face of marble hath peeled off, and I see brick-bowels within. I have seen beauty, and a strong breath from another tells me that complexion is from without, not from a sound constitution within. I have seen the state of princes, and all that is but ceremony; and I would be loath to put a master of ceremonies to define ceremony and tell me what it is, and to include so various a thing as ceremony in so constant a thing as a definition. I see a great officer, and I see a man of mine own profession, of great revenues, and I see not the interest of the money that was paid for it, I see not the pensions nor the annuities that are charged upon that office or that church. As he that fears God fears nothing else, so he that sees God sees everything else. When we shall see God *sicuti est*, as He is, we shall see all things *sicuti sunt*, as they are; for that's their essence, as they conduce to His glory. We shall be no more deluded with outward appearances: for when this sight which we intend here comes, there will be no delusory thing to be seen. All that we have made as though we saw in this world will be vanished, and I shall see nothing but God, and what is in Him.

~ JOHN DONNE

July 18

"I am as you are, my people as your people,
my horses as your horses."
1 KINGS 22:4

May the Lord make your love increase and overflow for each other and for
everyone else, just as ours does for you.
1 THESSALONIANS 3:12

She doeth little kindnesses
Which most leave undone or despise
For nought which sets one heart at ease,
And giveth happiness or peace,
Is low-esteemed in her eyes.
J. R. LOWELL

. . . how sometimes we have dreamed of a better state of things in which each man's independence should make the brotherhood of all men perfect. . . . . Must we wait for such a society as that until we get to heaven? Surely not!
. . . We may begin it in ourselves. Already we may give ourselves to Christ. We may own that we are His. We may see in all our bodily life—in the strength and glory of our youth if we are young and strong, in the weariness and depression of our age or feebleness if we are old and feeble—the marks of His ownership, the signs that we are His. We may wait for His coming to claim us, as the marked tree back in the woods waits till the ship-builder who has stuck his sign into it with his axe comes by and by to take it and make it part of the great ship that he is building. And while we wait we may make the world stronger by being our own, and sweeter by being our brethren's; and both, because and only because we are really not our own nor theirs, but Christ's.

~ PHILLIPS BROOKS

July 19

For everything God created is good,
and nothing is to be rejected if it is received with thanksgiving,
because it is consecrated by the word of God and prayer.
1 TIMOTHY 4:4

The Lord is good to all;
he has compassion on all he has made.
PSALMS 145:9

For every thing that lives is holy.
WILLIAM BLAKE

To see a world in a grain of sand
And heaven in a wild flower,
Hold infinity in the palm of your hand
And eternity in and hour.
WILLIAM BLAKE

I believe where the love of God is verily and the true spirit of government watchfully attended to, a tenderness towards all creatures made subject to us will be experienced; a care felt in us, that we do not lessen that sweetness of life in the animal creation, which the great Creator intends for them under our government . . . . To say we love God as unseen, and at the same time exercise cruelty toward the least creature moving His life, or by life derived from Him, was a contradiction in itself.

~ JOHN WOOLMAN

I would give nothing for that man's religion whose very dog and cat are not the better for it.

~ ROWLAND HILL

July 20

. . . they will wear themselves out but gain nothing.
JEREMIAH 12:13

Unless the Lord builds the house, its builders labor in vain.
PSALMS 127:1

Because I spent the strength Thou gavest me
In struggle which Thou never didst ordain,
And have but dregs of life to offer Thee—
O Lord, I do repent.
SARAH WILLIAMS

Mind, it is our best work that He wants, not the dregs of our exhaustion. I think He must prefer quality to quantity.

~ GEORGE MACDONALD

If the people about you are carrying on their business or their benevolence at a pace which drains the life out of you, resolutely take a slower pace; be called a laggard, make less money, accomplish less work than they, but be what you were meant to be and can be. You have your natural limit of power as much as an engine—ten-horse power, or twenty, or a hundred. You are fit to do certain kinds of work, and you need a certain kind and amount of fuel, and a certain kind of handling.

~ GEORGE S. MERRIAM

In your occupations, try to possess your soul in peace. It is not a good plan to be in haste to perform any action that it may be the sooner over. On the contrary, you should accustom yourself to do whatever you have to do with

tranquility, in order that you may retain the possession of yourself and of settled peace.

~ MADAME GUYON

July 21

Therefore we do not lose heart. Though outwardly we are wasting away, yet inwardly we are being renewed day by day.
2 CORINTHIANS 4:16

And now in age I bud again,
After so many deaths I live and write;
I once more smell the dew and rain,
And relish versing: O my only light,
It cannot be
That I am he
On whom thy tempests fell all night.
GEORGE HERBERT

In my attempts to promote the comfort of my family, the quiet of my spirit has been disturbed. Some of this is doubtless owing to physical weakness; but, with every temptation, there is a way of escape; there is never any need to sin. Another thing I have suffered loss from—entering into the business of the day without seeking to have my spirit quieted and directed. So many things press upon me, this is sometimes neglected shame to me that it should be so.

This is of great importance, to watch carefully—now I am so weak—not to over-fatigue myself, because then I cannot contribute to the pleasure of others; and a placid face and a gentle tone will make my family more happy than anything else I can do for them. Our own will gets sadly into the performance of our duties sometimes.

~ ELIZABETH T. KING

July 22

"He is good; His love endures forever."
2 CHRONICLES 5:13

The one remains, the many change and pass;
Heaven's light forever shines, earth's shadows fly;
Life, like a dome of many-colored glass,
Stains the white radiance of eternity,
Until Death tramples it to fragments—Die,
If thou wouldst be with that which thou dost seek.
PERCY BYSSHE SHELLEY

Wondered over again for the hundredth time what could be the principle which, in the wildest, most lawless, fantastically chaotic, apparently capricious work of nature, always kept it beautiful. The beauty of holiness must be at the heart of it somehow, I thought. Because our God is so free from stain, so loving, so unselfish, so good, so altogether what He wants us to be, so holy, therefore all His works declare Him in beauty; His fingers can touch nothing but to mould it into loveliness; and even the play of His elements is in grace and tenderness of form.

~ GEORGE MACDONALD

"Shall we accept good from God, and not trouble?"
JOB 2:10

*"Love the Lord your God with all your heart and with all your soul and
with all your strength and with all your mind."*
LUKE 10:27

*Teach us, good Lord, to serve Thee as Thou deservest;
To give and not to count the cost;
To fight and not to heed the wounds;
to toil and not to seek for rest;
To labor and not ask for any reward
Save that of knowing that we do Thy will.*
ST. IGNATIUS OF LOYOLA

To love God "with all our heart," is to know the spiritual passion of mea-
sureless gratitude for loving-kindness, and self-devotedness to goodness; to
love Him "with all our mind," is to know the passion for Truth that is the
enthusiasm of Science, the passion for Beauty that inspires the poet and
the artist, when all truth and beauty are regarded as the self-revealings of
God; to love Him "with all our soul," is to know the saint's rapture of
devotion and gaze of penitential awe into the face of the All-holy, the
saint's abhorrence of sin, and agony of desire to save a sinner's soul and to
love Him "with all our strength," is the supreme spiritual passion that
tests the rest; the passion for reality, for worship in spirit and in truth, for
being what we adore, for doing what we know to be God's word; the loyalty that exacts the living sacrifice, the whole burnt-offering that is our reasonable service, and in our coldest hours keeps steadfast to what seemed
good when we were aglow.

~ J. H. THOM

*And I pray that you, being rooted and established in love,
may have power, together with all the saints, to grasp how wide
and long and high and deep is the love of Christ, and to know this love
that surpasses knowledge.*
EPHESIANS 3:17-19

*Thou camest not to thy place by accident,
It is the very place God meant for thee;
And shouldst thou there small scope for action see,
Do not for this give room to discontent.*
R. C. TRENCH

Accept the place the divine providence has found for you, the society of
your contemporaries, the connection of events.

~ RALPH WALDO EMERSON

Adapt thyself to the things with which thy lot has been cast; and love the
men with whom it is thy portion to live, and that with a sincere affection.
. . . No longer be either dissatisfied with thy present lot, or shrink from
the future.

~ MARCUS ANTINONUS

I love best to have each thing in its season, doing without it at all other times. I have never got over my surprise that I should have been born into the most estimable place in all the world, and in the very nick of time too.

~ HENRY DAVID THOREAU

July 25

The light shines in the darkness,
but the darkness has not understood it.
JOHN 1:5

A man's steps are directed by the Lord.
How then can anyone understand his own way?
PROVERBS 20:24

Be quiet, why this anxious heed
About thy tangled ways?
God knows them all,
He giveth speed,
And He allows delays.
E. W.

But indeed Conviction, were it never so excellent, is worthless till it convert itself into Conduct. Nay properly Conviction is not possible till then; inasmuch as all Speculation is by nature endless, formless, a vortex amid vortices: only by a felt indubitable certainty of Experience does it find any center to revolve round, and so fashion itself into a system. Most true is it, as a wise man teaches us, that "Doubt of any sort cannot be removed except by Action." On which ground, too, let him who gropes painfully in darkness or uncertain light, and prays vehemently that the dawn may ripen into day, lay this other precept well to heart, which to me was of invaluable service: "Do the Duty which lies nearest thee," which thou knowest to be a Duty! Thy second Duty will already have become clearer.

~ THOMAS CARLYLE

July 26

But blessed is the man who trusts in the Lord,
whose confidence is in him.
JEREMIAH 17:7

Those who trust in the Lord are like Mount Zion,
which cannot be shaken but endures forever.
PSALMS 125:1

How on a rock they stand,
Who watch His eye, and hold His guiding hand!
Not half so fixed amid her vassal hills,
Rises the holy pile that Kedron's valley fills.
J. KEBLE

That is the way to be immovable in the midst of troubles, as a rock amidst the waves. When God is in the midst of a kingdom or city, He makes it firm as Mount Sion, that cannot be removed. When He is in the midst of a soul, though calamities throng about it on all hands, and roar like the billows of the sea, yet there is a constant calm within, such a peace as the world can neither give nor take away. What is it but want of lodging God in the soul, and that in His stead the world is in men's hearts, that makes them shake like leaves at every blast of danger?

~ R. LEIGHTON

July 27

*A man who has riches without understanding is
like the beasts that perish.*
PSALMS 49:20

*. . . for wisdom is more precious than rubies,
and nothing you desire can compare with her.*
PROVERBS 8:11

*O World, thou choosest not the better part!
It is not wisdom to be only wise,
And on the inward vision close the eyes,
But it is wisdom to believe the heart.*
GEORGE SANTAYANA

Knowledge is proud that he has learn'd so much; Wisdom is humble that he knows no more.

~ WILLIAM COWPER

To be a philosopher is not merely to have subtle thoughts, nor even to found a school, but so to love wisdom as to live accordingly to its dictates, a life of simplicity, independence, magnanimity and trust.

~ HENRY DAVID THOREAU

The wisest man is he that does not fancy that he is so at all.

~ NICOLAS BOILEAU-DESPREAUX

I want, by understanding myself, to understand others. I want to be all that I am capable of becoming . . . This all sounds very strenuous and serious. But now that I have wrestled with it, it's no longer so. I feel happy—deep down. All is well.

~ KATHERINE MANSFIELD

July 28

*Listen, I tell you a mystery:
We will not all sleep, but we will all be changed . . .*
1 CORINTHIANS 15:51

*. . . we believe that God will bring with Jesus those who
have fallen asleep in him.*
1 THESSALONIANS 4:14

Now I lay me down to sleep,
I pray the Lord my soul to keep;
If I should die before I wake,
I pray the Lord my soul to take.
NEW ENGLAND PRIMER

Death be not proud, though some have called thee
Mighty and dreadful, for thou art not so,
For those whom thou think'st thou dost overthrow,
Die not, poor death, nor yet canst thou kill me.
JOHN DONNE

We give back, to you, O God, those whom you gave to us. You did not lose them when you gave them to us, and we do not lose them by their return to you. Your dear Son has taught us that life is eternal and love cannot die. So death is only an horizon, and an horizon is only the limit of our sight. Open our eyes to see more clearly, and draw us closer to you that we may know that we are nearer to our loved ones, who are with you. You have told us that you are preparing a place for us: prepare us also for that happy place, that where you are we may also be always, O dear Lord of life and death.

~ WILLIAM PENN

O Lord, you have made us very small, and we bring our years to an end like a tale that is told; help us to remember that beyond our brief day is the eternity of your love.

~ REINHOLD NIEBUHR

July 29

What I mean, brothers, is that the time is short.
1 CORINTHIANS 7:29

Nor love thy life, nor hate; but what thou liv'st
Live well; how long or short permit to Heaven.
JOHN MILTON

My blessed task from day to day
Is humbly, gladly, to obey.
HARRIET MCEWEN KIMALL

Oh, my dear friends, you who are letting miserable misunderstandings run on from year to year, meaning to clear them up some day; you who are keeping wretched quarrels alive because you cannot quite make up your mind that now is the day to sacrifice your pride and kill them; you who are passing men sullenly upon the street, not speaking to them out of some silly spite, and yet knowing that it would fill you with shame and remorse if you heard that one of those men were dead to-morrow morning; you who are letting your neighbor starve, till you hear that he is dying of starvation; or letting your friend's heart ache for a word of appreciation or sympathy, which you mean to give him some day—if you only could know and see and feel, all of a sudden, that "the time is short," how it would break the spell! How you would go instantly and do the thing which you might never have another chance to do.

~ PHILLIPS BROOKS

*"O my God, I am too ashamed and
disgraced to lift up my face to you my God,
because our sins are higher than our heads and
our guilt has reached to the heavens."*
EZRA 9:6

*Look upon my affliction and my distress and
take away all my sins.*
PSALMS 25:18

*When on my aching, burdened heart
My sins lie heavily,
My pardon speak, new peace impart,
In love remember me.*
T. HAWEIS

We need to know that our sins are forgiven. And how shall we know
this? By feeling that we have peace with God, by feeling that we are able
so to trust in the divine compassion and infinite tenderness of our Father,
as to arise and go to Him, whenever we commit sin, and say at once to
Him, "Father, I have sinned; forgive me." To know that we are forgiven,
it is only necessary to look at our Father's love till it sinks into our heart,
to open our soul to Him till He shall pour His love into it; to wait on
Him till we find peace, till our conscience no longer torments us, till the
weight of responsibility ceases to be an oppressive burden to us, till we
can feel that our sins, great as they are, cannot keep us away from our
Heavenly Father.

~ J. F. CLARKE

*He is the atoning sacrifice for our sins,
and not only for ours but also for the sins of the whole world.*
1 JOHN 2:2

*"Look, the Lamb of God,
who takes away the sin of the world!"*
JOHN 1:29

*Little Lamb, who made thee?
Dost thou know who made thee?
. . . Gave thee such a tender voice
Making all the vales rejoice!
Little Lamb who made thee?
Dost thou know who made thee?*

*Little Lamb, I'll tell thee,
Little Lamb, I'll tell thee:
He is called by thy name,
For he calls himself a Lamb.
He is meek and he is mild;
He became a little child.
I a child, and thou a lamb,*

We are called by his name.
Little Lamb, God bless thee!
Little Lamb, God bless thee!
WILLIAM BLAKE

O lord God gracious and merciful, give us, I entreat Thee, a humble trust in Thy mercy, and suffer not our heart to fail us. Though our sins be seven, though our sins be seventy times seven, though our sins be more in number than the hairs of our head, yet give us grace in loving penitence to cast ourselves down into the depth of Thy compassion. Let us fall into the hand of the Lord. Amen.

~ CHRISTINA G. ROSSETTI

Joshua said to them, "Do not be afraid; do not be discouraged.
Be strong and courageous. This is what the Lord will do to all
the enemies you are going to fight."
JOSHUA 10: 25

A man of knowledge uses words with restraint,
and a man of understanding is even-tempered.
PROVERBS 17:27

But, children, you should never let
Such angry passions rise;
Your little hands were never made
To tear each other's eyes.
ISAAC WATTS

A thing moderately good is not so good as it ought to be. Moderation in temper is always a virtue; but moderation in principle is always a vice.

~ THOMAS PAINE

When thou art offended or annoyed by others, suffer not thy thoughts to dwell thereon, or on anything relating to them. For example, "that they ought not so to have treated thee; who they are, or whom they think themselves to be," or the like; for all this is fuel and kindling of wrath, anger, and hatred.

~ LORENZO SCUPOLI

Struggle diligently against your impatience, and strive to be amiable and gentle, in season and out of season, towards every one, however much they may vex and annoy you, and be sure God will bless your efforts.

~ ST. FRANCIS DE SALES

Surely God is my salvation; I will trust and not be afraid. The Lord, the
Lord, is my strength and my song; he has become my salvation.
ISAIAH 12:2

Trust in him at all times, O people; pour out your hearts to him,
for God is our refuge.
PSALMS 62:8

A mighty fortress is our God,
A bulwark never failing.
Our helper He amid the flood
Of mortal ills prevailing.
MARTIN LUTHER

Go on in all simplicity; do not be so anxious to win a quiet mind, and it will be all the quieter. Do not examine so closely into the progress of your soul. Do not crave so much to be perfect, but let your spiritual life be formed by your duties, and by the actions which are called forth by circumstances. Do not take overmuch thought for to-morrow. God, who has led you Safely on so far, will lead you on to the end. Be altogether at rest in the loving holy confidence which you ought to have in His heavenly Providence.

~ ST. FRANCIS DE SALES

August 3

Clap your hands, all you nations; shout to God with cries of joy.
PSALMS 47:1

Surely you have granted him eternal blessings and made him glad with the joy of your presence.
PSALMS 21:6

When with his smiles my soul he deigns to bless,
Nor cares nor crosses can my peace destroy,
Possessing all things if I him possess,
Enjoying all things if I him enjoy.
ANONYMOUS

A new day rose upon me. It was as if another sun had risen into the sky; the heavens were indescribably brighter, and the earth fairer; and that day has gone on brightening to the present hour. I have known the other joys of life, I suppose, as much as most men; I have known art and beauty, music and gladness; I have known friendship and love and family ties; but it is certain that till we see GOD in the world—GOD in the bright and boundless universe—we never know the highest joy. It is far more than if one were translated to a world a thousand times fairer than this;for that supreme and central Light of Infinite Love and Wisdom, shining over this world and all worlds, alone can show us how noble and beautiful, how fair and glorious they are.

~ ORVILLE DEWEY

August 4

"Come, all you who are thirsty,
come to the waters . . . Listen,
listen to me, and eat what is good,
and your soul will delight in the richest of fare . . .
come to me; hear me, that your soul may live."
ISAIAH 55:1-3

As the deer pants for streams of water,
so my soul pants for you, O God.
My soul thirsts for God, the living God.
PSALMS 42:1-2

Hunger and thirst, O Christ, for sight of thee
Came between me and all the feasts of earth.
Give thou Thyself the Bread, thyself the Wine,
Thou, sole provision for the unknown way.
Long hunger wasted the world wanderer,
With sight of thee may he be satisfied.
RADBOD, BISHOP OF UTRECHT

O God, the Life of the Faithful, the Bliss of the Righteous, mercifully receive the prayers of Thy suppliants, that the souls which thirst for Thy promises may evermore be filled from Thy abundance. Amen.

~ GELASIAN

Lord, I have sought and thought with all my poor heart! And, Lord, in my meditation the fire of desire kindled for to know thee, not only the bitter bark without, but in feeling and tasting in my soul. And this unworthiness I ask not for me, for I am wretched and sinful and most unworthy of all other. But, Lord, as a whelp eateth of the crumbs that fall from the board of his lord: of the heritage that is for to come, a crop of that heavenly joy to comfort my thirsty soul that burneth in love-longing to thee!

~ THE CLOUD OF UNKNOWING

August 5

Thanks be to God for his indescribable gift!
2 CORINTHIANS 9:15

Every good and perfect gift is from above, coming down from the Father of the heavenly lights . . .
JAMES 1:17

O Giver of each perfect gift!
This day our daily bread supply
While from the Spirit's tranquil depths
We drink unfailing draughts of joy.
LYRA CATHOLICA

O holy Spirit . . . which with thy holy breath cleanest men's minds, comforting them when they be in sorrow, cheering them up with pure gladness, when they be in heaviness, leading them into all truth, when they be out of the way, kindling in them the fire of charity, when they be a cold, knitting them together with the glue of peace, when they be at variance, and garnishing and enriching them with sundry gifts, which by thy means profess the name of the Lord Jesus: by whose working all things live, which live in deed: whose delight is to dwell in the hearts of the simple, which thou hast vouchsafed to consecrate for temples, to thyself. I beseech thee, maintain thy gifts in me, and increase the things daily, which thou hast vouchsafed to bestow upon me . . .

~ ERASMUS

August 6

O Lord, you are my God;
I will exalt you and praise your name,
for in perfect faithfulness you have
done marvelous things . . . .
ISAIAH 25:1

Praise the Lord,
O my soul, and forget not all his benefits—
PSALMS 103:2

Sweet is the breath of vernal shower,
The bee's collected treasures sweet,
Sweet music's melting fall, but sweeter yet
The still small voice of gratitude.

THOMAS GRAY

Into all our lives, in many simple, familiar, homely ways, God infuses this element of joy from the surprises of life, which unexpectedly brighten our days, and fill our eyes with light. He drops this added sweetness into his children's cup, and makes it to run over. The success we were not counting on, the blessing we were not trying after, the strain of music in the midst of drudgery, the beautiful morning picture or sunset glory thrown in as we pass to or from our daily business, the unsought word of encouragement or expression of sympathy, the sentence that meant for us more than the writer or speaker thought—these and a hundred others that every one's experience can supply are instances of what I mean. You may call it accident or chance—it often is; you may call it human goodness—it often is; but always, always call it God's love for that is always in it. These are the overflowing riches of His grace, these are His free gifts.

~ S. LONGFELLOW

August 7

"What is impossible with men is possible with God."
LUKE 18:27

"Nothing will be impossible for you."
MATTHEW 17:20

So nigh is grandeur to our dust,
So near is God to man,
When Duty whispers low, Thou must,
The youth replies, I can.

RALPH WALDO EMERSON

Now that "Impossible," where truth and mercy and the everlasting voice of nature order, has no place in the brave man's dictionary. That when all men have said "Impossible," and tumbled noisily else whither, and thou alone art left, then first thy time and possibility have come. It is for thee now: do thou that, and ask no man's counsel, but thy own only and God's. Brother, thou hast possibility in thee for much: the possibility of writing on the eternal skies the record of a heroic life.

~ THOMAS CARLYLE

In the moral world there is nothing impossible, if we bring a thorough will to it. Man can do everything with himself; but he must not attempt to do too much with others.

~ WILLIAM VON HUMBOLDT

August 8

*He whose walk is blameless and who does what is righteous, who speaks the
truth from his heart and has no slander on his tongue,
who does his neighbor no wrong and casts no slur on his fellowman.
. . . He who does these things will never be shaken.*
PSALMS 15:2-5

*The arrogant mock me without restraint, but I do not turn from your law
. . . Your decrees are the theme of my song wherever I lodge.*
PSALMS 119:51-54

*They are slaves who fear to speak
For the fallen and the weak;
They are slaves who will not choose
Hatred, scoffing, and abuse,
Rather than in silence shrink
From the truth they needs must think;
They are slaves who dare not be
In the right with two or three.*
J. R. LOWELL

The real corrupters of society may be, not the corrupt, but those who have
held back the righteous leaven, the salt that has lost its savor, the innocent
who have not even the moral courage to show what they think of the
effrontery of impurity—the serious, who yet timidly succumb before some
loud-voiced scoffer—the heart trembling all over with religious sensibilities
that yet suffers itself through false shame to be beaten down into outward
and practical acquiescence by some rude and worldly nature.

~ J. H. THOM

August 9

"First seek the counsel of the Lord."
1 KINGS 22:5

*You guide me with your counsel,
and afterward you will take me into glory.*
PSALMS 73:24

*I've many a cross to take up now,
And many left behind;
But present troubles move me not,
Nor shake my quiet mind.
And what may be to-morrow's cross
I never seek to find;
My Father says, "Leave that to me,
And keep a quiet mind."*
ANONYMOUS

The mind never puts forth greater power over itself than when, in great
trials, it yields up calmly its desires, affections, interests to God. There are
seasons when to be still demands immeasurably higher.strength than to
act. Composure is often the highest result of power. Think you it demands
no power to calm the stormy elements of passion, to moderate the vehemence of desire, to throw off the load of dejection, to suppress every repin-

ing thought, when the dearest hopes are withered, and to turn the wounded spirit from dangerous reveries and wasting grief, to the quiet discharge of ordinary duties? Is there no power put forth, when a man, stripped of his property, of the fruits of a life's labors, quells discontent and gloomy forebodings, and serenely and patiently returns to the tasks which Providence assigns?

~ WILLIAM E. CHANNING

August 10

"I have told you these things, so that in me you may have peace.
In this world you will have trouble.
But take heart! I have overcome the world."
JOHN 16:33

Surely it was for my benefit that I suffered such anguish.
In your love you kept me from the pit of destruction;
you put all my sins behind your back.
ISAIAH 38:17

WE shall overcome, we shall overcome,
We shall overcome some day
Oh, deep in my heart I do believe
We shall overcome some day.
ANONYMOUS, ADAPTED BY C. ALBERT TINDLEY

The very least and the very greatest sorrows that God ever suffers to befall thee, proceed from the depths of His unspeakable love; and such great love were better for thee than the highest and best gifts besides that He has given thee, or ever could give thee, if thou couldst but see it in this light. So that if your little finger only aches, if you are cold, if you are hungry or thirsty, if others vex you by their words or deeds, or whatever happens to you that causes you distress or pain, it will all help to fit you for a noble and blessed state.

~ J. TAULER

August 11

The Lord will repay him for what he has done.
2 TIMOTHY 4:14

. . . the Lord your God will bless you in all your work and in
everything you put your hand to.
DEUTERONOMY 15:10

God give me work
Till my life shall end
And life
Till my work is done.
ON THE GRAVE OF WINIFRED HOLTBY

I think I find most help in trying to look on all interruptions and hindrances to work that one has planned out for oneself as discipline, trials sent by God to help one against getting selfish over one's work. Then one can feel that perhaps one's true work—one's work for God—consists in doing some trifling haphazard thing that has been thrown into one's day. It is not waste of time, as one is tempted to think, it is the most important part of the work of the day—the part one can best offer to God. After such a hindrance, do not rush after the planned work; trust that the time to finish it will be given sometime, and keep a quiet heart about it.

~ ANNIE KEARY

August 12

"Teacher . . . what must I do to inherit eternal life?"
LUKE 10:25

Anyone who does not love remains in death.
Anyone who hates his brother is a murderer, and you know that no murderer has eternal life in him.
1 JOHN 3:14-15

What shall I do to gain eternal life?
Discharge aright
The simple dues with which each day is rife
Yea, with thy might.
F. VON SCHILLER

Be diligent, after thy power, to do deeds of love. Think nothing too little, nothing too low, to do lovingly for the sake of God. Bear with infirmities, ungentle tempers, contradictions; visit, if thou mayest, the sick; relieve the poor; forego thyself and thine own ways for love; and He whom in them thou lovest, to whom in them thou ministerest, will own thy love, and will pour His own love into thee.

~ E. B. PUSEY

It is no great matter to associate with the good and gentle, for this is naturally pleasing to all, and every one willingly enjoyeth peace, and loveth those best that agree with him. But to be able to live peaceably with hard and perverse persons, or with the disorderly, or with such as go contrary to us, is a great grace, and a most commendable and manly thing.

~ ST. THOMAS A. KEMPIS

August 13

"Do it again," he said, and they did it again. "Do it a third time,"
he ordered, and they did it the third time.
1 KINGS 18:34

Brothers, as an example of patience in the face of suffering, take the prophets who spoke in the name of the Lord. As you know, we consider blessed those who have persevered. You have heard of Job's perseverance and have seen what the Lord finally brought about.
JAMES 5:10-11

What though thy way be dark, and earth
With ceaseless care do cark, till mirth
To thee no sweet strain singeth;

Still hide thy life above, and still
Believe that God is love; fulfil
Whatever lot He bringeth.
ALBERT E. EVANS

The soul loses command of itself when it is impatient. Whereas, when it submits without a murmur it possesses itself in peace, and possesses God. To be impatient, is to desire what we have not, or not to desire what we have. When we acquiesce in an evil, it is no longer such. Why make a real calamity of it by resistance? Peace does not dwell in out-ward things, but within the soul. We may preserve it in the midst of the bitter-est pain, if our will remains firm and submissive. Peace in this life springs from acquiescence even in disagreeable things, not in an exemption from bearing them.

~ FENELON

August 14

But where sin increased, grace increased all the more, so that, just as sin reigned in death, so also grace might reign through righteousness to bring eternal life through Jesus Christ our Lord.
ROMANS 5:20-21

. . . by the power of God, who has saved us and called us to a holy life—not because of anything we have done but because of his own purpose and grace.
TIMOTHY 1:8-9

Amazing grace! How sweet the sound
That saved a wretch like me!
I once was lost, but now am found,
Was blind, but now I see.
JOHN NEWTON

Religion in its humility restores man to his only dignity,
the courage to live by grace.

~ GEORGE SANTAYANA

Will is to grace as the horse is to the rider.

~ ST. AUGUSTINE

O Lord, who has taught us that to gain the whole world and to lose our souls is great folly, grant us the grace so to lose ourselves that we may truly find ourselves anew in the life of grace, and so to forget ourselves that we may be remembered in your kingdom.

~ REINHOLD NIEBUHR

Give me grace, O God, to hearken to thy calling, and to follow thy guid-ing. For thou leadest us to store of all good things: thou offerest thyself and all thy goods; give us grace to receive them.

~ LUDOVICUS VIVES

August 15

For God did not give us a spirit of timidity, but a spirit of power,
of love and of self-discipline.
2 TIMOTHY 1:7

Therefore, prepare your minds for action;
be self-controlled . . .
1 PETER 1:13

Onward, Christian soldiers,
Marching as to war,
With the Cross of Jesus
Going on before!
SABINE BARING-GOULD

Once it was the Apostles' turn. It was St. Paul's turn once. He had all
cares upon him all at once; covered from head to foot with cares, as Job
with sores. And, as if all this were not enough, he had a thorn in the flesh
added—some personal discomfort ever with him. Yet he did his part well
—he was as a strong and bold wrestler in his day, and at the close of it
was able to say, "I have fought a good fight, I have finished my course, I
have kept the faith." . . . Such is our state; angels are looking on, Christ
has gone before—Christ has given us an example, that we may follow in
His steps. He went through far more, infinitely more, than we can be
called to suffer. Our brethren have gone through much more; and they
seem to encourage us by their success, and to sympathize in our essay.
Now it is our turn; and all ministering spirits keep silence and look on.
O let not your foot slip, or your eye be false, or your ear dull, or your
attention flagging!

~ JOHN HENRY NEWMAN

August 16

. . . those who plow evil and those who sow trouble reap it.
JOB 4:8

The Lord is with you when you are with him.
If you seek him, he will be found by you,
but if you forsake him, he will forsake you.
2 CHRONICLES 15:2

The life above, when this is past,
Is the ripe fruit of life below.
Sow love, and taste its fruitage pure;
Sow peace, and reap its harvest bright
Sow sunbeams on the rock and moor,
And find a harvest-home of light.
H. BONAR

Lord, make me an instrument of Your peace. Where there is hatred let me
sow love; where there is injury, pardon; where there is doubt, faith; where
there is despair, hope; where there is darkness, light; and where there is
sadness, joy. O divine Master, grant that I may not so much seek to be
consoled as to console; to be understood as to understand; to be loved as

to love. For it is in giving that we receive; it is in pardoning that we are pardoned; and it is in dying that we are born to eternal life.

~ ST. FRANCIS OF ASSISI

August 17

Turn to me and have mercy on me . . .
PSALMS 86:16

*Do not withhold your mercy from me,
O Lord; may your love and
your truth always protect me.*
PSALMS 40:11

*No ceremony that to great ones longs,
Not the king's crown, nor the deputed sword,
The marshal's truncheon, nor the judge's robe,
Become them with one half so good a grace
As mercy does.*
WILLIAM SHAKESPEARE

"I will sing of thy mercy and judgment," says David. When we fix ourselves upon the meditation and the modulation of the mercy of God, even His judgments cannot put us out of tune, but we shall sing and be cheerful even in them. As God made grass for beasts before He made beasts, and beasts for man before He made man; as in that first generation, the creation, so in the regeneration, our re-creating, He begins with that which was necessary for that which follows, mercy before judgment. Nay, even to say that mercy was first is to post-date mercy; to prefer mercy but so, is to diminish mercy. The names of first or last derogate from it, for first and last are but rags of time, and His mercy has no relation to time, no limitation in time; it is not first nor last, but eternal, everlasting. Let the devil make me so far desperate as to conceive a time when there was no mercy, and he hath made me so far an atheist as to conceive a time when there was no God. If I despoil Him of His mercy any one minute and say, "Now God hath no mercy," for that minute I discontinue His very Godhead, and His being . . . . Mercy considered externally, and in the practice and in the effect, began not at the helping of man, when man was fallen and became miserable, but at the making of man, when man was nothing . . . .
Particular mercies are feathers of His wings, and that prayer "Lord, let Thy mercy lighten upon us, as our trust is in Thee", is our birdlime. Particular mercies are that cloud of quails which hovered over the host of Israel, and that prayer, "Lord, let Thy mercy lighten upon us" is our net to catch, our garner to fill of, those quails.

~ JOHN DONNE

August 18

*Dear friends, if our hearts do not condemn us,
we have confidence before God . . .*
1 JOHN 3:21

The fruits of righteousness will be peace; the effect of righteousness will be quietness and confidence forever.
ISAIAH 32:17

My Father, I abandon myself to you. Do with me as you will.
Whatever you may do with me, I thank you.
I am prepared for anything, I accept everything.
Provided your will is fulfilled in me and in all
creatures I ask for nothing more my God.
I place my soul in your hands.
I give it to you, my God,
with all the love of my heart
because I love you.
And for me it is a necessity of love,
this gift of myself,
this placing of myself in your hands
without reserve
in boundless confidence
because you are my Father.
CHARLES DE FOUCAULD

Nothing doth so much establish the mind amidst the rollings and turbulency of present things, as both a look above them, and a look beyond them; above them to the good and steady Hand by which they are ruled, and beyond them to the sweet and beautiful end to which, by that Hand, they shall be brought. . . . Study pure and holy walking, if you would have your confidence firm, and have boldness and joy in God. You will find that a little sin will shake your trust and disturb your peace more than the greatest sufferings: yea, in those sufferings, your assurance and joy in God will grow and abound most if sin be kept out. So much sin as gets in, so much peace will go out.

~ R. LEIGHTON

August 19

The path of the righteous is level;
O upright One, you make the way of the righteous smooth.
ISAIAH 26:7

"I will lead them beside streams of water on a level path where they will not stumble, because I am Israel's father . . ."
JEREMIAH 31:9

Lead, kindly Light, amid the encircling gloom;
Lead Thou me on!
The night is dark, and I am far from home,
Lead Thou me on!
Keep Thou my feet; I do not ask to see
The distant scene; one step enough for me.
JOHN HENRY CARDINAL NEWMAN

O God by whom the meek are guided in judgment, and light riseth up in the darkness for the godly; grant us, in all our doubts and uncertainties, the grace to ask what thou wouldst have us do; that the Spirit of Wisdom may save us from all false choices and that in thy light we may see light, and in thy straight path may not stumble; through Jesus Christ our Lord.

~ WILLIAM BRIGHT

God only is holy; He alone knows how to lead His children in the paths of holiness....He knows how to mould you to His will, and lead you onwards to perfect sanctification; He knows exactly how each event, each trial, each temptation, will tell upon you, and He disposes all things accordingly. The consequences of this belief, if fully grasped, will influence your whole life. You will seek to give yourself up to God more and more unreservedly, asking nothing, refusing nothing, wishing nothing, but what He wills; not seeking to bring things about for yourself, taking all He sends joyfully, and believing the "one step" set before you to be enough for you.

~ JEAN NICOLAS GROU

August 20

Awake, awake, O Zion, clothe yourself with strength.
ISAIAH 52:1

It is God who arms me with strength and makes my way perfect.
PSALMS 18:32

Leaning on Him, make with reverent meekness
His own thy will,
And with strength from Him shall thy utter weakness
Life's task fulfill.
J. G. WHITTIER

My strength is as the strength of ten,
Because my heart is pure.
ALFRED, LORD TENNYSON

Should we feel at times disheartened and discouraged, a confiding thought, a simple movement of heart towards God will renew our powers. Whatever he may demand of us, he will give us at the moment the strength and the courage that we need.

~ FENELON

We require a certain firmness in all circumstances of life, even the happiest, and perhaps contradictions come in order to prove and exercise this; and, if we can only determine so to use them, the very effort brings back tranquility to the soul, which always enjoys having exercised its strength in conformity to duty.

~ WILLIAM VON HUMBOLDT

August 21

For none of us lives to himself alone and none of us dies to himself alone.
ROMANS 14:7

Brothers, if someone is caught in a sin, you who are spiritual should restore him gently. But watch yourself, or you also may be tempted. Carry each other's burdens, and in this way you will fulfill the law of Christ.
GALATIANS 6:1-2

If there be some weaker one,
Give me strength to help him on;
If a blinder soul there be,
Let me guide him nearer Thee.
J. G. WHITTIER

No man is an island, entire of itself; every man is a piece of the continent, a part of the main; if a clod be washed away by the sea, Europe is the less, as well as if a promontory were, as well as if a manor of thy friends or of thine own were; any man's death diminishes me, because I am involved in mankind; and therefore never send to know for whom the bell tolls; it tolls for thee.

~ JOHN DONNE

Try to put yourself in another's place . . . Cultivate the habit of sympathy.
~ G.H. WILKINSON

August 22

Therefore I urge you, brothers, in view of God's mercy, to offer your bodies as living sacrifices, holy and pleasing to God—this is your spiritual act of worship.
ROMANS 12:1

For we are God's workmanship,
created in Christ Jesus to do good works . . .
EPHESIANS 2:10

O GOD, what offering shall I give
To Thee, the Lord of earth and skies?
My spirit, soul, and flesh receive,
A holy, living sacrifice.
J. LANGE

May it not be a comfort to those of us who feel we have not the mental or spiritual power that others have, to notice that the living sacrifice mentioned in Romans 12:1 is our "bodies"? Of course, that includes the mental power, but does it not also include the loving, sympathizing glance, the kind, encouraging word the ready errand for another, the work of our hands, opportunities for all of which come oftener in the day than for the mental power we are often tempted to envy? May we be enabled to offer willingly that which we have.

~ ANONYMOUS

August 23

. . . nor is it honorable to seek one's own honor.
PROVERBS 25:27

"Should you then seek great things for yourself? Seek them not."
JEREMIAH 45:5

My crown is in my heart, not on my head;
Not deck'd with diamonds and Indian stones,
Nor to be seen: my crown is call'd content;
A crown it is that seldom kings enjoy.
WILLIAM SHAKESPEARE

Know of a truth that if thine own honor is of more importance to thee and dearer than that of another man, thou doest wrongfully. Know this, that if thou seekest something that is thine own, thou seekest not God only; and thou wilt never find Him. Thou art acting as though thou madest of God a candle to seek for something and, when thou hast found it, thou castest the candle away. Therefore, when thou doest this, that which thou seekest with God, whatever it may be, it is nothing; gain, reward, favor, or whatever it may be, thou seekest nothing, therefore thou wilt find nothing. There is no other cause for finding nothing but that thou seekest nothing. All creatures are absolutely nothing. I do not say that they are small or anything else, but that they are absolutely nothing. That which has no being is nothing. And creatures have no being, because they have their being in God; if God turned away for a moment, they would cease to exist. He who desired to have all the world with God would have nothing more than if he had God alone . . . .

~ JOHANN TAULER

Sink into the sweet and blessed littleness, where thou livest by grace alone. Contemplate with delight the holiness and goodness in God, which thou dost not find in thyself. How lovely it is to be nothing when God is all!

~ G. TERSTEEGEN

August 24

". . . it is easier for a camel to go through the eye of a needle than
for a rich man to enter the kingdom of God."
MATTHEW 19:24

"The seed that fell among thorns stands for those who hear,
but as they go on their way they are choked by life's worries,
riches and pleasures, and they do not mature."
LUKE 8:14

Preserve me from my calling's snare,
And hide my simple heart above,
Above the thorns of choking care,
The gilded baits of worldly love.
C. WESLEY

Anything allowed in the heart which is contrary to the will of God, let it seem ever so insignificant, or be ever so deeply hidden, will cause us to fall before our enemies. Any root of bitterness cherished towards another, any self-seeking, any harsh judgments indulged in, any slackness in obeying the voice of the Lord, any doubtful habits or surroundings, any one of these things will effectually cripple and paralyze our spiritual life. I believe our blessed Guide, the indwelling Holy Spirit, is always secretly discovering these things to us by continual little twinges and pangs of conscience, so that we are left without excuse.

~ H. W. S.

"Speak, Lord, for your servant is listening."
1 SAMUEL 3:9

See to it that you do not refuse him who speaks.
HEBREWS 12:25

O God of mountains, stars, and boundless spaces,
O God of freedom and of joyous hearts,
When thy face looketh forth from all men's faces,
There will be room enough in crowded marts!
Brood thou around me, and the noise is o'er,
Thy universe my closet with shut door.
GEORGE MACDONALD

When therefore the smallest instinct or desire of thy heart calleth thee towards God, and a newness of life, give it time andleave to speak; and take care thou refuse not Him that speaketh . . . Be retired, silent, passive, and humbly attentive to this new risen light within thee.

~ WILLIAM LAW

It is hardly to be wondered at that he should lose the finer consciousness of higher powers and deeper feelings, not from any behavior in itself wrong, but from the hurry, noise, and tumult in the streets of life, that, penetrating too deep into the house of life, dazed and stupefied the silent and lonely watcher in the chamber of conscience, far apart. He had no time to think or feel.

~ GEORGE MACDONALD

Do not be quick with your mouth, do not be hasty in your heart to utter anything before God.
ECCLESIASTES 5:2

Be still before the Lord . . .
ZECHARIAH 2:13

From the world of sin and noise
And hurry I withdraw;
For the small and inward voice
I wait with humble awe
Silent am I now and still,
Dare not in Thy presence move;
To my waiting soul reveal
The secret of Thy love.
C. WESLEY

It is only with the pious affection of the will that we can be spiritually attentive to God. As long as the noisy restlessness of the thoughts goes on, the gentle and holy desires of the new nature are overpowered and inactive.

~ J. P. GREAVES

There is hardly ever a complete silence in our soul. God is whispering to us wellnigh incessantly. Whenever the sounds of the world die out in the soul, or sink low, then we hear these whisperings of God. He is always whispering to us, only we do not always hear, because of the noise, hurry, and distraction which life causes as it rushes on.

~ F. W. FABER

157

August 27

". . . he who stands firm to the end will be saved."
MATTHEW 10:22

You need to persevere so that when you have done the will of God, you will receive what he has promised.
HEBREW 10:36

Teach me, O God, so to use all the circumstances of my life today that they may bring forth in me the fruits of holiness rather than the fruits of sin.

Let me use disappointments as material for patience:
Let me use success as material for thankfulness:
Let me use suspense as material for perseverance:
Let me use danger as material for courage:
Let me use reproach as material for longsuffering:
Let me use praise as material for humility:
Let me use pleasure as material for temperance:
Let me use pains as material for endurance.
JOHN BAILLIE

If any sincere Christian cast himself with his whole will upon the Divine Presence which dwells within him, he shall be kept safe unto the end. What is it that makes us unable to persevere? Is it want of strength? By no means. We have with us the strength of the Holy Spirit. When did we ever set ourselves sincerely to any work according to the will of God, and fail for want of strength? It was not that strength failed the will, but that the will failed first. If we could but embrace the Divine will with the whole love of ours; cleaving to it, and holding fast by it, we should be borne along as upon "the river of the water of life". We open only certain chambers of our will to the influence of the Divine will. We are afraid of being wholly absorbed into it. And yet, if we would have peace, we must be altogether united to Him.

~ H. E. MANNING

August 28

Yet this I call to mind and therefore I have hope: Because of the Lord's great love we are not consumed, for his compassions never fail.
LAMENTATIONS 3:21-22

Those who know your name will trust in you, for you, Lord, have never forsaken those who seek you.
PSALMS 9:10

Through Jesus Christ the Just,
My faint desires receive;
And let me in thy goodness trust,
And to thy glory live.
ANONYMOUS

He is immortal, not because he alone among creatures has an inexhaustible voice, but because he has a soul, a spirit capable of compassion and sacrifice and endurance.

~ WILLIAM FAULKNER

Mine are the heavens and mine is the earth. Mine are the nations, the just are mine and mine the sinners. The angels are mine and the Mother of God and all things are mine; and God himself is mine and all for me, because Christ is mine and all for me. What do you ask then and seek, my soul?

~ ST. JOHN OF THE CROSS

August 29

Am I my brother's keeper?
GENESIS 4:9

If anyone says, "I love God," yet hates his brother, he is a liar.
JOHN 5:20

Because I held upon my selfish road,
And left my brother wounded by the way,
And called ambition duty, and pressed on—
Lord, I do repent.
SARAH WILLIAMS

Dearest Lord, may I see you today and every day in the person of your sick, and whilst nursing them, minister unto you.

Though you hide yourself behind the unattractive disguise of the irritable, the exacting, the unreasonable, may I still recognize you and say: "Jesus, my patient, how sweet it is to serve you."

. . . O beloved sick, how doubly dear you are to me, when you personify Christ; and what a privilege is mine to be allowed to tend you.

. . . And, O God, while you are Jesus, my patient, deign also to be to me a patient Jesus, bearing with my faults, looking only to my intention, which is to love and serve you in the person of each of your sick. Lord, increase my faith, bless my efforts and work, now and for evermore.

~ DAILY PRAYER OF MOTHER TERESA

August 30

. . . I urge you to live a life worthy of the calling you have received.
Be completely humble and gentle;
be patient, bearing with one another in love.
EPHESIANS 4:1-2

Help us, O Lord, with patient love to bear
Each other's faults, to suffer with true meekness;

Help us each other's joys and griefs to share,
But let us turn to Thee alone in weakness.
ANONYMOUS

Give us grace and strength to forbear and to persevere . . . Give us courage
and gaiety and the quiet mind, spare to us our friends, soften to us our
enemies.

~ ROBERT LOUIS STEVENSON

How many are the sufferers who have fallen amongst misfortunes along
the wayside of life! By chance, we come that way; chance, accident,
Providence, has thrown them in our way; we see them from a distance,
like the Priest, or we come upon them suddenly, like the Levite; our business, our pleasure, is interrupted by the sight, is troubled by the delay;
what are our feelings, what our actions towards them? . . . "Who is thy
neighbor?" It is the sufferer, wherever, whoever, whatsoever he be.
Wherever thou hearest the cry of distress, wherever thou seest any one
brought across thy path by the chances and changes of life (that is, by the
Providence of God), whom it is in thy power to help—he, stranger or
enemy though he be—he is thy neighbor.

~ A.P. STANLEY

August 31

He was oppressed and afflicted, yet he did not open his mouth.
ISAIAH 53:7

Go, bury thy sorrow,
The world hath its share
Go, bury it deeply,
Go, hide it with care
Go, bury thy sorrow,
Let others be blest
Go, give them the sunshine,
And tell God the rest.
ANON.

Oh! be little, be little; and then thou wilt be content with little; and if
thou feel, now and then, a check or a secret smiting—in that is the
Father's love; be not over-wise, nor over-eager, in thy own willing, running,
and desiring, and thou mayest feel it so; and by degrees come to the
knowledge of thy Guide, who will lead thee, step by step, in the path of
life, and teach thee to follow. Be still, and wait for light and strength.

~ I. PENINGTON

Strive to realize a state of inward happiness,
independent of circumstances.

~ J. P. GREAVES

The Lord is full of compassion and mercy.
JAMES 5:11

*"As a mother comforts her child,
so will I comfort you . . ."*
ISAIAH 66:13

*"Rejoice with Jerusalem and be glad for her,
all you who love her;
rejoice greatly with her,
all you who mourn over her.
For you will nurse and be satisfied
at her comforting breasts;
you will drink deeply
and delight in her overflowing abundance . . .
I will extend peace to her like a river,
and the wealth of nations like a flooding stream;
you will nurse and be carried on her arm
and dandled on her knees."*
ISAIAH 66:10-12

O Lord God, our heavenly Father, regard, we beseech thee, with thy divine pity the pains of all thy children, and grant that the passion of our Lord and his infinite merits may make fruitful for good the miseries of the innocent, the sufferings of the sick and the sorrows of the bereaved; through him who suffered in our flesh and died for our sake, thy Son our Savior Jesus Christ.

~ SCOTTISH PRAYER BOOK

My soul could not incline itself on the one side or the other . . . but only nourished itself with the daily providences of God.

~ MME. GUYON

I have calmed and quieted my soul, like a child quieted at its mother's breast: like a child that is quieted is my soul.

~ ANONYMOUS
(BASED ON PSALMS 131:3)

*If it is possible, as far as it depends on you,
live at peace with everyone.*
ROMANS 12:18

*"Blessed are the peacemakers,
for they will be called sons of God."*
MATTHEW 5:9

*O God of many names
Lover of all nations
We pray for peace
in our hearts
in our homes*

in our nations
in our world
The peace of your will
The peace of your need.
GEORGE APPLETON

O God, who art Peace everlasting, whose chosen reward is the gift of peace, and who hast taught us that the peacemakers are Thy children, pour Thy sweet peace into our souls, that everything discordant may utterly vanish, and all that makes for peace be sweet to us forever. Amen.

~ GELASIAN

Have you ever thought seriously of the meaning of that blessing given to the peacemakers? People are always expecting to get peace in heaven; but you know whatever peace they get there will be ready-made. Whatever making of peace they can be blest for, must be on the earth here: not the taking of arms against, but the building of nests amidst, its 'sea of troubles' like the halcyons. Difficult enough, you think? Perhaps so, but I do not see that any of us try. We complain of the want of many things—we want votes, we want liberty, we want amusement, we want money. Which of us feels or knows that he wants peace?

~ JOHN RUSKIN

September 3

He who ignores discipline despises himself,
but whoever heeds
correction gains understanding.
PROVERBS 15:32

Whoever loves discipline loves knowledge,
but he who hates correction is stupid.
PROVERBS 12:1

. . . Chasten us, Father, but be merciful.
Go thou before thy flock, and come behind:
Thy fold that walk upon the harmless road
Keep to eternity.
ST. PAULINUS OF AQUILEIA

The crosses of the present moment always bring their own special grace and consequent comfort with them; we see the hand of God in them when it is laid upon us. But the crosses of anxious foreboding are seen out of the dispensation of God; we see them without grace to bear them; we see them indeed through a faithless spirit which banishes grace. So, everything in them is bitter and unendurable; all seems dark and helpless. Let us throw self aside; no more self-interest, and then God's will, unfolding every moment in everything, will console us also every moment for all that He shall do around us, or within us, for our discipline.

~ FENELON

September 4

But his delight is in the law of the Lord . . .
He is like a tree planted by streams of water,
which yields its fruit in season and whose leaf does not wither.
Whatever he does prospers.
PSALMS1:2-3

The wind that blows can never kill
The tree God plants;
It bloweth east; it bloweth west
The tender leaves have little rest,
But any wind that blows is best.
The tree God plants
Strikes deeper root, grows higher still,
Spreads wider boughs, for God's good-will
Meets all its wants.
LILLIE E. BARR

I have learned
To look on nature, not as in the hour
Of thoughtless youth; but hearing oftentimes
The still, sad music of humanity,
Nor harsh nor grating, though of ample power
To chasten and subdue. And I have felt
A presence that disturbs me with the joy
Of elevated thoughts; a sense sublime
Of something far more deeply interfused,
Whose dwelling is the light of setting suns,
And the round ocean and the living air,
And the blue sky, and in the mind of man:
A motion and a spirit, that impels
All thinking things, all objects of all thought,
And rolls through all things.
WILLIAM WORDSWORTH

It is not by change of circumstances, but by fitting our spirits to the circumstances in which God has placed us, that we can be reconciled to life and duty.

~ F. W. ROBERTSON

September 5

"Come unto me, all you who are weary and burdened,
and I will give you rest.
Take my yoke upon you and learn from me,
for I am gentle and humble in heart,
and you will find rest for your souls."
MATTHEW 11:28-29

Blessed mood,
In which the burthen of the mystery,
In which the heavy and the weary weight
Of all this unintelligible world,
Is lightened.
WILLIAM WORDSWORTH

Oh, look not at thy pain or sorrow, how great soever; but look from them, look off them, look beyond them, to the Deliverer! whose power is over them, and whose loving, wise, and tender spirit is able to do thee good by them. The Lord lead thee, day by day, in the right way, and keep thy mind stayed upon Him, in whatever befalls thee; that the belief of His love and hope in His mercy, when thou art at the lowest ebb, may keep up thy head above the billows.

~ ISAAC PENINGTON

September 6

Test me, O Lord, and try me,
examine my heart and my mind . . .
PSALMS 26:2

Not a broken, brief obedience
Does the Lord of heaven demand;
He requires our whole allegiance,
Words and deeds, and heart and hand:
God will hold divided sway With no deity of clay.
ANONYMOUS

Although I must indeed confess that very often, even through my bodily sensibilities, God has made my life uncommonly hard, I must also at once acknowledge that He has, on the other hand, been near me with quite uncommon aids of grace, so that I have been able to get through so many decades of this painful life already. Here, then, surely, there is room only for humble and adoring thankfulness.

A retrospect of my whole life, from the earliest period of my recollection down to the present hour, leaves me with this impression, that I have been, and am being, guided by a gracious and a mighty Hand, which has made, and is making, that possible to me which otherwise to me had been impossible. Oh that I had at all times unhesitatingly trusted and yielded myself to its guidance!

~ RICHARD ROTHE

September 7

For the Lord comforts his people
and will have compassion on his afflicted ones.
ISAIAH 49:13

Religion that God our Father accepts
as pure and faultless is this:
to look after orphans and widows in their distress . . .
JAMES 1:27

Awake, my charity, and feed
The hungry soul, and clothe the poor;
In heaven are found no sons of need,
There all these duties are no more.
ANONYMOUS

Make us generous with the resources you have entrusted to us. Let your work of rescue be done in us and through us all.
~ CONTEMPORARY PRAYERS FOR PUBLIC WORSHIP

O merciful and loving Father of all, look down we pray thee on the many millions who are hungry in the world today and are at the mercy of disase. Grant that we who have lived so comfortably and gently all our lives may have true sympathy with them and do all in our power, as individuals and as a nation, to help them to that abundant life which is thy will for them; through Jesus Christ our Lord.

~ G. A.

September 8

Devote yourselves to prayer, being watchful and thankful.
COLOSSIANS 4:2

Be on your guard; stand firm in the faith; be men of courage; be strong.
1 CORINTHIANS 16:13

Arm me with jealous care,
As in thy sight to live:
And oh, thy servant, Lord, prepare,
A strict account to give.

Help me to watch and pray,
And on thyself rely;
Assured if I my trust betray,
I shall for ever die.
ANONYMOUS

It is impossible for us to make the duties of our lot minister to our sanctification without a habit of devout fellowship with God. This is the spring of all our life, and the strength of it. It is prayer, meditation, and converse with God, that refreshes, restores, and renews the temper of our minds, at all times, under all trials, after all conflicts with the world. By this contact with the world unseen we receive continual accesses of strength. As our day, so is our strength. Without this healing and refreshing of spirit, duties grow to be burdens, the events of life chafe our temper, employments lower the tone of our minds, and we become fretful, irritable, and impatient.

~ I. E. MANNING

September 9

This is a trustworthy saying. And I want you to stress these things, so that those who have trusted in God may be careful to devote themselves to doing what is good.
TITUS 3:8

Whate'er is noble, pure, refined,
Just, generous, amiable, and kind,
That may my constant thoughts pursue,
That may I love and practice too.
ANONYMOUS

One secret act of self-denial, one sacrifice of inclination to duty, is worth all the mere good thoughts, warm feelings, passionate prayers, in which idle people indulge themselves.

~ J. H. NEWMAN

It is impossible for us to live in fellowship with God without holiness in all the duties of life. These things act and react on each other. Without a diligent and faithful obedience to the calls and claims of others upon us, our religious profession is simply dead. To disobey conscience when it points to relative duties irritates the whole temper, and quenches the first beginnings of devotion. We cannot go from strife, breaches, and angry words, to God. Selfishness, an imperious will, want of sympathy with the sufferings and sorrows of other men, neglect of charitable offices, suspicions, hard censures of those with whom our lot is cast, will miserably darken our own hearts, and hide the face of God from us.

~ H. E. MANNING

September 10

Do you not know that your body is a temple of the Holy Spirit,
who is in you, whom you have received from God?. . .
Therefore honor God with your body.
CORINTHIANS 6:19-20

Here, Lord, before you tonight are the bodies of sleeping men:
The pure body of the tiny child,
The soiled body of the prostitute,
The vigorous body of the athlete,
The exhausted body of the factory worker,
The soft body of the playboy,
The surfeited body of the poor man,
The paralyzed body of the cripple,
All bodies, Lord, of all ages.

I offer them all to you, Lord, and ask you to bless them,
. . . May these bodies be developed, purified, transfigured,
By those who dwell in them.
MICHEL QUOIST

The human body is an instrument for the production of art in the life of the human soul.

~ ALFRED NORTH WHITEHEAD

If a man may attain thereunto, to be unto God as his hand is to a man, let him be therewith content, and not seek further. That is to say, let him strive and wrestle with all his might to obey God and His commandments so thoroughly at all times, and in all things, that in him there be nothing, spiritual or natural, which opposeth God; and that his whole soul and body, with all their members, may stand ready and willing for that to which God hath created them . . .

~ THEOLOGIA GERMANICA

When the mind thinks nothing, when the soul covets nothing, and the body acteth nothing that is contrary to the will of God, this is perfect sanctification.

~ ANONYMOUS, IN AN OLD BIBLE

September 11

. . . your kingdom come,
your will be done on earth as it is in heaven.
MATTHEW 6:10

To do his heavenly Father's will
Was his employment and delight;
Humility and holy zeal
Shone through his life divinely bright.
ANONYMOUS

My child, thou mayest not measure out thine offering unto me by what others have done or left undone; but be it thine to seek out, even to the last moment of thine earthly life, what is the utmost height of pure devotion to which I have called thine own self. Remember that, if thou fall short of this, each time thou utterest in prayer the words, "Hallowed be Thy name, Thy kingdom come," thou dost most fearfully condemn thyself, for is it not a mockery to ask for that thou wilt not seek to promote even unto the uttermost, within the narrow compass of thine own heart and spirit?

~ THE DIVINE MASTER

If you do not wish for His kingdom, don't pray for it. But if you do, you must do more than pray for it; you must work for it.

~ JOHN RUSKIN

September 12

She obeys no one, she accepts no correction.
She does not trust in the Lord,
she does not draw near to her God.
ZEPHANIAH 3:2

We must have holy hearts and hands,
And feet that go where he commands;
A holy will to keep his ways,
And holy lips to speak his praise.
ANONYMOUS

If God requires anything of us, we have no right to draw back under the pretext that we are liable to commit some fault in obeying. It is better to obey imperfectly than not at all. Perhaps you ought to rebuke someone

dependent on you, but you are silent for fear of giving way to vehemence;
— or you avoid the society of certain persons, because they make you
cross and impatient. How are you to attain self control, if you shun all
occasions of practicing it? Is not such self-choosing a greater fault than
those into which you fear to fallI? Aim at a steady mind to do right, go
wherever duty calls you, and believe firmly that God will forgive the faults
that take our weakness by surprise in spite of our sincere desire to
please Him.

~ JEAN NICOLAS GROU

September 13

. . . it is good to wait quietly for the salvation of the Lord.
LAMENTATIONS 3:26

My soul finds rest in God alone; my salvation comes from him.
PSALMS 62:1

Lord, we would strive, and hope, and wait,
The offending still to reinstate;
And when a broken heart we view,
Our Christian friendship quick renew.
ANONYMOUS

The true use to be made of all the imperfections of which you are conscious is neither to justify, nor to condemn them, but to present them
before God, conforming your will to His, and remaining in peace; for
peace is the divine order, in whatever state we may be.

~ FENELON

The prayer of faith is a sincere, sweet, and quiet view of divine, eternal
truth. The soul rests quiet, perceiving and loving God sweetly rejecting all
the imaginations that present themselves, calming the mind in the Divine
presence, and fixing it only on God.

~ M. MOLINOS

September 14

Listen and hear my voice; pay attention and hear what I say.
ISAIAH 28:23

"Call to me and I will answer you and tell you great and
unsearchable things you do not know."
JEREMIAH 33:3

Prayer is the soul's sincere desire,
Uttered or unexpressed;
The motion of a hidden fire
That trembles in the breast.
JAMES MONTGOMERY

If you have any trial which seems intolerable, pray—pray and it be relieved
or changed. There is no harm in that. We may pray for anything, not
wrong in itself, with perfect freedom, if we do not pray selfishly. One dis-

abled from duty by sickness may pray for health, that he may do his work; or one hemmed in by internal impediments may pray for utterance, that he may serve better the truth and the right. Or, if we have a besetting sin, we may pray to be delivered from it, in order to serve God and man, and not be ourselves Satans to mislead and destroy. But the answer to the prayer may be, as it was to Paul, not the removal of the thorn, but, instead, a growing insight into its meaning and value. The voice of God in our soul may show us, as we look up to Him, that His strength is enough to enable us to bear it.

~ J. F. CLARKE

September 15

"My Father, if it is possible, may this cup be taken from me. Yet not as I will, but as you will."
MATTHEW 26:39

Whatever my God ordains is right;
Though I the cup must drink
That bitter seems to my faint heart,
I will not fear nor shrink.
S. RODIGAST

He is Thy best servant who looks not so much to hear that from Thee which is conformable to his own will, as rather to conform his will to what he heareth from Thee.
. . .Thou calledst and shoutedst and didst pierce my deafness. Thou flashedst and shonest and didst dispel my blindness. Thou didst send forth Thy fragrance, and I drew in breath and panted for Thee. I tasted, and still I hunger and thirst. Thou touchedst me, and I burned for Thy peace . . . . And now my whole life is in nothing but in Thine exceeding great mercy. Give what Thou commandest, and command what Thou wilt.

~ ST. AUGUSTINE

September 16

"I tell you the truth, if you have faith as small as a mustard seed, you can say to this mountain, 'Move from here to there' and it will move. Nothing will be impossible for you."
MATTHEW 17:20

We find great things are made of little things,
And little things go lessening till at last
Comes God behind them.
ROBERT BROWNING

He showed a little thing, the quantity of a hazel-nut, lying in the palm of my hand, as meseemed, and it was as round as a ball. I looked thereon with the eye of my understanding, and thought, "What may this be?" and it was answered generally thus, "It is all that is made." I marvelled how it might last; for methought it might suddenly have fallen to naught for littleness. And I was answered in my understanding, "It lasteth, and ever shall: For God loveth it. And so hath all thing being by the Love of God."

In this little thing I saw three properties. The first is, that God made it. The second is, that God loveth it. The third is, that God keepeth it. For this is the cause which we be not all in ease of heart and soul: for we seek here rest in this thing which is so little, where no rest is in—and we know not our God that is all Mighty, all Wise, and all Good, for he is very rest. God wills to be known, and it pleaseth Him that we rest us in Him. For all that is beneath Him, sufficeth not us.

~ MOTHER JULIANA

September 17

. . . whoever wants to become great among you must be your servant, and whoever wants to be first must be slave of all.
MATTHEW 10:43

All service ranks the same with God:
With God, whose puppets, best and worst,
Are we, there is no last or first.
ROBERT BROWNING

Let every man lovingly cast all his thoughts and cares, and his sins too, as it were, on the Will of God. Morevoer, if a man, while busy in this lofty inward work, were called by some duty in the Providence of God to cease there from, and cook a broth for some sick person, or any other such service, he should do so willingly and with great joy. If I had to forsake such work, and go out to preach or aught else, I Should go cheerfully, believing not only that God would be with me, but that he would vouchsafe me it may be even greater grace and blessing in that external work undertaken out of true love in the service of my neighbor, than I should perhaps receive in my season of loftiest contemplation.

~ JOHN TAULER

September 18

All the ways of the Lord are loving and faithful
for those who keep the demands of his covenant.
PSALMS 25:10

In peace, Love tunes the shepherd's reed;
In war, he mounts the warrior's steed;
In halls, in gay attire is seen;
In hamlets, dances on the green.
Love rules the court, the camp, the grove,
And men below, and saints above;
For love is heaven, and heaven is love.
SIR WALTER SCOTT

To recognize with delight all high and generous and beautiful actions; to find a joy even in seeing the good qualities of your bitterest opponents, and to admire those qualities even in those with whom you have least sympathy, be it either the Romanist or the Unitarian, this is the only spirit which can heal the love of slander and of calumny.

~ F. W. ROBERTSON

"Pray that the Lord your God will tell us where we should go and what we should do."
JEREMIAH 42:3

Lord God Almighty,
I pray thee for thy great mercy and by the token of the holy rood,
Guide me to thy will, to my soul's need, better than I can myself;
And shield me against my foes, seen and unseen;
And teach me to do thy will that I may inwardly love thee before all things
with a clean mind and a clean body.
For thou art my maker and my redeemer,
my help, my comfort, my trust, and my hope.
Praise and glory be to thee now, ever and ever, world without end.
KING ALFRED

"We can't choose happiness either for ourselves or for another; we can't tell where that will lie. We can only choose whether we will indulge ourselves in the present moment, or whether we will renounce that, for the sake of obeying the Divine voice within us,—for the sake of being true to all the motives that sanctify our lives. I know this belief is hard; it has slipped away from me again and again; but I have felt that if I let it go forever, I should have no light through the darkness of this life."

~ GEORGE ELIOT

Rescue me from my enemies, O Lord, for I hide myself in you.
PSALMS 143:9

Eternal King, grant me true quietness
For thou art rest and quiet without end.
Eternal light, grant me the abiding light,
And may I live and quicken in thy good.
ANGILBERT

If you could once make up your mind in the fear of God never to undertake more work of any sort than you can carry on calmly, quietly, without hurry or flurry, and the instant you feel yourself growing nervous and like one out of breath, would stop and take breath, you would find this simple common-sense rule doing for you what no prayers or tears could ever accomplish.

~ ELIZABETH PRENTISS

I long to dwell in your tent forever and
take refuge in the shelter of your wings.
PSALMS 61:4

Within Thy circling arms we lie,
O God I in Thy infinity:

Our souls in quiet shall abide,
Beset with love on every side.
ANONYMOUS

Like an ant on a stick both ends of which are burning, I go to and fro without knowing what to do and in great despair. Like the inescapable shadow which follows me, the dead weight of sin haunts me. Graciously look upon me. Thy love is my refuge.

~ ANONYMOUS

September 22

When your words came, I ate them;
they were my joy and my heart's delight,
For I bear your name, O Lord God Almighty.
JEREMIAH 15:16

The grass withers and the flowers fall,
but the word of God stands forever.
ISAIAH 40:8

Bless'd are the souls that hear and know
The gospel's joyful sound;
Peace shall attend the path they go,
And light their steps surround.
ANONYMOUS

The gospel is like a fresh, mild, and cool air in the extreme heat of summer, a solace and comfort in the anguish of the conscience. But as this heat proceeds from the rays of the sun, so likewise the terrifying of the conscience must proceed from the preaching of the law, to the end that we may know we have offended against the laws of God.

~ MARTIN LUTHER

September 23

Show me your ways, O lord, teach me your paths;
guide me in your truth and teach me, for you are God my Savior,
and my hope is in you all day long.
PSALMS 25:4-5

O Holy Spirit,
Giver of light and life,
impart to us thoughts higher than our own thoughts,
and prayers better than our own prayers,
and powers beyond our own powers,
that we may spend and be spent
in the ways of love and goodness,
after the perfect image
of our Lord and Savior Jesus Christ.
ERIC MILNER-WHITE

There is nothing like the first glance we get at duty, before there has been any special pleading of our affections or inclinations. Duty is never uncertain at first. It is only after we have got involved in the mazes and sophistries of wishing that things were otherwise than they are, that it seems indistinct. Considering a duty is often only explaining it away. Deliberation is often only dishonesty. God's guidance is plain, when we are true.

~ F. W. ROBERTSON

September 24

. . . I will sing of your strength,
in the morning I will sing of your love;
for you are my fortress,
my refuge in times of trouble.
PSALMS 59:16

. . . wake up and shout for joy.
ISAIAH 26:19

England! awake! awake! awake!
Jerusalem calls!
Why wilt thou sleep the sleep of death
And close her from thy ancient walls?
WILLIAM BLAKE

With his first waking consciousness, he can set himself to take a serious, manly view of the day before him. He ought to know pretty well on what lines his difficulty is likely to come, whether in being irritable, or domineering, or sharp in his bargains, or self absorbed, or whatever it be; and now, in this quiet hour, he can take a good, full look at his enemy, and make up his mind to beat him. It is a good time, too, for giving his thoughts a range quite beyond himself—beyond even his own moral struggles—a good time, there in the stillness, for going into the realm of other lives. His wife—what needs has she for help, for sympathy, that he can meet? His children, how can he make the day sweeter to them? This acquaintance, who is having a hard time; this friend, who dropped a word to you yesterday that you hardly noticed in your hurry, but that comes up to you now, revealing in him some finer trait, some deeper hunger, than you had guessed before—now you can think these things over. So you get your day somewhat into right perspective and proportion before you begin it.

~ G. S. MERRIAM

September 25

There, in the presence of the Lord your God,
you and your families shall eat and
rejoice in everything you have put your hand to,
because the Lord your God has blessed you.
DEUTERONOMY 12:7

'Mid pleasures and palaces though we may roam,
Be it ever so humble, there's no place like home.
JOHN HOWARD PAYNE

Is there any tie which absence has loosened, or which the wear and tear of every-day intercourse, little uncongenialities, unconfessed misunderstandings, have fretted into the heart, until it bears something of the nature of a fetter? Any cup at our home-table whose sweetness we have not fully tasted, although it might yet make of our daily bread a continual feast? Let us reckon up these treasures while they are still ours, in thankfulness to God.

~ ELIZABETH CHARLES

We ought daily or weekly to dedicate a little time to the reckoning up of the virtues of our belongings—wife, children, friends—and contemplating them then in a beautiful collection. And we should do so now, that we may not pardon and love in vain and too late, after the beloved one has been taken away from us to a better world.

~ JEAN PAUL RICHTER

September 26

Go and enjoy choice food and sweet drinks, and send some to those who have nothing prepared. This day is sacred to our Lord. Do not grieve, for the joy of the Lord is your strength.

NEHEMIAH 8:10

Creator Spirit I by whose aid
The world's foundations first were laid,
Come, visit every humble mind;
Come, pour thy joys on human kind:
From sin and sorrow set us free,
And make us temples worthy thee.

ANONYMOUS

As the hand is made for holding and the eye for seeing, thou hast fashioned me for joy. Share with me the vision that shall find it everywhere: in the wild violet's beauty; in the lark's melody; in the face of a steadfast man; in a child's smile; in a mother's love; in the purity of Jesus.

~ GAELIC PRAYER

September 27

. . . and so our God gives light to our eyes and a little relief in our bondage . . . He has shown us kindness in the sight of kings of Persia: He has granted us new life to rebuild the house of our God.

EZRA 9:8-9

In him was life, and that life was the light of men.

JOHN 1: 4

Behold the Highest, parting hence away,
Lightens the dark clouds, which He treads upon,
Nor doth He by ascending, show alone,
But first He, and He first enters the way.
O strong Ram, which hast battered heaven for me,
Mild Lamb, which with Thy blood hast marked the path;
Bright Torch, which shin'st, that I the way may see,

Oh, with Thine own blood quench Thine own just wrath,
And if Thy holy Spirit, my Muse did raise,
Deign at my hands this crown of prayer and praise.
ANONYMOUS

Suppose you are bewildered and know not what is right nor what is true. Can you not cease to regard whether you do or not, whether you be bewildered, whether you be happy? Cannot you utterly and perfectly love, and rejoice to be in the dark, and gloom-beset, because that very thing is the fact of God's Infinite Being as it is to you? Cannot you take this trial also into your own heart, and be ignorant, not because you are obliged, but because that being God's will, it is yours also? Do you not see that a person who truly loves is one with the Infinite Being—cannot be uncomfortable or unhappy? It is that which is that he wills and desires and holds best of all to be. To know God is utterly to sacrifice self.

~ JAMES HINTON

September 28

Dear children, let us not love with words or
tongue but with actions and in truth.
I JOHN 3:18

O Lord God
when we pray unto thee
desiring well and meaning truly,
if thou seest a better way
to thy glory and our good,
then be thy will done,
and not ours:
as with thy dear Son
in the Garden of Agony,
even Jesus Christ our Lord.
ERIC MILNER-WHITE

Do not let your deeds belie your words, lest when you speak in church someone may say to himself, "Why do you not practice what you preach."

~ SAINT JEROME

Grant, O merciful Father, that thy divine Spirit may enlighten, inflame, and cleanse our hearts; that he may penetrate us with his heavenly dew, and make us fruitful in good works. Through Jesus Christ our Lord.

~ THE GOLDEN MANUEL

'Twant me, 'twas the Lord. I always told him, "I trust to you. I don't know where to go or what to do, but I expect you to lead me," and he always did.

~ HARRIET TUBMAN

September 29

"These people come near to me with their mouth
and honor me with their lips, but their hearts are far from me."
ISAIAH 29:13

Blessed are the pure in heart, for they will see God.
MATTHEW 5:8

> *Joy to the world! the Lord is come;*
> *Let earth receive her King.*
> *Let ev'ry heart prepare Him room,*
> *And heav'n and nature sing.*
ISAAC WATTS

Lord, take my lips and speak through them; take my mind and think through it; take my heart and set it on fire.

~ W. H. H. AITKEN

O Lord God, who hast given me the gift of sight, grant that I may see not only with the eyes of my head but with the eyes of the heart also, that I may perceive the beauty and meaning of all that I behold, and glorify Thee, the Creator of all, who art blessed for evermore.

~ GEORGE APPLETON

O God, I know that if I do not love thee with all my heart, with all my mind, with all my soul and with all my strength, I shall love something else with all my heart and mind and strength. Grant that putting thee first in all my lovings I may be liberated from all lesser loves and loyalties, and have thee as my first love, my chiefest good and my final joy.

~ GEORGE APPLETON

September 30

"Let us meet in the house of God, inside the temple . . ."
NEHEMIAH 6:10

". . . for God's temple is sacred, and you are that temple."
1 CORINTHIANS 3:17

> *When once thy foot enters the church, be bare.*
> *God is more there than thou; for thou art there*
> *Only by His permission. Then beware,*
> *And make thyself all reverence and fear.*
> *Kneeling ne'er spoiled silk stockings; quit thy state.*
> *All equal are within the church's gate . . .*
GEORGE HERBERT

One great sign of the practical recognition of the "divine moment", and of our finding God's habitation in it, is constant calmness and peace of mind. Events and things come with the moment; but God comes with them too. So that if He comes in the sunshine, we find rest and joy; and if He comes in the storm, we know He is King of the storms, and our hearts are not troubled. God Himself, though possessing a heart filled with the tenderest feelings, is, nevertheless, an everlasting tranquility; and when we enter into His holy tabernacle, our souls necessarily enter into the tabernacle of rest.

~ T. C. UPHAM

"Now strengthen my hands."
NEHEMIAH 6:9

Lazy hands make a man poor, but diligent hands bring wealth.
PROVERBS 10:4

For what is life if measured by the space,
Not by the act?
Or masked man, if valued by his face,
Above his fact?
Here's one outlived his peers
And told forth fourscore years:
He vexed time, and busied the whole state,
Troubled both foes and friends,
But ever to no ends:
What did this stirrer but die late?
How well at twenty had he fall'n or stood!
For three of his four score, he did no good.
BEN JOHNSON

The situation that has not its duty, its ideal, was never yet occupied by
man. Yes, here, in this poor, miserable, hampered, despicable Actual,
wherein thou even now standest, here or nowhere is thy Ideal: work
it out therefrom; and working, believe, live, be free. Fool! the Ideal is in
thyself, the impediment too is in thyself: thy condition is but the stuff
thou art to shape that same Ideal out of: what matters whether such stuff
be of this sort or that, so the form thou givest it be heroic, be poetic. O
thou that pinest in the imprisonment of the Actual, and criest bitterly to
the gods for a kingdom wherein to rule and create, know this of a truth:
the thing thou seekest is already with thee, "here or nowhere," couldst
thou only see!

~ THOMAS CARLYLE

"My words come from an upright heart;
my lips sincerely speak what I know."
JOB 33:3

I have resolved that my mouth will not sin.
PSALMS 17:3

When, like committed linnets, I
With shriller throat shall sing
The sweetness, mercy, majesty
And glories of my King;
When I shall voice aloud how good
He is, how great should be,
Enlarged winds, that curl the flood,
Know no such liberty.
RICHARD LOVELACE

Do not flatter yourself that your thoughts are under due control, your desires properly regulated, or your dispositions subject as they should be to Christian principle, if your intercourse with others consists mainly of frivolous gossip, impertinent anecdotes, speculations on the character and affairs of your neighbours, the repetition of former conversations, or a discussion of the current petty scandal of society; much less, if you allow yourself in careless exaggeration on all these points, and that grievous inattention to exact truth, which is apt to attend the statements of those whose conversation is made up of these materials.

~ H. WARE, JR.

October 3

. . . you who pass judgment on someone else, for at whatever point you judge the other, you are condemning yourself, because you who pass judgment do the same things.

ROMANS 2:1

Brothers, do not slander one another. Anyone who speaks against his brother or judges him speaks against the law and judges it . . . There is only one lawgiver and Judge . . .

JAMES 4:11

> *Judge not; the workings of his brain*
> *And of his heart thou canst not see;*
> *What looks to thy dim eyes a stain,*
> *In God's pure light rnay only be*
> *A scar, brought from some well-won field,*
> *Where thou wouldst only faint and yield.*

ADELAIDE A. PROCTER

The world has often seen examples of the presumptuous religious individual who is perfectly secure in his own God-relationship, flippantly assured of his own salvation, but self-importantly engaged in doubting the salvation of others and in offering to help them. However, I believe it would be a fitting expression for a genuinely religious attitude if the individual were to say: "I do not doubt the salvation of any human being; the only one I have fears about is myself. Even when I see a man sink very low, I should never presume to doubt his salvation; but if it were myself, I should doubtless have to suffer this terrible thought." A genuine religious personality is always mild in his judgment of others, and only in his relation to himself is he cold and strict as a master inquisitor. His attitude towards others is like that of a benevolent patriarch to the younger generation; in relation to himself he is old and incorruptible.

~ SØREN KIERKEGAARD

October 4

"For I know the plans I have for you," declares the Lord,
"Plans to prosper you and not harm you,
plans to give you hope and a future."

JEREMIAH 29:11

Therefore, a man cannot discover anything about his future.
ECCLESIASTES 7:14

Why shouldst thou fill to-day with sorrow
About to-morrow,
My heart!
One watches all with care most true,
Doubt not that He will give thee too
Thy part.
PAUL FLEMMING

Watch your way then, as a cautious traveler; and don't be gazing at that mountain or river in the distance, and saying, "How shall I ever get over them?" but keep to the present little inch that is before you, and accomplish that in the little moment that belongs to it. The mountain and the river can only be passed in the same way; and, when you come to them, you will come to the light and strength that belong to them.

~ M. A. KELTY

Let not future things disturb thee, for thou wilt come to them, if it shall be necessary, having with thee the same reason which thou now usest for present things.

~ MARCUS ANTONINUS

October 5

They approach and come forward;
each helps the other and says to his brother,
"Be strong!"
ISAIAH 41:5-6

. . . say to those with fearful hearts, "Be strong, do not fear . . . "
ISAIAH 35:4

When weaker Christians we despise,
We do the great Redeemer wrong;
For God, the gracious and the wise,
Receives the feeble with the strong.
ANONYMOUS

I think we often fail by our own foolishness, impulsiveness, or selfishness, and hurt people needlessly (some are called to punish as a duty, that is another matter), and still God may overrule it; yet that will be no excuse for our self-confidence, or rudeness, or hastiness, or lack of humility, or whatever the fault was. I must humble myself before God for the fault; but then it is very pride and a still worse fault to go on fidgeting about the forgiven fault, calling myself all the bad names in the dictionary. It may be quite true in fact, but it is not true in humility and gratitude for God's love of me a sinner, to go on dwelling upon my badness, the obstinate contemplation of which shuts out the sight of God's goodness and beauty. . . . I am very glad if it may possibly be that my fault may do good somehow to someone else, because God overrules evil for good; but the evil is not God's work but mine. But if I am sorry and own it, I will not dwell on it as if evil were the victorious power, but will thank God for His pardoning love, and try to be more humble and simple, and to keep my spirit in obedience to the Spirit of Christ for the future. It is possible to go on simply, and avoid a thousand perplexing questions, pains and doubts, which are unnecessary and unreal. It is possible because we can learn to abide in Christ more closely, and so to be subject to His wise and gracious inspiration, instead of at the mercy of our own tempests.

~ G. CONGREVE

October 6

May the God of peace . . . equip you with everything good for doing his will . . .
HEBREWS 13:20-21

In everything that he undertook in the service of God's temple and in obedience to the law and the commands, he sought his God and worked wholeheartedly. And so he prospered.
2 CHRONICLES 31:21

Be strong!
We are not here to play, to dream, to drift;
We have hard work to do and loads to lift;
Shun not the struggle – face it; 'tis God's gift.
MALTBIE DAVENPORT BABCOCK

Let us be very careful of thinking, on the one hand, that we have no work assigned us to do, or, on the other hand, that what we have assigned to us is not the right thing for us. If ever we can say in our hearts to God, in reference to any daily duty, "This is not my place; I would choose something dearer; I am capable of something higher"; we are guilty notonly of rebellion, but of blasphemy. It is equivalent to saying, not only, "My heart revolts against Thy commands," but "Thy commands are unwise; Thine Almighty guidance is unskilful; Thine omniscient eye has mistaken the capacities of Thy creature; Thine infinite love is indifferent to the welfare of Thy child."

~ ELIZABETH CHARLES

October 7

How beautiful on the mountains
are the feet of those who bring good news,
who proclaim peace,
who bring good tidings,
who proclaim salvation,
who say to Zion,
"Your God reigns!"
ISAIAH 52:7

So let our lips and lives express
The holy gospel we profess;
So let our works and virtues shine
To prove the doctrine all divine.
ANONYMOUS

But you will not leave in haste or go in flight;
for the Lord will go before you . . .
ISAIAH 52:12

The plans of the diligent lead to profit
as surely as haste leads to poverty.
PROVERBS 21:5

Holy Spirit, Peace divine!
Still this restless heart of mine;
Speak to calm this tossing sea,
Stayed in Thy tranquility.
S. LONGFELLOW

In whatever you are called upon to do, endeavor to maintain a calm, collected, and prayerful state of mind. Self-recollection is of great importance. "It is good for a man to quietly wait for the salvation of the Lord." He who is in what may be called a spiritual hurry, or rather who runs without having evidence of being spiritually sent, makes haste to no purpose.

~ T. C. UPHAM

Haste, haste, has no blessing.

~ ANONYMOUS PROVERB

If anyone does not know how to manage his own family,
how can he take care of God's church?
1 TIMOTHY 3:5

He who brings trouble on his family will inherit only wind . . .
PROVERBS 11:29

O Happy house! and happy servitude!
Where all alike one Master own;
Where daily duty, in Thy strength pursued,
Is never hard or toilsome known;
Where each one serves Thee, meek and lowly,
Whatever Thine appointment be,
Till common tasks seem great and holy,
When they are done as unto Thee,
C. J. P. SPITTA

. . . for there is nothing greater and better than this— when a husband and wife keep a household in oneness of mind, a great woe to their enemies and joy to their friends and win high renown.

~ HOMER

The family, like the home in which they live, needs to be kept in repair, lest some little rift in the walls should appear and let in the wind and rain. The happiness of a family depends very much on attention to little things. Order, comfort, regularity, cheerfulness, good taste, pleasant conversation —these are the ornaments of daily life, deprived of which it degenerates into a wearisome routine. There must be light in the dwelling, and brightness and pure spirits and cheerful smiles. Home is not usually the place of toil, but the place to which we return and rest from our labors; in which parents and children meet together and pass a joyful and careless hour . . . Sympathy, too, is the noblest exercise; of it is the Spirit of God working together with our spirit; it is warmth as well as light, putting into us a new heart, and taking away the stony heart which is dead to its natural surroundings.

~ BENJAMIN JOWETT

October 10

Now may the Lord of peace himself give you peace at all times and in every way.
2 THESSALONIANS 3:16

. . . there is a future for the man of peace.
PSALMS 37:37

In the heart's depths a peace serene and holy
Abides, and when pain seems to have its will,
Or we despair,—oh, may that peace rise slowly,
Stronger than agony, and we be still.
SAMUEL JOHNSON

God send that there may be an end at last; God send that there may be peace again. God in heaven send us peace.

~ DIARY OF HARTICH SIERK, A PEASANT

O Lord, calm the waves of this heart; calm its tempests. Calm thyself, O my soul, so that the divine can act in thee. Calm thyself, O my soul, so that God is able to repose in thee, so that his peace may cover thee. Yes, Father in heaven, often have we found that the world cannot give us peace, O but make us feel that thou art able to give peace; let us know the truth of thy promise: that the whole world may not be able to take away they peace.

~ SØREN KIERKEGAARD

October 11

". . . and anyone who does not take his cross and follow me is not worthy of me."
MATTHEW 10:38

The way to bliss lies not on beds of down,
And he that had no cross deserves no crown.
FRANCIS QUARLES

Jesus hath now many lovers of the heavenly kingdom, but few bearers of His Cross. He hath many desirous of consolation, but few of tribulation. He findeth many companions of His table, but few of His abstinence. All desire to rejoice with Him, few are willing to endure anything for Him, or with Him. Many follow Jesus unto the breaking of bread, but few to the drinking of the cup of His Passion. Many reverence His miracles, few follow the ignominy of His Cross. Many love Jesus so long as no adversities befall them, many praise and bless Him so long as they receive any consolations from Him; but if Jesus hide Himself and leave them but a little while, they fall either into complaining or into too much dejection of mind. . . . If thou bear the Cross cheerfully, it will bear thee, and lead thee to the desired end, namely, where there shall be an end of suffering, though here there shall not be. If thou bear it unwillingly, thou makest for thyself a burden and increasest thy load, and yet notwithstanding thou must bear it. If thou cast away one cross, without doubt thou shalt find another, and that perhaps a more heavy one.

~ THOMAS A. KEMPIS

October 12

*They will enter Zion with singing;
everlasting joy will crown their heads. Gladness and joy will overtake them,
and sorrow and sighing will flee away.*
ISAIAH 51:11

He put a new song in my mouth, a hymn of praise to our God.
PSALMS 40:3

*Sing to the Lord a new song;
sing to the Lord, all the earth.
Sing to the Lord, praise his name;
proclaim his salvation day after day.
Declare his glory among the nations,
his marvelous deeds among all peoples.*
PSALMS 96:1-3

*Sing, my tongue, the Savior's glory,
Of His Flesh the mystery sing;
Of the Blood, all price exceeding,
Shed by our immortal King.*
ST. THOMAS AQUINAS

Let our mouth be filled with thy praise, O Lord, that we may sing of thy glory, because thou hast counted us worthy to partake of thy holy, divine, immortal and life-giving mysteries: preserve us in thy holiness, that we may learn of thy righteousness all the day long. Alleluia, alleluia, alleluia.

~ LITURGY OF ST. JOHN CHRYSOSTOM

October 13

*We want each of you to show this same diligence to the very end, in order to
make your hope sure. We do not want you to become lazy . . .*
HEBREWS 6:11-12

*Long though my task may be,
Cometh the end.
God 'tis that helpeth me,
His is the work, and He
New strength will lend.*
ANONYMOUS

When I am assailed with heavy tribulations, I rush out among my pigs rather than remain alone by myself. The human heart is like a millstone in a mill: when you put wheat under it, it turns and grinds and bruises the wheat to flour; if you put no wheat, it still grinds on, but then 'tis itself it grinds and wears away. So the human heart, unless it be occupied with some employment, leaves space for the devil, who wriggles himself in and brings with him a whole host of evil thoughts, temptations, and tribulations, which grind out the heart.

~ MARTIN LUTHER

Set yourself steadfastly to those duties which have the least attractive exterior; it matters not whether God's holy will be fulfilled in great or small matters. Be patient with yourself and your own failings; never be in a hurry, and do not yield to longings after that which is impossible to you. My dear sister, go on steadily and quietly; if our dear Lord means you to run, He will "strengthen your heart."

~ FRANCIS DE SALES

October 14

And forgive your people who have sinned against you.
2 CHRONICLES 6:39

*For the wages of sin is death,
but the gift of God is eternal life in Christ Jesus our Lord.*
ROMANS 6:23

*Hark! the herald angels sing
Glory to the newborn King;
Peace on earth and mercy mild
God and sinners reconciled!*
CHARLES WESLEY

Sin itself is hell, and death, and misery to the soul, as being a departure from goodness and holiness itself; I mean from God, in conjunction with whom the happiness, and blessedness, and heaven of a soul doth consist. Avoid it, therefore, as you would avoid being miserable.

~ SAMUEL SHAW

"I couldn't live in peace if I put the shadow of a wilful sin between myself and God."

~ GEORGE ELIOT

Unholy tempers are always unhappy tempers.

~ JOHN WESLEY

October 15

*. . . because your people have sinned against you,
and when they pray toward this place and confess your name
and turn from their sin . . . then hear from heaven
and forgive the sin of your servants, your people of Israel.*
2 CHRONICLES 6:26-27

For sin shall not be your master,
because you are not under law, but under grace.
ROMANS 6:14

O Lord, forgive my sin,
And deign to put within
A calm, obedient heart, a patient mind;
That I may murmur not,
Though bitter seem my lot;
For hearts unthankful can no blessing find.
RUTILIUS

Yes, this sin which has sent me wearyhearted to bed and desperate in heart to morning work, that has made my plans miscarry until I am a coward, that cuts me off from prayer, that robs the sky of blueness and the earth of spring-time, and the air of freshness, and human faces of friendli-ness—this blasting sin which perhaps has made my bed in hell for me so long—this can be conquered. I do not say annihilated, but, better than that, conquered, captured and transfigured into a friend: so that I at last shall say, "My temptation has become my strength! for to the very fight with it I owe my force."

~ W. C. GANNETT

October 16

Let us fall into the hands of the Lord, for his mercy is great . . .
2 SAMUEL 24:14

But in your great mercy you did not put an end to them or
abandon them, for you are a gracious and merciful God.
NEHEMIAH 9:31

The quality of mercy is not strain'd
It droppeth as the gentle rain from heaven
Upon the place beneath: it is twice bless'd;
It blesseth him that gives and him that takes:
'Tis mightiest in the mightiest; it becomes
The throned monarch better than his crown;
His scepter shows the force of temporal power,
The attribute to awe and majesty,
Wherein doth sit the dread and fear of kings;
But mercy is above this sceptered sway,
It is enthroned in the hearts of kings,
It is an attribute to God himself,
And earthly power doth then show likest God's
When mercy seasons justice . . . we do pray for mercy,
And that same prayer doth teach us all to render
The deeds of mercy.
WILLIAM SHAKESPEARE

We hand folks over to God's mercy, and show none ourselves.
~ GEORGE ELIOT

Who will not mercy unto others show, how can he mercy ever hope to have?
~ EDMUND SPENSER

October 17

"Does the Lord delight in burnt offerings and sacrifices as much as in obeying the voice of the Lord? To obey is better than sacrifice . . ."
1 SAMUEL 15:22

Walk in his ways, and keep his decrees and commands, his laws and requirements, as written in the Law of Moses, so that you may prosper in all you do and wherever you go . . .
1 KINGS 2:3

Dearest Lord, teach me to be generous;
Teach me to serve thee as thou deservest;
To give and not to count the cost,
To fight and not to heed the wounds,
To toil and not to seek for rest,
To labor and not to seek reward,
Save that of knowing that I do thy will.
ST. IGNATIUS LOYOLA

O God, thou knowest that I do not want anything else but to serve thee and men, always, all my life.

~ TEMPLE GARDNER OF CAIRO

Lord make thy will our will in all things.

~ DEAN VAUGHAN

It is not the multitude of hard duties, it is not constraint and contention that advance us in our Christian course. On the contrary, it is the yielding of our wills without restriction and without choice, to tread cheerfully every day in the path in which Providence leads us, to seek nothing, to be discouraged by nothing, to see our duty in the present moment, to trust all else without reserve to the will and power of God.

~ FENELON

October 18

I put this in human terms because you are weak in your natural selves. Just as you used to offer the parts of your body in slavery to impurity and to ever-increasing wickedness, so now offer them in slavery to righteousness leading to holiness.
ROMANS 6:19

Your righteousness reaches to the skies,
O God, you who have done great things. Who, O God, is like you?
PSALMS 71:19

Be strong, live happy, and love, but first of all
Him whom to love is to obey, and keep
His great command; take heed lest passion sway
Thy judgment to do aught which else free will
Would not admit; thine and of all thy sons
The weal or woe in thee is placed; beware.
I in thy persevering shall rejoice,
And all the blest. Stand fast; to stand or fall

Free in thine own arbitrement it lies.
Perfect within, no outward aid require;
And all temptation to transgress repel.
JOHN MILTON

You perhaps will say that all people fall short of the perfection of the Gospel, and therefore you are content with your failings. But this is saying nothing to the purpose: for the question is not whether Gospel perfection can be fully attained, but whether you come as near it as a sincere intention and careful diligence can carry you. Whether you are not in a much lower state than you might be if you sincerely intended and carefully labored to advance yourself in all Christian virtues.

~ WILLIAM LAW

We know not exactly how low the least degree of obedience is, which will bring a man to heaven; but this we are quite sure of, that he who aims no higher will be sure to fall short even of that, and that he who goes farthest beyond it will be most blessed.

~ JOHN KEBLE

October 19

In all your ways acknowledge him,
and he will make your paths straight.
PROVERBS 3:6

I am the Lord your God, who teaches you what is best for you,
who directs you in the way you should go.
ISAIAH 48:17

Out of the light that dazzles me,
Bright as the sun from pole to pole,
I thank the God I know to be
For Christ the conqueror of my soul.

Since His the sway of circumstance,
I would not wince nor cry aloud.
Under that rule which men call chance
My head with joy is humbly bowed.

Beyond this place of sin and tears
That life with Him! And His the aid,
Despite the menace of the years,
Keeps, and shall keep me, unafraid.

I have no fear, though strait the gait,
He cleared from punishment the scroll.
Christ is the Master of my fate,
Christ is the Captain of my soul.
DOROTHEA DAY

Of all paths a man could strike into, there is, at any given moment, a best path for every man; a thing which, here and now, it were of all things wisest for him to do; which could he but be led or driven to do, he were then doing "like a man," as we phrase it. His success, in such case, were complete, his felicity a maximum. This path, to find this path, and walk in it, is the one thing needful for him.

~ THOMAS CARLYLE

Every man has his own vocation. There is one direction in which all space is open to him. He has faculties silently inviting him thither to endless exertion. He is like a ship in a river; he runs against obstructions on every side but one; on that side all obstruction is taken away, and he sweeps serenely over a deepening channel into an infinite sea.

~ RALPH WALDO EMERSON

October 20

"You have heard that it was said, 'Love your neighbor and hate your enemy.' But I tell you: Love your enemies and pray for those who persecute you, that you may be sons of your Father in Heaven."
MATTHEW 5:43

Do not be overcome with evil, but overcome evil with good.
ROMANS 12:21

'Tis the human touch in this world that counts,
The touch of your hand and mine,
Which means far more to the fainting heart
Than shelter and bread and wine;
For shelter is gone when the night is o'er,
And bread lasts only a day,
But the touch of the hand and the sound of the voice
Sing on in the soul alway.
SPENCER MICHAEL FREE

If we wish to overcome evil, we must overcome it by good. There are doubtless many ways of overcoming the evil in our own hearts, but the simplest, easiest, most universal, is to overcome it by active occupation in some good word or work. The best antidote against evil of all kinds, against the evil thoughts which haunt the soul, against the needless per- plexities which distract the conscience, is to keep hold of the good we have. Impure thoughts will not stand against pure words, and prayers, and deeds. Little doubts will not avail against great certainties. Fix your affec- tions on things above, and then you will be less and less troubled by the cares, the temptations, the troubles of things on earth.

~ A. P. STANLEY

October 21

I will be careful to lead a blameless life . . .
PSALMS 101:2

I am God Almighty;
walk before me, and be blameless.
GENESIS 17:1

Come, in this accepted hour
Bring Thy heavenly kingdom in

Fill us with Thy glorious power,
Rooting out the seeds of sin.
C. WESLEY

But one day, as I was passing in the field, and that too with some dashes on my conscience, fearing lest yet all was not right, suddenly this sentence fell upon my soul, Thy righteousness is in heaven; and methought withal, I saw, with the eyes of my soul, Jesus Christ at God's right hand. There, I say, was my righteousness; so that wherever I was, or whatever I was adoing, God could not say of me, He wants my righteousness, for that was just before Him. I also saw, moreover, that it was not my good frame of heart that made my righteousness better, nor yet my bad frame that made my righteousness worse; for my righteousness was Jesus Christ Himself, the same yesterday, and today, and for ever. Now did my chains fall off my legs indeed; I was loosed from my affliction and irons; my temptations also fled away; now went I also home rejoicing, for the grace and love of God.

~ JOHN BUNYAN

October 22

Be joyful always, pray continually; give thanks in all circumstances, for this is God's will for you in Christ Jesus.
1 THESSALONIANS 5:16-18

Lord, you have assigned my portion and my cup; you have made my lot secure.
PSALMS 16:5

To fret thy soul with crosses and with cares;
To eat thy heart through comfortless despairs;
To fawn, to crouch, to wait, to ride, to run,
To spend, to give, to want, to be undone.
Unhappy wight, born to disastrous end,
That doth his life in so long tendance spend.
EDMUND SPENSER

I have noticed that wherever there has been a faithful following of the Lord in a consecrated soul, several things have inevitably followed, sooner or later. Meekness and quietness of spirit become in time the characteristics of the daily life. A submissive acceptance of the will of God as it comes in the hourly events of each day; pliability in the hands of God to do or to suffer all the good pleasure of his will; sweetness under provocation; calmness in the midst of turmoil and bustle; yieldingness to the wishes of others, and an insensibility to slights and affronts; absence of worry or anxiety; deliverance from care and fear—all these, and many similar graces, are invariably found to be the natural outward development of that inward life which is hid with Christ in God.

~ H. W. S.

October 23

Teach me to do your will, for you are my God;
may your good Spirit lead me on level ground.
PSALMS 143:10

. . . for it is God who works in you to will and
to act according to his good purpose.
PHILIPPIANS 2:13

Just as Thou wilt is just what I would will;
Give me but this, the heart to be content,
And, if my wish is thwarted, to lie still,
Waiting till puzzle and till pain are spent,
And the sweet thing made plain which the Lord meant.
SUSAN COOLIDGE

"You are seeking your own will, my daughter. You are seeking some good
other than the law you are bound to obey. But how will you find good?
It is not a thing of choice; it is a river that flows from the foot of the
Invisible Throne, and flows by the path Of obedience. I say again, man
cannot choose his duties. You may choose to forsake your duties, and
choose not to have the sorrow they bring. But you will go forth, and what
will you find, my daughter? Sorrow without duty—bitter herbs, and no
bread with them."

~ GEORGE ELIOT

However dark and profitless, however painful and weary, existence may
have become; however any man, like Elijah, may be tempted to cast himself down beneath the juniper-tree, and say, "It is enough, O Lord"—life is
not done, and our Christian character is not won, so long as God has anything left for us to suffer, or anything left for us to do.

~ F. W. ROBERTSON

October 24

But let all who take refuge in you be glad; let them ever sing for joy.
Spread your protection over them, that those who love your name may
rejoice in you. For surely, Oh Lord, you bless the righteous; you surround
them with your favor as with a shield.
PSALMS 5:11-12

Well may Thy happy children cease
From restless wishes, prone to sin,
And, in Thy own exceeding peace,
Yield to Thy daily discipline.
A. L. WARING

Holy purity of heart sees God, and true devotion enjoys Him. If thou
lovest, thou shalt be loved. If thou servest, thou shalt be served. If thou
fearest, thou shalt be feared. If thou dost good to others, fitting it is that
others should do good to thee. But blessed is he who truly loves and
desires not to be loved again. Blessed is he who serves and desires not to
be served. Blessed is he who fears and desires not to be feared. Blessed is
he who does good to others and desires not that others should do good to

him. But because these things are very sublime and of high perfection, therefore they that are foolish can neither understand them nor attain unto them. There are three things that are very sublime and very profitable, which he who has once acquired shall never fall. The first is that thou bear willingly and gladly, for the love of Christ, every affliction that shall befall thee. The second is that thou daily humble thyself in everything thou doest, and in everything thou seest. The third is that thou love faithfully with all thy heart that invisible and supreme Good which thou canst not behold with thy bodily eyes.

~ BROTHER GILES

October 25

And earth has nothing I desire besides you. My flesh and my heart my fail, but God is the strength of my heart and my portion forever.
PSALMS 73:25-26

The opening heavens around me shine
With beams of sacred bliss,
While Jesus shows his heart is mine,
And whispers, I am his.
ANONYMOUS

Be of good faith, my dear Friends, look not out at any thing; fear none of those things ye may be exposed to suffer, either outwardly or inwardly; but trust the Lord over all, and your life will spring, and grow, and refresh you, and ye will learn obedience and faithfulness daily more and more, even by your exercises and sufferings; yea, the Lord will teach you the very mystery of faith and obedience; the wisdom, power, love, and goodness of the Lord ordering every thing for you, and ordering your hearts in everything.

~ I. PENINGTON

October 26

Be still before the Lord and wait patiently for him . . .
PSALMS 37:7

. . . in quietness and trust is your strength . . .
ISAIAH 30:15

O Power to do; 0 baffled will!
O prayer and action! ye are one.
Who may not strive, may yet fulfil
The harder task of standing still,
And good but wished with God is done.
J. G. WHITTIER

To get alone—to dare to be alone—with God, this, I am persuaded, is one of the best ways of doing anything in the world. . . . If we are ever to be or to do anything, if we are ever to be full of deep, permanent, rational enthusiasm, we must know God. If we are ever to know each other, we must know Him first. . . . I believe that we do most for those whom God has begun to teach us to love, not by constantly thinking of their goodness, their grace, their simplicity, but by never thinking of them apart from God, by always connecting their beauty and purity with a higher Beauty and a higher Purity, by seeing God in them. Let us learn to make every thought of admiration and love a kind of prayer of intercession and thanksgiving. Thus human love will correct itself with, and find its root in, divine love. But this we can do only if we are willing to be alone with Him.

~ FORBES ROBINSON

October 27

"My grace is sufficient for you, my power is made perfect in your weakness."... That is why, for Christ's sake, I delight in weaknesses, in insults, in hardships, in persecutions, in difficulties. For when I am weak, then I am strong.

2 CORINTHIANS 12:9-10

To suffer woes which Hope thinks infinite;
To forgive wrongs darker than death or night;
To defy Power, which seems omnipotent;
To love, and bear; to hope till Hope creates
From its own wreck the thing it contemplates;
Neither to change, nor falter, nor repent;
This, like thy glory, Titan, is to be
Good, great and joyous, beautiful and free;
This is alone Life, Joy, Empire, and Victory.

PERCY BYSSHE SHELLEY

Let us dwell upon times and seasons, times of trouble, times of joy, times of trial, times of refreshment. How did He cherish us as children! How did He guide us in that dangerous time when the mind began to think for itself, and the heart to open to the world! How did He with His sweet discipline restrain our passions, mortify our hopes, calm our fears, enliven our heavinesses, sweeten our desolateness, and strengthen our infirmities! How did He gently guide us towards the strait gate! How did He allure us along His everlasting way, in spite of its strictness, in spite of its loneliness, in spite of the dim twilight in which it lay! He has been all things to us, He has been, as He was to Abraham, Isaac and Jacob, our God, our shield, and great reward, promising and performing, day by day. "Hitherto hath He helped us." "He hath been mindful of us, and He will bless us." He has not made us for naught; He has brought us thus far, in order to bring us further, in order to bring us to the end.

~ JOHN HENRY CARDINAL NEWMAN

October 28

How precious to me are your thoughts, O God!
How vast is the sum of them!
Were I to count them they would
outnumber the grains of sand.

PSALMS 139:17-18

Thy thoughts are good, and Thou art kind,
Even when we think it not;
How many an anxious, faithless mind
Sits grieving o'er its lot,
And frets, and pines by day and night,

As God had lost it out of sight,
And all its wants forgot.
P. GERHARDT

I have no knowledge to take up the Lord in all His strange ways, and passages of deep and unsearchable providences. For the Lord is before me, and I am so bernisted. that I cannot follow Him; He is behind me and following at my heels, and I am not aware of Him; He is above me, but His glory so dazzleth my twilight of short knowledge that I cannot look up to Him. He is upon my right hand, and I see Him not; He is upon my left hand, and within me, and goeth and cometh, and His going and coming are a dream to me; He is round about me, and compasseth all my goings, and still I have Him to seek. He is every way higher and deeper and broader than the shallow and ebb hand-breadth of my short and dim light can take up; and therefore I would that my heart could be silent and sit down in the learnedly-ignorant wondering at the Lord whom men and angels cannot comprehend. I know that the noon-day light of the highest angels, who see Him face to face, seeth not the borders of His infiniteness. They apprehend God near at hand; but they cannot comprehend Him. And therefore it is my happiness to look afar off, and to come near to the Lord's back parts, and to light my candle at His brightness, and to have leave to sit and content myself with a traveller's light, without the clear vision of an enjoyer. I would seek no more till I were in my country than a little watering and sprinkling of a withered soul, with some half out-breakings and half out-lookings of the beams, and small ravishing smiles, of a revealed and believed-in Godhead. A little of God would make my soul bankfull.

~ SAMUEL RUTHERFORD

October 29

Be joyful in hope,
patient in affliction,
faithful in prayer.
ROMANS 12:12

See, I have refined you, though not as silver;
I have tested you in the furnace of affliction.
ISAIAH 48:10

Be patient, suffering soul ! I hear thy cry.
The trial fires may glow, but I am nigh.
I see the silver, and I will refine
Until My image shall upon it shine.
Fear not, for I am near, thy help to be
Greater than all thy pain, My love for Thee.
H. W. C.

To love sufferings and afflictions for the love of God is the highest point of most holy charity; for in this there is nothing lovable save the love of God only; there is a great contradiction on the part of our nature; and not only do we forsake all pleasures, but we embrace torments and labors. Our mortal enemy knew well what was the farthest and finest act of love when, having heard from the mouth of God that "Job was a perfect and upright man, one that feareth God, and escheweth evil," he made no account of this in comparison with bearing afflictions, by which he made the last and surest trial of this great servant of God; and to make these afflictions extreme he formed them out of the loss of all his goods, and of all his children, abandonment by all his friends, an arrogant contradiction by his most intimate associates, ... Now, say I, hear the great Job crying out: "Shall we receive good at the hand of God, and shall we not receive evil?"

~ ST. FRANCIS DE SALES

October 30

Guard the good deposit that was entrusted to you—guard it with the help of the Holy Spirit who lives in us.
2 TIMOTHY 1:14

We know that we live in him and he in us because he has given us of his Spirit.
1 JOHN 4:13

. . . O Spirit of God, mighty fire,
glow in me, burn in me,
until thy radiance fills my soul.
O Spirit of God, mighty fire,
may thy light illumine my mind.
O Spirit of God, mighty fire,
may thy heat consume my will
until I burn for thee.
May the flames of thy love
ever blaze upon the altar
of my heart.
CHARLES DEVANESAN

Thy spirit should become, while yet on earth, the peaceful throne of the Divine Being; think, then, how quiet, how gentle and pure, how reverent, thou shouldest be.

~ GERHARD TERSTEEGEN

The Spirit of the Lord fills the whole world, alleluia, alleluia.
In him all things.

~ FEAST OF PENTACOST, WESTERN RITE

October 31

"Whoever finds his life will lose it,
and whoever loses his life for my sake will find it."
MATTHEW 10:39

"I tell you the truth, whoever hears my word and believes . . . will not be condemned; he has crossed over from death to life."
JOHN 5:24

No coward soul is mine,
No trembler in the world's storm-troubled sphere:
I see Heaven's glories shine,
And faith shines equal arming me from fear . . . .

There is not room for Death.
Nor atom that his might could render void:
Thou—Thou art Being and Breath,
And what Thou art may never be destroyed.
EMILY BRONTE

. . . Heaven seems to be awakened in you. It is a tender plant. It requires stillness, meekness, and the unity of the heart, totally given up to the unknown workings of the Spirit of God, which will do all its work in the calm soul, that has no hunger or desire but to escape out of the mire of its earthly life into its lost union and life in God.

~ WILLIAM LAW

Is it possible for any of us in these modern days to so live that we may walk with God? Can we walk with God in the shop, in the office, in the household, and on the street? . . . [Religion] should be more than a plank to sustain us in the rushing tide, and land us exhausted and dripping on the other side. It ought, if it come from above, to be always, day by day, to our souls as the wings of a bird, bearing us away from and beyond the impediments which seek to hold us down. If the Divine Love be a conscious presence, an indwelling force with us, it will do this.

~ CHRISTIAN UNION

"In my Father's house are many rooms; if it were not so, I would have told you. I am going there to prepare a place for you."
JOHN 14:2

Consequently, you are no longer foreigners and aliens, but fellow citizens with God's people and members of God's household . . .
EPHESIANS 2:19

My church has but one temple,
Wide as the world is wide,
Set with a million stars,
Where a million hearts abide.

My church has no creed to bar
A single brother man
But says, "Come thou and worship"
To everyone who can.

My church has no roof or walls,
Nor floors save the beautiful sod—
For fear, I would seem to limit
The love of the illimitable God.
E. O. G.

Our first step is the sociableness, the communicableness of God; He loves holy meetings, He loves the communion of saints, the household of the faithful: "deliciae eius," says Solomon, "His delight is to be with the sons of men, and that the sons of men should be with Him." Religion is not a melancholy: the Spirit of God is not a damp: the Church is not a grave: it is a fold, it is an ark, it is a net, it is a city, it is a kingdom, not only a house but a house that hath many mansions in it. Always it is a plural thing, consisting of many. And very good grammarians amongst the Hebrews have thought and said that that name by which God notifies Himself to the world in the very beginning of Genesis, which is Elohim, as it is a plural word there, so it hath no singular. They say we cannot name God but plurally; so sociable, so communicable, so extensive, so derivative of Himself, is God, and so manifold are the beams and the emanations that flow from Him.

~ JOHN DONNE

. . . [Christ] is all for every one, and He is One for all.

~ JOHN KER

Therefore, since we are surrounded by such a great cloud of witnesses, let us throw off everything that hinders and the sin that so easily entangles, and let us run with perseverance the race marked out for us.
HEBREWS 12:1

When the powers of hell prevail
O'er our weakness and unfitness,
Could we lift the fleshly veil,

Could we for a moment witness
Those unnumbered hosts that stand
Calm and bright on either hand;

Oh, what joyful hope would cheer,
Oh, what faith serene would guide us!
Great may be the danger near.
Greater are the friends beside us.
ANONYMOUS

In the discharge of thy place set before thee the best examples; for imitation is a globe of precepts. And after a time set before thee thine own example; and examine thyself strictly, whether thou didst not best at first. Neglect not also the examples of those that have carried themselves ill in the same place; not to set off thyself by taxing their memory, but to direct thyself what to avoid. . . . Embrace and invite helps and advices touching the execution of thy place; and do not drive away such as bring thee information, as meddlers; but accept of them in good part.

~ FRANCIS BACON

"He went about doing good." So we might say in our own age of two or three who have been personally known to us, "He or she went about doing good." They are the living witnesses to us of His work. If we observe them we shall see that they did good because they were good—because they lived for others and not for themselves, because they had a higher standard of truth and therefore men could trust them, because their love was deeper and therefore they drew others after them. These are they of whom we read in Scripture that they bear the image of Christ until His coming again, and of a few of them that they have borne the image of His sufferings, and to us they are the best interpreters of His life.

~ BENJAMIN JOWETT

November 3

Therefore each of you must put off falsehood and speak truthfully to his neighbor, for we are all members of one body.
EPHESIANS 4:25

"You shall not give false testimony against your neighbor."
EXODUS 20:16

In conversation be sincere;
Keep conscience as the noontide clear;
Think how All-seeing God thy ways
And all thy secret thoughts surveys.
THOMAS KEN

We begin, I think, when we set out to lie and deceive, by having an increased sense of power. . . . I suppose the successful liar may continue to enjoy this feeling of triumph and superiority, so that he does not notice what is happening to him. But something very terrible is happening. The lie does not stay outside his soul; it does not remain the mere instrument used so cleverly by the self; it invades the self and becomes part of it. I have heard that actors who have played one part for a long time sometimes become temporarily deranged and cannot distinguish their real selves from the person whom they were representing in the drama.

Something of the same kind happens to the man who has cultivated insincerity, but his is not a temporary derangement. . . . What has happened to him? He has lost the power to know himself, and with it the power to repent, unless the grace of God should, in some flash of revelation, dissolve the blinding veil he has bound upon his own eyes. One who cannot know himself cannot repent—that is why the Heavenly City includes none "that loveth or maketh a lie."

~ W. R. MATTHEWS

November 4

Be wise in the way you act toward outsiders; make the most of every opportunity. Let your conversation be always full of grace, seasoned with salt, so that you may know how to answer everyone.
COLOSSIANS 4:5-6

If ever you have look'd on better days,
If ever been where bells have knoll'd to church,
If ever sat at any good man's feast,
If ever from your eyelids wip'd a tear,
And know what 'tis to pity, and be pitied,
Let gentleness my strong enforcement be.
WILLIAM SHAKESPEARE

Neither say nor do aught displeasing to thy neighbor; and if thou hast been wanting in charity, seek his forgiveness, or speak to him with gentleness. Speak always with mildness and in a low tone of voice.

~ LORENZO SCUPOLI

Injuries hurt not more in the receiving than in the remembrance. A small injury shall go as it comes; a great injury may dine or sup with me; but none at all shall lodge with me. Why should I vex myself because another hath vexed me? Grief for things past that cannot be remedied, and care for things to come that cannot be prevented, may easily hurt, can never benefit me. I will therefore commit myself to God in both, and enjoy the present.

~ JOSEPH HALL

November 5

For we are the temple of the living God.
2 CORINTHIANS 6:16

Wilt thou love God, as He thee? then digest,
My soul, this wholesome meditation,
How God the Spirit, by angels waited on
In heaven, doth make His Temple in thy breast.
JOHN DONNE

This pearl of eternity is the church or temple of God within thee, the consecrated place of divine worship, where alone thou canst worship God in spirit and in truth. When once thou art well grounded in this inward worship, thou wilt have learned to live unto God above time and place. For every day will be Sunday to thee, and, wherever thou goest, thou wilt have a priest, a church, and an altar along with thee. For when God has all that he should have of thy heart, when thou art wholly given up to the obedience of the light and spirit of God within thee, to will only in His will, to love only in His love, to be wise only in His wisdom, then it is that everything thou dost is as a song of praise, and the common business of thy life is a conforming to God's will on earth as angels do in heaven.

~ WILLIAM LAW

November 6

Evening, morning and noon, I cry out in distress, and he hears my voice.
PSALMS 55:17

Then my enemies will turn back when I call for help, by this I will know that God is for me.
PSALMS 56:9

Speak to Him thou for He hears, and Spirit with
Spirit can meet—
Closer is He than breathing, and nearer than
hands and feet.
ALFRED, LORD TENNYSON

. . . Thus for some months I had great troubles; there remaining in me an unsubjected will, which rendered my labors fruitless, till at length through the merciful continuance of heavenly visitations, I was made to bow down in spirit before the Lord. I remember one evening I had spent some time in reading a pious author; and, walking out alone, I humbly prayed to the Lord for His help, that I might be delivered from all those vanities which so ensnared me. Thus, being brought low, He helped me; and as I learned to bear the Cross, I felt refreshment to come from His presence; but, not keeping in that strength which gave victory, I lost ground again; the sense of which greatly affected me; and I sought deserts and lonely places, and there with tears did confess my sins to God and humbly craved help of Him. And I may say with reverence, He was near to me in my troubles, and in those times of humiliation opened my ear to discipline . . .

~ JOHN WOOLMAN

November 7

For God does speak— now one way,
now another—though man may not perceive it.
JOB 33:14

God moves in a mysterious way,
His wonders to perform;
He plants his footsteps in the sea,
And rides upon the storm.
Deep in unfathomable mines
Of never-failing skill,
He treasures up his bright designs,
And works his sovereign will. . . .
WILLIAM COWPER

All these longings and doubts, and this inward distress, are the voice of the Good Shepherd in your heart, seeking to call you out of all that is contrary to His will. Oh, let men treat of you not to turn away from His gentle pleadings.

~ H. W. S.

. . . In this state of universal uncertainty, where a thousand dangers hover about us, and none can tell whether the good that he pursues is not evil in disguise, or whether the next step will lead him to safety or destruction, nothing can afford any rational tranquility but the conviction that, however we amuse ourselves with unideal sounds, nothing in reality is governed by chance, but that the universe is under the perpetual superintendence of Him who created it; that our being is in the hands of omnipotent Goodness, by whom what appears casual to us is directed for ends ultimately kind and merciful; and that nothing can finally hurt him who debars not himself from the divine favor.

~ SAMUEL JOHNSON

November 8

"Here I am, I have come to do your will."
HEBREWS 10:9

There is no chance, no destiny, no fate,
Can circumvent or hinder or control
The firm resolve of a determined soul.
Gifts count for nothing; will alone is great;
. . . Each wellborn soul must win what it deserves.
Let the fool prate of luck. The fortunate
Is he whose earnest purpose never swerves,
Whose slightest action or inaction serves
The one great aim. Why, even Death stands still,
And waits an hour sometimes for such a will.
ELLA WHEELER WILCOX

I had such a sense how sweet and blessed a thing it was to walk in the way of duty; to do that which was right and meet to be done and agreeable to the holy mind of God; that it caused me to break forth into a kind of loud weeping, which held me some time, so that I was forced to shut myself up and to fasten doors. I could not but, as it were, cry out, "How happy are they which do right in the sight of God!" I had at the same time a very affecting sense how meet and suitable it was that God should govern the world, and order all things according to His own pleasure; and I rejoiced in it that God reigned, and that His will was done.

~ JONATHAN EDWARDS

When we have learned to offer up every duty connected with our situation in life as a sacrifice to God, a settled employment becomes just a settled habit of prayer.

~ THOMAS ERSKINE

"The Lord, the Lord, the compassionate and gracious God . . .
maintaining love to thousands, and forgiving wickedness,
rebellion and sin."
EXODUS 34:6-7

I asked the Lord, "Could I be
important to one so great as Thee?"
"Yes!" said the Lord, "Yes!" said He,
"Each one is dear who believes in me."
E. C. M.

Give, free and bold play to those instincts of the heart which believe that the Creator must care for the creatures He has made, and that the only real effective care for them must be that which takes each of them into His love, and knowing it separately surrounds it with His separate sympathy. There is not one life which the Life-giver ever loses out of His sight; not one which sins so that He casts it away; not one which is not so near to Him that whatever touches it touches Him with sorrow or with joy.

~ PHILLIPS BROOKS

You have made known to me the path of life;
you will fill me with joy . . .
PSALMS 16:11

"For in him we live and
move and have our being."
ACTS 17:28

Among so many, can He care?
Can special love be everywhere?
A myriad homes,—a myriad ways,
And God's eye over every place?

I asked: my soul bethought of this;—
In just that very place of His
Where He hath put and keepeth you,
God hath no other thing to do!
A. D. T. WHITNEY

Where then is our God? You say, He is everywhere: then show me anywhere that you have met Him. You declare Him everlasting: then tell me any moment that He has been with you. You believe Him ready to succor them that are tempted, and to lift those that are bowed down: then in what passionate hour did you subside into His calm grace? in what sorrow lose yourself in His "more exceeding" joy? These are the testing questions by which we may learn whether we too have raised our altar to an "unknown God" and pay the worship of the blind; or whether we commune with Him "in whom we live, and move, and have our being."

~ JAMES MARTINEAU

Be strong and do the work.
1 CHRONICLES 28:10

*And we pray this in order that you may live a life worthy of the
Lord and may please him in every way:
bearing fruit in every good work . . .*
COLOSSIANS 1:10

*To be the thing we seem,
To do the thing we deem
Enjoined by duty;
To walk in faith, nor dream
Of questioning God's scheme
Of truth and beauty.*
ANONYMOUS

A soul cannot be regarded as truly subdued and consecrated in its will, and
as having passed into union with the Divine will, until it has a disposition
to do promptly and faithfully all that God requires, as well as to endure
patiently and thankfully all that He imposes.

~ T. C. UPHAM

"Do the duty which lies nearest thee," which thou knowest to be a duty.
Thy second duty will already have become clearer.

~ THOMAS CARLYLE

Do your duty, and leave the rest to heaven.

~ PIERRE CORNEILLE

*"My food," said Jesus,
"is to do the will of him who sent me and to finish his work."*
JOHN 4:34

*"As long as it is day, we must do the work of him who sent me.
Night is coming, when no one can work."*
JOHN 9:4

*He who intermits
The appointed task and duties of the day
Untunes full oft the pleasures of the day
Checking the finer spirits that refuse
To flow, when purposes are lightly changed.*
WILLIAM WORDSWORTH

Give us constancy and steadiness of purpose, that our thoughts may nott
be fleeting, fond and ineffectual, but that we may perform all things with
an unmovable mind, to the glory of thy holy name. Through Jesus Christ
our Lord.

~ LUDOVICUS VIVES

O Lord, without whom our labor is but lost, and with whom thy little ones go forth as the mighty; be present to all works in thy Church which are undertaken according to thy will . . . and grant to thy laborers a pure intention, patient faith, sufficient success upon earth and the bliss of serving thee in heaven; through Jesus Christ our Lord.

~ WILLIAM BRIGHT

November 13

Blessed is the man you discipline, O Lord, the man you teach from your law; you grant him relief from days of trouble . . .
PSALMS 94:12-13

Then welcome each rebuff
That turns earth's smoothness rough,
Each sting that bids nor sit nor stand, but go!
Be our joys three parts pain!
Strive, and hold cheap the strain;
Learn, nor account the pang; dare, never grudge
the throe!
ROBERT BROWNING

Better it is to be heavy-laden and near one that is strong than relieved of one's load and near one that is weak. When thou art heavy-laden, thou art near to God, who is thy strength and is with them that are in trouble. When thou art relieved, thou art near but to thyself, who art thine own weakness. For the virtue and strength of the soul grows and is confirmed by trials of patience.

He that desires to be alone without the support of a master and guide will be like the tree that is alone in the field and has no owner. However much fruit it bears, passers-by will pluck it all, and it will not mature. The tree that is cultivated and kept with the favour of its owner gives in due season the fruit that is expected of it.

~ ST. JOHN OF THE CROSS

Do not run to this and that for comfort when you are in trouble, but bear it. Be uncomfortably quiet—be uneasily silent—be patiently unhappy.

~ J. P. GREAVES

November 14

"O Lord, you are God!
You have promised these good things to your servant.
Now you have been pleased to bless the house of your servant, that it may
continue forever in your sight; for you, O Lord, have blessed it,
and it will be blessed forever."
1 CHRONICLES 17:26-27

Servant of God, well done, well hast thou fought
The better fight, who single hast maintained
Against revolted multitudes the cause
Of truth, in word mightier than they in arms.
JOHN MILTON

Accept His will entirely, and never suppose that you could serve Him better in any other way. You can never serve Him well, save in the way He chooses. Supposing that you were never to be set free from such trials, what would you do? You would say to God, "I am Thine—if my trials are acceptable to Thee, give me more and more." I have full confidence that this is what you would say, and then you would not think more of it—at any rate, you would not be anxious. Well, do the same now. Make friends with your trials, as though you were always to live together; and you will see that when you cease to take thought for your own deliverance, God will take thought for you ; and when you cease to help yourself eagerly, He will help you.

~ FRANCIS DE SALES

November 15

So do not fear, for I am with you;
do not be dismayed for I am your God. I will strengthen you and help you;
I will uphold you with my righteous right hand.
ISAIAH 41:10

LORD, be Thou near and cheer my lonely way;
With Thy sweet peace my aching bosom fill;
Scatter my cares and fears; my griefs allay,
And be it mine each day
To love and please Thee still.
P. CORNEILLE

O Lord, we beseech thee to deliver us from the fear of the unknown future, from fear of failure; from fear of poverty; from fear of bereavement; from fear of lonliness; from fear of sickness and pain; from fear of age; and from fear of death. Help us, O Father, by thy grace to love and fear thee only, fill our hearts with cheerful courage and loving trust in thee; through our Lord and Master Jesus Christ.

~ AKANU IBAIM

November 16

You will keep in perfect peace him whose mind is steadfast,
because he trusts in you. Trust in the Lord forever, for the Lord,
the Lord, is the Rock eternal.
ISAIAH 26:4

Serene, I fold my hands and wait,
Nor care for wind, nor tide, nor sea;
I rave no more 'gainst time or fate,
For lo! my own shall come to me.
JOHN BURROUGHS

God is a tranquil Being, and abides in a tranquil eternity. So must thy spirit become a tranquil and clear little pool, wherein the serene light of God can be mirrored. Therefore shun all that is disquieting and distracting, both within and without. Nothing in the whole world is worth the loss of thy peace; even the faults which thou hast committed should only humble, but not disquiet thee. God is full of joy, peace, and happiness.

Endeavor then to obtain a continually joyful and peaceful spirit. Avoid all anxious care, vexation, murmuring, and melancholy, which darken thy soul, and render thee unfit for the friendship of God. If thou dost perceive such feelings arising, turn gently away from them.

~ G. TERSTREGEN

November 17

*My mouth is filled with your praise,
declaring your splendor all day long.*
PSALMS 71:8

*Lord, I my vows to Thee renew
Disperse my sins as morning dew
Guard my first springs of thought and will,
And with Thyself my spirit fill.*
THOMAS KEN

O most glorious and exalted Lord, you are glorified in the heights above by ministers of fire and spirit in most holy fashion, yet in your love you wished to be glorified by mankind on earth as well, so that you might exalt our mortal race and make us like supernal beings and brothers in your dominion. Free us, Lord, in your compassion from whatever cares hinder the worship of you, and teach us to seek the kingdom and its righteousness in accordance with your holy commandments that bring life; and may we become worthy of that kingdom along with all the saints who have done your will, and may we sing your praises.

~ MARONITE SHEMINTO

November 18

This is how you can recognize the Spirit of God: Every spirit that acknowledges that Jesus Christ has come in the flesh is from God . . .
I JOHN 4:2

*Within! within, oh turn
Thy spirit's eyes, and learn
Thy wandering senses gently to control;
Thy dearest Friend dwells deep within thy soul,
And asks thyself of thee,
That heart, and mind, and sense, He may make whole
In perfect harmony.*
G. TERSTEEGEN

To the person that begins to understand spiritual and divine things, and that begins to know them, I understand that befalls which befalls those persons who, having by some accident lost the sight of their eyes, begin to recover it. I would say that, as those persons go knowing the being of things, according as they go recovering the sight of their eyes, first confusedly, as it befell to the blind man in the Gospel who, beginning to open his eyes, saw men and it seemed to him that they were trees; and afterwards less confusedly, until such time as little by little they come to see and know things in their own proper being; in the selfsame manner these persons go on knowing spiritual and divine things accordingly as they go purifying their minds with faith and with love and with union with God. First they know them confusedly, and afterwards less confusedly, and so by little and little they go advancing in the knowledge of them, until such time as they arrive unto such pass, as they come to know God and the things that are God's in that manner which may be in this present life. And hence, so I understand, it proceeds that that thing which a person without the Spirit holds for holy and just and good in the things of God, another person who hath the Spirit condemns and reputes defective and evil. . . . Going on thus from one step to another, the clearness of that judgment increases which spiritual persons have of divine matters . . . no less than that of the blind man who begins to recover the sight of his eyes, when in the things which he begins to see he forms his conceptions according to that which they appeared unto him at the first, not expecting to see them better and more clearly.

~ JUAN DE VALDES

November 19

The mouth of the righteous is a fountain of life,
but violence overwhelms the mouth of the wicked.
PROVERBS 10:11

A fool's mouth is his undoing, and his lips are a snare to his soul.
PROVERBS 18:7

No sinful word, nor deed of wrong,
Nor thoughts that idly rove;
But simple truth be on our tongue,
And in our hearts be love.
ST. AMBROSE

The Wise Man observes that there is a time to speak and a time to keep silence. One meets with people in the world who seem never to have made the last of these observations. And yet these great talkers do not at all speak from their having anything to say, as every sentence shows, but only from their inclination to be talking. Their conversation is merely an exercise of the tongue: no other human faculty has any share in it. It is strange these persons can help reflecting that unless they have in truth a superior capacity, and are in an extraordinary manner furnished for conversation, if they are entertaining, they are entertaining at their own expense. Is it possible that it should never come into people's thoughts to suspect whether or no it be to their advantage to show so very much of themselves? Oh that you would altogether hold your peace, and it should be your wisdom! Remember likewise that there are persons who love fewer words, an inoffensive sort of people, and who deserve some regard, though of too still and composed tempers for you. . . .

~ JOSEPH BUTLER

November 20

But hope that is seen is no hope at all. Who hopes for what he already
has? But if we hope for what we do not yet have, we wait for it patiently.
ROMANS 8:24-25

"Hope" is the thing with feathers—
That perches in the soul—
And sings the tune without the words—
And never stops—at alló.
EMILY DICKINSON

Patience endues her scholars with content of mind, and evenness of temper, preventing all repining grumbling, and impatient desires, and inordinate affections; disappointments here are no crosses, and all anxious thoughts are disarmed of their sting; in her habitations dwell quietness, submission, and long-suffering, all fierce turbulent inclinations are hereby allayed. The eyes of the patient fixedly wait the inward power of God's providence, and they are thereby mightily enabled towards their salvation and preservation.

~ THOMAS TRYON

November 21

As the deer pants for streams of water, so my soul pants for you,
O God. My soul thirsts for God, the living God.
PSALMS 42:1-2

"It is written, 'Man does not live on bread alone, but on every word that
comes from the mouth of God.'"
MATTHEW 4:4

Tamely, frail body, abstain today; today
My soul eats twice, Christ hither and away.
JOHN DONNE

We need or think we need a thousand things we could very well do without, and there are a thousand people importuning us to spend our money on them—thrusting them into our very hands on the most tempting terms. Plainly there are many people who find the temptation to spend so strong that they simply cannot keep their money in their pockets. It is drawn from them as by an irresistible attraction. They have no bad conscience about it, but they just do not know where it goes. It goes on dress, on traveling, on trinkets, on personal adornments, and indulgence of every kind . . . But the true moral of this is . . . that it is not the way to become rich toward God.

~ JAMES DENNEY

Is that beast better, that hath two or three mountains to graze on, than a little bee, that feeds on dew or manna, and lives, upon what falls every morning from the storehouse of heaven, clouds, and providence?

~ JEREMY TAYLOR

November 22

"And when you pray, do not keep on babbling, like pagans, for they think
they will be heard because of their many words. Do not be like them, for
your Father knows what you need before you ask him."
MATTHEW 6:7-8

> *. . . Must helpless man, in ignorance sedate,*
> *Roll darling down the torrent of his fate?*
> *Must no dislike alarm, no wishes rise,*
> *No cries invoke the mercies of the skies?*
> *Inquirer, cease; petitions yet remain,*
> *Which Heaven may hear, nor deem religion vain.*
> *Still raise for good the supplicating voice,*
> *But leave to Heaven the measure and the choice.*
> *Safe in His power, whose eyes discern afar*
> *The secret ambush of a specious prayer.*
> *Implore His aid, in His decisions rest,*
> *Secure, whate'er He gives, He gives the best . . .*
> SAMUEL JOHNSON

As soon as we are with God in faith and in love, we are in prayer.
~ FENELON

That prayer which does not succeed in moderating our wish, in changing the passionate desire into still submission, the anxious, tumultuous expectation into silent surrender is no true prayer, and proves that we have not the spirit of true prayer. That life is most holy in which there is least of petition and desire, and most of waiting upon God; that in which petition most often passes into thanksgiving. Pray till prayer makes you forget your own wish, and leave it or merge it in God's will. The Divine wisdom has given us prayer, not as a means whereby to obtain the good things of earth, but as a means whereby we learn to do without them; not as a means whereby we escape evil, but as a means whereby we become strong to meet it.
~ F. W. ROBERTSON

November 23

> *Blessed is the man who finds wisdom,*
> *the man who gains understanding,*
> *for she is more profitable than silver and*
> *yields better returns than gold.*
> PROVERBS 3:13-14

> *O World, thou choosest not the better part!*
> *It is not wisdom to be only wise,*
> *And on the inward vision close the eyes,*
> *But it is wisdom to believe the heart.*
> GEORGE SANTAYANA

To be ignorant of one's ignorance is the malady of the ignorant.
~ AMOS BRONSON ALCOTT

Where there is charity and wisdom, there is neither fear nor ignorance.
Where there is patience and humility, there is neither anger nor vexation.
Where there is poverty and joy, there is neither greed nor avarice.
Where there is peace and meditation, there is neither anxiety nor doubt.
~ ST. FRANCIS OF ASSISI

Father in heaven! Thou dost speak to man in many ways; thou to whom alone belongeth wisdom and understanding yet desirest theyself to be understood by man. Even when thou art silent, still thou speakest to him

. . . so that in thy silence as in thy word thou art still the same Father and that it is still the same paternal love that thou guidest by thy voice and that thou dost instruct by thy silence.

~ SØREN KIERKEGAARD

November 24

Be strong and take heart, all you who hope in the Lord.
PSALMS 31:24

"Do not let your hearts be troubled and do not be afraid."
JOHN 14:27

In heavenly love abiding,
No change my heart shall fear
And safe is such confiding,
For nothing changes here.
A. L. WARING

The devout soul is always safe in every state, if it makes everything an occasion either of rising up, or falling down into the hands of God, and exercising faith, and trust, and resignation to Him. The pious soul, that eyes only God, that means nothing but being His alone, can have no stop put to its progress; light and darkness equally assist him: in the light he looks up to God, in the darkness he lays hold on God, and so they both do him the same good.

~ WILLIAM LAW

Oh, my friend, look not out at what stands in the way; what if it look dreadfully as a lion, is not the Lord stronger than the mountains of prey? but look in, where the law of life is written, and the will of the Lord revealed, that thou mayest know what is the Lord's will concerning thee.

~ I. PENINGTON

November 25

Be strong and courageous. Do not be afraid or
terrified because of them, for the Lord your God goes with you;
he will never leave you nor forsake you.
DEUTERONOMY 31:6

My soul there is a country
Far beyond the stars,
Where stands a winged sentry
All skillful in the wars.
There, above the noise and danger,
Sweet Peace sit crowned with smiles,
And One born in a manger
Commands the beauteous files.
. . . Leave then thy foolish ranges;
For none can thee secure
But One who never changes,
Thy God, thy life, thy cure.
HENRY VAUGHAN

The lessons of the moral sentiment are, once for all, an emancipation from that anxiety which takes the joy out of all life. It teaches a great peace. It comes itself from the highest place. It is that, which being in all sound natures, and strongest in the best and most gifted men, we know to be implanted by the Creator of men. It is a commandment at every moment, and in every condition of life, to do the duty of that moment, and to abstain from doing the wrong.

~ RALPH WALDO EMERSON

November 26

"I am with you and will watch over you wherever you go."
GENESIS 28:15

. . . he will watch over your life; the Lord will watch over your coming and going, both now and forevermore.
PSALMS 121:7-8

I never spoke with God
Nor visited in Heaven—
Yet certain am I of the spot
As if the Checks were given . . .
EMILY DICKINSON

What a strength and spring of life, what hope and trust, what glad, unresting energy, is in this one thought—to serve Him who is "my Lord," ever near me, ever looking on; seeing my intentions before He beholds my failures; knowing my desires before He sees my faults; cheering me to endeavour greater things, and yet accepting the least; inviting my poor service, and yet, above all, content with my poorer love. Let us try to realize this, whatsoever, wheresoever we be. The humblest and the simplest, the weakest and the most encumbered, may love Him not less than the busiest and strongest, the most gifted and laborious. If our heart be clear before Him; if He be to us our chief and sovereign choice, dear above all, and beyond all desired; then all else matters little. That which concerneth us He will perfect in stillness and in power.

~ H. E. MANNING

November 27

I was pushed back and about to fall, but the Lord helped me.
The Lord is my strength and my song; he has become my salvation.
PSALMS 118:13-14

Christ, be with me, Christ before me, Christ behind me,
Christ in me, Christ beneath me, Christ above me,
Christ on my right, Christ on my left,
Christ where I lie, Christ where I sit, Christ where I arise . . .
Salvation is of the Lord,
Salvation is of the Lord,
Salvation is of the Christ,
May your salvation, O Lord, be ever with us.
ST. PATRICK

Dear Jesus, as a hen covers her chicks with her wings to keep them safe, do thou this dark night protect us under your golden wings.

~ PRAYER FROM INDIA

O God, who has been the refuge of my fathers through many generations, be my refuge today in every time and circumstance of need. Be my guide through all that is dark and doubtful. Be my guard against all that threatens my spirit's welfare. Be my strength in time of testing. Gladden my heart with thy peace; through Jesus Christ my Lord.

~ JOHN BAILLIE

November 28

. . . our God gives light to our eyes and
a little relief in our bondage . . . He has shown us kindness.
EZRA 9:9

. . . I have drawn you with loving-kindness.
I will build you up again and you will be rebuilt.
JEREMIAH 31:3-4

The heart benevolent and kind
The most resembles God.
ROBERT BURNS

What wisdom can you find that is greater than kindness?

~ JEAN JACQUES ROUSSEAU

If ever human love was tender, and self-sacrificing, and devoted; if ever it could bear and forbear; if ever it could suffer gladly for its loved ones; if ever it was willing to pour itself out in a lavish abandonment for the comfort or pleasure of its objects; then infinitely more is Divine love tender, and self-sacrificing, and devoted, and glad to bear and forbear, and to suffer, and to lavish its best of gifts and blessings upon the objects of its love. Put together all the tenderest love you know of, the deepest you have ever felt, and the strongest that has ever been poured out upon you, and heap upon it all the love of all the loving human hearts in the world, and then multiply it by infinity, and you will begin, perhaps, to have some faint glimpse of what the love of God is.

~ H. W. S.

November 29

He chose David his servant and took him from the sheep pens;
from tending the sheep he brought him to be the shepherd of his people . . .
And David shepherded them with integrity of heart;
with skillful hands he led them.
PSALMS 78:70-72

Love bade me welcome; yet my soul drew back,
Guilty of dust and sin.
But quick-eyed Love, observing me grow slack
From my first entrance in,
Drew nearer to me, sweetly questioning

If I lack'd anything.

"A guest," I answer'd, "worthy to be here."
Love said, "You shall be he."
"I, the unkind, ungrateful? Ah, my dear,
I cannot look on Thee."
Love took my hand and smiling did reply,
"Who made the eyes but I?"

"Truth, Lord, but I have marr'd them: let my shame
Go where it doth deserve."
"And know you not," says Love, "Who bore the blame?"
"My dear, then I will serve."
"You must sit down," says Love, "and taste my meat."
So I did sit and eat.
GEORGE HERBERT

Love taketh up no malign elements; its spirit prompteth it to cover in mercy all things that ought not to be exposed, to believe all of good that can be believed, to hope all things that a good God makes possible, and to endure all things that the hope may be made good.

~ J. H. THOM

November 30

Why are you downcast, O my soul?
Why so disturbed within me? Put your hope in God . . .
PSALMS 42:5

We are hard-pressed on every side,
but not crushed; perplexed, but not in despair . . .
2 CORINTHIANS 4:8

OH my soul, why are thou vexed?
Let things go e'en as they will;
Though to thee they seem perplexed,
Yet His order they fulfil.
A. H. FRANCKE

The vexation, restlessness, and impatience which small trials cause, arise wholly from our ignorance and want of self-control. We may be thwarted and troubled, it is true, but these things put us into a condition for exercising patience and meek submission, and the self-abnegation wherein alone the fullness of God is to be found.

~ DE RENTY

The Will can only be made submissive by frequent self-denials, which must keep in subjection its sallies and inclinations. Great weakness is often produced by indulgences which seem of no importance.

~ M. MOLINOS

Hard words will vex; unkindness will pierce; neglect will wound; threatened evils will make the soul quiver; sharp pain or weariness will rack the body, or make it restless. But what says the Psalmist? "When my heart is vexed, I will complain." To whom? Not of God, but to God.

~ E. B. PUSEY

213

Above all, love each other deeply, because love covers over a multitude of sins. Offer hospitality to one another without grumbling.
1 PETER 4:8-9

If you want to live in the kind of a town
That's the kind of a town you like,
You needn't slip your clothes in a grip
And start on a long, long hike.

You'll find elsewhere what you left behind,
For there's nothing that's really new.
It's a knock at yourself when you knock your town;
It isn't your town—it's you.

Real towns are not made by men afraid
Lest somebody else gets ahead.
When everybody works and nobody shirks
You can raise a town from the dead.

And if while you make your stake
Your neighbor can make one, too,
Your town will be what you want to see,
It isn't your town—it's you.
R.W. GLOVER

If, on hearing of the fall of a brother, however differing or severed from us, we feel the least inclination to linger over it, instead of hiding it in grief and shame, or veiling it in the love which covereth a multitude of sins; if, in seeing a joy or a grace or an effective service given to others, we do not rejoice, but feel depressed, let us be very watchful; the most diabolical of passions may mask itself as humility, or zeal for the glory of God.
~ ELIZABETH CHARLES

You, therefore, have no excuse, you who pass judgment on someone else, for at whatever point you judge the other, you are condemning yourself, because you who pass judgment do the same things.
ROMANS 2:1

If I knew you and you knew me—
If both of us could clearly see,
And with an inner sight divine
The meaning of your heart and mine—
I'm sure that we would differ less
And clasp our hands in friendliness;
Our thoughts would pleasantly agree
If I knew you, and you knew me.

If I knew you and you knew me,
As each one knows his own self, we
Could look each other in the face
And see therein a truer grace.
Life has so many hidden woes,

So many thorns for every rose;
The "why" of things our hearts would see,
If I knew you and you knew me.

NIXON WATERMAN

Know that when unhappily thou thinkest any evil of thy brother, some root of that same evil is in thine own heart which, in proportion as it is ill disposed, readily receives any like object which it meets with. Therefore whenever it comes into thy mind to judge others for some fault, be wroth against thyself as guilty of the same, and say in thine heart, "How is it that I, wretched being, buried in this and far heavier faults, dare to lift up my head to see and judge the faults of others?" And thus the weapons which, directed against others, would have wounded thee, being used against thyself, will bring healing to thy wounds. . . . And be very sure that all good and kindly feeling towards thy neighbor is the gift of the Holy Spirit; and all contempt, rash judgment, and bitterness towards him comes from thine own evil and from the suggestions of Satan.

~ LORENZO SCUPOLI

December 3

May the God of hope fill you with all joy and
peace as you trust in him, so that you may overflow with
hope by the power of the Holy Spirit.

ROMANS 15:13

I leant upon a coppice gate
When Frost was specter-gray,
And Winter's dregs made desolate
The weakening eye of day.
The tangled bine-stems scored the sky
Like strings of broken lyres,
and all mankind that haunted nigh
Had sought their household fires. . . .

At once a voice arose among
The bleak twigs overhead
In a full-hearted evensong
Of joy illimited;
An aged thrush, frail, gaunt, and small,
In blast-beruffled plume,
Had chosen thus to fling his soul
Upon the growing gloom.

So little cause for carolings
Of such ecstatic sound
Was written on terrestrial things
Afar or nigh around,
That I could think there trembled through
His happy good-night air
Some blessed Hope, whereof he knew
And I was unaware.

THOMAS HARDY

Grovel not in things below, among earthly cares, pleasures, anxieties, toils, if thou wouldst have a good strong hope on high. Lift up thy cares with thy heart to God, if thou wouldst hope in Him. Then see what in thee is most displeasing to God. This it is which holdeth thy hope down. Strike firmly, repeatedly, in the might of God, until it give way. Thy hope will soar at once with thy thanks to God who delivereth thee.

~ E. B. PUSEY

December 4

Be strong and courageous. Do not be afraid or discouraged.
1 CHRONICLES 22:13

Let me do my work each day;
And if the darkened hours of despair overcome me,
May I not forget the strength that comforted me
In the desolation of other times.
May I still remember the bright hours that found me
Walking over the silent hills of my childhood,
Or dreaming on the margin of the quiet river,
When a light glowed within me,
And I promised my early God to have courage
Amid the tempests of the changing years. . . .
MAX EHRMANN

Never let us be discouraged with ourselves; it is not when we are conscious of our faults that we are the most wicked; on the contrary we are then less so. We see by a brighter light; and let us remember for our consolation that we never perceive our sins till we begin to cure them. We must neither flatter nor be impatient with ourselves in the correction of our faults. Despondency is not a state of humility; on the contrary, it is the vexation and despair of a cowardly pride—nothing is worse; whether we stumble or whether we fall, we must think only of rising again and going on in our course. Our faults may be useful to us, if they cure us of a vain confidence in ourselves, and do not deprive us of a humble and salutary confidence in God. Let us bless God with as true thankfulness if He have enabled us to make any progress in virtue as if we had made it through our own strength, and let us not be troubled with the weak agitations of self-love; let them pass; do not think of them. God never makes us feel our weakness but that we may be led to seek strength from Him. What is involuntary should not trouble us; but the great thing is never to act against the light within us, and to desire to follow where God would lead us.

~ FENELON

December 5

May our Lord Jesus Christ himself and God our Father,
who loved us and by his grace gave us eternal encouragement and
good hope, encourage your hearts and strengthen you in every
good deed and word.
THESSALONIANS 2:16

. . . Only Thou art above, and when towards Thee
By Thy leave I can look, I rise again;
But our old subtle foe so tempteth me

That not one hour myself I can sustain;
Thy grace may wing me to prevent his art,
And thou like adamant draw mine iron heart.

JOHN DONNE

Grace strikes us when we are in great pain and restlessness. . . .
Sometimes at that moment a wave of light breaks into our darkness, and
it is as though a voice were saying: "You are accepted."

~ PAUL TILLICH

Take steadily some one sin, which seems to stand out before thee, to root
it out, by God's grace, and every fiber of it. Purpose strongly, by the grace
and strength of God, wholly to sacrifice this sin or sinful inclination to the
love of God, to spare it not, until thou leave of it none remaining, neither
root nor branch. Fix, by God's help, not only to root out this sin, but to set
thyself to gain, by that same help, the opposite grace. If thou art tempted
to be angry, try hard, by God's grace, to be very meek; if to be proud, seek
to be very humble.

~ E. B. PUSEY

December 6

. . . for the Lord will be your confidence and
will keep your foot from being snared.

PROVERBS 3:26

Though I may stumble, I may fall,
My weakness is His strength;
No one is lost who hears His call:
His grace, my recompense.

E.C.M.

Faults may be useful to us, if they cure us of a vain confidence in ourselves, and do not deprive us of a humble and salutary confidence in God.
Let us bless God with as true thankfulness if He have enabled us to make
any progress in virtue as if we had made it through our own strength, and
let us not be troubled with the weak agitations of self-love; let them pass;
do not think of them. God never makes us feel our weakness but that we
may be led to seek strength from Him. What is involuntary should not
trouble us; but the great thing is never to act against the light within us,
and to desire to follow where God would lead us.

~ FENELON

He has kept and folded us from ten thousand ills when we did not know
it: in the midst of our security we should have perished every hour, but
that He sheltered us "from the terror by night and from the arrow that flieth by day"—from the powers of evil that walk in darkness, from snares of
our own evil will. He has kept us even against ourselves, and saved us
even from our own undoing. . . .

~ H. E. MANNING

December 7

"If you really knew me, you would know my Father as well."
JOHN 14:7

*"Now we can see that you know all things and that you do
not even need to have anyone ask you questions. This makes us
believe that you came from God."*
JOHN 16:30

*Unite, My roving thoughts, unite
In silence soft and sweet;
And thou, my soul, sit gently down
At thy great Sovereign's feet.*
P. DODDRIDGE

Almost all men are slaves: they are mastered by foolish ambitions, vile
appetites, jealousies, prejudices, the conventions and opinions of other
men. These things obsess them, so that they cannot see anything in its
right perspective. For most men the world is centered in self, which is misery: to have one's world centered in God is the peace that passeth understanding.

~ DONALD HANKEY

My wants seem to be gradually narrowing down, my personal wants, I
mean, and I often think I could be quite content in the Poor-house! I do
not know whether this is piety or old age, or a little of each mixed together, but honestly the world and our life in it does seem of too little account
to be worth making the least fuss over, when one has such a magnificent
prospect close at hand ahead of one; and I am tremendously content to let
one activity after another go, and to await quietly and happily the opening
of the door at the end of the passage way, that will let me in to my real
abiding place. So you may think of me as happy and contented, surrounded with unnumbered blessings, and delighted to be seventy-one years old.

~ MRS. PEARSALL SMITH

December 8

Blessed are all who take refuge in him.
PSALMS 2:12

*Blessed is the man who perseveres under trial, because when he has stood
the test, he will receive the crown of life . . .*
JAMES 1:12

*How oft in this great city's din
Have I, my Savior, let you in?
Nor stopped nor paused amidst the fray
too busy e'er to kneel and pray.
But from my garden nature sings
Awake, my soul! remembering,
in chorus to join with the rest,
to thank God for His blessedness.*
E. C. M.

Yes! blessed are those holy hours in which the soul retires from the world to be alone with God. God's voice, as Himself, is everywhere. Within and without, He speaks to our souls, if we would hear. Only the din of the world, or the tumult of our own hearts, deafens our inward ear to it. Learn to commune with Him in stillness, and He, whom thou hast sought in stillness, will be with thee when thou goest abroad.

~ E. B. PUSEY

The elements of happiness in this present life no man can command, even if he could command himself, for they depend on the action of many wills, on the purity of many hearts, and by the highest law of God the holiest must ever bear the sins and sorrows of the rest; but over the blessedness of his own spirit circumstance need have no control; God has therein given an unlimited power to the means of preservation, of grace and growth, at every man's command.

~ J. H. THOM

December 9

For with much wisdom comes much sorrow;
the more knowledge, the more grief.
ECCLESIASTES 1:18

I walked a mile with Pleasure;
She chattered all the way,
But left me none the wiser
For all she had to say.

I walked a mile with Sorrow
And ne'er a word said she;
But oh, the things I learned from her
When Sorrow walked with me!
ROBERT BROWNING HAMILTON

. . . for affliction is a treasure, and scarce any man has enough of it. No man hath affliction enough that is not matured and ripened by it, and made fit for God by that affliction. If a man carry treasure in bullion, or in a wedge of gold, and have none coined into current money, his treasure will not defray him as he travels. Tribulation is treasure in the nature of it, but it is not current money in the use of it, except as we get nearer and nearer our home, heaven, by it. Another man may be sick too, and sick to death, and this affliction may lie in his bowels, as gold in a mine, and be of no use to him; but this bell, that tells me of his affliction, digs out and applies that gold to m if by this consideration of another's danger I take mine own into contemplation, and so secure myself, by making my recourse to my God, who is our only security.

~ JOHN DONNE

December 10

He who heeds discipline shows the way to life,
but whoever ignores correction leads others astray.
PROVERBS 10:17

Endure hardship as discipline; God is treating you as sons. For what son is not disciplined by his father? . . . How much more should we submit to the Father of our spirits and live!
HEBREWS 12:7-9

Be not o'ermastered by thy pain,
But cling to God, thou shalt not fall.
The floods sweep over thee in vain,
Thou yet shalt rise above them all
For when thy trial seems too hard to bear,
Lo! God, thy King, hath granted all thy prayer.
Be thou content.
P. GERHARDT

Be not afraid of these trials which God may see fit to send upon thee. It is with the wind and storm of tribulation that God separates the true wheat from the chaff. Always remember, therefore, that God comes to thee in thy sorrows, as really as in thy joys. He lays low, and He builds up. Thou wilt find thyself far from perfection, if thou dost not find God in everything.

~ M. MOLINOS

Be not troubled; for if troubles abound, and there be tossing, and storms, and tempests, and no peace, nor anything visible left to support; yet, lie still, and sink beneath, till a secret hope stir, which will stay the heart in the midst of all these; until the Lord administer comfort, who knows how and what relief to give to the weary traveler, that knows not where it is, nor which way to look, nor where to expect a path.

~ I. PENINGTON

December 11

. . . any of you who does not give up everything he has cannot be my disciple.
LUKE 14:33

Set your minds on things above, not on earthly things.
COLOSSIANS 3:2

Yield to the Lord, with simple heart,
All that thou hast, and all thou art:
Renounce all strength, but strength divine,
And peace shall be for ever thine.
ANONYMOUS

Offer up to God all pure affections, desires, regrets, and all the bonds which link us to home, kindred, and friends, together with all our works, purposes, and labors. These things, which are not only lawful, but sacred, become then the matter of thanksgiving and oblation. Memories, plans for the future, wishes, intentions; works just begun, half done, all but completed; emotions, sympathies, affections—all these things throng tumultuously and dangerously in the heart and will. The only way to master them is to offer them up to Him, as once ours, under Him, always His by right.

~ H. E. MANNING

December 12

I desire to do your will, O my God, your law is within my heart.
PALMS 40:8

Sing and make music in your heart to the Lord,
always giving thanks to God the Father for everything,
in the name of our Lord Jesus Christ.
EPHESIANS 5:19-20

Thou that hast given so much to me,
Give one thing more, a grateful heart.
Not thankful when it pleaseth me,
As if thy blessings had spare days;
But such a heart, whose pulse may be
Thy praise.
GEORGE HERBERT

That piety which sanctifies us, and which is a true devotion to God, consists in doing all His will precisely at the time, in the situation, and under the circumstances, in which He has placed us. Perfect devotedness requires, not only that we do the will of God, but that we do it with love. God would have us serve Him with delight; it is our hearts that He asks of us.

~ FENELON

Devotion is really neither more nor less than a general inclination and readiness to do that which we know to be acceptable to God. . . . To be truly devout, we must not only do God's will, but we must do it cheerfully.

~ FRANCIS DE SALES

Resignation to the Divine Will signifies a cheerful approbation and thankful acceptance of everything that comes from God. . . .

~ WILLIAM LAW

December 13

I have learned the secret of being content in any and every situation,
whether well fed or hungry, whether living in plenty or in want. I can do
everything through him who gives me strength.
PHILIPPIANS 4:12-13

I am content with what I have,
Little be it or much:
And, Lord, contentment still I crave,
Because thou savest such.
JOHN BUNYAN

Every day let us renew the consecration to God's service; every day let us, in His strength, pledge ourselves afresh to do His will, even in the veriest trifle, and to turn aside from anything that may displease Him. . . . He does not bid us bear the burdens of to-morrow, next week, or next year. Every day we are to come to Him in simple obedience and faith, asking help to keep us, and aid us through that day's work; and to-morrow, and to-morrow, and to-morrow, through years of long tomorrows, it will be but the same thing to do; leaving the future always in God's hands, sure that He can care for it better than we. Blessed trust! that can thus confidingly say, "This hour is mine with its present duty; the next is God's, and when it comes, His presence will come with it."

~ ANONYMOUS

December 14

And what does the Lord require of you? To act justly and to love mercy and to walk humbly with your God.
MICAH 6:8

. . . To love life and men as God loves them . . . to obey the order when it is given and never look back—then he can use you—then, perhaps, he will use you. And if he doesn't use you—what matter. In his hand, every moment has its meaning, its greatness, its glory, its peace, its co-inherence.
DAG HAMMARSKJÖLD

Begin at once; before you venture away from this quiet moment, ask your King to take you wholly into His service, and place all the hours of this day quite simply at His disposal, and ask Him to make and keep you ready to do just exactly what He appoints. Never mind about to-morrow; one day at a time is enough. Try it to-day, and see if it is not a day of strange, almost curious peace, so sweet that you will be only too thankful, when to-morrow comes, to ask Him to take it also—till it will become a blessed habit to hold yourself simply and "wholly at Thy commandment for any manner of service." The "whatsoever" is not necessarily active work. It may be waiting (whether half an hour or half a lifetime), learning, suffering, sitting still. But shall we be less ready for these, if any of them are His appointments for to-day? Let us ask Him to prepare us for all that He is preparing for us.

~ F. R. HAVERGAL

December 15

And he will be their peace.
MICAH 5:5

Be at rest once more, O my soul, for the Lord has been good to you.
PSALMS 116:7

. . . Ere I am old, O! let me give
My life to learning how to live;
Then shall I meet with willing heart,
An early summons to depart.
Or find my lengthened days consoled
By God's sweet peace—when I am old.
CAROLINE ATHERTON BRIGGS MASON

As a result of this strong faith, the inner life of Catherine of Genoa was characterized, in a remarkable degree, by what may be termed rest, or quietude; which is only another form of expression for true interior peace. It was not, however, the quietude of a lazy inaction, but the quietude of an inward acquiescence; not a quietude which feels nothing and does nothing, but that higher and divine quietude which exists by feeling and acting in the time and degree of God's appointment and God's will. It was a principle in her conduct, to give herself to God in the discharge of duty; and to leave all results without solicitude in His hands.

~ T. C. UPHAM

December 16

If I have the gift of prophecy and can fathom all mysteries and all knowledge, and if I have a faith that can move mountains, but have not love, I am nothing. If I give all I possess to the poor and surrender my body to the flames, but have not love, I gain nothing.

1 CORINTHIANS 13:2-3

What love is this of Thine, that cannot be
In Thine infinity, O Lord, confined,
Unless it in Thy very Person see
Infinity and finity conjoined?
What! hath Thy Godhead, as not satisfied,
Married our manhood, making it its bride?

Oh matchless love! Filling heaven to the brim!
O'errunning it: all running o'er beside
This world! Nay, overflowing hell, wherein,
For Thine elect, there rose a mighty tide!
That there our veins might through Thy Person bleed,
To quench the flames that else would on us feed.

Oh! that Thy love might overflow my heart!
To fire the same with love for love I would.
But oh! my straightened breast! my lifeless spark!
My fireless flame! What chilly love and cold!
In measure small! In manner chilly! See!
Lord, blow the coal: Thy love enflame in me.

EDWARD TAYLOR

If we do a thing because we think it is our duty, we generally fail; that is the old law which makes slaves of us. The real spring of our life, and of our work in life, must be love—true, deep love—not love of this or that person, or for this or that reason, but deep human love, devotion of soul to soul, love of God realized where alone it can be—in love of those whom He loves. Everything else is weak, passes away; that love alone supports us, makes life tolerable, binds the present together with the past and future, and is, we may trust, imperishable.

~ MAX MULLER

December 17

But the fruit of the Spirit is love, joy,
peace, patience, kindness,
goodness, faithfulness, gentleness and self-control.

GALATIANS 5:22

This is to my Father's glory, that you bear much fruit,
showing yourselves to be my disciples.
JOHN 15:8

O BREATH from out the Eternal Silence! blow
Softly upon our spirits' barren ground;
The precious fullness of our God bestow,
That fruits of faith, love, reverence may abound.
G. TERSTEEGEN

Whoever is happy will make others happy too. He who has courage and faith will never perish in misery!

~ ANNE FRANK

We aim at something more sublime and more equitable—the common good, or the community of goods. . . . We demand, we would have, the communal enjoyment of the fruits of the earth, fruits which are for everyone.

~ FRANCOIS NOEL BABEUF, AKA "GRACCHUS"

The happiness of life is made up of minute fractions—the little soon forgotten charities of a kiss or smile, a kind look, a heartfelt compliment, and the countless infinitesimals of pleasurable and genial feeling.

~ SAMUEL TAYLOR COLERIDGE

December 18

There is no fear in love, but perfect love drives out fear.
1 JOHN 4:18

Whoever does not love does not know God,
because God is love.
1 JOHN 4:8

They sin who tell us love can die;
With life all other passions fly,
All others are but vanity.
ROBERT SOUTHEY

Would not the carrying out of one single commandment of Christ, "Love one another," change the whole aspect of the world, and sweep away prisons and workhouses, and envying and strife, and all the strongholds of the devil? Two thousand years have nearly passed, and people have not yet understood that one single command of Christ, "Love one another"!

~ MAX MULLER

Is it possible we should be ignorant whether we feel tempers contrary to love or no?—whether we rejoice always, or are burdened and bowed down with sorrow?—whether we have a praying, or a dead, lifeless spirit?—whether we can praise God, and be resigned in all trials, or feel murmurings, fretfulness, and impatience under them?—is it not easy to know if we feel anger at provocations, or whether we feel our tempers mild, gentle, peaceable, and easy to be entreated, or feel stubbornness, self-will, and pride? whether we have slavish fears, or are possessed of that perfect love which casteth out all fear that hath torment?

~ HESTER ANN ROGERS

December 19

. . . let the wise listen and add to their learning.
PROVERBS 1:5

Hail to thee, blithe spirit!
Bird thou never wert,
That from heaven, or near it,
Pourest thy full heart
In profuse strains of unpremeditated art. . . .

Teach me half the gladness
That thy brain must know,
Such harmonious madness
From my lips would flow,
The world should listen then, as I am listening now.
PERCY BYSSHE SHELLEY

The attention of the listener serves as accompaniment to the music of the discourse. Everyone should be provided with that sort of indulgence, and that readiness to listen, which makes the thoughts of others bloom. It is a bad sort of cleverness which deprives the character of kindness, indulgence, and sympathy, which makes it difficult for us to live and talk with others, to make them pleased with us and pleased with themselves—in a word, to love and be lovable. The gentle mind is patient, gives itself without hurry to the task of understanding, is open to conviction, afraid of obstinacy, and would rather learn than take the lead.

~ JOSEPH JOUBERT

December 20

" . . . do not worry about what to say or how to say it. At that time you
will be given what to say, for it will not be you speaking, but the Spirit of
your Father speaking through you."
MATTHEW 10:19-20

I must speak only what God puts in my mouth.
NUMBERS 22:38

O creator past all telling . . .
You make eloquent the tongues of children.
Then instruct my speech and touch my lips with graciousness.
Make me keen to understand, quick to learn, able to remember;
make me delicate to interpret and ready to speak.
ST. THOMAS AQUINAS

My Lord, I have nothing to do in this world, but to seek and serve thee; I have nothing to do with a heart and its affections, but to breathe after thee; I have nothing to do with my tongue and pen, but to speak to thee, and for thee, and to publish thy glory and thy will.

~ RICHARD BAXTER

Resolved, that I will live so as I shall wish I had done when I come to die.
Resolved, never to speak in narrations anything but the pure and
simple verity.

~ JONATHAN EDWARDS

"There is nothing," says Plato, "so delightful as the hearing or the speaking of truth." For this reason there is no conversation so agreeable as that
of the man of integrity, who hears without any intention to betray, and
speaks without any intention to deceive.

~ JOSEPH ADDISON

December 21

Teach me your way, O Lord, and I will walk in your truth.
PSALMS 86:11

Teach me, my Lord, to further go,
Than I think I am able,
Like Mary who didst bear our Lord,
In nothing but a stable.

When I am weak and cry out "No!"
Teach me, my Lord, to see
That where I think I cannot go,
There waits my God for me.
~ E. C. M.

Ah! Lord Jesus, King of bliss, how shall I be eased? Who shall teach me
and tell me that [thing] me needeth to know, if I may not at this time see
it in Thee?

~ JULIAN OF NORWICH

My Father, teach us not only thy will, but how to do it. Teach us the best
way of doing the best thing, lest we spoil the end by unworthy means.

~ REV. J. H. JOWETT

Teach us to love without wanting to control; to love without limit; to love
you, our friends, and also our enemies. Teach us to be patient in love
when love is not returned; teach us to be patient when even you are apparently far away. Teach us loving, waiting, patience when there is no answer
to our questionings and our doubt.

~ MICHAEL HOLLINGS AND ETTA GULLICK

December 22

Who can discern his errors? Forgive my hidden faults.
PSALMS 19:12

Forgive us our debts, as we also have forgiven our debtors.
And lead us not into temptation, but deliver us from the evil one.
MATTHEW 6:9

The night is come, like to the day,
Depart not Thou, great God, away.

Let not my sins, black as the night,
Eclipse the lustre of Thy light:
Keep still in my horizon; for to me
The sun makes not the day, but Thee.
. . . Howe'er I rest, great God, let me
Awake again at last with Thee;
And thus assured, behold I lie
Securely, or to wake or die.
These are my drowsy days; in vain
I do now wake to sleep again:
O come that hour when I shall never
Sleep again, but wake for ever.

SIR THOMAS BROWNE

There are but two things that we can do against temptations. The first is
to be faithful to the light within us, in avoiding all exposure to temptation
which we are at liberty to avoid. . . . The other is to turn our eyes to God
in the moment of temptation, to throw ourselves immediately upon the
protection of heaven, as a child when in danger flies to the arms of its parent. The habitual conviction of the presence of God is the sovereign remedy; it supports, it consoles, it calms us. We must not be surprised that we
are tempted. We are placed here to be proved by temptations. . . but Jesus
Christ combats with us. We must let temptations, like a tempest, beat
upon our heads, and stiff move on; like a traveler surprised on the way by
a storm, who wraps his cloak about him, and goes on his journey in spite
of the opposing elements.

In a certain sense, there is little to do in doing the will of God. Still it
is true that it is a great work, because it must be without any reserve. His
Spirit enters the secret folding of our hearts, and even the most upright
affections and the most necessary attachments must be regulated by His
will; but it is not the multitude of hard duties, it is not the constraint and
contention, that advances us on our course. On the contrary it is the
yielding of our wills without restriction to tread cheerfully every day in the
path in which Providence leads us; to seek nothing, to be discouraged by
nothing, to see our duty in the present moment, to trust all else without
reserve to the will and power of God.

~ FENELON

December 23

Endure hardship with us like a good soldier of Christ Jesus.
2 TIMOTHY 2:3

Where our Captain bids us go,
'Tis not ours to murmur, 'No'.
He that gives the sword and shield,
Chooses too the battle-field
On which we are to fight the foe.

ANONYMOUS

Soldiers of the cross, it is not for us, but for our Leader and our Lord, to
choose the field; it is ours, taking the station which He assigns, to make it
the field of truth and honor, though it be the field of death.

~ J. MARTINEAU

As soon as we lay ourselves entirely at His feet, we have enough light given us to guide our own steps; as the foot-soldier, who hears nothing of the councils that determine the course of the great battle he is in, hears plainly enough the word of command which he must himself obey.

~ GEORGE ELIOT

Here on earth we are as soldiers, fighting in a foreign land, that understand not the plan of the campaign, and have no need to understand it; seeing well what is at our hand to be done. Let us do it like soldiers, with submission, with courage, with a heroic joy.

~ THOMAS CARLYLE

December 24

. . . joyfully giving thanks to the Father, who has qualified you to share in the inheritance of the saints in the kingdom of light.
COLOSSIANS 1:12

Give thanks to the Lord, for he is good; his love endures forever.
PSALMS 118:29

Let those refuse to sing
Who never knew the Lord;
To Heav'n my thanks will ring
In voiced harmonious chord!
E. C. M.

The feast which Levi gave to our Lord on his conversion is such a cheerful type to me of the Christian life. It is a festival of joy and gratitude for a conversion. We are sinners forgiven; there is a reason for perpetual praise. A feast represents a forgiven sinner's whole course; he is welcomed home, and he has brought more joy to heaven than there was before. His sorrow for sin is not a mortified, humiliated, angry disgust with himself. It is a humble, hopeful sorrow, always "turning into joy." So if his very sorrows are the material of joy, his life may be represented by the feast which Levi the Publican gave to our Lord, who had forgiven and called him. . . . our life ought to be full of the joy of grateful love; the remembrance of sin means the remembrance of the love that called us out of our sins and forgave us the whole debt. And besides, Levi made Him a great feast. It is not that we are to be cheerful for our own gratification, but our life is to be full of praise and thanksgiving, singing and making melody in our hearts to the Lord, for the honor of Jesus. Levi made Him a feast. Our habitual joy is due to God, and honors God; and our joy means not a reflection of the joy of God, but is the very joy of God. . . . If we are sinners forgiven, we ought to behave as forgiven, welcomed home, crowned with wonderful love in Christ, and so cheer and encourage all about us, who often go heavily because we reflect our gloom upon them instead of our grateful love, hope, confidence.

~ FATHER CONGREVE

"Do not be afraid. I bring you good news of great joy that will be for all the people. Today in the town of David a Savior has been born to you; he is Christ the Lord."

LUKE 1:10-11

This is the month, and this the happy morn,
Wherein the Son of Heav'n's eternal King,
Of wedded maid and virgin mother born,
Our great redemption from above did bring;
For so the holy sages once did sing,
That He our deadly forfeit should release,
And with His Father work us a perpetual peace.

JOHN MILTON

. . . Christ believed it possible to bind men to their kind, but on one condition—that they were first bound fast to Himself. He stood forth as the representative of men, He identified Himself with the cause and with the interests of all human beings, He was destined, as He began before long obscurely to intimate, to lay down His life for them. Few of us sympathize originally and directly with this devotion; few of us can perceive in human nature itself any merit sufficient to evoke it. But it is not so hard to love and venerate Him who felt it. So vast a passion of love, a devotion so comprehensive, has not elsewhere been in any degree approached, save by some of His imitators. And as love provokes love, many have found it possible to conceive for Christ an attachment the closeness of which no words can describe, a veneration so possessing and absorbing the man within them, that they have said "I live no more, but Christ lives in me." Now such a feeling carries with it of necessity the feeling of love for all human beings. It matters no longer what quality men may exhibit; amiable or unamiable, as the brothers of Christ, as belonging to His sacred and consecrated kind, as the objects of His love in life and death, they must be dear to all to whom He is dear.

~ SIR JOHN SEELEY

He that forgets his friend is ungrateful unto him: but he that forgets his Savior is unmerciful unto himself.

~ JOHN BUNYAN

Let the peace of Christ rule in your hearts,
since as members of one body you were called to peace.

COLOSSIANS 3:15

For God was pleased to have all his fullness dwell in him,
and through him to reconcile to himself all things,
whether things on earth or things in heaven,
by making peace through his blood, shed on the cross.

COLOSSIANS 1:19-20

What comforts, Lord, to those are given,
Who seek in Thee their home and rest!

They find on earth an opening heaven,
And in Thy peace are amply blest.
W. C. DESSLER

I do so earnestly call upon you to learn the true and proper definition of Christ out of these words of Paul, "which gave Himself for our sins." If He gave Himself to death for our sins, then undoubtedly He is no tyrant or judge which will condemn us for our sins. He is no caster-down of the afflicted, but a raiser-up of those that are fallen, a merciful reliever and comforter of the heavy and the broken-hearted. Else should Paul lie in saying, "which gave Himself for our sins." If I define Christ thus, I define Him rightly, and take hold of the true Christ, and possess Him indeed. And here I let pass all curious speculations touching the divine majesty, and stay myself in the humanity of Christ, and so I learn truly to know the will of God. Here is then no fear, but altogether sweetness, joy, peace of conscience, and suchlike. And herewithal there is a light opened, which showeth me the true knowledge of God, of myself, of all creatures, and of all the iniquity of the devil's kingdom. We teach no new thing, but we repeat and establish old things, which the apostles and all godly teachers have taught us. And would to God we could so teach and establish them that we might not only have them in our mouth, but also well grounded in the bottom of our heart, and especially that we might be able to use them in the agony and conflict of death.

~ MARTIN LUTHER

December 27

As a father has compassion on his children,
so the Lord has compassion on those who fear him . . .
PSALMS 103:13

So you are no longer a slave, but a son;
and since you are a son,
God has made you also an heir.
GALATIANS 4:7

Not by the terrors of a slave
God's sons perform His will,
But with the noblest powers they have
His sweet commands fulfill.
ISAAC WATTS

God hath provided a sweet and quiet life for His children, could they improve and use it; a calm and firm conviction in all the storms and troubles that are about them, however things go, to find content, and be careful for nothing.

~ R. LEIGHTON

Grant us, O Lord, we beseech Thee, always to seek Thy kingdom and righteousness, and of whatsoever Thou seest us to stand in need, mercifully grant us an abundant portion. Amen.

Be content to be a child, and let the Father proportion out daily to thee
what light, what power, what exercises, what straits, what fears, what
troubles He sees fit for thee.

~ I. PENINGTON

Aim to be ever this little child, contented with what the Father gives of
pleasure or of play; and when restrained from pleasure or from play, and
led for a season into the chamber of sorrow, rest quiet on His bosom, and
be patient, and smile, as one who is nestled in a sweet and secure asylum.

~ ANONYMOUS

December 28

So, firm in steadfast hope, in thought secure,
in full accord to all Thy world of joy,
May I be nerved to labors high and pure,
And thou Thy child to do Thy work employ.
J. STERLING

The return from your work must be the satisfaction which that work
brings you and the world's need of that work. With this life is heaven, or
as near heaven as you can get.

~ W. E. B. DUBOIS

Be with God in thy outward works, refer them to Him, offer them to Him,
seek to do them in Him and for Him, and He will be with thee in them,
and they shall not hinder, but rather invite His presence in thy soul. Seek
to see Him in all things, and in all things He will come nigh to thee.

~ E. B. PUSEY

Do everything for God, uniting yourself to Him by a mere upward glance,
or by the overflowing of your heart towards Him. Never be in a hurry; do
everything quietly and in a calm spirit.

~ FRANCIS DE SALES

December 29

Finally brothers, whatever is true, whatever is noble, whatever is right,
whatever is pure, whatever is lovely, whatever is admirable—if anything is
excellent or praiseworthy—think about such things.
PHILIPPIANS 4:8

Love thyself last: cherish those hearts that hate thee;
Corruption wins not more than honesty.
Still in thy right hand carry gentle peace,
To silence envious tongues: be just, and fear not.
Let all the ends thou aim'st at be thy country's, Thy God's, and truth's . . .
WILLIAM SHAKESPEARE,

Truth does not, and cannot, come from ourselves. In all that is spiritual it
comes from God, or from those spirits, the friends of God, on whom His

light has shone; in what is material, from the things where God has placed it. Therefore in all that is spiritual we must first take counsel of God, then of the wise, and lastly of our own souls; and in all that is material we must search things to their depths.

~ JOSEPH JOUBERT

Strive to see God in all things without exception . . .

~ FRANCIS DE SALES

. . . [There] was a moment when we were in harmony with all around, reconciled to ourselves and to our God; when we sympathized with all that was pure, all that was beautiful, all that was lovely. This was not stagnation, it was fullness of life—life in its most expanded form, such as nature witnessed in her first hour. This is life in that form of benevolence which expands into the mind of Christ. And when this is working in the soul, it is marvelous how it distils into a man's words and countenance. . .

~F.W. ROBERTSON

December 30

Be joyful always, pray continually, give thanks in all circumstances, for this is God's will for you in Christ Jesus.
1 THESSALONIANS 5:16-18

As you have heard from the beginning, his command is that you walk in love.
2 JOHN 1:6

I praise Thee while my days go on;
I love Thee while my days go on;
Through dark and dearth, through fire and frost,
With emptied arms and treasure lost,
I thank Thee while my days go on.
E.B. BROWNING

Mirth is like a flash of lightning, that breaks through a gloom of clouds, and glitters for a moment; cheerfulness keeps up a kind of daylight in the mind, and fills it with a steady and perpetual serenity.

~ JOSEPH ADDISON

We know nothing of tomorrow, our business is to be good and happy today.

~ SYDNEY SMITH

Religion begins in knowledge, proceeds in practice, and ends in happiness. We never better enjoy ourselves than when we most enjoy God.

Nothing should alienate us from one another but that which alienates us from God.

It is impossible for a man to be made happy by putting him into a happy place, unless he be first in a happy state.

~ BENJAMIN WHICHCOTE

*Forgetting what is behind and straining toward what is ahead,
I press on toward the goal . . .*
PHILIPPIANS 3:14

*The time of life is short;
To spend that shortness basely were too long.*
WILLIAM SHAKESPEARE

*That ye may live, which will be many days,
Both in one faith unanimous; though sad
With cause for evils past, yet much more cheered
With meditation on the happy end.*
JOHN MILTON

It is not by regretting what is irreparable that true work is to be done, but by making the best, of what we are. It is not by complaining that we have not the right tools, but by using well the tools we have. What we are, and where we are, is God's providential arrangement, God's doing, though it may be man's misdoing; and the manly and the wise way is to look your disadvantages in the face, and see what can be made out of them. Life, like war, is a series of mistakes, and he is not the best Christian nor the best general who makes the fewest false steps. He is the best who wins the most splendid victories by the retrieval of mistakes. Forget mistakes; organize victory out of mistakes.

~ F. W. ROBERTSON

Words of Wisdom for the Times of Your Life

Birth

*A woman giving birth to a child has pain because her time has come;
but when her baby is born she forgets the anguish because of her joy that a
child is born into the world.*
JOHN 16:21

238

Sweet Infancy!
O Fire of heaven! O sacred Light
How fair and bright,
How great am I,
Whom all the world doth magnify!

O Heavenly Joy!
O great and sacred blessedness
Which I possess!
So great a joy
Who did into my arms convey!
THOMAS TRAHERNE

A mother's care is the closest, nearest, and surest—for it is the truest.
This care never might, nor could, nor should, be fully done except by him
alone. We know our own mother bore us into pain and dying. But our
true Mother Jesus, who is all love, bears us into joy and endless living.
Blessed may he be!

And so he nourished us with himself for love, and he labored until the
full term, because he willed to suffer the sharpest pangs and deepest pains
that ever were or ever shall be. And at the end he died. And when he had
done this—and so borne us into bliss—yet even all this could not assuage
his marvelous love. And he showed this in those high, wonderful words of
love: "If I could have suffered more, I would have suffered more."
~ JULIAN OF NORWICH

---

*In the beginning was the Word,
and the Word was with God, and the Word was God.
He was in the beginning with God.
All things came into being through him,
and without him not one thing came into being.
What has come into being in him was life,
and the life was the light of all people.*
JOHN 1:1-4

And you, Jesus, are you not also a mother?
Are you not the mother who, like a hen,
gathers her chickens under her wings?
Truly, Lord, you are a mother;
for both they who are in labor
and they who are brought forth
are accepted by you.
You have died more than they, that they may labor to bear.
It is by your death that they have been born,
for if you had not been in labor
you could not have borne death;
and if you had not died, you would not have brought forth.
For, longing to bear sons into life,
you tasted of death,
and by dying you begot them.
You did this in your own self,
your servants by your commands and help.
You as the author, they as the ministers.
So you, Lord God, are the great mother.

ST. ANSELM OF CANTERBURY

Mothers of families, even if they had a thousand sons and daughters, would still find room for every single one in their hearts, because that is how true love works. It even seems that the more children a mother has, the greater is her love and care for each one individually . . .

~ ST. ANGELA MERICI

Our awesome responsibility to ourselves, to our children, and to the future is to create ourselves in the image of goodness, because the future depends on the nobility of our imaginings.

I THESSALONIANS

Maiden, yet a Mother,
Daughter of thy Son,
High beyond all other—
Lowlier is none;
Thou the consummation
Planned by God's decree,
When our lost creation
Nobler rose in thee!

DANTE ALIGHIERI

From birth I have relied on you;
you brought me forth from my mother's womb.
I will ever praise you.

PSALMS 71:6

Behold the father is his daughter's son,
The bird that built the nest is hatched therein,
The old of years an hour hath not outrun,
Eternal life to live doth now begin,
The Word is dumb, the mirth of heaven doth weep,
Might feeble is, and force doth faintly creep.

O dying souls, behold your living spring;
O dazzled eyes, behold your sun of grace;
Dull ears, attend what word this Word doth bring;
Up, heavy hearts, with joy your joy embrace.
From death, from dark, from deafness, from despairs,
This life, this light, this Word, this joy repairs.

ST. ROBERT SOUTHWELL

Here he tells us that the new birth is first of all "not of blood." You don't get it through the blood stream, through heredity. Your parents can give you much, but they cannot give you this. Being born in a Christian home does not make you a Christian.

~ E. STANLEY JONES

May your father and mother be glad;
may she who gave you birth rejoice!

PROVERBS 23:25

The circle of a girl's arms
has changed the world
the round and sorrowful world
to a cradle of God.

CARYLL HOUSELANDER

Blessed be the Child who today delights Bethlehem,
Blessed be the Newborn who today made humanity young again.
Blessed be the Fruit who bowed Himself down for our hunger.
Blessed be the Gracious One who suddenly enriched all of our poverty and
     filled our need.
Blessed be He whose mercy inclined Him to heal our sickness . . .
Blessed is He whom freedom crucified, when He permitted it.
Blessed is He whom also the wood bore, when He allowed it.
   Blessed is He whom even the grave enclosed, when He set limits to
Himself.
Blessed is He whose will brought Him to the womb and to birth and to the
     bosom and to growth.
Blessed is He whose changes revived our humanity.
Blessed is He who engraved our soul and adorned and betrothed her
     to Him.
Blessed is He who made our body a Tabernacle for His hiddenness.
Blessed is He who with our tongue interpreted His secrets.

~ ST. EPHRAEM THE SYRIAN

He chose to give us birth through the word of truth, that we might be a kind of first fruits of all he created.

JAMES 1:18

Every night and every morn
Some to misery are born;
Every morn and every night
Some are born to sweet delight;
Some are born to sweet delight,
Some are born to endless night.
Joy and woe are woven fine,
A clothing for the soul divine;
Under every grief and pine
Runs a joy with silken twine.
It is right it should be so;
Man was made for joy and woe;
And when this we rightly know
Safely through the world we go.

WILLIAM BLAKE

Let us pray.

O God, you have taught us through your blessed Son that whoever receives a little child in the name of Christ receives Christ himself: We give thanks for the blessing you have bestowed upon this family in giving them a child. Confirm their joy by a lively sense of your presence with them, and give them calm strength and patient wisdom as they seek to bring this child to love all that is true and noble, just and pure, lovable and gracious, excellent and admirable, following the example of our Lord and Savior, Jesus Christ.

Amen.

~ THE BOOK OF COMMON PRAYER

Sons are a heritage from the Lord, children a reward from him. Like arrows in the hands of a warrior are sons born in one's youth. Blessed is the man whose quiver is full of them.

PSALMS 127:3–5

We mothers,
we gather seed of desire
from oceanic night,
we are gatherers
of scattered goods.

NELLY SACHS

⁓

There is a time for everything,
and a season for every activity under heaven:
a time to be born and a time to die,
a time to plant and a time to uproot.
ECCLESIASTES 3:1-2

I sing the birth was born tonight,
The Author both of life and light;
The angels so did sound it,
And like the ravished shepherds said,
Who saw the light, and were afraid,
Yet searched, and true they found it.

The Son of God, the eternal King,
That did us all salvation bring,
And freed the soul from danger;
He whom the whole world could not take,
The Word, which heaven and earth did make,
Was now laid in a manger.

The Father's wisdom willed it so,
The Son's obedience knew no "No,"
Both wills were in one stature;
And as that wisdom had decreed,
The Word was now made Flesh indeed,
And took on Him our nature.

BEN JONSON

Prayer for a child not yet baptized:
O eternal God, you have promised to be a father to a thousand generations
of those who love and fear you: Bless this child and preserve his life;
receive him and enable him to receive you, that through the Sacrament of
Baptism he may become the child of God; through Jesus Christ our Lord.
Amen.

~ THE BOOK OF COMMON PRAYER

Can a mother forget the baby at her breast and
have no compassion on the child she has borne?
ISAIAH 49:15

God, who created me
Nimble and light of limb,
In three elements free,
To run, to ride, to swim;
Not when the sense is dim,
But now from the heart of joy,
I would remember him:
Take the thanks of a boy.

H. C. BEECHING

⁓

*Pierced by the light of God
Mary Virgin,
drenched in the speech of God,
your body bloomed,
swelling with the breath of God.*

*For the Spirit purged you
of the poison Eve took.
She soiled all freshness when she caught
that infection
from the devil's suggestion.*

*But in wonder within you
you hid an untainted
child of God's mind
and God's Son blossomed in your body.*

*The Holy One was his midwife:
His birth broke the laws
Of flesh that Eve made. He was coupled
to wholeness
in the seedbed of holiness.*

HILDEGARD OF BINGEN

---

*We know that anyone born of God does not continue to sin;
the one who was born of God keeps him safe, and the evil
one cannot harm him.*

1 JOHN 5:18

---

*Sweet dreams form a shade,
O'er my lovely infants head.
Sweet dreams of pleasant streams,
By happy silent moony beams.*

*Sweet sleep with soft down,
Weave they brows in infant crown.
Sweet sleep Angel mild,
Hover o'er my happy child.*

*Sweet smiles in the night,
Hover over my delight.
Sweet smiles Mothers smiles
All the livelong night beguiles.*

*Sweet moans, dovelike sighs,
Chase not slumber from thy eyes.
Sweet moans, sweeter smiles,
All the dovelike moans beguiles.*

WILLIAM BLAKE

Blessed is the man who fears the Lord,

*who finds great delight in his commands.
His children will be mighty in the land;
the generation of the upright will be blessed.*
PSALMS 112:1-2

Prayer for a child already baptized:
Into your hands, O God, we place your child. Support him in his success-
es and in his failures, in his joys and in his sorrows. As he grows in age,
may he grow in grace, and in the knowledge of his Savior Jesus Christ.
Amen.

~ THE BOOK OF COMMON PRAYER

---

*He settles the barren woman in her home as a
happy mother of children. Praise the Lord.*
PSALMS 113:9

---

*Of course you are the messenger, you who
Shed the grey brightness which the sun breaks through.
As when pale dawn provokes the birds to play
Their music glorifies the shape of day,
So your birth violates your father's tongue
Till, from his lips, a shriek of praise is wrung.
And as the sun burns red when the last gleam
Of styptic dawn admits a blood-red stream,
Your blood, too, gushes on the world whose fate
The sun you herald will illuminate.*
ANDREZJ MORSZTYN

. . . Blessed be thy holy Name, O Lord my God! For ever blessed be thy
holy Name, for that I am made the work of thy hands, curiously wrought,
by thy divine Wisdom, enriched by thy Goodness, being more thine than I
am mine own, O Lord! Thou hast given me a Body, wherein the glory of
the Power shineth, wonderfully composed above the Beasts, within distinguished into useful parts, beautified without with many Ornaments.
Limbs rarely poised, and made for Heaven: arteries filled with celestial
spirits . . . For all the art which thou hast hidden in this little piece of red
clay. For the workmanship of thy hand, who didst thy self form man of the
dust of the ground, and breath into his nostrils the breath of Life. For the
high Exaltation whereby thou hast glorified every body, especially mine,
as thou didst they Servant Adam's in Eden. Thy Works themselves
speaking to me the same thing that was said unto him in the beginning,
WE ARE THINE.

~ THOMAS TRAHERNE

---

*May the Lord make you increase, both you and your children.
May you be blessed by the Lord, the Maker of heaven and earth.*
PSALMS 115:14-15

Sleep sleep happy child.
All creation slept and smil'd.
Sleep sleep, happy sleep,
While o're thee thy mother weep.

Sweet babe in thy face,
Holy image I can trace.
Sweet babe once like thee,
Thy maker lay and wept for me,

Wept for me for thee for all,
When he was an infant small.
Thou his image ever see,
Heavenly face that smiles on thee.

Smiles on thee on me on all,
Who became an infant small,
Infant smiles are his own smiles,
Heaven & earth to peace beguiles.

WILLIAM BLAKE

Of all nature's gifts to the human race, what is sweeter to a man
than his children?

~ MARCUS TULLIUS CICERO

[Jesus] said to them,
"Let the little children come to me,
and do not hinder them, for the kingdom of God
belongs to such as these. I tell you the truth,
anyone who will not receive the kingdom of
God like a little child will never enter it."

MARK 10:14-15

You are a child of the universe no less than the trees and the stars; you
have a right to be here. And whether or not it is clear to you, no doubt the
universe is unfolding as it should.

~ MAX EHRMANN

Neither circumcision nor uncircumcision means anything;
what counts is a new creation.

GALATIANS 6:15

Had I the heavens' embroidered cloths,
Enwrought with golden and silver light,
The blue and the dim and the dark cloths
Of night and light and the half-light,
I would spread the cloths under your feet:

But I, being poor, have only my dreams;
I have spread my dreams under your feet;
Tread softly because you tread on my dreams.
WILLIAM BUTLER YEATS

Make thyself manifest, O Lord, in this water and grant to him who is baptized in it so to be transformed, that he may put off the old man, which is corrupted by deceitful lusts, and may put on the new man, which is formed fresh according to the image of the Creator. Grafted through baptism into the likeness of thy death, may be become a partaker also in thy resurrection. May he guard the gift of thy Holy Spirit, may he increase the measure of grace which has been entrusted to him, and so may he receive the prize which is God's calling to life above, being numbered among the first born whose names are written in heaven.

~ BLESSING OF THE BAPTISMAL FONT, EASTERN ORTHODOX.

Though he brings grief, he will show compassion,
so great is his unfailing love. For he does not willingly bring
affliction or grief to the children of men.
LAMENTATIONS 3:32-33

They told her how a glorious light,
Streaming from a heavenly throng,
Around them shone, suspending night;
While sweeter than a mother's song,
Blessed angels heralded the Savior's birth,
Glory to God on high! and peace on earth.

She listened to the tale divine,
And closer still the babe she pressed;
And while she cried, "The babe is mine!"
The milk rushed faster to her breast:
Joy rose within her, like a summer's morn:
Peace, peace on earth! the Prince of peace is born.
SAMUEL TAYLOR COLERIDGE

In our birth these two things are commingled . . . the body which we share with the animals, and the Reason and Thought which we share with the Gods, many decline towards this unhappy kinship with the dead, few rise to the blessed kinship with the Divine. Since then every one must deal with each thing according to the view which he forms about it, those few who hold that they are born for fidelity, modesty, and unerring sureness in dealing with the things of sense, never conceive aught base or ignoble of themselves: but the multitude the contrary. Why, what am I? . . . A wretched human creature; with this miserable flesh of mine. Miserable indeed! but you have something better than that paltry flesh of yours. Why then cling to the one, and neglect the other?

~ EPICTETUS

⁓

At that time the disciples came to Jesus and asked, "Who is the greatest in the kingdom of heaven?" He called a little child and had him stand among them. And he said: "I tell you the truth, unless you change and become like little children, you will never enter the kingdom of heaven."
MATTHEW 18:1-3

O child! O new-born denizen
Of life's great city! on thy head
The glory of the morn is shed,
Like a celestial benison!
Here at the portal thou dost stand,
And with thy little hand
Thou openest the mysterious gate
Into the future's undiscovered land.
HENRY WADSWORTH LONGFELLOW

Scripture says that the Word of God was made flesh, that is that he was united to flesh, which had a rational soul. The Word of God took to himself descent from Abraham and shared in flesh and blood, forming for himself a body from a woman, so that he should not only be God but should become man too and be regarded as one of our race because of his union with us.

Emmanuel therefore is made up of two realities, divinity and humanity, as we must acknowledge. But the Lord Jesus Christ is one, the one true Son, who is both God and man. He is not deified as we are by graced, but rather is true God made manifest in human form for us. St. Paul confirms this with his words: "When the fullness of time came, God sent forth his Son, born of a woman, born under the law; to redeem those who were under the law, so that we might receive adoption as sons."
~ ST. CYRIL OF ALEXANDRIA

Whoever welcomes a little child like this in my name welcomes me.
MATTHEW 18:5

Our new baby has done his job well, the job all babies are assigned:
he has broken open my heart.
~ DEBORAH KEENAN

Whoever humbles himself like this child is the greatest
in the kingdom of heaven.
MATTHEW 18:4

I am Thine, and born for Thee:
What wilt Thou have done with me?
Sovereign Lord upon Thy throne,

Endless Wisdom, One and Whole,
Goodness that dost feed my soul,
Good and great, One God alone:
Vile Thou seest me, yet Thine own,
As I sing my love for Thee,
What wilt Thou have done with me?
Thine I am, for Thou didst make me;
Thine, for Thou alone didst save me;
Thine - Thou couldst endure to hae me;
For Thine own didst deign to take me.

ST. TERESA OF AVILA

O God, make the door of this house wide enough to receive all who need human love and fellowship, and a heavenly Father's care; and narrow enough to shut out all envy, pride and hate. Make its threshold smooth enough to be no stumbling block to children, or to straying feet, but rugged enough to turn back the tempter's power: make it a gateway to thine eternal kingdom.

~ BISHOP THOMAS KEN

Repent and be baptized, every one of you, in the name of Jesus Christ for the forgiveness of your sins. And you will receive the gift of the Holy Spirit. The promise is for you and your children and for all who are far off—for all whom the Lord our God will call.

ACTS 2:38-39

You drew us out of your holy mind
like a flower
petaled with our soul's three powers,
and into each power
you put the whole plant,
so that they might bear fruit in your garden,
might come back to you
with the fruit you gave them.
And you would come back to the soul
to fill her with your blessedness.
There the soul dwells-
like the fish in the sea
and the sea in the fish.

ST. CATHERINE OF SIENA

Prayer for a safe delivery:

O gracious God, we give you humble and hearty thanks that you have preserved through the pain and anxiety of childbirth your servant, who desires now to offer you her praises and thanksgivings. Grant, most merciful Father, that by your help she may live faithfully according to your will in this life, and finally partake of everlasting glory in the life to come; through Jesus Christ our Lord. Amen.

~ THE BOOK OF COMMON PRAYER

☙

If anyone causes one of these little ones who believe in me to sin, it would be better for him to have a large millstone hung around his neck and to be drowned in the depths of the sea.
MATTHEW 18:6

Like as the fountain of all light created
Doth pour out streams of brightness undefined
Through all the conduits of transparent kind,
That heaven and air are both illuminated,
And yet his light is not thereby abated;
So God's eternal bounty every shined
The beams of being, moving, life, sense, mind,
And to all things himself communicated
But for the violent diffusive pleasure
Of goodness, that left not till God had spent
Himself, by giving us himself his treasure
In making man a God omnipotent.
How might this goodness draw ourselves above
Which drew down God with such attractive love!

WILLIAM ALABASTER

He never despises what he has made. Neither is he reluctant to serve our simplest office that belongs to our body in kind, because he loves our soul that he made in his own likeness. For just as the body is clad in clothes and the flesh in skin and the bones in flesh with the heart in the breast, so are we, soul and body, clothed and wrapped around in the goodness of God. Yet it is even more intimate than this; because they all disappear once they decay. But the goodness of God is always whole and more near to us without any comparison.

~ JULIAN OF NORWICH

The Spirit himself testifies with our spirit that we are God's children.
ROMANS 8:16

You gave us memory
so that we might be able to hold your blessings
and so bring forth the flower of glory to your name
and the fruit of profit to ourselves.
You gave us understanding
to understand your truth
and your will—
your will that wants only that we be made holy—
so that we might bear first the flower of glory
and then the fruit of virtue.
And you gave us our will
so that we might be able to love
what our understanding has seen
and what our memory has held.

ST. CATHERINE OF SIENA

Birth

~

If the new man, made in the likeness of sinful flesh, had not taken our old nature; if he, one in substance with the Father, had not accepted to be one in substance the mother; if he who was alone free from sin had not united our nature to himself—then men would still have been held captive under the power of the devil. We would have been incapable of profiting by the victor's triumph if the battle had been fought outside our nature.

But, by means of this marvelous sharing, the mystery of our rebirth shone out upon us. We would be reborn in newness of spirit through the same Spirit through whom Christ was conceived and born.

Consequently the evangelist speaks of those who believe as those "who were born, not of blood nor the will of the flesh nor of the will of man, but of God."

~ ST. LEO THE GREAT

What I am saying is that as long as the heir is a child, he is no different from a slave, although he owns the whole estate. He is subject to guardians and trustees until the time set by his father. So also, when we were children, we were in slavery under the basic principles of the world. But when the time had fully come, God sent his Son, born of a woman, born under law, to redeem those under law, that we might receive the full rights of sons.

GALATIANS 4:1–5

How have I labored?
How have I not labored
To bring her soul to birth,
To give these elements a name and a center!
She is beautiful as the sunlight, and as fluid.
She has no name, and no place.
How have I labored to bring her soul into separation
To give her a name and her being!

Surely you are bound and entwined,
You are mingled with the elements unborn;
I have loved a stream and a shadow.
I beseech you enter your life.
I beseech you learn to say 'T,
When I question you;
For you are no part, but a whole,
No portion, but a being.

EZRA POUND

Prayer for the Gift of a Child:
Heavenly Father, you sent; your own Son into this world. We thank you for the life of this child, entrusted to our care. Help us to remember that we are all your children, and so to love and nurture him, that he may attain to that full stature intended for him in your eternal kingdom; for the sake of your dear Son, Jesus Christ our Lord. Amen.

~ THE BOOK OF COMMON PRAYER

⌒

We know that the whole creation has been groaning as in the pains of childbirth right up to the present time. Not only so, but we ourselves, who have the firstfruits of the Spirit, groan inwardly as we wait eagerly for our adoption as sons, the redemption of our bodies. For in this hope we were saved.

ROMANS 8:22-24

You, all-accomplishing
Word of the Father,
are the light of primordial
daybreak over the spheres.
You, the foreknowing
mind of divinity,
foresaw all your works
as you willed them,
your prescience hidden
in the heart of your power,
your power like a wheel around the world,
whose circling never began and never slides to an end.

ST. HILDEGARD OF BINGEN

What boundless love! The innocent hands and feet of Christ were pierced by the nails; he suffered the pain. I suffer neither pain nor anguish; yet by letting me participate in his pain he gives me the gift of salvation.

No one should think, then, that his baptism is merely for the remission of sins and for adoption as sons in the way that John's baptism brought only remission of sins. We know well that not merely does it cleanse sins and bestow on us the gift of the Holy Spirit—it is also the counterpart of Christ's suffering. This is why, as we heard just now, Paul cried out: "Do you not know that all of us who have been baptized into death? We were buried therefore with him by baptism into death."

~ LETTER TO DIOGNETUS, C. 2ND CENTURY

The Lord God formed the man from the dust of the ground and breathed into his nostrils the breath of life, and the man became a living being.

GENESIS 2:7

Words of Wisdom

Growing
&
Changing

Therefore, I urge you, brothers, in view of God's mercy,
to offer your bodies as living sacrifices, holy and pleasing to God—this is
your spiritual act of worship.
Do not conform any longer to the pattern of this world, but be transformed
by the renewing of your mind. Then you will be able to test and approve
what God's will is—his good, pleasing and perfect will.
ROMANS 12:1-2

O Lord our God,
fill us with hope in the shadow of your wings;
protect us and sustain us.
You will uphold us, right from our childhood until our old age,
because our present strength,
if it comes from you, is strength indeed;
but if it is merely our own strength then it is weakness.
When we are close to you we find living goodness,
but at the very moment we turn aside from you
we become corrupt.
So, Lord, make us retrace our steps,
so that we are not defeated.
ST. AUGUSTINE

With all my heart and soul, O God, I thank you that in all the changes
and chances of this mortal life I can look up to you and cheerfully resign
my will to yours. I have trusted you, O Father, with myself. My soul is in
your hand, which I truly believe you will preserve from all evil, my body
and all that belongs to it are of much less value. I do therefore, with as
great a sense of security as satisfaction, trust all I have to you.

~ THOMAS WILSON

All over the world this gospel is bearing fruit and growing,
just as it has been doing among you since the day you heard it and
understood God's grace in all its truth.
COLOSSIANS 1:6

But let all who take refuge in you be glad;
let them ever sing for joy.
Spread your protection over them,
that those who love your name may rejoice in you.
For surely, O Lord, you bless the righteous;
you surround them with your favor as with a shield.
PSALMS 5:11-12

*That night the Lord appeared to him and said,
"I am the God of your father Abraham. Do not be afraid,
for I am with you; I will bless you and will increase the number of your
descendants for the sake of my servant Abraham."*

GENESIS 26:24

O God, by whom the meek are guided in judgement and light rises up in
darkness for the godly; grant us, in all our doubts and uncertainties, the
grace to ask what you would have us do; that the Spirit of Wisdom may
save us from all false choices and that in your light we may see light and
in your straight path may not stumble; through Jesus Christ our Lord.

~ WILLIAM BRIGHT

---

*Be devoted to one another in brotherly love.
Honor one another above yourselves.
Never be lacking in zeal, but keep your spiritual fervor,
serving the Lord.
Be joyful in hope, patient in affliction, faithful in prayer.
Share with God's people who are in need.
Practice hospitality.
Bless those who persecute you; bless and do not curse.
Rejoice with those who rejoice; mourn with those who mourn.
Live in harmony with one another.*

ROMANS 12:10-13

---

*Grant, Lord God, that we may cleave to you without parting,
worship you without wearying,
serve you without failing,
faithfully find you, for ever possess you, the one only God,
blessed for all eternity. Amen.*

ST. ANSELM

---

*This day I call heaven and earth as witnesses against you that I have set
before you life and death, blessings and curses. Now choose life, so that you
and your children may live and that you may love the Lord your God, listen
to his voice, and hold fast to him. For the Lord is your life, and he will give
you many years in the land he swore to give to your fathers, Abraham,
Isaac and Jacob.*

DEUTERONOMY 30:19-20

---

*Your beginnings will seem humble, so prosperous will your future be.
Ask the former generations and find out what their fathers learned,
for we were born only yesterday and know nothing,
and our days on earth are but a shadow.
Will they not instruct you and tell you? Will they not
bring forth words from their understanding?*

JOB 8:7-10

Batter my heart, three-person'd God, for you
as yet but knock! Breathe, shine and seek to mend;
that I may rise and stand, o'erthrow me, and bend
your force to break, blow, burn and make me new.
I, like an usurp'd town, to another due
Labor to admit you, but O, to no end!
Reason, your viceroy in me, me should defend,
but is captiv'd and proves weak or untrue.
Yet dearly I love you, and would be loved fain,
but am betrothed unto your enemy;
divorce me, untie or break that knot again,
take me to you, imprison me, for I
except you enthrall me, never shall be free,
nor ever chaste, except you ravish me.

JOHN DONNE

I will surely bless you and make your descendants as numerous as the stars in the sky and as the sand on the seashore. Your descendants will take possession of the cities of their enemies, and through your offspring all nations on earth will be blessed, because you have obeyed me.

GENESIS 22:17-18

The righteous will flourish like a palm tree,
they will grow like a cedar of Lebanon;
planted in the house of the Lord,
they will flourish in the courts of our God.

PSALMS 92:12-13

Take my life and let it be
Consecrated, Lord, to thee:
Take my moments and my days,
Let them flow in ceaseless praise.

Take my hands and let them move
At the impulse of thy love;
Take my feet and let them be
Swift and beautiful for thee.

Take my voice and let me sing
Always, only, for my King;
Take my lips and let them be
Filled with messages from thee.

FRANCES RIDLEY HAVERGAL

O God . . . I acknowledge my utter dependence upon you. I have nothing that I have not received. By you I am sustained in nature and grace, day by day, and moment by moment. Suffer not the work of your hands to perish. Let your Spirit empty me of all that is not yours, that Christ may dwell in me and I in him.

~ W. GRAY ELMSLIE

I delight greatly in the Lord;
my soul rejoices in my God.
For he has clothed me with garments of salvation
and arrayed me in a robe of righteousness,
as a bridegroom adorns his head like a priest,
and as a bride adorns herself with her jewels.
For as the soil makes the sprout come up and a garden
causes seeds to grow, so the Sovereign Lord
will make righteousness and praise spring up before all nations.
ISAIAH 61:10-11

Lead us, O Father, in the paths of peace,
Without your guiding hand we go astray,
And doubts appall and sorrows still increase;
Lead us through Christ, the true and living Way.
WILLIAM BURLEIGH

O Lord, this is our desire, to walk along the path of life that you have appointed us, in steadfastness of faith, in lowliness of heart, in gentleness of love. Let not the cares or duties of this life press on us too heavily; but lighten our burdens, that we may follow your way in quietness, filled with thankfulness for your mercy; through Jesus Christ our Lord.

~ MARIA HARE

What good will it be for a man
if he gains the whole world,
yet forfeits his soul?
Or what can a man
give in exchange for his soul?
MATTHEW 16:26

O though, from whom to be turned is to fall,
to whom to be turned is to rise,
and in whom to stand is to abide for ever;
grant us in all our duties thy help,
in all our perplexities thy guidance,
in all our dangers thy protection,
and in all our sorrows thy peace;
through Jesus Christ our Lord.
ST. AUGUSTINE

Take, Lord, all my liberty. Receive my memory, my understanding and my whole will. Whatever I have and possess, you have given me; to you I restore it wholly and to your will I surrender it for my direction. Give me the love of you only, with your grace and I am rich enough; nor ask I anything beside.

~ ST. IGNATIUS LOYOLA

Young men, in the same way be submissive to those who are older. All of you, clothe yourselves with humility toward one another, because, "God opposes the proud but gives grace to the humble."
1 PETER 5:5

The ultimate measure of a man is not where he stands in moments of comfort and convenience, but where he stands at times of challenge and controversy.

~ MARTIN LUTHER KING JR.

Let us make our way together, Lord;
wherever you go
I must go:
and through whatever you pass,
there too I will pass.
ST. TERESA OF AVILA

Do not be afraid to throw yourself on the Lord!
He will not draw back and let you fall!
Put your worries aside and throw yourself on him;
He will welcome you and heal you.

~ ST. AUGUSTINE

For you are great and do marvelous deeds; you alone are God. Teach me your way, O Lord, and I will walk in your truth; give me an undivided heart, that I may fear your name. I will praise you, O Lord my God, with all my heart; I will glorify your name forever.
PSALMS 86:10-12

You have persevered and have endured hardships for my name, and have not grown weary.
REVELATION 2:3

Holy Spirit:
As the wind is your symbol, so forward our goings.
As the dove so launch us heavenwards.
As water so purify our spirits.
As a cloud so abate our temptations.
As dew so revive our languor.
As fire so purge out our dross.
CHRISTINA ROSSETTI

---

*Consider it pure joy, my brothers, whenever you face trials
of many kinds, because you know that the testing of your
faith develops perseverance.*
JAMES 1:2-3

In the way of virtue, there is no standing still; anyone who does not daily advance, loses ground. To remain at a standstill is impossible; he that gains not, loses; he that ascends not, descends. If one does not ascend the ladder, one must descend; if one does not conquer, one will be conquered.

~ ST. BONAVENTURE

---

*Turn from evil and do good; then you will dwell in the land forever.
For the Lord loves the just and will not forsake his faithful ones.
They will be protected forever, but the offspring of the wicked will be cut off;
the righteous will inherit the land and dwell in it forever.*
PSALMS 37:27-29

---

*Save us, O Lord, from the snares of a double mind.
Deliver us from all cowardly neutralities.
Make us to go in the paths of your commandments,
and to trust for our defense in your mighty arm alone,
through Jesus Christ our Lord.*
RICHARD HURRELL FROUDE

---

*You have led me through my crowded travels of the day
To my evening's loneliness.
I wait for its meaning through the stillness of the night.*
RABINDRANATH TAGORE

If thou meet with the cross on thy journey, in what manner soever it be, be not daunted, and say, Alas, what shall I do now? But rather take courage, knowing that by the cross is the way to the kingdom.

~ JOHN BUNYAN

---

*And we pray this in order that you may live a life worthy of the Lord and
may please him in every way: bearing fruit in every good work, growing in
the knowledge of God.*
COLOSSIANS 1:10

---

*My heart leaps up when I behold
A rainbow in the sky:
So was it when my life began;
So is it now I am a man;*

So be it when I shall grow old,
Or let me die!
And I could wish my days to be
Bound to each to each by natural piety.
WILLIAM WORDSWORTH

In fact, though by this time you ought to be teachers, you need someone to teach you the elementary truths of God's word all over again.
You need milk, not solid food! Anyone who lives on milk, being still an infant, is not acquainted with the teaching about righteousness. But solid food is for the mature, who by constant use have trained themselves to distinguish good from evil.

HEBREWS 5:12–14

Bad I am, but yet thy child.
Father, be thou reconciled.
Spare thou me, since I see
With thy might that thou art mild.
I have life before me still
And thy purpose to fulfil;
Yea a debt to pay thee yet:
Help me, sir, and so I will.
GERARD MANLEY HOPKINS

One thing I do: Forgetting what is behind and straining toward what is ahead, I press on toward the goal to win the prize for which God has called me heavenward in Christ Jesus. All of us who are mature should take such a view of things. And if on some point you think differently, that too God will make clear to you. Only let us live up to what we have already attained.

PHILIPPIANS 3:13-16

Teach me, my God and King,
In all things Thee to see,
And what I do in anything
To do it as for Thee.
Not rudely, as a beast
To run into an action;
But still to make Thee prepossest
And give it his perfection.
A man that looks on glass
On it may stay his eye,

Or if he pleaseth, through it pass,
And then the heaven espy.
All may of Thee partake
Nothing can be so mean
Which with his tincture, for Thy sake,
Will not grow bright and clean

GEORGE HERBERT

Blessed be Jesus, who is always near in times of stress. Even when we cannot feel his presence he is close. Jesus said within my heart, "I will never leave you either in happiness or distress. I will always be there to help you and watch over you. Nothing in heaven or earth can part you from me. When you are quiet and still I can speak to your heart."

~ MARGERY KEMPE

We ought always to thank God for you, brothers,
and rightly so, because your faith is growing more and more,
and the love every one of you has for each other is increasing.

2 THESSALONIANS 1:3

It is not growing like a tree
In bulk, doth make Man better be . . .
In small proportions we just beauties see;
And in short measures life may perfect be.

BEN JONSON

Consider it pure joy, my brothers, whenever you face trials of many kinds,
because you know that the testing of your faith develops
perseverance. Perseverance must finish its work so that you may be mature
and complete, not lacking anything.

JAMES 1:2-4

God has created me to do Him some definite service;
He has committed some work to me which He has not committed to
another. I have my mission — I may never know it in this life,
but I shall be told it in the next.
I am a link in a chain, a bond of connection between persons.
He has not created me for nothing. I hall do good. I shall do His work.
I shall be an angel of peace, a preacher of truth in my own place,
if I do but keep His commandments.
Therefore, I will trust Him.
Whatever, wherever I am. I can never be thrown away.
If I am in sickness, my sickness may serve Him.
In perplexity, my perplexity may serve Him;
if I am in sorrow, my sorrow may serve Him.
He does nothing in vain. He knows what he is about.
He may take away my friends, throw me among strangers.

He may make me feel desolate, make my spirits sink,
hide my future from me, still He knows what He is about.
JOHN HENRY NEWMAN

The slow work of transfiguring the cosmos has had a beginning in us. The whole creation has been waiting for this moment: the revelation of the glory of the children of God. It is going on in secret and quite unpretentiously; and yet already in Spirit and truth.

~ ANDRÉ LOUF

All over the world this gospel is bearing fruit and growing, just as it has been doing among you since the day you heard it and understood God's grace in all its truth.
COLOSSIANS 1:6

Tell me not, in mournful numbers,
Life is but an empty dream!
For the soul is dead that slumbers,
And things are not what they seem.
Life is real! Life is earnest!
And the grave is not its goal;
Dust thou art, to dust returnest,
Was not spoken of the soul.
Not enjoyment, and not sorrow,
Is our destined end or way;
But to act, that each tomorrow
Finds us farther than today.
Lives of great men all remind us
We can make our lives sublime,
And, departing, leave behind us
Footprints on the sands of time;
Footprints, that perhaps another,
Sailing o'er life's solemn main,
A forlorn and shipwrecked brother,
Seeing, shall take heart again.
Let us, then, be up and doing,
With a heart for any fate;
Still achieving, still pursuing,
Learn to labour and to wait.
HENRY WADSWORTH LONGFELLOW

It was he who gave some to be apostles, some to be prophets,
some to be evangelists, and some to be pastors and teachers, to prepare
God's people for works of service, so that the body of Christ may be built up
until we all reach unity in the faith and in the knowledge of the Son of God
and become mature, attaining to the whole measure of the fullness of Christ.
Then we will no longer be infants, tossed back and forth by the waves,
and blown here and there by every wind of teaching and by the cunning and
craftiness of men in their deceitful scheming. Instead, speaking the

truth in love, we will in all things grow up into him who is the Head, that is, Christ.
EPHESIANS 4:11-15

O, may this bounteous God
Through all our life be near us,
With ever joyful hearts
And blessed peace to cheer us,
And keep us in his grace,
And guide us when perplexed,
And free us from all ills
In this world and the next.
MARTIN RINKART

Give me thy grace, good Lord, to set the world at nought, to set my mind fast upon thee. And not to hang upon the blast of men's mouths. To be content to be solitary, not to long for worldly company, little and little utterly to cast off the world, and rid my mind of all the business thereof. Not to long to hear of any worldly things, but that the hearing of worldly phantasies may be to me displeasant. Gladly to be thinking of God, piteously to call for his help, to lean unto the comfort of God, busily to labour to love him. To know mind own vileness and wretchedness, to humble and meeken myself under the might hand of God, to bewail my sins passed, for the purging of them, patiently to suffer adversity. Gladly to bear my purgatory here, to be joyful of tribulations, to walk the narrow way that leadeth to life.

~ THOMAS MORE

The seed that fell among thorns stands for those who hear, but as they go on their way they are choked by life's worries, riches and pleasures, and they do not mature.
LUKE 8:14

That which creates a happy life
Is substance left, not gained by strife,
A fertile and a thankful mold,
A chimney always free from cold;
Never to be the client, or
But seldom times the counselor.
A mind content with what is fit,
Whose strength doth most consist in wit;
A body nothing prone to be
Sick; a prudent simplicity.
Such friends as of one's own rank are;
Homely fare, not sought from far;
The table without art's help spread;
A night in wine not buried,
Yet drowning cares; a bed that's blest
With true joy, chastity, and rest;

Such short, sweet slumber as may give
Less time to die in't, more to live:
Thine own estate whate'er commend,
And wish not for, nor fear thine end.
THE EARL OF WESTMORELAND

Since the long-enduring patience of God summons you to improvement, we hope that with increase of understanding, your heart and mind may be turned to obey the commands of God.

~ ST. GREGORY VII

I made you grow like a plant of the field.
You grew up and developed and became the most beautiful of jewels.
EZEKIEL 16:7

Help, lord, my Faith, my Hope increase;
And fill my portion in thy peace.
Give love for life; nor let my dayes
Grow, but in new powres to thy name & praise.
RICHARD CRASHAW

Lord, you are my God and my Lord, and never have I seen you. You have created me and recreated me and you have given me all the good things I possesss, and still I do not know you. In fine, I was made in order to see you, and I have not yet accomplished what I was made for . . . Look upon us Lord; hear us, enlighten us, show yourself to us. Give yourself to us that it may be well with us, for without you it goes so ill for us. Have pity upon our effort and our strivings toward you, for we can avail nothing without you. Teach me to seek you, and reveal yourself to me as I seek, because I can neither seek you if you do not teach me how, nor find you unless you reveal yourself. Let me seek you in desiring you; let me desire you in seeking you; let me find you in loving you; let me love in finding you.

Thou, therefore, O Lord Jesu Christ, which art the greatest of all lights, the only true light, the light from whence springeth the light of the day, and the sun: thou light, which enlighteneth every man that cometh into the world: thou light, whereon there cometh no night nor eventide, but continuest ever bright and clear, as at mid-day: thou light, wherewithout all things are deep darkness, and whereby all things were made lightsome: thou mind and wisdom of the heavenly Father, enlighten my mind, that (being blind to all other things) I may see nothing but that which belongeth to thee, and that I may thereby walk in thy ways, without fantasying or liking of any other light else. Lord, I beseech thee, enlighten mine eyes, that I may never slumber in darkness, lest my ghostly enemy say at any time, I have prevailed against him.

~ ST. ANSELM OF CANTERBURY

If you really change your ways and your actions and deal with each other justly, if you do not oppress the alien, the fatherless or the widow and do not shed innocent blood in this place, and if you do not follow other gods to your own harm, then I will let you live in this place, in the land I gave your forefathers for ever and ever.

JEREMIAH 7:5-7

Lord, make me an instrument of your peace.
Where there is hatred, let me sow love,
Where there is injury, pardon,
Where there is doubt, faith;
Where there is despair, hope;
Where there is darkness, light;
Where there is sadness, joy.
O divine Master, Grant that I may not so much seek
To be consoled, as to console,
To be understood, as to understand,
To be loved, as to love,
For it is in giving that we receive;
It is in pardoning that we are pardoned;
It is in dying that we are born to eternal life.

ST. FRANCIS OF ASSISI

Almighty God, who hast created man in thine own image, and made him a living soul that he might seek after thee and have dominion over thy creatures, teach us to study the works of thy hands, that we may subdue the earth to our use, and strengthen our reason for thy service; and so to receive thy blessed word that we may believe on Him whom thou hast sent to give us the knowledge of salvation and the remission of our sins. All which we ask in the name of the same Jesus Christ our Lord.

~ JAMES CLERK MAXWELL

Words of Wisdom

Love
&
Friendship

❧

Let no debt remain outstanding, except the continuing debt to love one another, for he who loves his fellowman has fulfilled the law.
ROMANS 13:8

What can I give Him?
Poor as I am?
If I were a shepherd
I would bring a lamb,
If I were a wise man,
I would do my part,—
Yet what I can I give Him,
Give my heart.
CHRISTINA G. ROSSETTI

Paul puts love at the head of the list; love is the first thing, the first in that precious cluster of fruit. Someone has said that all the other eight can be put in terms of love. Joy is love exulting; peace is love in repose; longsuffering is love on trial; gentleness is love in society; goodness is love in action; faith is love on the battlefield; meekness is love at school; and temperance is love in training. So it is love all the way; love at the top, love at the bottom, and all the way along down this list of graces. If we just brought forth the fruit of the Spirit, what a world we would have!
~ D. L. MOODY

We need have no fear of someone who loves us perfectly;
his perfect love for us eliminates all dread of what he might do to us.
If we are afraid, it is for fear of what he might do to us
and shows that we are not fully convinced that he really loves us.
So you see, our love for him
comes as a result of his loving us first.
1 JOHN 4:18-19

Shall I compare thee to a summer's day?
Thou art more lovely and more temperate:
Rough winds do shake the darling buds of May,
And summer's lease hath all too short a date:
Sometime too hot the eye of heaven shines,
And often is his gold complexion dimm'd;
And every fair from fair sometime declines,
By chance or nature's changing course untrimm'd;
But thy eternal summer shall not fade
Nor lose possession of that fair thou owest;
Nor shall Death brag thou wander'st in his shade,
When in eternal lines to time thou growest:
So long as men can breathe or eyes can see,
So long lives this and this gives life to thee.
WILLIAM SHAKESPEARE

"You ask me, why should God be loved?" I answer: "the reason for loving God is God Himself." If we ask why God is entitled to our love, we should answer, 'Because He first loved us.'"

~ BERNARD OF CLAIRVAUX

And above all things have fervent love for one another,
for love will cover a multitude of sins.
1 PETER 4:8

Father of spirits, this my sovereign plea
I bring again and yet again to Thee.
Fulfill me now with love, that I may know
A daily inflow; daily overflow.
For love, for love, my Lord was crucified,
With cords of love he bound me to His side.
Pour through me now; I yield myself to Thee,
O Love that led my Lord to Calvary.
A. CARMICHAEL

If we love God and give ourselves to Him, we must give ourselves to the whole world. Otherwise we would divide off our personal experience of God from his Greatness and Infinite Presence and turn what ought to be dedication into private enjoyment.

One of the holy miracles of love is that once it is really started on its path, it cannot stop; it spreads and spreads in ever-widening circles till it embraces the whole world in God. We begin by loving those nearest to us, end by loving those who seem farthest. And as our love expands, so our whole personality will grow, slowly but truly. Every fresh soul we touch in love is going to teach us something fresh about God.

One of the mystics said: God cannot lodge in a narrow heart: our hearts are as great as our love. Let us take that into our meditation and measure our prayer and service against the unmeasured generosity of God.

~ E. UNDERHILL

Love is patient, love is kind. It does not envy,
it does not boast, it is not proud. It is not rude,
it is not self seeking, it is not easily angered,
it keeps no record of wrongs.
CORINTHIANS XIII. 4.

When weight of all the garner'd years
Bows me, and praise must find relief
In harvest-song, and smiles and tears
Twist in the band that binds my sheaf;

Thou known Unknown, dark, radiant sea
In whom we live, in whom we move,

My spirit must lose itself in Thee,
Crying a name—Life, Light, or Love.
E. DOWDEN

Too late have I loved You, O Beauty so ancient and so new, too late have I loved You! Behold, You were within me, while I was outside: it was there that I sought You, and a deformed creature, rushed headlong upon these things of beauty which you have made. You were with me, but I was not with You. They kept me far from You, those fair things which, if they were not in You, would not exist at all. You have called to me, and have cried out, and have shattered my deafness. You have blazed forth with light, and have shone upon me, and You have put my blindness to flight! You have sent forth fragrance, and I have drawn in my breath, and I pant after You. I have tasted You, and I hunger and thirst after You. You have touched me, and I have burned for Your peace.

~ ST. AUGUSTINE

And now abide faith, hope, love, these three:
but the greatest of these is love.
CORINTHIANS 13:13

Lord, it is my chief complaint;
That my love is weak and faint;
Yet I love thee and adore,
Oh for grace to love thee more!
W. COWPER

If you love those who love you, what credit is that to you?
Even "sinners" love those who love them.
LUKE 6:32

Love divine, all loves excelling,
Joy of heaven, to earth come down;
Fix in us Thy humble dwelling,
All Thy faithful mercies crown:
Jesus, Thou art all compassion,
Pure, unbounded love Thou art;
Visit us with Thy salvation,
Enter every trembling heart.
Breath, O breathe Thy loving Spirit
Into ever troubled breast;
Let us all in Thee inherit,
Let us find the promised rest;
Take away the love of sinning,
Alpha and Omega be;
End of faith, as its beginning,
Set our hearts at liberty.

Come, Almighty, to deliver,
Let us all They life receive;
Suddenly return, and never,
Nevermore Thy temples leave.
Thee we would be always blessing,
Serve Thee as Thy hosts above,
Pray, and praise Thee without ceasing,
Glory in Thy perfect love.
C. WESLEY

It is easy to love the people far away. It is not always easy to love those close to us . . . Bring love into your home for this is where our love for each other must start.

~ MOTHER TERESA

"Love the Lord your God with all your heart and with all your soul and with all your strength and with all your mind; and, Love your neighbor as yourself."
LUKE 10:26-28.

Beloved, let us love one another: for love is of God.
He that loveth not knoweth not God; for God is love.
God is love; and he that dwelleth in love dwelleth in God,
and God in him.
Perfect love casteth out fear.
W. TYNDALE

Love does not delight in evil but rejoices with the truth.
I CORINTHIANS 13:6

Feelings are not entirely ours to command. We are attracted towards some against our will, while towards others we can never experience a spontaneous affection. If we are moved solely by our feelings, that is not love. Real love means that we are still master of our acts, and we use our inclinations and attractions simply as guides in the direction which we choose to take. And the same is true when reason tells us what direction love must take. It is not reason which impels us to love, it is we ourselves who choose to love, taking reason as our guide.

~ ST. AEIRED

Since you have purified your souls in obeying the truth through the Spirit in sincere love of the brethren, love one another fervently with a pure heart.
1 PETER 1:22

In some green bower
Rest, and be not alone, but have thou there
The One who is thy choice of all the world:
There linger, listening, gazing, with delight
Impassioned, but delight how pitiable!
Unless this love by a still higher love
Be hallowed, love that breathes not without awe;
Love that adores, but on the knees of prayer,
By heaven inspired; that frees from chains the soul,
Life, in union with the purest, best,
Of earth-born passions, on the wings of praise
Bearing a tribute to the Almighty's Throne.
WILLIAM WORDSWORTH

[Christian love] is in itself generous and disinterested; springing from no view of advantage to himself, from no regard to profit or praise—no, nor even the pleasure of loving. This is the daughter, not the parent, of his affection. By experience he knows that social love, if it means the love of our neighbor, is absolutely different from self-love, even of the most allowable kind—just as different as the objects at which they point. And yet it is sure that, if they are under due regulations, each will give additional force to the other till they mix together never to be divided.

~ J. WESLEY

Jesus taught:
"But I tell you who hear me: Love your enemies, do good to those who hate you, bless those who curse you, pray for those who mistreat you. If someone strikes you on one cheek, turn to him the other also. If someone takes your cloak, do not stop him from taking your tunic. Give to everyone who asks you, and if anyone takes what belongs to you, do not demand it back. Do you unto others as you would have them do to you."
LUKE 6:27-31

Love flows from God to man without effort
As a bird glides through the air
Without moving its wings—
Thus they go whithersoever they will
United in body and soul

Yet in their form separate—
As the Godhead strikes the note
Humanity sings,
The Holy Spirit is the harpist
And all the strings must sound
Which are strung in love.
MECHTHILD OF MAGDEBURG

"Thou shalt love the Lord the God with thy whole heart, with they whole soul and with thy whole mind." This is the commandment of the great

God, and He cannot command the impossible. Love is a fruit in season at all times, and within reach of every hand.

~ MOTHER TERESA

Do not seek revenge or bear a grudge against one of your people,
but love your neighbor as yourself.
I am the Lord.
LEVITICUS 19:18

I have loved Thee with two loves—
a selfish love and a love that is worthy of Thee.
As for the love which is selfish,
Therein I occupy myself with Thee,
to the exclusion of all others.
But in the love which is worthy of Thee,
Thou does raise the veil that I may see Thee.
Yet is the praise not mine in this or that,
But that praise is to Thee in both that and this.
RABI'A

The Lord is slow to anger, abounding in love and forgiving sin and rebellion. Yet he does not leave the guilty unpunished; he punishes the children for the sin of the fathers to the third and fourth generation.
NUMBERS 14:17-19

'Forth from the last corporeal are we come
Into the heaven, that is unbodied light;
Light intellectual, replete with love;
Love of true happiness, replete with joy;
Joy, that transcends all sweetness of delight.
Here shalt thou look on either mighty host
Of Paradise.
DANTE ALIGHIERI

Love the Lord your God with all your heart and
with all your soul and with all your strength.
DEUTERONOMY 6:5

'We bow down our heads before His edict and ordinance,
We stake precious life to gain His favor.
While the thought of the Beloved fills our hearts,
All our work is to do Him service and spend life for Him.
Wherever He kindles His destructive torch,
Myriads of lovers' souls are burnt therewith.
The lovers who dwell within the sanctuary

Are moths burnt with the touch of the Beloved's face.'
O heart, haste thither, for God will shine upon you.
RUMI

You do not yet see God, but by loving your neighbor you gain the sight of God; by loving your neighbor you purify your eye for seeing God, as John says clearly: "If you do not love the brother whom you see, how will you be able to love God whom you do not see?"

You are told: love God. If you say to me: "Show me the one I am to love," what shall I answer, except what John himself says: "No one has ever seen God"? Do not think that you are altogether unsuited to seeing God - no, for John states: "God is love, and he who dwells in love is dwelling in God." Love your neighbor therefore, and observe the source of that love in you; there, as best you can, you will see God . . .

By loving your neighbor and being concerned about your neighbor, you make progress on your journey. Where is your journey, if not to the Lord God, to him whom we must love with all our heart, and with all our soul, and with all our mind? We have not yet reached the Lord, but we have our neighbor with us. So then, support him with whom you are travelling so that you may come to him with whom you long to dwell.

~ ST. AUGUSTINE OF HIPPO

You have heard that it was said,
"Love your neighbor and hate your enemy."
But I tell you: Love your enemies and
pray for those who persecute you.
MATTHEW 5:43-44

I gave myself to Love Divine,
And lo! my lot so changed is
That my Beloved One is mine
And I at last am surely His.
When that sweet Hunstman from above
First wounded me and left me prone,
Into the very arms of Love
My stricken soul forthwith was thrown.
Since then my life's no more my own
And all my lot so changed is
That my Beloved One is mine
And I at last am surely His.
ST TERESA OF AVILA

Serve nobly, wish for nothing else, and fear nothing else: and let Love freely take care of herself! For Love rewards to the full, even though she often comes late. Let no doubt or disappointment ever turn you away from performing acts of virtue; let no ill success cause you to fear that you yourself will not come to conformity with God. You must not doubt this, and you must not believe in men on earth, saints, or angels, even if they work wonders (Gal. 1:8); for you were called early, and your heart feels, at least sometimes, that you are chosen, and that God has begun to sustain your soul in abandonment.

~ HADEWIJCH OF ANTWERP

A heart that to God's will
Submits in patience mute
Loves to be touched by Him:
It serves God as His lute.
ANGELUS SILESIUS

God is one and there is no other but him. To love him with all your heart,
with all your understanding and with all your strength,
and to love your neighbor as yourself is more important than all burnt
offerings and sacrifices.
MARK 12:32-33

The dart wherewith He wounded me
Was all embarbed round with love,
And thus my spirit came to be
One with its Maker, God above.
No love but this I need to prove:
My life to God surrender'd is
And my Beloved One is mine
And I at last am surely His
ST. TERESA OF AVILA

Love your enemies, do good to them, and lend to them without expecting to
get anything back. Then your reward will be great, and you will be sons of
the Most High, because he is kind to the ungrateful and be merciful, just
as your Father is merciful.
LUKE 6:35-26

Fear not, dear friend, but freely live your days
Though lesser lives should suffer. Such am I,
A lesser life, that what is his of sky
Gladly would give for you, and what of praise.
Step, without trouble, down the sunlit ways.
We that have touched your raiment, are made whole
From all the selfish cankers of man's soul,
And we would see you happy, dear, or die.
Therefore be brave, and therefore, dear, be free;
Try all things resolutely, till the best,
Out of all lesser betters, you shall find;
And we, who have learned greatness from you, we,
Your lovers, with a still, contented mind,
See you well anchored in some port of rest.
ROBERT LOUIS STEVENSON

Late have I loved you, Beauty so ancient and so new, late have I loved you!
Lo, you were within, but I outside, seeking there for you, and upon the
shapely things you have made I rushed headlong, I misshapen. You were
with me, but I was not with you. They held me back from you, those
things which would have no being were they not in you. You called, shout-
ed, broke though my deafness; you flared, blazed, banished my blindness;
you lavished your fragrance, I gasped, and now I pant for you; I tasted you,
and I hunger and thirst; you touched me, and I burned for your peace.

~ ST. AUGUSTINE OF HIPPO

---

*For God so loved the world that he gave his one and only Son,
that whoever believes in him shall not perish but have eternal life.*
JOHN 3:16

"Love seeketh not Itself to please,
Nor for itself hath any care;
But for another gives its ease,
And builds a Heaven in Hell's despair."
So sang a little Clod of Clay,
Trodden with the cattle's feet;
But a Pebble of the brook,
Warbled out these metres meet:
"Love seeketh only Self to please,
To bind another to Its delight:
Joys in another's loss of ease,
And builds a Hell in Heaven's despite."
WILLIAM BLAKE

Having received a commandment—to love God—we possess the power to
love implanted in us at the moment we were constituted. The proof of
this is not external, but anyone can learn it from himself and within himself. For by nature we desire beautiful things though we differ as to what is
supremely beautiful, and without being taught, we have affection toward
those near and dear to us, and we spontaneously show goodwill to all our
benefactors.

Now was is more marvelous than the divine beauty? What thought
has more charm than the magnificence of God? What yearning of the soul
is so keen and intolerable as that which comes from God upon the soul
that is cleansed from all evil and cries with true affection: "I am wounded
with love"? Ineffable wholly and inexplicable are the flashes of the divine
beauty.

~ ST. BASIL THE GREAT

Jesus replied,
"If anyone loves me, he will obey my teaching.
My Father will love him,
and we will come to him and make our home with him."
JOHN 14:23

Yet, love, mere love, is beautiful indeed,
And worthy of acceptation. Fire is bright indeed,
Let temple burn, or flax! An equal light
Leaps in the flame from cedar-plank or weed.
And love is fire: and when I say at need
I love thee . . . mark! . . . I love thee! . . . in thy sight
I stand transfigured, glorified aright,
With conscience of the new rays that proceed
Out of my face toward thine. There's nothing low
In love, when love the lowest; meanest creatures
Who love God, God accepts while loving so.
And what I feel, across inferior features
Of what I am, doth flash itself, and show
How that great work of Love enhances Nature's.
ELIZABETH BARRETT BROWNING

Where do you pasture your flock, O good shepherd, you who take on your shoulders the whole flock, for the whole of human nature that you take on your shoulders forms one sheep. Show me the place of green pastures and the restful waters, lead me to the grass that nourishes, call me by name, so that I who am your sheep may hear your voice. Give me by your voice eternal life. Speak to me, you whom my soul loves.

This is how I name you, for your name is above every name and cannot be uttered or comprehended by any rational nature. Your name, which reveals your goodness, is the love my soul has for you. How can I not love you who loved me, even though I was black, so much that you laid down your life for the other sheep whose shepherd you are? Greater love than this cannot be conceived, that you should purchase my salvation with your life.

~ ST. GREGORY OF NYSSA

Greater love has no one than this, that he lay down his life for his friends.
JOHN 15:13

This is the miracle that happens every time to those who really love: the more they give, the more they possess of that precious, nourishing love from which flowers and children have their strength and which could help all human beings if they would take it without doubting.

~ RAINER MARIA RILKE

The man who says,
"I know him," but does not do what he commands is a liar,
and the truth is not in him. But if anyone obeys his word,
God's love is truly made complete in him.
This is how we know we are in him:
Whoever claims to live in him must walk as Jesus did.
JOHN 2:4-6

Life may change, but it may fly not;
Hope may vanish, but can die not;
Truth be veiled, but still it burneth;
PERCY BYSSHE SHELLEY

At this time our Lord showed me an inward sight of his homely loving. I saw that he is everything that is good and comforting to us. He is our clothing. In his love he wraps and holds us. He enfolds us in love, and he will never let us go.

And then he showed me a little thing, the size of a hazelnut in the palm of my hand—and it was as round as a ball. I looked at it with my mind's eye and I thought: "What can this be?" and answer came: "It is all that is made." I marveled that it could last, for I thought it might have crumbled to nothing, it was so small. And the answer came into my mind: "It lasts, and ever shall, because God loves it." And so all things have being through the love of God.

In this little thing I saw three truths. The first is that God made it. The second is that God loves it. And the third is that God looks after it.

~ JULIAN OF NORWICH

Now that you have purified yourselves by obeying the truth so that you have sincere love for your brothers, love one another deeply, from the heart.
PETER 1:22

God loves you with an intensity beyond anything that I could describe to you. He loves you, and He loves you so much that He gave His only Son, Jesus Christ to die on that cross; and the thing that kept Christ on that cross was love, not the nail.

~ BILLY GRAHAM

Whoever would love life and see good days must keep his tongue from evil and his lips from deceitful speech.
PETER 3:10

In love's snare the soul doth lie
it is no sin for eye to see:
though far Thy face from outward eye,
with inward sight I gaze on Thee.
My soul is drunken with the wine
quaffed on that first primeval day
when Thou wast mine, and I was Thine,
and promised so to be for aye.
I cannot let my Lover go,
though I am doomed to banishment:
the sprk betrays the ember's glow,
this blush, my soul's bewilderment.

Thy languorous eye is lover's bane,
the earth Thou treadest, China's throne:
whate'er Thou willest, Thou dost reign,
and humbly I obedience own
IRAQI

Death is given power over everything finite, especially in our period of history. But death is given no power over love. Love is stronger.

~ PAUL TILLICH

Let us consider how we may spur one another on toward
love and good deeds.
HEBREWS 10:24

"Would you know your Lord's meaning in this? Learn it well. Love was his meaning. Who showed it you? Love. What did he show you? Love. Why did he show you? For love. Hold fast to this and you shall never know nor learn about anything except love forever." So was I taught that love was our Lord's meaning. And I saw full surely that before ever God made us, he loved us. And this love was never quenched, nor ever shall be. And in this love he has done all his works. And in this love he has made all things profitable to us. And in this love our life is everlasting. In our making we had beginning, but the love in which he made us was in him from without beginning. In which love we have our beginning. And all this shall we see in God without end—which Jesus grant us.

~ JULIAN OF NORWICH

God demonstrates his own love for us in this:
While we were still sinners, Christ died for us.
ROMANS 5:8

Words of Wisdom

Marriage

Let love and faithfulness never leave you; bind them around your neck, write them on the tablet of your heart.
PROVERBS 3:3

The ring, so worn as you behold,
So thin, so pale, is yet of gold:
The passion such it was to proveó
Worn with life's care, love yet was love.
GEORGE CRABBE

If anyone does not provide for his relatives, and especially for his immediate family, he has denied the faith and is worse than an unbeliever.
I TIMOTHY 5:8

Let us go into the fields, my beloved, for the
Time of harvest approaches, and the sun's eyes
Are ripening the grain.
Let us tend the fruit of the earth, as the
Spirit nourishes the gains of Joy from the
Seeds of Love, sowed deep in our hearts.
KAHLIL GIBRAN

Marriage is rightly recommended to the faithful for its fruits, the gift of children, and for the conjugal modesty of which the mutual fidelity of the spouses is the guarantee and bond.

But there is another reason too. In this union there is also a mystery that makes it sacred and causes the Apostle to say: "Husbands, love your wives as Christ has loved the Church." The effect of such a marriage is that man and woman once they are committed and bound to one another remain irrevocably united for their whole lives without being permitted to separate, except for the reason of adultery.

Is it not perhaps the same as with the union of Christ and his Church? They are alive together eternally; no divorce can ever separate them.

~ ST. AUGUSTINE OF HIPPO

So ought men to love their wives as their own bodies. He that loveth his wife loveth himself.
EPHESIANS 5:28

At night in each other's arms,
Content, overjoyed, resting deep deep down in the darkness,
Lo! the heavens opened and He appeared—
Whom no mortal eye may see,
Whom no eye clouded with Care,

Whom none who seeks after this or that,
whom none who has not escaped from self.
There—in the region of Equality,
in the world of Freedom no longer limited,
Standing as a lofty peak in heaven above the clouds,
From below hidden, yet to all who pass into
that region most clearly visible—
He the Eternal appeared.
EDWARD CARPENTER

For when two persons who mutually love embrace each other with supreme longing and take supreme delight in each other's love, then the supreme joy of the first is in intimate love of the second, and conversely the excellent joy of the second is in love of the first. As long as only the first is loved by the second, he alone seems to possess the delights of his excellent sweetness. Similarly, as long as the second does not have some-one who shares in love for a third, he lacks the sharing of excellent joy. In order that both may be able to share delights of that kind, it is necessary for them to have someone who shares in love for a third.

~ RICHARD OF ST. VICTOR

For this cause shall a man leave his father and mother, and shall be joined
unto his wife, and they two shall be one flesh.
EPHESIANS 5:31

We are weaned from our timidity
In the flush of love's light
we dare be brave
And suddenly we see
that love costs all we are
and will ever be.
Yet it is only love
which sets us free.
MAYA ANGELOU

Children, obey your parents in the Lord: for this is the right. Honor thy
father and mother, which is the first commandment with promise;
That it may be well with thee, and thou mayest live long on the earth.
And, ye fathers, provoke not your children to wrath: but bring them up in
the nurture and admonition of the Lord.
EPHESIANS 6:1-4

The Vested Priest before the Altar stands;
Approach, come gladly, ye prepared, in sight
Of God and chosen friends, your troth to plight
With the symbolic ring, and willing hands
Solemnly joined. Now sanctify the bands

O Father!—to the Espoused thy blessing give,
That mutually assisted they may live
Obedient, as here taught, to thy commands.
So prays the Church, to consecrate a Vow
"The which would endless matrimony make";
Union that shadows forth and doth partake
A mystery potent human love to endow
With heavenly, each more prized for the other's sake;
Weep not, meek Bride! uplift thy timid brow.

WILLIAM WORDSWORTH

Fair weather weddings make fair weather lives.

~ RICHARD HOVEY

In that age they will neither marry nor be given in marriage, but will be as the angels. We are destined to a better state — destined to rise to a spiritual consortship. So we, who shall be with God, shall be together: since we shall all be with the one God, though there be many mansions in the house of the same Father; and, in eternal life, God will still less separate them whom He has joined together, than, in this lesser life, He allows them to be separated.

~ TERTULLIAN

When I was a child, I spake as a child, I understood as a child: but when I became a man, I put away childish things.

I CORINTHIANS 13:11

Let me not to the marriage of true minds
Admit impediments. Love is not love
Which alters when it alteration finds,
Or bends with the remover to remove:
O no! it is an ever-fixed mark
That looks on tempests and is never shaken;
It is the star to every wandering bark,
Whose worth's unknown, although his height be taken.
Love's not Time's fool, though rosy lips and cheeks
Within his bending sickle's compass come:
Love alters not with his brief hours and weeks,
But bears it out even to the edge of doom.
If this be error and upon me proved,
I never writ, nor no man ever loved.

WILLIAM SHAKESPEARE

May almighty God bless you by the word of His mouth, and unite your hearts in the enduring bond of pure love.

May you be blessed in your children and may the love that you lavish on them be returned a hundredfold.

May the peace of Christ dwell always in your hearts and in your home; may you have true friends to stand by you, both in joy and sorrow. May you be ready with help and consolation for all those who come to you in need; and may the blessings promised to the compassionate descend in abundance on your house.

~ TERTULLIAN

*Marriage is honorable in all, and the bed undefiled:
but whoremongers and adulterers God will judge.*
HEBREWS 13:4

*If ever two were one, then surely we.
If ever man were loved by wife, then thee;
If ever wife was happy in a man,*

May your fountain be blessed, and may you rejoice in the wife of your youth. A loving doe, a graceful deer— may her breasts satisfy you always, may you ever be captivated by her love.
PROVERBS 5:18-19

*To these whom death again did wed
This grave 's the second marriage-bed.
For though the hand of Fate could force
'Twixt soul and body a divorce,
It could not sever man and wife,
Because they both lived but one life.
Peace, good reader, do not weep;
Peace, the lovers are asleep.
They, sweet turtles, folded lie
In the last knot that love could tie.
Let them sleep, let them sleep on,
Till the stormy night be gone,
And the eternal morrow dawn;
Then the curtains will be drawn,
and they wake into a light
Whose day shall never die in night.*
RICHARD CRASHAW

When those who love mutually are of such great benevolence that, as we have said, they wish every perfection to be shared, then it is necessary, as has been said, that each with equal desire and for a similar reason seek out someone with whom to share love, and that each devotedly possess such a one, according to the fullness of his power.

~ RICHARD OF ST. VICTOR

All weddings are similar, but every marriage is different.
~ JOHN BERGER

If a man has recently married, he must not be sent to war or have any other duty laid on him. For one year he is to be free to stay at home and bring happiness to the wife he has married.
DEUTERONOMY 24:5

Come, my beloved: let us drink the last of Winter's
Tears from the cupped lilies, and soothe our spirits
With the shower of notes from the birds . . .
Let us sit by that rock, where violets hide; let us
Pursue their exchange of the sweetness of kisses.
KAHLIL GIBRAN

We assemble not in the church to pass away the time, but to gain some great benefit for our souls. If therefore we depart without profit, our zeal in frequenting the church will prove our condemnation. That so great a judgment comes not upon you, when ye go hence ponder the things ye have heard, and exercise yourselves in confirming our instruction — friend with friend, fathers with their children, masters with their slaves — so that, when ye return hither and hear from us the same counsels, ye may not be ashamed, but rejoice and be glad in the conviction that ye have put into practice the greater part of our exhortation. Not only must we meditate upon these things here — for this short exhortation sufficeth not to eradicate the evil — but at home let the husband be reminded of them by the wife, and the wife by the husband, and let an emulation obtain in families to the fulfilment of the divine law.
~ ST. JOHN CHRYSOSTOM

He who finds a wife finds what is good and receives favor from the Lord.
PROVERBS 18:22

My true love hath my heart, and I have his,
By just exchange, one for another given.
I hold his dear, and mine he cannot miss:
There never was a better bargain driven.

His heart in me, keeps me and him in one.
My heart in him, his thoughts and senses guides:
He loves my heart, for once it was his own:

I cherish his because in me it bides.

His heart his wound received from my sight:
My heard was wounded, with his wounded heart,
For as from me, on him his hurt did light,
So still me thought in me his hurt did smart:
Both equal hurt, in this change sought our bliss:
My true love hath my heart and I have his.
SIR PHILIP SIDNEY

Love is self-sufficient; it is pleasing to itself and on its own account. Love is its own payment, its own reward. Love needs no extrinsic cause or result. Love is the result of love, it is intrinsically valuable. I love because I love; I love in order to love. Love is a valuable thing only if it returns to its beginning, consults its origin, and flows back to its source. It must always draw from that endless stream. Love is the only one of the soul's motions, senses, and affections by which the creature in his inadequate fashion may respond to his Creator and pay him back in kind. When God loves, he wishes only to be loved in return; assuredly he loves for no other purpse than to be loved. He knows that those who love him are happy in their love.

~ ST. BERNARD OF CLAIRVAUX

Marriage should be honored by all, and the marriage bed kept pure, for God will judge the adulterer and all the sexually immoral.
HEBREWS 13:4

My godlike friend nay, do not stare,
You think the phrase is odd-like;
But "God is love," the saints declare,
Then surely thou art god-like.
And is thy ardour still the same?
And kindled still at Anna?
Others may boast a partial flame,
But thou art a volcano!
Ev'n Wedlock asks not love beyond
Death's tie-dissolving portal;
But thou, omnipotently fond,
May'st promise love immortal!
Thy wounds such healing powers defy,
Such symptoms dire attend them,
That last great antihectic try,
Marriage perhaps may mend them.
ROBERT BURNS

May you be blessed in your work and enjoy its fruits. May cares never cause you distress, nor the desire for earthly possessions lead you astray; but may your hearts' concern be always for the treasures laid for you in the life of heaven.

May the Lord grant you fullness of years, so that you may reap the harvest of a good life, and after you have served Him with loyalty in His king down on earth, may He take you up into His eternal dominions in Heaven.

~ TERTULLIAN

Houses and wealth are inherited from parents,
but a prudent wife is from the Lord.
PROVERBS 19:14

Within the life of the church, the paths of the single and the married should not be allowed to diverge. The shared life of the Christian community must become a context in which the differing gifts can be used for each other.

~ OLIVER O'DONOVAN

Jesus said: "At the beginning of creation God 'made them male and female.' For this reason a man will leave his father and mother and be united to his wife, and the two will become one flesh.' So they are no longer two, but one. Therefore what God has joined together, let man not separate."
MARK 10:6-9

How do I love thee? Let me count the ways.
I love thee to the depth and breadth and height
My soul can reach, when feeling out of sight
For the ends of Being and ideal Grace.
I love thee to the level of everyday's
Most quiet need, by sun and candle-light.
I love thee freely, as men strive for Right;
I love thee purely, as they turn from Praise.
I love thee with the passion put to use
In my old griefs, and with my childhood's faith.
I love thee with a love I seemed to lose
With my lost saints, – I love thee with the breath,
Smiles, tears, of all my life! – and, if God choose,
I shall love thee better after death.
ELIZABETH BARRETT BROWNING

I have always considered marriage as the most interesting event of one's life, the foundation of happiness or misery.

~ GEORGE WASHINGTON

A wife of noble character who can find? She is worth far more than rubies. Her husband has full confidence in her and lacks nothing of value.
PROVERBS 31:10-11

In short, without your presence: without your coming
suddenly, incitingly, to know my life, gust of a rosebush, wheat of wind:

since then I am because you are,
since then you are, I am, we are,
and through love I will be, you will be, we'll be.
PABLO NERUDA

However welcome the hospitality that welcomes you
You are permitted to receive it but a little while
Afoot and lighthearted, take to the open road,
Healthy, free, the world before you,
The long brown path before you,
leading wherever you choose.
Say only to one another:
Camerado, I give you my hand!
I give you my love, more precious than money,
I give you myself before preaching or law:
Will you give me yourself?
Will you come travel with me?
Shall we stick by each other as long as we live?
WALT WHITMAN

A vocation to marriage is a vocation to glorify God in a particular state with its necessary rights and duties. It can only be combined with the vocation of a pioneer missionary of the classic type if matrimony is felt to be spiritually neutral, irrelevant to God's calling.
~ DAVID M. PATON.

Enjoy life with your wife, whom you love,
all the days of this meaningless life that
God has given you under the sun.
ECCLESIASTES 9:9

Come live with me and be my love,
And we will all the pleasures prove
That valleys, grooves, hills and fields,
Woods, or steepy mountain yields.
And we will sit upon the rocks,
Seeing the shepherds feed their flocks
By shallow rivers, to whose falls
Melodius birds sing madrigals.
And I will make thee beds of roses

And a thousand fragrant posies;
A cap of flowers and a kirtle
Embroidered all with leaves of myrtle.
A gown made of the finest wool
Which from our pretty lambs we pull;
Fair-lined slippers for the cold,
With buckles of the purest gold;
A belt of straw and ivy buds
With coral clasps and amber studs:
And if these pleasures may thee move,
Come live with me and be my love.
CHRISTOPHER MARLOWE

There isn't time—so brief is life—for bickerings, apologies, heartburnings, callings to account. There is only time for loving—and but an instant, so to speak, for that.

~ MARK TWAIN

What is the beginning? —Love.
What the course. —Love still.
What the goal. —The goal is Love.
On a happy hill
Is there nothing then but Love?
Search we sky or earth
There is nothing out of Love
Hath perpetual worth;
All things flag but only Love,
All things fail and flee;
There is nothing left but Love
Worthy you and me.
CHRISTINA ROSSETTI

Your lips drop sweetness as the honeycomb, my bride; milk and honey are under your tongue. The fragrance of your garments is like that of Lebanon.
SONG OF SOLOMON 4:11

When two people are at one
in their inmost hearts,
they shatter even the strength of iron or bronze.
And when two people understand each other
in their inmost hearts,
their words are sweet and strong,
like the fragrance of orchids.
I CHING

---

*Anyone who divorces his wife and marries another woman commits
adultery, and the man who marries a divorced woman commits adultery.*
LUKE 16:18

Lovers prostrate themselves before the crucified. For with him is all the
strength of love and all the strength that turns the disillusion of love into
that love that is stronger than death, into that unique love of Christ that
can feed on its own fire and stay alive.

~ KARL RAHNER

---

*For great is your love, reaching to the heavens;
your faithfulness reaches to the skies.*
PSALMS 57:10

---

*What need of clamorous bells, or ribands gay,
These humble nuptials to proclaim or grace?
Angels of love, look down upon the place;
Shed on the chosen vale a sun-bright day!
Yet no proud gladness would the Bride display
Even for such promise:—serious is her face,
Modest her mien; and she, whose thoughts keep pace
With gentleness, in that becoming way
Will thank you. Faultless does the Maid appear;
No disproportion in her soul, no strife:
But, when the closer view of wedded life
Hath shown that nothing human can be clear
From frailty, for that insight may the Wife
To her indulgent Lord become more dear.*
WILLIAM WORDSWORTH

Many are his visits to the man of inward life. With such a one he holds
delightful converse, granting him sweet comfort, much peace, and an intimacy astonishing beyond measure. Come then, faithful soul, prepare your
heart for this your Spouse, so that he may vouchsafe to come to you and
swell within you. For so he says: "if any man love me, he will keep my
word; and we will come to him and make our dwelling with him." Make
room therefore for Christ, and refuse entrance to all others. When you
have Christ, you are rich and have need of nought else. He will provide for
you, and be in all things your faithful procurator; you shall not need to
look to men. Put your whole trust in God; let him be your fear and your
love.

~ THOMAS A. KEMPIS

---

*The husband should fulfill his marital duty to his wife,
and likewise the wife to her husband.*
1 CORINTHIANS 7:3

So dark the night! At rest
and hushed my house, I went with no one knowing upon a lover's quest
—Ah the sheer grace!—so blest,
my eager heart with love aflame and glowing.
In darkness, hid from sight
I went by secret ladder safe and sure
—Ah grace of sheer delight!—
so softly veiled by night,
hushed now my house, in darkness and secure.
Hidden in that glad night,
regarding nothing as I stole away,
no one to see my flight,
no other guide or light
save one that in my heart burned bright as day.
Surer than noonday sun,
guiding me from the start this radiant light
led me to that dear One
waiting for me, well-known,
somewhere apart where no one came in sight.
ST. JOHN OF THE CROSS

A Prayer For those we Love:
Almighty God, we entrust all who are dear to us to thy never-failing care
and love, for this life and the life to come, knowing that thou art doing for
them better things than we can desire or pray for; through Jesus Christ
our Lord. Amen.

~ THE BOOK OF COMMON PRAYER

You have become mine forever.
Yes, we have become partners.
I have become yours.
Hereafter, I cannot live without you.
Do not live without me.
Let us share the joys.
We are word and meaning, unite.
You are thought and I am sound.

May the nights be honey-sweet for us.
May the mornings be honey-sweet for us.
May the plants be honey-sweet for us.
May the earth be honey-sweet for us.
AUTHOR UNKNOWN

People talk about beautiful friendships between two persons of the same
sex. What is the best of that sort, as compared with the friendship of man
and wife, where the best impulses and highest ideals of both are the same.
There is no place for comparison between the two friendships; the one is
earthly, the other divine.

~ MARK TWAIN

The wife's body does not belong to her alone but also to her husband. In the same way, the husband's body does not belong to him alone but also to his wife.

1 CORINTHIANS 7:4

Dark of the night, my guide,
fairer by far than dawn when stars grow dim!
Night that has unified
the Lover and the Bride,
transforming the Beloved into him.
There on my flowered breast
that none by he might ever own or keep,
he stayed, sinking to rest,
and softly I caressed
my Love while cedars gently fanned his sleep.
Breeze from the turret blew
ruffling his hair. Then with his tranquil hand
wounding my neck, I knew
nothing: my senses flew
at touch of peace too deep to understand.
Forgetting all, my quest
ended, I stayed lost to myself at last.
All ceased: my face was pressed
upon my Love, at rest,
with all my cares among the lilies cast.

ST. JOHN OF THE CROSS

I love you for what you are, but I love you yet more for what you are going to be . . . not so much for your realities as for your ideals. You are going forward toward something great. I am on the way with you and therefore I love you.

~ CARL SANDBURG

Husbands, love your wives, just as Christ loved the church and gave himself up for to make her holy, cleansing her by the washing with water through the world, and to present her to himself as a radiant church, without stain or wrinkle or any other blemish, but holy and blameless.

EPHESIANS 5:25-27

Stone walls do not a prison make,
Nor iron bars a cage;
Minds innocent and quiet take
That for an hermitage;
If I have freedom in my love,
And in my soul am free,
Angels alone that soar above,
Enjoy such liberty.

RICHARD LOVELACE

O gracious and everliving God, you have created us male and female in
your image: Look mercifully upon this man and this woman who come to
you seeking your blessing, and assist them with your grace, that with true
fidelity and steadfast love they may honor and keep the promises and
vows they make; through Jesus Christ our Savior, who lives and reigns
with you in the unity of the Holy Spirit, one God, for ever and ever.
Amen.

~ THE BOOK OF COMMON PRAYER

To the married I give this command (not I, but the Lord):
A wife must not separate from her husband.
But if she does, she must remain
unmarried or else be reconciled to her husband.
And a husband must not divorce his wife.
1 CORINTHIANS 7:10-11

The fountains mingle with the river,
—And the rivers with the ocean;
The winds of heaven mix forever
—With a sweet emotion;
Nothing in the world is single:
—All things by a law divine
In another's being mingle—
—Why not I with thine?
See, the mountains kiss high heaven,
—And the waves clasp one another;
No sister flower could be forgiven
—If it disdained its brother;
And the sunlight clasps the earth,
—And the moonbeams kiss the sea;—
What are all these kissings worth,
—If thou kiss not me?
PERCY BYSSHE SHELLEY

Lord, make us instruments of your peace. Where there is hatred, let us
sow love; where there is injury, pardon; where there is discord, union;
where there is doubt, faith; where there is despair, hope; where there is
darkness, light; where there is sadness, joy; O Divine Master, grant that
we may not so much seek to be consoled as to console, to be understood
as to understand, to be loved as to love. For it is in giving that we receive;
it is in pardoning that we are pardoned; and it is in dying that we are born
to eternal life. Amen.

~ ST. FRANCIS OF ASSISI

Each one of you also must love his wife as he loves himself,
and the wife must respect her husband.
EPHESIANS 5:33

Love lives beyond
The tomb, the earth, which fades like dew.
I love the fond,
The faithful, and the true
Love lives in sleep,
The happiness of healthy dreams
Eve's dews may weep,
But love delightful seems.
'Tis heard in Spring
When light and sunbeams, warm and kind,
On angels' wing
Bring love and music to the mind.
And where is voice,
So young, so beautiful and sweet
As nature's choice,
Where Spring and lovers meet?
Love lives beyond
The tomb, the earth, the flowers, and dew.
I love the fond,
The faithful, young and true

JOHN CLARE

A Christian marriage . . . means a marriage in which selfish people can accept selfish people without constantly trying to change them—and even accept themselves, because they realize personally that they have been accepted by Christ.

~ KEITH MILLER

---

*I will declare that your love stands firm forever,
that you established your faithfulness in heaven itself.*
PSALMS 89:2

The union of husband and wife in heart, body, and mind is intended by God for their mutual joy; for the help and comfort given one another in prosperity and adversity; and, when it is God's will, for the procreation of children and their nurture in the knowledge and love of the Lord. Therefore marriage is not to be entered into unadvisedly or lightly, but reverently, deliberately, and in accordance with the purposes for which it was instituted by God.

~ THE BOOK OF COMMON PRAYER

To the rest I say this (I, not the Lord): If any brother has a wife who is not a believer and she is willing to live with him, he must not divorce her. And if a woman has a husband who is not a believer and he is willing to live with her, she must not divorce him. For the unbelieving husband has been sanctified through his wife, and the unbelieving wife has been sanctified through her believing husband. Otherwise your children would be unclean, but as it is, they are holy.
1 CORINTHIANS 7:12-14

May the road rise to meet you,
May the wind be always at your back.
May the sun shine warm upon your face,
The rains fall soft upon your fields.
And until we meet again,
May God hold you in the palm of his hand.
May God be with you and bless you;
May you see your children's children.
May you be poor in misfortune,
Rich in blessings,
May you know nothing but happiness
From this day forward.
May the road rise to meet you
May the wind be always at your back
May the warm rays of sun fall upon your home
And may the hand of a friend always be near.
May green be the grass you walk on,
May blue be the skies above you,
May pure be the joys that surround you,
May true be the hearts that love you.
TRADITIONAL IRISH BLESSING

The value of marriage is not that adults produce children but that children produce adults.

~ PETER DE VRIES

Many a man claims to have unfailing love,
but a faithful man who can find?
PROVERBS 20:6

The entire sum of existence is the magic of being
needed by just one other person.
VI PUTNAM

Charm is deceptive, and beauty is fleeting; but a woman who fears the Lord
is to be. Give her the reward she has earned, and let her works bring her
praise at the city gate.
PROVERBS 31:30-31

She walks in beauty, like the night
Of cloudless climes and starry skies;
And all that's best of dark and bright
Meet in her aspect and her eyes:
Thus mellow'd to that tender light
Which heaven to gaudy day denies.

One shade the more, one ray the less,
Had half impair'd the nameless grace

Which waves in every raven tress,
Or softly lightens o'er her face;
Where thoughts serenely sweet express
How pure, how dear their dwelling-place.

And on that cheek, and o'er that brow,
So soft, so calm, yet eloquent,
The smiles that win, the tints that glow,
But tell of days in goodness spent,
A mind at peace with all below,
A heart whose love is innocent!

LORD BYRON

For marriage ordained by fate for a man and a woman is greater than an oath and guarded by Justice.

~ AESCHYLUS

Wives, in the same way be submissive to your husbands so that, if any of them do not believe the word, they may be won over without words by the behavior of their wives, when they see the purity and reverence of your lives.

1 PETER 3:1-2

Oh, my love is like a red, red rose,
That's newly sprung in June:
Oh my love is like a melody,
That's sweetly played in tune.

As fair art thou, my bonnie lass,
So deep in love am I,
And I will love thee still, my dear,
Till all the seas gang dry.

Till all the seas gang dry, my Dear,
And the rocks melt with the sun:
I will love thee still, my Dear,
While the sands of life shall run.

And fare thee well, my only love,
And fare thee well a while!
And I will come again, my love.
Though it were ten thousand mile!

ROBERT BURNS

Words of Wisdom

Parenting

Children, obey your parents in the Lord, for this is right.
"Honor your father and mother"—which is the first commandment
with a promise—— "that it may go well with you and
that you may enjoy long life on the earth."
Fathers, do not exasperate your children;
instead, bring them up in the training and
instruction of the Lord.

EPHESIANS 6:1-4

Last night my little boy confessed to me
Some childish wrong;
And kneeling at my knee,
He prayed with tears—
"Dear God, make me a man
Like Daddy—wise and strong;
I know You can."

Then while he slept
I knelt beside his bed,
Confessed my sins,
And prayed with low-bowed head.
"O God, make me a child
Like my child here—
Pure, guileless,
Trusting Thee with faith sincere."

ANDREW GILLIES

Heavenly Father, bless our children with healthful bodies, with good
understandings, with the graces and gifts of your Spirit, with sweet dispositions and holy habits; and sanctify them throughout in their bodies,
souls and spirits, and keep them blameless to the coming of our Lord
Jesus Christ.

~ JEREMY TAYLOR

God our Father,
maker of all that is living
we praise you for the wonder and joy of creation.
THE ALTERNATIVE SERVICE BOOK

O Lord God almighty who hast made us out of nothing and redeemed us
by the precious blood of thine only Son, preserve, I beseech thee, the work
of thy hands and defend both me and the tender fruit of my womb from
all perils and evils. I beg thee, for myself, thy grace, protection and a happy
delivery; and for my child, that thou wouldest preserve it for baptism,
sanctify it for thyself and make it thine for ever. Through Jesus Christ, thy
Son, our Lord.

~ THE CHRISTIAN'S GUIDE TO HEAVEN

≈

*Children's children are a crown to the aged,
and parents are the pride of their children.*
PROVERBS 17:6

---

*Piping down the valleys wild
Piping songs of pleasant glee
On a cloud I saw child,
And he laughing said to me,
"Pipe a song about a Lam";
So I piped with merry cheer.
"Piper pipe that song again"
So I piped, he wept to hear.
"Drop thy pipe thy happy pipe
Sing thy songs of happy cheer";
So I sung the same again
While he wept with joy to hear.
"Piper sit thee down and write
In a book that all may read";
So he vanish'd from my sight.
And I pluck'd a hollow reed,
And I made a rural pen,
And I stain'd the water clear,
And I wrote my happy songs
Every child may joy to hear . . .*
DAVID BATES

As Jesus was getting into the boat, the man who had been demon-possessed begged to go with him. Jesus did not let him, but said, "Go home to your family and tell them how much the Lord has done for you, and how he has had mercy on you." So the man went away and began to tell in the Decapolis how much Jesus had done for him. And all the people were amazed.
MARK 5:18-20

---

*Almighty God and heavenly Father,
we thank you for the children which you have given us:
give us also grace to train them in your faith, fear and love;
that as they advance in years they may grow in grace,
and may hereafter be found in the number of your elect children;
through Jesus Christ our Lord.*
BISHOP COSIN

. . . Fatherly and motherly hearts often beat warm and wise in the breasts of bachelor uncles and maiden aunts; and it is my privated opinion that these worthy creatures are a beautiful provision of nature for the cherishing of other people's children . . .

~ LOUISA MAE ALCOTT

꠰

*Jesus said to him, "Let the dead bury their own dead,
but you go and proclaim the kingdom of God."*

*Still another said, "I will follow you, Lord;
but first let me go back and say good-by to my family."*

*Jesus replied, "No one who puts his hand to the plow and
looks back is fit for service in the kingdom of God."*
LUKE 9:60-62

---

*You are young, and I am older;
You are hopeful, I am not—
Enjoy life, ere it grow colder—
Pluck the roses ere they rot.*

*Teach your beau to heed the lay—
That sunshine soon is lost in shade—
That now's as good as any day—
To take thee, Rosa, ere she fade.*
ABRAHAM LINCOLN

---

*I think I must let go.
Must fear not, must be quiet so that my children
can hear the Sound of Creation and dance the dance that is in them.*
RUSSELL HOBAN

Almighty God, heavenly Father, you have blessed us with the joy and care of children: Give us calm strength and patient wisdom as we bring them up, that we may teach them to love whatever is just and true and good, following the example of our Savior Jesus Christ. Amen.
~ THE BOOK OF COMMON PRAYER

---

*Through all the changing scenes of life,
In trouble and in joy,
The praises of my God shall still
My heart and tongue employ.*
NAHUM TATE AND NICHOLAS BRADY

It is difficult to give children a sense of security unless you have it yourself. If you have it, they catch it from you.
~ WILLIAM C. MENNINGER

Each of us individually has risen into moral life from a mode of being which was purely natural; in other words, each of us also has fallen — fallen, presumably in ways determined by his natural constitution, yet certainly, as conscience assures us, in ways for which we are morally answerable, and to which, in the moral constitution of the world, consequences attach which we must recognize as our due. They are not only results of our action, but results which that action has merited; and there is no moral hope for us unless we accept them as such.

~ JAMES DENNEY

Jesus said, "Let the little children come to me, and do not hinder them, for the kingdom of heaven belongs to such as these."
MATTHEW 19:14

Unto us a Child is born!
Ne'er has earth beheld a morn,
Among all the morns of time,
Half so glorious in its prime!

Unto us a Son is given!
He has come from God's own heaven,
Bringing with Him, from above,
Holy peace and holy love.
HORATIUS BONAR

Wisdom comes . . . not from trying to do great things for God . . . but more from being faithful to the small, obscure tasks few people ever see.

~ CHARLES R. SWINDOLL

Oh, how precious is time, and how it pains me to see it slide away, while I do so little to any good purpose. Oh, that God would make me more fruitful and spiritual.

~ DAVID BRAINERD

Joseph said to his brothers,
"I am Joseph! Is my father still living?"
But his brothers were not able to answer him, because they
were terrified at his presence.
GENESIS 45:3

Lord, teach me to love my grandchildren as a grandmother should:
not interfering, only understanding;
not pushing myself, just being there when wanted.
teach me to be the sort of grandmother
my children and my children's children
would want me to be.
ROSA GEORGE

Parenting

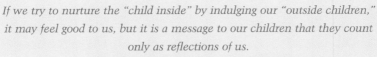

If we try to nurture the "child inside" by indulging our "outside children,"
it may feel good to us, but it is a message to our children that they count
only as reflections of us.
JEAN ILLSLEY CLARKE AND CONNIE DAWSON

Fill us with sensitive respect for the great gift of human life . . . help us to listen with patience to their worries and problems and give us tolerance to allow them to develop as individuals, as your Son did under the loving guidance of Mary and Joseph.

~ MICHAEL BUCKLEY

"Abraham is our father," they answered. "If you were Abraham's children," said Jesus, "then you would do the things Abraham did."
JOHN 8:39

Grant, O Lord, that we may
live in your fear,
die in your favor,
rest in your peace,
rise in your power,
reign in your glory;
for your own beloved Son's sake,
Jesus Christ our Lord.
ARCHBISHOP LAUD

God our Father, you see your children growing up in an unsteady and confusing world: Show them that your ways give more life than the ways of the world, and that following you is better than chasing after selfish goals. Help them to take failure, not as a measure of their worth, but as a chance for a new start. Give them strength to hold their faith in you, and to keep alive their joy in your creation; through Jesus Christ our Lord. Amen.

~ THE BOOK OF COMMON PRAYER

O Lord our God,
fill us with hope in the shadow of your wings;
protect and sustain us.
You will uphold us, right from our childhood until our old age,
because our present strength,
if it comes from you, is strength indeed;
but if it is merely our own strength then it is weakness.
When we are close to you we find living goodness,
but at the very moment we turn aside from you
we become corrupt.
So, Lord, make us retrace our steps,
so that we are not defeated.
ST. AUGUSTINE

Think often on God, by day, by night, in your business and even in your diversions. He is always near you and with you; leave him not alone.

~ BROTHER LAWRENCE

But let all who take refuge in you be glad; let them ever sing for joy. Spread your protection over them, that those who love your name may rejoice in you. For surely, O Lord, you bless the righteous; you surround them with your favor as with a shield.

PSALM 5:11-12

Lord of all hopefulness, Lord of all joy,
Whose trust, ever childlike, no cares could destroy,
Be there at our waking, and give us, we pray,
Your bliss in our hearts, Lord, at the break of the day.

JAN STRUTHER

A mother is the truest friend we have, when trials, heavy and sudden, fall upon us; when adversity takes the place of prosperity; when friends who rejoice with us in our sunshine, desert us when troubles thicken around us, still will she cling to us, and endeavor by her kind precepts and counsels to dissipate the clouds of darkness, and cause peace to return to our hearts.

~ WASHINGTON IRVING

When they had gone, an angel of the Lord appeared to Joseph in a dream. "Get up," he said, "take the child and his mother and escape to Egypt. Stay there until I tell you, for Herod is going to search for the child to kill him."

So he got up, took the child and his mother during the night and left for Egypt, where he stayed until the death of Herod. And so was fulfilled what the Lord had said through the prophet: "Out of Egypt I called my son."

MATTHEW 2:13-15

Open my eyes that I may see,
Incline my heart that I may desire,
Order my steps that I may follow
The way of your commandments.

LANCELOT ANDREWES

O God, make the door of this house wide enough
to receive all who need human love and fellowship,
and a heavenly Father's care;
and narrow enough to shut out all envy, pride and hate.

❧

Make its threshold smooth enough
to be no stumbling block to children or to straying feet,
but rugged enough to turn back the tempter's power;
make it a gateway to thine eternal kingdom.
THOMAS KEN

So it is written: "The first man Adam became a living being"; the last
Adam, a life-giving spirit. The spiritual did not come first, but the natur-
al, and after that the spiritual.
The first man was of the dust of the earth, the second man from heaven.
As was the earthly man, so are those who are of the earth; and as is the
man from heaven, so also are those who are of heaven. And just as we
have borne the likeness of the earthly man, so shall we bear the likeness of
the man from heaven.
1 CORINTHIANS 15:45-49

The baby woke me with her teething cries
and I can't get back to sleep.
All around there's a silent expectation,
Soon light will come and there will be the dawn chorus
and your gift of a new day.
It's rather like your Son's dying and rising.
TONY CASTLE

Father, whose Son called children to him,
we pray for boys and girls everywhere,
that their childhood may
be filled with laughter and happiness . . .

may they learn of your love,
and how to serve Jesus as Master and Lord.
BERNARD THOROGOOD

Give, I pray thee, to all children grace reverently to love their parents, and
lovingly obey them. Teach us all that filial duty never ends or lessens; and
bless all parents in their children and all children in their parents.
~ CHRISTINA ROSSETTI

Lord, keep us safe this night,
Secure from all our fears;
May angels guard us while we sleep,
Till morning light appears.
JOHN LELAND

O Lord Jesus Christ, our watchman and keeper, take us into thy care, and grant that, our bodies sleeping, our minds may watch in thee and be made merry by some sight of that celestial and heavenly life wherein thou art the King and Prince, together with the Father and the Holy Ghost, where the angels and holy souls be most happy citizens. O purify our souls, keep clean our bodies, that in both we may please thee, sleeping and waking, forever.

~ CHRISTIAN PRAYERS

If you remain in me and my words remain in you, ask whatever you wish, and it will be given you. This is to my Father's glory, that you bear much fruit, showing yourselves to be my disciples. As the Father has loved me, so have I loved you. Now remain in my love.

JOHN 15:7-9

This night is yours, and we are yours;
You are our Father, Brother Friend.
You love enfolds your children now,
This night, tomorrow, without end.

LILIAN COX

Abide with me, fast falls the eventide;
The darkness deepens, Lord, with me abide;
When other helpers fail and comforts flee,
Help of the helpless, O abide with me.
Reveal yourself before my closing eyes,
Shine through the gloom and point me to the skies;
Heaven's morning breaks and earth's vain shadows flee—-
In life, in death, O Lord, abide with me.

HENRY LYTE

Naked I came from my mother's womb, and naked I will depart.
The Lord gave and the Lord has taken away;
may the name of the Lord be praised.

JOB 1:21

Glory to thee, my God, this night
For all the blessings of the light;
Keep me, O keep me, King of kings,
Beneath thine own almighty wings.

Forgive me, Lord, for thy dear Son,
The ill that I this day have done,
That with the world, myself and thee
I, ere I sleep, at peace may be.

O may my soul on thee repose,

≈

And with sweet sleep mine eyelids close,
Sleep that may me more vigorous make
To serve my God when I awake.
THOMAS KEN

Watch over little children, support the sick, comfort the grieved, guide the harassed among us, for the sake of Christ. Amen.

~ RITA SNOWDEN

Honor your father and your mother, so that you may live long in the land the Lord your God is giving you.
EXODUS 20:12

Jesus, tender Shepherd, hear me,
Bless your little lamb tonight;
Through the darkness please be near me,
Watch my sleep till morning light.

All this day your hand has led me,
And I thank you for your care;
You have clothed me, warmed and fed me,
Listen to my evening prayer.

Let my sings be all forgiven;
Bless the friends I love so well;
Take me, when I die, to heaven,
Happy there with you to dwell.
MARY L. DUNCAN

Go with each of us to rest; if any awake, temper to them the dark hours of watching; and when the day returns, return to us, our sun and comforter, and call us up with morning faces and with morning hearts, eager to labor, eager to be happy, if happiness should be our portion, and if the day be marked for sorrow, strong to endure it.

~ ROBERT LOUIS STEVENSON

For you have been my hope, O Sovereign Lord, my confidence since my youth. From birth I have relied on you; you brought me forth from my mother's womb. I will ever praise you. I have become like a portent to many, but you are my strong refuge.
PSALMS 71:5-7

Hurt no living thing;
Ladybird nor butterfly,
Nor moth with dusty wing,

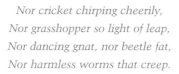

Nor cricket chirping cheerily,
Nor grasshopper so light of leap,
Nor dancing gnat, nor beetle fat,
Nor harmless worms that creep.
CHRISTINA ROSSETTI

Lord, behold our family here assembled. We thank thee for this place in which we dwell; for the love that unites us; for the peace accorded us this day; for the hope with which we expect the morrow; for the health, the work, the food, and the bright skies, that make our life delightful; for our friends in all parts of the earth and our friendly helpers in this foreign isle. Let peace abound in our small community. Purge out of every heart the lurking grudge. Give us strength to forbear and to persevere . . . Give us courage, gaiety and the quiet mind.

~ ROBERT LOUIS STEVENSON

I lie down and sleep; I wake again, because the Lord sustains me. I will not fear the tens of thousands drawn up against me on every side.
PSALMS 3:5-6

. . . Suddenly the splendour of that sun fell on me and immediately freed me of all misery. And I believe that I was sustained by Christ my Lord, and that His Spirit was even then crying out in my behalf, and I hope it will be so on the day of my tribulation, as is written in the Gospel: On that day, the Lord declares, it is not you that speak, but the Spirit of your Father that speaketh in you.

~ ST. PATRICK

Come, my Light, my Feast, my strength:
Such a Light, as shows a feast:
Such a Feast, as mends in length:
Such a Strength, as makes his guest.

Come, my Joy, my Love, my Heart:
Such a Joy, as none can move:
Such a Love, as none can part:
Such a Heart, as joys in love.
GEORGE HERBERT

Oh, how great peace and quietness would he possess who should cut off all vain anxiety and place all his confidence in God.

~ THOMAS A. KEMPIS

⊸

If a child sees his parents day in and day out living without self-restraint or self-discipline, then he will come in the deepest fibers of being to believe that that is the way to live.

~ M. SCOTT PECK

But I have stilled and quieted my soul; like a weaned child with its mother, like a weaned child is my soul within me. O Israel, put your hope in the Lord both now and forevermore.

PSALMS 131:2-3

May you walk
with beauty before you,
beauty behind you, all
around you, and
The Most Great Beauty keep
you His concern.

ROBERT HAYDEN

My son, keep your father's commands and
do not forsake your mother's teaching.

Bind them upon your heart forever;
fasten them around your neck.

PROVERBS 6:20-21

The joys of parents are secret, and so are their griefs and fears.

~ FRANCIS BACON

Even such is Time, that takes in trust
Our youth, our joys, our all we have,
And pays us but with earth and dust;
Who in the dark and silent grave,
When we have wandered all our ways,
Shuts up the story of our days;
But from this ear, this grave, this dust,
My God will raise me up, I trust.

SIR WALTER RALEIGH

For the unbelieving husband has been sanctified through his wife, and the unbelieving wife has been sanctified through her believing husband. Otherwise your children would be unclean, but as it is, they are holy.

1 CORINTHIANS 7:14

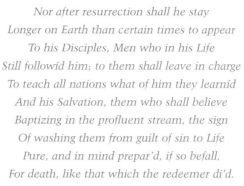

Nor after resurrection shall he stay
Longer on Earth than certain times to appear
To his Disciples, Men who in his Life
Still follow'd him; to them shall leave in charge
To teach all nations what of him they learn'd
And his Salvation, them who shall believe
Baptizing in the profluent stream, the sign
Of washing them from guilt of sin to Life
Pure, and in mind prepar'd, if so befall,
For death, like that which the redeemer di'd.

JOHN MILTON

Do not let your happiness depend on something you may lose . . .
only [upon] the Beloved who will never pass away.

C. S. LEWIS

Almighty and everlasting God, by whose Spirit the whole body of the Church is governed and sanctified: Receive our supplications and prayers, which we offer before thee for all in thy holy Church, that every member of the same, in his vocation and ministry, may truly and godly serve thee; through our Lord and Savior Jesus Christ.

~ BOOK OF COMMON PRAYER

And everyone who has left houses or brothers or sisters or father or mother or children or fields for my sake will receive a hundred times as much and will inherit eternal life.

MATTHEW 19:29

Because I feel that in the heavens above
The angels, whispering one to another,
Can find among their burning terms of love,
None so devotional as that of "Mother,"
Therefore by that dear name I have long called you,
You who are more than mother unto me,
And filled my heart of hearts, where death installed you,
In setting my Virginia's spirit free.
My mother — my own mother, who died early,
Was but the mother of myself; but you
Are the mother to the one I loved so dearly,
And thus are dearer than the mother I knew
But that infinity with which my wife
Was dearer to my soul that its soul-life.

EDGAR ALLAN POE

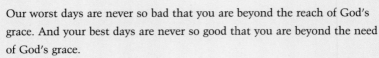

Our worst days are never so bad that you are beyond the reach of God's grace. And your best days are never so good that you are beyond the need of God's grace.

~ JERRY BRIDGES

Greater love has no one than this,
that he lay down his life for his friends.
JOHN 15:13

No child can be understood without knowing the parent; no revolution canbe understood without knowing the ancient regime; no colony can be understood without knowing the mother country; no new world can be understood without first knowing the old world that went before.

~ ORSON SCOTT CARD

Do all the good you can,
By all the means you can,
In all the ways you can,
In all the places you can,
At all the times you can,
To all the people you can,
As long as ever you can.
JOHN WESLEY

God knows that a mother needs fortitude and courage and tolerance and flexibility and patience and firmness and nearly every other brave aspect of the human soul. But because I happen to be a parent of almost fiercely maternal nature, I praise casualness.

~ PHYLLIS MCGINLEY

He who robs his father and drives out his mother is a son who brings
shame and disgrace.
PROVERBS 19:26

My son, if your heart is wise, then my heart will be glad; my inmost being
will rejoice when your lips speak what is right. Do not let your heart envy
sinners, but always be zealous for the fear of the Lord. There is surely a
future hope for you, and your hope will not be cut off. Listen, my son, and
be wise, and keep your heart on the right path. Do not join those who
drink too much wine or gorge themselves on meat, for drunkards and glut-

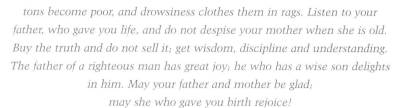

tons become poor, and drowsiness clothes them in rags. Listen to your
father, who gave you life, and do not despise your mother when she is old.
Buy the truth and do not sell it; get wisdom, discipline and understanding.
The father of a righteous man has great joy; he who has a wise son delights
in him. May your father and mother be glad;
may she who gave you birth rejoice!

PROVERBS 23:15-25

313

Birth is the sudden opening of a window, through which you look out
upon a stupendous prospect. For what has happened? A miracle. You have
exchanged nothing for the possibility of everything.

~ WILLIAM MACNEILE DIXON

I thank the goodness and the grace
Which on my birth have smiled,
And made me, in these Christian days,
A happy Christian child.

JANE TAYLOR

As you do not know the path of the wind, or how the body is formed in a
mother's womb, so you cannot understand the work of God,
the Maker of all things.

ECCLESIASTES 11:5

The heart of a mother is a deep abyss at the bottom of which you will
always find forgiveness.

HONORÉ DE BALZAC

Heavenly Father, maker of all things, you enable us to share in your work
of creation. Bless this couple in the gifts and care of children, that their
home maybe a place of love, security and truth . . .

ALTERNATIVE SERVICE BOOK

Blessings
&
Graces

*May the grace of the Lord Jesus Christ, and the love of God,
and the fellowship of the Holy Spirit be with you all.*
2 CORINTHIANS 13:14

---

*Blessed is the man who does not walk in the counsel of the wicked or
stand in the way of sinners or sit in the seat of mockers. But his delight is
in the law of the Lord, and on his law he meditates day and night. He is
like a tree planted by streams of water, which yields its fruit in season and
whose leaf does not wither. Whatever he does prospers. Not so the wicked!
They are like chaff that the wind blows away. Therefore the wicked will
not stand in the judgment, nor sinners in the assembly of the righteous.
For the Lord watches over the way of the righteous, but the way of the
wicked will perish.*
PSALMS 1

The peace of God, which passeth all understanding, keep your hearts and
minds in the knowledge and love of God, and of his Son, Jesus Christ our
Lord: and the blessing of God Almighty, the Father, the Son, and the Holy
Ghost, be among you and remain with you always.

~ HOLY COMMUNION

---

*See, I am setting before you today a blessing and a curse: the blessing if
you obey the commands of the Lord your God that I am giving you today;
the curse if you disobey the commands of the Lord your God and turn from
the way that I command you today by following other gods,
which you have not known.*
DEUTERONOMY 11:26-28

---

*Shout for joy to the Lord, all the earth.
Worship the Lord with gladness; come before him with joyful songs.
Know that the Lord is God. It is he who made us, and we are his;
we are his people, the sheep of his pasture.
Enter his gates with thanksgiving and his courts with praise;
give thanks to him and praise his name.
For the Lord is good and his love endures forever;
his faithfulness continues through all generations.*
PSALM 100

May God the Father, and the eternal High Priest Jesus Christ, build us up
in faith and truth and love, and grant us our portion among the saints
with all those who believe on our Lord Jesus Christ. We pray for all saints,
for kings and rulers, for the enemies of the cross of Christ, and for ourselves we pray that our fruit may abound and we be made perfect in
Christ Jesus our Lord.

~ POLYCARP

The Lord bless you and keep you;
the Lord make his face shine upon you and be gracious to you;
the Lord turn his face toward you and give you peace.
NUMBERS 6:24-26

Work, and thou wilt bless the day
Ere the toil be done;
They that work not, can not pray,
Cannot feel the sun.
God is living, working still,
All things work and move;
Work, or lose the power to will,
Lose the power to love.
JOHN SULLIVAN DWIGHT

O God of all power, who has called from death the great pastor of the sheep, our Lord Jesus: comfort and defend the flock which he has redeemed by the blood of the eternal testament.

Increase the number of true preachers; lighten the hearts of the ignorant; relieve the pains of such as be afflicted, especially of those that suffer for the testimony of the truth; by the power of our Lord Jesus Christ.

~ JOHN KNOX

Since the people began to bring their contributions to the temple of the Lord, we have had enough to eat and plenty to spare, because the Lord has blessed his people, and this great amount is left over.
2 CHRONICLES 31:10

We commend unto you, O Lord,
our souls and our bodies,
our minds and our thoughts,
our prayers and our hopes,
our health and our work,
our life and our death,
our parents and brothers and sisters,
our benefactors and friends,
our neighbors, our countrymen,
and all Christian folk,
this day and always.
LANCELOT ANDREWES

May the grace of Christ our Savior,
And the Father's boundless love,
With the Holy Spirit's favor,
Rest upon us from above.
JOHN NEWTON

May the God of peace, who through the blood of the eternal covenant brought back from the dead our Lord Jesus, that great Shepherd of the sheep, equip you with everything good for doing his will, and may he work in us what is pleasing to him, through Jesus Christ, to whom be glory for ever and ever.

~ HEBREWS 13:20-21

May the Lord direct your hearts into God's love and Christ's perseverance.
2 THESSALONIANS 3:5

Be an honor to the church, follow Christ's word,
Clear in thy task and careful in thy speech.
Be thine an open hand, a merry heart,
Christ in thy mouth, life that all men may know
A lover of righteousness and compassion
Let none come to thee and go sad away.
Hope of poor men, and solace to the sad,
Go thou before God's people to God's realm,
That he who follows thee may come to the stars.
Sow living seeds, words that are quick with life,
That faith may be the harvest in men's hearts.
In word and in example let thy light
Shine in the black dark like the morning star.
Let not the wealth of the world nor its dominion
Flatter thee into silence as to truth,
Nor king, nor judge, yea, nor thy dearest friend
Muzzle thy lips from righteousness.

ALCUIN OF YORK

The blessing of the Lord rest and remain upon all his people, in every land, of every tongue; the Lord meet in mercy all that seek him; the Lord comfort all who suffer and mourn; the Lord hasten his coming, and give us, his people, the blessing of peace.

~ BISHOP HANDLEY MOUL

And God blessed the seventh day and made it holy, because on it he rested from all the work of creating that he had done.
GENESIS 2:3

May God be gracious to us and bless us
and make his face shine upon us, Selah
that your ways may be known on earth,
your salvation among all nations.
May the peoples praise you, O God;
may all the peoples praise you.
May the nations be glad and sing for joy,

for you rule the peoples justly and guide the nations of the earth.
Selah May the peoples praise you,
O God; may all the peoples praise you.
Then the land will yield its harvest, and God, our God, will bless us.
God will bless us, and all the ends of the earth will fear him.
PSALM 67:1-7

The Lord Jesus Christ be near to defend thee, within thee to refresh thee, around thee to preserve thee, before thee to guide thee, behind thee to justify thee, above thee to bless thee; who liveth and reigneth with the Father and the Holy Spirit, God for evermore.

~ AUTHOR UNKNOWN

Loving Shepherd of your sheep
Keep your lamb in safety, keep;
Nothing can your power withstand,
None can pluck me from your hand.
JANE ELIZA LEESON

Incline us O God! To think humbly of ourselves, to be saved only in the examination of our own conduct, to consider our fellow-creatures with kindness, and to judge of all they say and do with the charity which we would desire from them ourselves.

~ JANE AUSTEN

Now may the Lord of peace himself give you peace at all times
and in every way.
2 THESSALONIANS 3:16

God send that there may be an end at last; God send that there may be peace again. God in heaven send us peace.

~ SIERK HARTICH

Lord, take my lips and speak through them; take my mind and think through it; take my heart and set it on fire.

~ W. H. H. AITKEN

May the right hand of the Lord keep us ever in old age, the grace of Christ continually defend us from the enemy. O Lord, direct our heart in the way of peace; through Jesus Christ our Lord.

~ BISHOP AEDELWALD

---

*Blessed is the man who perseveres under trial, because when he
has stood the test, he will receive the crown of life that God has promised to
those who love him.*
JAMES 1:12

*Blessed are the dead who die in the Lord from now on.
"Yes," says the Spirit, "they will rest from their labor,
for their deeds will follow them."*
REVELATION 14:13

*Eternal King, grant me true quietness
For thou art rest and quiet without end.
Eternal light, grant me the abiding light,
And may I live and quicken in thy good.*
ANGILBERT

Almighty Father, Son and Holy Ghost, eternal ever blessed gracious God;
to me the least of saints, to me allow that I may keep a door in paradise.
That I may keep even the smallest door, the furthest, the darkest, the
coldest door, the door that is least used, the stiffest door. If so it be but in
thine house, O God, if so be that I can see thy glory even afar, and hear
thy voice O God, and know that I am with thee, thee O God.

~ ST. COLUMBA

*God blessed them and said, "Be fruitful and increase in number and fill the
water in the seas, and let the birds increase on the earth."*
GENESIS 1:22

*Hail, holy Lady,
Most holy Queen,
Mary, Mother of God,
Ever Virgin;
Chosen by the most holy Father in heaven,
Consecrated by him,
With his most holy beloved Son
And the Holy Spirit, the comforter.
On you descended and in you still remains
All the fullness of grace
And every good.
Hail, his Palace.
Hail, his Tabernacle.
Hail, his Robe.
Hail, his Handmaid.
Hail, his Mother.
And hail, all holy virtues,
Who by the grace*

And inspiration of the Holy Spirit,
Are poured into the hearts of the faithful
So that, faithless no longer,
They may be made faithful servants of God
Through you.
ST. FRANCIS OF ASSISI

Grant us, O Lord, not to mind earthly things, but to love things heavenly;
and even now, while we are placed among things that are passing away, to
cleave to those that shall abide; through Jesus Christ our Lord.

~ LEONINE SACRAMENTARY

May God himself, the God of peace, sanctify you through and through.
May your whole spirit, soul and body be kept blameless at the coming of
our Lord Jesus Christ.
1 THESSALONIANS 5:23

In the same way, let your light shine before men, that they may see your
good deeds and praise your Father in heaven.
MATTHEW 5:16

For each new morning with its light,
For rest and shelter of the night,
For health and food, for love and friends,
For everything Thy goodness sends.
RALPH WALDO EMERSON

My father, for another night
Of quiet sleep and rest,
For all the joy of morning light,
Your holy name be blest.
HENRY WILLIAM BAKER

Walk while you have the light, before darkness overtakes you.
The man who walks in the dark does not know where he is going. Put your
trust in the light while you have it, so that you may
become sons of light.
JOHN 12:35-36

There is one body and one Spirit —just as you were called to one hope when you were called— one Lord, one faith, one baptism; one God and Father of all, who is over all and through all and in all. But to each one of us grace has been given as Christ apportioned it. This is why it says: "When he ascended on high, he led captives in his train and gave gifts to men."

EPHESIANS 4:4-8

First then behold the world as thine, and well
Note that where thou dost dwell.
See all the beauty of the spacious case,
Lift up thy pleas'd and ravisht eyes,

Admire the glory of the Heavenly place
And all its blessings prize.
That sight well seen thy spirit shall prepare,
The first makes all the other rare.

THOMAS TRAHERN

From the fullness of his grace we have all received one blessing after another.

JOHN 1:16

For blessings ever wait on virtuous deeds, and though a late,
a sure reward succeeds.

~ WILLIAM CONGREVE

Spirit of truth, and love,
Life-giving, holy Dove,
Speed forth Thy flight!
Move on the waters' face
Bearing the lamp of grace,
And in earth's darkest place
Let there be light!

Holy and blessed Three,
Glorious Trinity,
Wisdom, Love, Might!
Boundless as ocean's tide
Rolling in fullest pride,
Through the earth, far and wide,
Let there be light

JOHN MARRIOTT

❧

Your father's blessings are greater than the blessings of the ancient mountains, than the bounty of the age-old hills.
GENESIS 49:26

If you wish to be on good terms with God, and have his grace direct your life, and come to the joy of love, then fix this name "Jesus" so firmly in your heart that it never leaves your thought. And when you speak to him using your customary name "Jesu," in your ear it will be joy, in your mouth honey, and in your heart melody, because it will seem joy to you to hear that name being pronounced, sweetness to speak it, cheer and singing to think it.

~ ST. ROSE OF LIMA

For by the grace given me I say to every one of you:
Do not think of yourself more highly than you ought,
but rather think of yourself with sober judgment, in accordance with the
measure of faith God has given you.
ROMANS 12:3

Thou that givest food to all flesh,
which feedst the young raves that cry unto thee
and hast nourished us from our youth up;
fill our hearts with good and gladness
and establish our hearts with thy grace.
BISHOP LANCELOT ANDREWES

Blessings crown the head of the righteous,
but violence overwhelms the mouth of the wicked.
PROVERBS 10:6

Ye fearful saints, fresh courage take,
The clouds ye so much dread
Are big with mercy, and shall break
In blessings on your head.

Judge not the Lord by feeble sense,
But trust him for his grace;
Behind a frowning providence
He hides a smiling face.
WILLIAM COWPER

Most holy and eternal God, lord and sovereign of all the creatures, I humbly present to thy divine majesty, myself, my soul and body, my thoughts and my words, my actions and intentions, my passions and my sufferings, to be disposed by thee to thy glory; to be blessed by thy providence; to be guided by thy counsel; to be sanctified by thy Spirit; and afterwards that my body and soul may be received into glory; for nothing can perish which is under thy custody, and the enemy of sols cannot devour, what is thy portion, nor take it out of thy hands. This day, O Lord, and all the days of my life, I dedicate to thy honor, and the actions of my calling to the uses of grace, and the religion of all my days to be united to the merits and intercession of my holy Savior, Jesus; that, in him and for him, I may be pardoned and accepted.

~ JEREMY TAYLOR

As God's fellow workers we urge you not to receive
God's grace in vain.
CORINTHIANS 6:1

O thou who kindly dost provide
For every creature's want!
We bless Thee, God of Nature wide,
For all Thy goodness lent:
And if it please Thee, Heavenly Guide,
May never worse be sent;
But, whether granted, or denied,
Lord, bless us with content.
Amen
ROBERT BURNS

Give me grace, O God, to hearken to thy calling, and to follow thy guiding. For thou leadest us to store of all good things: thou offerest thyself and all thy goods; give us grace to receive them. Thou shewest us the way to most singular benefits; suffer us not to turn aside, until we have taken possession of them.

Give us constancy and steadiness of purpose, that our thoughts may not be fleeting, fond and ineffectual, but that we may perform all things with an unmovable mind, to the glory of thy holy name. Through Jesus Christ our Lord.

~ LUDOVICUS VIVES

Do not repay evil with evil or insult with insult, but with blessing,
because to this you were called so that you may inherit a blessing.
PETER 3:9

So am I as the rich, whose blessed key
Can bring him to his sweet up-locked treasure,
The which he will not every hour survey,
For blunting the fine point of seldom pleasure.
Therefore are feasts so solemn and so rare,
Since, seldom coming, in that long year set,

Like stones of worth they thinly placed are,
Or captain jewels in the carconet.
So is the time that keeps you as my chest,
Or as the wardrobe which the robe doth hide,
To make some special instant special blest
By new unfolding his imprison'd pride.
Blessed are you, whose worthiness gives scope,
Being had, to triumph; being lack'd, to hope
WILLIAM SHAKESPEARE

Grant us grace, our Father, to do our work this day as workmen who need not be ashamed. Give us the spirit of diligence and honest enquiry in our quest for the truth, the spirit of charity in all our dealings with our fellows, and the spirit of gaiety, courage, and a quiet mind in facing all tasks and responsibilities.

~ REINHOLD NIEBUHR

And God is able to make all grace abound to you,
so that in all things at all times, having all that you need,
you will abound in every good work.
CORINTHIANS 9:8

Whate'er the path these mortal feet may trace,
Breathe through my soul the blessing of thy grace,
Glad, through a perfect love, a faith sincere
Drawn from the wisdom that begins with fear,
Glad to expand; and, for a season, free
From finite cares, to rest absorbed in Thee!
WILLIAM WORDSWORTH

The grace of Jesus Christ, which is the efficacious principle of every kind of good, is necessary for every good work; without it, not only is nothing done, but nothing can be done.

~ CLEMENT

For it is by grace you have been saved, through faith—and this not from
yourselves, it is the gift of God.
EPHESIANS 2:8

No graces are granted except through faith. Faith is the first grace and the source of all others.

~ CLEMENT

May the Lord bless you with all good and keep you from all evil; may He give light to your heart with loving wisdom, and be gracious to you with eternal knowledge; may He lift up his loving countenance upon you for eternal peace.

~ DEAD SEA SCROLLS

But just as you excel in everything—in faith, in speech, in knowledge, in complete earnestness and in your love for us—see that you also excel in this grace of giving.
CORINTHIANS 8:7

Our entire striving is to be directed towards inward joys, to keep ourselves from seeking outward rewards and becoming conformed to this world and forfeiting the promise of a blessedness which is the more solid and enduring as it is interior, and by which God chose us to be made conformable to the image of His Son.

~ ST. AUGUSTINE OF HIPPO

Sun of my soul, Thou Saviour dear,
It is not night if Thou be near;
Oh may no earth-born cloud arise
To hide Thee from Thy servant's eyes!
Abide with me from morn till eve,
For without Thee I cannot live;
Abide with me when night is nigh,
For without Thee I dare not die.
Watch by the sick; enrich the poor
With blessings from Thy boundless store;
Be every mourner's sleep to-night,
Like infant slumbers, pure and light.
Come near and bless us when we wake,
Ere through the world our way we take,
Till in the ocean of Thy love
We lose ourselves in heaven above.
JOHN KEBLE

The peace of God which passeth all understanding, keep your hearts and minds in the knowledge and love of God, and of his Son Jesus Christ our Lord, and the blessing of God Almighty, the Father, the Son and the Holy Ghost, be amongst you and remain with you always.

~ THE BOOK OF COMMON PRAYER

Words of Wisdom

Comfort
&
Strength

❧

The Lord is my rock, my fortress and my deliverer; my God is my rock, in whom I take refuge, my shield and the horn of my salvation. He is my stronghold, my refuge and my savior — from violent men you save me. I call to the Lord, who is worthy of praise, and I am saved from my enemies. The waves of death swirled about me; the torrents of destruction overwhelmed me. The cords of the grave coiled around me; the snares of death confronted me. In my distress I called to the Lord; I called out to my God. From his temple he heard my voice; my cry came to his ears.

2 SAMUEL 22:2-7

Comfort, O merciful Father, by thy Word and Holy Spirit, all who are afflicted or distressed, and so turn their hearts unto thee, that they may serve thee in truth and bring forth fruit to thy glory. Be thou, O Lord, their succor and defense, through Jesus Christ our Lord.

PHILIP MELANCHTHON

O God . . . I acknowledge my utter dependence upon you. I have nothing that I have not received. By you I am sustained in nature and grace, day by day, and moment by moment. Suffer not the work of your hands to perish. Let your Spirit empty me of all that is not yours, that Christ may dwell in me and I in him.

~ W. GRAY ELMSLIE

---

*Worship the Lord your God,
and his blessing will be on your food and water.
I will take away sickness from among you.*

EXODUS 23:25

"Bear with all, even as the Lord does with you. Support all in love."

ST. IGNATIUS OF ANTIOCH

---

*Oh! Blest beyond all daughters of the earth!
What were the Orient's thrones to that low seat,
Where thy hushed spirit drew celestial birth?
Mary! meek listener at the Savior's feet!
No feverish cares to that divine retreat
Thy woman's heart of silent worship brought,
But a fresh childhood, heavenly truth to meet,
With love, and wonder, and submissive thought.
Oh! For the holy quiet of thy breast,
Midst the world's eager tones and footsteps flying!
Thou, whose calm soul was like a wellspring, lying
So deep and still in its transparent rest,
That e'en when noontide burns upon the hills,
Some one bright solemn star all its lone mirror fills.*

FELICIA HEMANS

A man's spirit sustains him in sickness,
but a crushed spirit who can bear?
PROVERBS 18:14

Lord, I am a countryman
coming from my country to yours.
Teach me the laws of your country,
its way of life, its spirit,
so that I may feel at home there.
WILLIAM OF ST. THIERRY

Man that is born of a woman hath but a short time to live, and is full of misery. He cometh up and is cut down like a flower; he flieth as it were a shadow, and never continueth in one stay. In the midst of life we be in death: of whom may we seek for succor but of thee, O Lord, which for our sins justly art displeased. Yet, O Lord God most holy, O Lord most mighty, O holy and most merciful savior, deliver us not into the bitter pains of eternal death. Thou knowest, Lord, the secrets of our hearts, shut not up thy merciful eyes to our prayers: but spare us Lord most holy, O God most mighty, O holy and merciful savior, thou most worthy judge eternal, suffer us not at our last hour for any pains of death to fall from thee.

~ THE BOOK OF COMMON PRAYER

Jesus went through all the towns and villages,
teaching in their synagogues,
preaching the good news of the kingdom
and healing every disease and sickness.
MATTHEW 9:35

My dearest Lord,
be thou a bright flame before me,
be thou a guiding star above me,
be thou a smooth path beneath me,
be thou a kindly shepherd behind me,
today and for evermore.
ST. COLUMBA

Though our feelings come and go, His love for us does not. It is not wearied by our sins, or our indifference; and, therefore, it is quite relentless in its determination that we shall be cured of those sins, at whatever cost to us, at whatever cost to Him.

~ C. S. LEWIS

O Lord, whose way is perfect, help us, we pray, always to trust in your goodness, that walking with you and following you in all simplicity, we

✍

may possess quiet and contented minds and may cast all our care on you, who cares for us. Grant this, O Lord, for your dear Son's sake, Jesus Christ.

~ CHRISTINA ROSSETTI

Heal the sick who are there and tell them,
"The kingdom of God is near you."
LUKE 10:9

Dear Jesus, help us to spread your fragrance everywhere we go.
Flood our souls with your spirit and life.
Penetrate and possess our whole being so utterly that our lives may only
be a radiance of yours.
Shine through us and be so in us that every soul we come in contact with
may feel your presence in our soul.
Let them look up and see no longer us but only Jesus! Stay with us and
then we shall begin to shine as you shine; so to share as to be a light to
others; the light, O Jesus, will be all from you, none of it will be ours; it
will be you shining on others through us . . .
JOHN HENRY NEWMAN

Lord, here I am, do with me as seems best in your own eyes; only give me, I beseech you, a penitent and patient spirit to expect you. Make my service acceptable to you while I live, and my soul ready for you when I die.

~ ARCHBISHOP LAUD

In our journey towards God, we proceed like those small birds whose flight is in loops. They always seem to be about to drop, but the drop in their flight seems to urge them forward.

~ GERARD W. HUGHES

The Lord is my strength and my song; he has become my salvation. He is
my God, and I will praise him, my father's God, and I will exalt him.
EXODUS 15:2

Teach us, Lord,
to serve you as you deserve,
to give and not to count the cost,
to fight and not to heed the wounds
to toil and not to seek for rest,
to labor and not to seek for any reward
save that of knowing that we do your will.
ST. IGNATIUS LOYOLA

❧

O Lord, let me not henceforth desire health or life except to spend them for you and with you. You alone know what is good for me; do therefore what seems best to you. Give to me or take from me; I desire to adore equally all that comes to me from you, my Lord and God.

~ BLAISE PASCAL

From heaven he made you hear his voice to discipline you. On earth he showed you his great fire, and you heard his words from out of the fire. Because he loved your forefathers and chose their descendants after them, he brought you out of Egypt by his Presence and his great strength, to drive out before you nations greater and stronger than you and to bring you into their land to give it to you for your inheritance, as it is today.

DEUTERONOMY 4:36-38

---

*God is our refuge and strength,
an ever-present help in trouble.*

PSALMS 46:1

---

*Alone with none but thee, my God,
I journey on my way.
What need I fear, when thou are near
O King of night and day?
More safe am I within my hand
Than if a host did round me stand.*

ST. COLUMBA

---

*My flesh and my heart may fail,
but God is the strength of my heart and
my portion forever.*

PSALMS 73:26

---

*God does not lead His children around hardship,
but leads them straight through hardship.
But He leads!
And amidst the hardship,
He is nearer to them than ever before.*

OTTO DIBELIUS

But you, dear friends, build yourselves up in your most holy faith and pray in the Holy Spirit. Keep yourselves in God's love as you wait for the mercy of our Lord Jesus Christ to bring you to eternal life. Be merciful to those who doubt; snatch others from the fire and save them; to others show mercy, mixed with fear—hating even the clothing stained by corrupted flesh. To him who is able to keep you from falling and to present you before his glorious presence without fault and with great joy— to the only God our

Savior be glory, majesty, power and authority, through Jesus Christ our Lord, before all ages, now and forevermore! Amen.

JUDE 1:20-25

Through the night of doubt and sorrow
Onward goes the pilgrim band,
Singing songs of expectation,
Marching to the promised land.

BERNHARDT INGEMANN

Lord, teach me the art of patience whilst I am well, and give me the use of it when I am sick. In that day either lighten my burden or strengthen my back. Make me, who so often in my health have discovered my weakness presuming on my own strength, to be strong in my sickness when I rely solely on thy assistance.

~ THOMAS FULLER

On this mountain he will destroy the shroud that enfolds all peoples, the sheet that covers all nations; he will swallow up death forever. The Sovereign Lord will wipe away the tears from all faces; he will remove the disgrace of his people from all the earth. The Lord has spoken.

ISAIAH 25:7-8

Comfort, O merciful Father, by thy Word and Holy Spirit, all who are afflicted or distressed, and so turn their hearts unto thee, that they may serve thee in truth and bring forth fruit to thy glory. Be thou, O Lord, their succor and defense, through Jesus Christ our Lord.

PHILIP MELANCHTHON

As a father has compassion on his children,
so the Lord has
compassion on those who fear him;
for he knows how we are formed,
he remembers that we are dust.

PSALMS 103:13-14

While life's dark maze I tread,
And griefs around me spread,
Be Thou my guide;
Bid darkness turn to day,
Wipe sorrow's tears away,
Nor let me ever stray
From Thee aside.

When ends life's transient dream,
When death's cold, sullen stream
Shall o'er me roll;
Blest Saviour, then, in love,
Fear and distrust remove;
O bear me safe above,
A ransomed soul!

RAY PALMER

If I am to complain, let me complain to Jesus fastened on his cross. But in your presence, my Savior, what have I to complain of? What are my sufferings compared with those you bear without complaining? I might perhaps convince my fellow man that I am unjustly afflicted, but in your presence, Lord, I cannot, for my sins are known to you. You know my sufferings are far less than I deserve. And since all my afflictions proceed form you, to you I come; give me strength and hearten me to suffer in silence; as once you did yourself.

~ CLAUDE DE LA COLOMBIE

Oh, the depth of the riches of the wisdom and knowledge of God!
How unsearchable his judgments,
and his paths beyond tracing out!
"Who has known the mind of the Lord?
Or who has been his counselor?"
Who has ever given to God, that God should repay him?
For from him and through him and to him are all things.
ROMANS 11:33-36

I will rejoice at my tribulations and infirmities
and be strong in the Lord,
at all times giving thanks to God the Father
and to his only Son, our Lord Jesus Christ,
and to the Holy Spirit
for the great grace he has given me
in deigning to assure me, his unworthy servant,
while I am still alive, that his kingdom will be mine.
ST. FRANCIS OF ASSISI

My strength fails; I feel only weakness, irritation and depression. I am tempted to complain and to despair. What has become of the courage I was so proud of and that gave me so much self-confidence? In addition to my pain, I have to bear the shame of my fretful feebleness. Lord, destroy my pride; leave it no resource. How happy I shall be if you can teach me by these terrible trials that I am nothing, that I can do nothing and that you are all!

~ FRANÇOIS FENÉLON

Give us, O Lord, a humble spirit, that we may never presume upon your mercy, but live always as those who have been much forgiven. Make us tender and compassionate towards those who are overtaken by temptation, considering ourselves, how we have fallen in times past and may fall yet again. Make us watchful and sober-minded, looking ever unto you for grace to stand upright, and to persevere unto the end; through your Son, Jesus Christ our Lord.

DEAN VAUGHAN

O give us patience and steadfastness in adversity, strengthen our weakness, comfort us in trouble and distress, help us to fight; grant unto us that in true obedience and contentation of mind we may give over our own wills unto thee our Father in all things, according to the example of thy beloved Son; that in adversity we grudge not, but offer up ourselves unto thee without contradiction . . . O give us a willing and cheerful mind, that we may gladly suffer and bear all things for thy sake.

~ BISHOP MILES COVERDALE

As a prisoner for the Lord, then, I urge you to live a life worthy of the calling you have received. Be completely humble and gentle; be patient, bearing with one another in love. Make every effort to keep the unity of the Spirit through the bond of peace. There is one body and one Spirit— just as you were called to one hope when you were called— one Lord, one faith, one baptism; one God and Father of all, who is over all and through all and in all.

EPHESIANS 4:1-6

---

*All is silent
In the still and soundless air,
I fervently bow
To my almighty God.*

HSIEH PING-HSIN

We beg you, Lord, to help and defend us. Deliver the oppressed, pity the insignificant, raise the fallen, show yourself to the needy, heal the sick, bring back those of your people who have gone astray, feed the hungry, lift up the weak, take off the prisoners' chains. May every nation come to know that you alone are God, that Jesus Christ is your Child, that we are your people, the sheep that you pasture.

~ ST. CLEMENT OF ROME

God, in a man who is made partaker of His nature, desireth and taketh no
revenge for all the wrong that is or can be done unto Him.
This we see in Christ when He saith: "Father, forgive them,
for they know not what they do."
THEOLOGIA GERMANICA

There is time of weeping and there is time of laughing. But as you see, he
setteth the weeping time before, for that is the time of this wretched world
and the laughing time shall come after in heaven. There is also a time of
sowing, and a time of reaping too. Now must we in this world sow, that
we may in the other world reap: and in this short sowing time of this
weeping world, must we water our seed with the showers of our tears,
and then shall we have in heaven a merry laughing harvest for ever.

~ SIR THOMAS MORE

Some trust in chariots and some in horses, but we trust in the name of the
Lord our God. They are brought to their knees and fall,
but we rise up and stand firm.
PSALMS 20:7-8

If we with earnest effort could succeed
To make our life one long, connected prayer,
As lives of some, perhaps, have been and are;
If, never leaving Thee, we have no need
Our wandering spirits back again to lead
Into Thy presence, but continued there
Like angels standing on the highest stair
Of the Sapphire Throne: this were to pray indeed!
RICHARD CHENEVIX TRENCH

Contentment is not satisfaction. It is the grateful, faithful, fruitful use of
what we have, little or much. It is to take the cup of Providence, and call
upon the name of the Lord. What the cup contains is its contents. To get
all that is in the cup is the act and art of contentment. Not to drink
because one has but half a cup, or because one does not like its flavor, or
because somebody else has silver to one's own glass, is to lose the contents; and that is the penalty, if not the meaning, of discontent. No one is
discontented who employs and enjoys to the utmost what he has. It is
high philosophy to say, we can have just what we like if we like what we
have; but this much at least can be done, and this is contentment: to have
the most and best in life by making the most and best of what we have.

~ MALTBIE D. BABCOCK

Now we know that if the earthly tent we live in is destroyed,
we have a building from God, an eternal house in heaven,
not built by human hands.
2 CORINTHIANS 5:1

❧

Thou, who canst change the heart, and raise the dead!
As Thou art by to soothe our parting hour,
Be ready when we meet,
With Thy dear pardoning words.
JOHN KEBLE

It is no hard matter to adhere to God while you are in the enjoyment of His comforts and consolations; but if you would prove your fidelity to Him, you must be willing to follow Him through the paths of dryness and desertion. The truth of a friend is not known while he is receiving favors and benefits from us; but if he remain faithful to us when we treat him with coldness and neglect, it will be a proof of the sincerity of his attachment.

~ WILLIAM BACKHOUSE

Your love, O Lord, reaches to the heavens, your faithfulness to the skies. Your righteousness is like the mighty mountains, your justice like the great deep. O Lord, you preserve both man and beast. How priceless is your unfailing love! Both high and low among men find refuge in the shadow of your wings. They feast on the abundance of your house; you give them drink from your river of delights. For with you is the fountain of life; in your light we see light.
PSALMS 36:5-9

Since God offers to manage our affairs for us, let us once and for all hand them over to His infinite wisdom, in order to occupy ourselves only with Himself and what belongs to Him.
JEAN PIERRE DE CAUSSADE

Hear us, almighty and most merciful God and Savior. Extend thy accustomed goodness to this thy servant, which is grieved with sickness. Visit him, O Lord, as thou didst visit Peter's wife's mother, and the captain's servant. So visit and restore unto this sick person his former health (if it be thy will) or else give him grace so to take thy visitation, that after this painful life ended, he may dwell with thee in life everlasting. Amen.

~ THE BOOK OF COMMON PRAYER

"I Jesus have sent my angel to you
with this testimony for the churches.
I am the root and the offspring of David,
the bright morning star." The Spirit and the Bride say, "Come."
And let him who hears say, "Come."
And let him who is thirsty come,
let him who desires take the water of life without price.
REVELATION 22:16-27

I bind my heart, this tide, to the Galilean's side,
To the wounds of Calvary, to the Christ who died for me.

I bind my soul this day to the brother far away
And the brother near at hand, in this town and in this land.

I bind my heart in thrall to God, the Lord of all.—
To God, the poor man's friend, and the Christ whom He did send.

I bind myself to peace, to make strife and envy cease.
God, knit Thou sure the cord of my thralldom to my Lord!
LAUCHLAN MACLEAN WATT

Lord, make possible for me by grace what is impossible to me by nature. You know that I am not able to endure very much, and that I am downcast by the slightest difficulty. Grant that for your sake I may come to love and desire any hardship that puts me to the test, for salvation is brought to my soul when I undergo suffering and trouble for you.

~ THOMAS A. KEMPIS

I have set the Lord always before me.
Because he is at my right hand, I will not be shaken.
PSALMS 16:8

Pardon comes not to the soul alone; or rather, Christ comes not to the soul with pardon only! It is that which He opens the door and enters by, but He comes with a Spirit of life and power.
JOHN OWEN

The Lord redeems his servants;
no one will be condemned who takes refuge in him
PSALMS 34:22

The sun and moon I saw,
And reverential awe
Subdued me day and night,
"I am the perfect light."
JOHN BANISTER TABB

Give me a stout heart to bear my own burdens. Give me a willing heart to bear the burdens of others. Give me a believing heart to cast all burdens upon Thee, O Lord.

~ JOHN BAILLIE

A life devoted unto God, looking wholly unto Him in all our actions, and doing all things suitably to His glory, is so far from being dull and uncomfortable, that it creates new comforts in everything that we do.

~ WILLIAM LAW

I want to know Christ and the power of his resurrection and the fellowship of sharing in his sufferings, becoming like him in his death, and so, somehow, to attain to the resurrection from the dead. Not that I have already obtained all this, or have already been made perfect, but I press on to take hold of that for which Christ Jesus took hold of me. Brothers, I do not consider myself yet to have taken hold of it. But one thing I do: Forgetting what is behind and straining toward what is ahead.

PHILIPPIANS 3:10-13

I have held many things in my hands, and have lost them all; but whatever I have placed in God's hands, that I still possess.

MARTIN LUTHER

Thus was the Cross of Christ, in St. Paul's day, the glory of Christians; not as it signified their not being ashamed to own a master that was crucified, but as it signified their glorying in a religion which was nothing else but a doctrine of the Cross that called them to the same suffering spirit, the same sacrifice of themselves, the same renunciation of the world, the same humility and meekness, the same patient bearing of injuries, reproaches and contempts, and the same dying to all the greatness, honors, and happiness of this world, which Christ showed on the Cross.

~ WILLIAM LAW

He got up, rebuked the wind and said to the waves, "Quiet! Be still!" Then the wind died down and it was completely calm. He said to his disciples, "Why are you so afraid? Do you still have no faith?" They were terrified and asked each other, "Who is this? Even the wind and the waves obey him!"

MARK 4:39-41

*The sheep with their little lambs
Passed me by on the road;
All in the April evening
I thought on the Lamb of God.*

*The lambs were weary and crying
With a weak, human cry.
I thought on the Lamb of God
Going meekly to die.*

KATHERINE TYNAN

Do not pray for easy lives; pray to be stronger men. Do not pray for tasks equal to your powers; pray for powers equal to your tasks. Then the doing of your work shall be no miracle, but you yourself shall be a miracle. Every day you shall wonder at yourself, at the richness of life which has come to you by the grace of God.

~ PHILLIPS BROOKS

My eyes will be on the faithful in the land.
PSALM 101:6

Therefore do not worry about tomorrow, for tomorrow will worry about itself. Each day has enough trouble of its own.
MATTHEW 6:34

Give me an open ear, O God, that I may hear Thy voice
calling me to high endeavor.
Give me an open mind, O God, a mind ready to receive and to welcome
such new light of knowledge as it is Thy will to reveal to me.
JOHN BAILLIE

It has been well said that no man ever sank under the burden of the day. It is when tomorrow's burden is added to the burden of today that the weight is more than a man can bear.

~ GEORGE MACDONALD

In what way did He come but this, "The Word was made flesh, and dwelt among us"? Just as when we speak, in order that what we leave in our minds may enter through the ear into the mind of the hearer, the word which we have in our hearts becomes an outward sound and is called speech; and yet our thought does not lose itself in the sound, but remains complete in itself, and takes the form of speech without being modified in its own nature by the change: so the Divine Word, though suffering no change of nature, yet became flesh, that He might dwell among us.

~ ST. AUGUSTINE

Return to us, O God Almighty!
Look down from heaven and see!
Watch over this vine, the root your right hand has planted,

✍

the son you have raised up for yourself.
Your vine is cut down, it is burned with fire;
at your rebuke your people perish.
Let your hand rest on the man at your right hand,
the son of man you have raised up for yourself.
Then we will not turn away from you;
us, and we will call on your name.
PSALMS 80:14-18

For God says, "When you are dry, empty, sick, or weak,
at such a time is your prayer most pleasing to Me,
even though you find little enough to enjoy in it."
JULIAN OF NORWICH

Wherefore, since it is our duty fully to enjoy the truth which lives
unchangeably, and truth for the things which He has made, the soul must
be purified that it may have power to perceive that light, and to rest in it
when it is perceived. And let us look upon this purification as a kind of
journey or voyage to our native land. For it is not by change of place that
we can come nearer to Him who is in every place, but by the cultivation of
pure desires and virtuous habits.

~ ST. AUGUSTINE

When he heard this, Jesus said, "This sickness will not end in death.
No, it is for God's glory so that God's
Son may be glorified through it."
JOHN 11:4

" . . . to pick up the pieces of our lives and go on living,
we have to get over the irrational feeling that every misfortune is our fault
. . . We are really not that powerful. Not everything that happens in the
world is our doing."
RABBI HAROLD KUSHNER

Look at the birds of the air; they do not sow or reap or store away in barns,
and yet your heavenly Father feeds them. Are you not much more valuable
than they?
MATTHEW 6:26

God's child in Christ adopted—Christ my all—
What that earth boasts were not lost cheaply, rather
Than forfeit that blest name, by which I call
The Holy One, the Almighty God, my Father?—
Father! in Christ we live, and Christ in Thee—
Eternal Thou and everlasting we.

The heir of heaven, henceforth I fear not death:
In Christ I live! in Christ I draw the breath
Of the true life!—let then earth, sea, and sky
Make war against me! On my front I show
Their mighty Master's seal. In vain they try
To end my life, that can but end its woe.
Is that a death-bed where a Christian lies?
Yes, but not his—'tis Death itself there dies.
SAMUEL TAYLOR COLERIDGE

Steadfastness in believing doth not exclude all temptations from without. When we say a tree is firmly rooted, we do not say the wind never blows upon it.

~ JOHN OWEN

Some time after this, Jesus crossed to the far shore of the Sea of Galilee (that is, the Sea of Tiberias), and a great crowd of people followed him because they saw the miraculous signs he had performed on the sick.
JOHN 6:1-2

God does not die on the day when we cease to believe in a personal deity, but we die on the day when our lives cease to be illumined by the steady radiance, renewed daily, of a wonder, the source of which is beyond all reason.
DAG HAMMARSKJÔLD

O Holy God, whose mercy and pity made thee descend from the high throne down into this world for our salvation: mercifully forgive us all the sings that we have done and thought and said. Send us cleanness of heart and purity of soul; restore us with thy Holy Spirit, that we may henceforth live virtuously and love thee with all our hearts; through Jesus Christ thy Son.

~ RICHARD ROLLE

Blessed are those who mourn,
for they will be comforted.
MATTHEW 5:4

Sunshine let it be, or frost,
Storm or calm, as Thou shalt choose;
Though Thine every gift were lost,
Thee Thyself we cannot lose.
MARY ELIZABETH COLERIDGE

Father in heaven, when the thought of you wakes in our hearts, let it no wake like a frightened bird that flies about in dismay, but like a child waking form its sleep with a heavenly smile.

~ SØREN KIERKEGAARD

The Creed sets forth what Christ suffered in the sight of men, and then appositely speaks of that invisible and incomprehensible judgment which he underwent in the sight of God in order that we might know not only that Christ's body was given as the price of our redemption, but that he paid a greater and more excellent price in suffering in his soul the terrible torments of a condemned and forsaken man.

~ JOHN CALVIN

Praise be to the God and Father of our Lord Jesus Christ,
the Father of compassion and the God of all comfort,
who comforts us in all our troubles, so that we can comfort those in any
trouble with the comfort we ourselves have received from God.
For just as the sufferings of Christ flow over into our lives,
so also through Christ our comfort overflows.

2 CORINTHIANS 1:3-5

My spirit longs for thee
Within my troubled breast,
Though I unworthy be
Of so divine a guest.

Of so divine a guest
Unworthy though I be,
Yet has my heart no rest
Unless it comes from thee.

JOHN BYROM

Now the great thing is this: we are consecrated and dedicated to God in order that we may thereafter think, speak, meditate, and do, nothing except to his glory. For a sacred thing may not be applied to profane uses without marked injury to him.

~ JOHN CALVIN

Finish each day and be done with it. You have done what you could; some blunders and absurdities have crept in; forget them as soon as you can. Tomorrow is a new day; you shall begin it serenely and with too high a spirit to be encumbered with your old nonsense.

~ RALPH WALDO EMERSON

An angel from heaven appeared to him and strengthened him.
LUKE 22:43

Since God offers to manage our affairs for us, let us once and for all hand them over to His infinite wisdom, in order to occupy ourselves only with Himself and what belongs to Him.
JEAN PIERRE DE CAUSSADE

I can do everything through him who gives me strength.
PHILIPPIANS 4:13

At my first defense,
no one came to my support,
but everyone deserted me.
May it not be held against them.
But the Lord stood at my side and gave me strength,
so that through me the message might be fully proclaimed
and all the Gentiles might hear it.
And I was delivered from the lion's mouth.
The Lord will rescue me from every evil attack
and will bring me safely to his heavenly kingdom.
To him be glory for ever and ever. Amen.
2 TIMOTHY 4:16-18

It is to be acknowledged that many passages in the Bible are abstruse, and not to be easily understood. Yet we are not to omit reading the abstruser texts, which have any appearance of relating to us; but should follow the example of the Blessed Virgin, who understood not several of our Saviour's sayings, but kept them all in her heart. Were we only to learn humility thus, it would be enough; but we shall by degrees come to apprehend far more than we expected, if we diligently compare spiritual things to spiritual.

~ GEORGE D'OYLY AND RICHARD MANT

In a loud voice they sang:
"Worthy is the Lamb, who was slain,
to receive power and wealth and
wisdom and strength and honor and glory and praise!"
REVELATION 5:12

Dear Lord and Father of mankind,
Forgive our foolish ways!
Recloth us in our rightful mind;
In purer lives your service find,
In deeper reverence, praise.

❧

Drop your still dews of quietness
Till all our strivings cease:
Take from our lives the strain and stress,
And let our ordered lives confess
The beauty of your peace.
JOHN GREENLEAF WHITTIER

I am disposed to say grace upon twenty other occasions in the course of the day besides my dinner. I want a form for setting out upon a pleasant walk, for a moonlight ramble, for a friendly meeting or a solved problem. Why have we none for books, those spiritual repasts — a grace before Milton, a devotional exercise proper to be said before reading [Spenser]?

~ CHARLES LAMB

His mercy extends to those who fear him, from generation to generation. He has performed mighty deeds with his arm; he has scattered those who are proud in their inmost thoughts. He has brought down rulers from their thrones but has lifted up the humble. He has filled the hungry with good things but has sent the rich away empty. He has helped his servant Israel, remembering to be merciful to Abraham and his descendants forever, even as he said to our fathers.
LUKE 1:50-55

Twilight and evening bell,
And after that the dark!
And may there be no sadness of farewell,
When I embark;

For though from out our bourne of Time and Place
The flood may bear me far,
I hope to see my Pilot face to face
When I have crost the bar.
ALFRED, LORD TENNYSON

I believe in God as I believe in my friends, because I feel the breath of His affection, feel His invisible and intangible hand drawing me, leading me, grasping me.

~ MIGUEL DE UNAMUNO

Therefore, since we have been justified through faith, we have peace with God through our Lord Jesus Christ, through whom we have gained access by faith into this grace in which we now stand. And we rejoice in the hope of the glory of God. Not only so, but we also rejoice in our sufferings, because we know that suffering produces perseverance; perseverance, character; and character, hope.
ROMANS 5:1-4

If we believe, everything is illuminated and takes shape around us, risk no longer exists, and success takes on an incorruptible fullness; pain becomes a visit and a caress from God.

~ TEILHARD DE CHARDIN

...Lord brought us out of Egypt with a mighty hand.
DEUTERONOMY 6:21

347

The test of life are to make, not break us. Trouble may demolish a man's business but build up his character. The blow at the outward man may be the greatest blessing to the inner man. If God, then, puts or permits anything hard in our lives, be sure that the real peril, the real trouble, is that we shall lose if we flinch or rebel.

MALTBIE D. BABCOCK

For Christ's love compels us, because we are convinced that one died for all, and therefore all died. And he died for all, that those who live should no longer live for themselves but for him who died for them and was raised again. So from now on we regard no one from a worldly point of view. Though we once regarded Christ in this way, we do so no longer. Therefore, if anyone is in Christ, he is a new creation; the old has gone, the new has come!
2 CORINTHIANS 5:14-17

Receive every day as a resurrection from death, as a new enjoyment of life; meet every rising sun with such sentiments of God's goodness, as if you had seen it, and all things, new-created upon your account: and under the sense of so great a blessing, let your joyful heart praise and magnify so good and glorious a Creator.

~ WILLIAM LAW

Loss
&
Mourning

❧

The sun will no more be your light by day, nor will the brightness of the moon shine on you, for the Lord will be your everlasting light, and your God will be your glory. Your sun will never set again, and your moon will wane no more; the Lord will be your everlasting light, and your days of sorrow will end.

ISAIAH 60:19-20

Most loving Father,
Preserve us from faithless fears and worldly anxieties
and grant that no clouds of this mortal life
May hide from us the light of that love which is immortal
And which you have manifested unto us in your Son
Jesus Christ our Lord.

WILLIAM BRIGHT

Give me thy grace, good Lord, to make death no stranger to me. Give me, good Lord, a longing to be with thee, not for the avoiding of the calamities of this wretched world; nor so much for the avoiding of the pains of purgatory, nor of the pains of hell neither, nor so much for the attaining of the joys of heaven in respect of mid own commodity, as even for a very love to thee.

~ ST. THOMAS MORE

For the wages of sin is death,
but the gift of God is eternal life in Christ Jesus our Lord.

ROMANS 6:23

Do not be afraid to throw yourself on the Lord!
He will not draw back and let you fall!
Put your worries aside and throw yourself on him;
he will welcome you and heal you.

ST. AUGUSTINE

Behold, Lord, an empty vessel that needs to be filled. My Lord, fill it. I am weak in the faith; strengthen thou me. I am cold in love; warm me and make me fervent that my love may go out to my neighbor. I do not have a strong and firm faith; at times I doubt and am unable to trust thee altogether. O Lord, help me. Strengthen my faith and trust in thee. In thee I have sealed the treasures of all I have. I am poor; thou art rich and didst come to be merciful to the poor. I am a sinner; thou art upright. With me there is an abundance of sin; in thee is the fulness of righteousness. Therefore, I will remain with thee of who I can receive but to whom I may not give. Amen.

~ MARTIN LUTHER

My God, I pray that I may so know you and love you
that I may rejoice in you.
And if I may not do so fully in this life,
let me go steadily on
to the day when I come to that fulness . . .
let me receive
That which you promised through your truth,
that my joy may be full.

ST. ANSELM

O Lord Almighty, Father of our Lord Jesus Christ, grant us, we pray thee, to be grounded and settled in thy truth by the coming down of the Holy Spirit into our hearts. That which we know not do thou reveal, that which is wanting in us do thou fill up; that which we know do thou confirm, and keep us blameless in thy service, through the same Jesus Christ our Lord.

~ ST. CLEMENT OF ROME

I prayed to the Lord and said, "O Sovereign Lord, do not destroy your people, your own inheritance that you redeemed by your great power and brought out of Egypt with a mighty hand."

DEUTERONOMY 9:26

O God that art the only hope of the world,
The only refuge for unhappy men,
Abiding in the faithfulness of heaven,
Give me strong succor in this testing place.
O King, protect thy man from utter ruin
Lest the weak faith surrender to the tyrant,
Facing innumerable blows alone.
Remember I am dust, and wind, and shadow,
And life as fleeting as the flower of grass.
But may the eternal mercy which hath shone
From time of old
Rescue thy servant from the jaws of the lion.
Thou who didst come from on high in the cloak of flesh,
Strike down the dragon with that two-edged sword,
Whereby our mortal flesh can war with the winds
And beat down strongholds, with our Captain God.

VENERABLE BEDE

O give us patience and steadfastness in adversity, strengthen our weakness, comfort us in trouble and distress, help us to fight; grant unto us that in true obedience and contentation of mind we may give over our own wills unto thee our Father in all things, according to the example of thy beloved Son; that in adversity we grudge not, but offer up ourselves unto thee without contradiction . . . O give us a willing and cheerful mind, that we may gladly suffer and bear all things for thy sake.

~ BISHOP MILES COVERDALE

❧

Though the fig tree does not bud
and there are no grapes on the vines,
though the olive crop fails
and the fields produce no food,
though there are no sheep in the pen
and no cattle in the stalls,
yet I will rejoice in the Lord,
I will be joyful in God my Savior.
HABAKKUK 3:17-18

Grow old along with me!
The best is yet to be,
The last of life, for which the first was made:
Our times are in his hand
Who saith "A whole I planned,
Youth shows but half; trust God: see all nor be afraid!"
ROBERT BROWNING

We beg you, Lord, to help and defend us. Deliver the oppressed, pity the insignificant, raise the fallen, show yourself to the needy, heal the sick, bring back those of your people who have gone astray, feed the hungry, lift up the weak, take off the prisoners' chains. May every nation come to know that you alone are God, that Jesus Christ is your Child, that we are your people, the sheep that you pasture.

~ ST. CLEMENT OF ROME

For the Lord himself will come down from heaven, with a loud command,
with the voice of the archangel and with the trumpet call of God, and the
dead in Christ will rise first. After that, we who are still alive and are left
will be caught up together with them in the clouds to meet the Lord in the
air. And so we will be with the Lord forever. Therefore encourage each
other with these words.
1 THESSALONIANS 4:16-18

Come lovely and soothing death,
Undulate round the world, serenely arriving, arriving,
In the day, in the night, to all to each,
Sooner or later, delicate death.
WALT WHITMAN

Behold, Lord, and empty vessel that needs to be filled. My Lord, fill it. I am weak in the faith; strengthen thou me. I am cold in love; warm me and make me fervent that my love may go out to my neighbor. I do not have a strong and firm faith; at times I doubt and am unable to trust thee altogether. O Lord, help me. Strengthen my faith and trust in thee. In thee I have sealed the treasures of all I have. I am poor; thou art rich and didst come to be merciful to the poor. I am a sinner; thou art upright. With me there is an abundance of sin; in thee is the fullness of righteousness. Therefore, I will remain with thee of whom I can receive but to whom I may not give. Amen.

~ MARTIN LUTHER

Therefore you do not lack any spiritual gift
as you eagerly wait for our Lord Jesus Christ to be revealed.
He will keep you strong
to the end, so that you will be blameless
on the day of our Lord Jesus Christ.
1 CORINTHIANS 1:7-8

"He gives light to the sun."

~ ST. PATRICK

I'll praise my Maker while I've breath;
And when my voice is lost in death,
Praise shall employ my nobler powers:
My days of praise shall ne'er be past
While life, and thought, and being last
Or immortality endures.
ISAAC WATTS

Verily I say unto you, wheresoever this gospel shall be preached in the whole world, there shall also this, that this woman hath done, be told for a memorial of her.
MATTHEW 26:13

O, most loving Mary, star of the sea, most glorious mother of mercy, dwelling place of chasteness, pray for us to our Lord Jesus Christ your Son, that he may rescue us from evil, that he may make us rejoice in good, that he may cleanse us of vices and may strengthen us with virtues, that he may bring us tranquillity and may preserve us in a peaceful life with those who are his own. We entreat you that we may escape Satan's terrors, and that we may have you for our guide as we make our way to our home, lest the subtle enemy ensnare us on our road.

~ EDMUND COLLEDGE

I have been crucified with Christ and I no longer live, but Christ lives in me. The life I live in the body, I live by faith in the Son of God, who loved me and gave himself for me.
GALATIANS 2:20

Did not the Christ have to suffer these things and
then enter his glory?
LUKE 24:26

Almighty God, from whom all thoughts of truth and peace proceed:
Kindle, we pray you, in the hearts of all people the true love of peace; and
guide with your pure and peaceable wisdom those who take counsel for
the nations of the earth; that in tranquillity your kingdom may go forward,
till the earth be filled with the knowledge of your love:
through Jesus Christ our Lord.
FRANCIS PAGET

The religion of a Christian does more command fortitude than ever did
any institution; for we are commanded to be willing to die for Christ, to
die for the brethren, to die rather than give offence or scandal: the effect of
which is this, that he that is instructed to do the necessary parts of his
duty, is, by the same instrument, fortified against death . . .

~ JEREMEY TAYLOR

Because through Christ Jesus the law of the Spirit of life set me free from
the law of sin and death.
ROMANS 8:2

Rest and peace eternal give them,
Lord Our God: and light for
Evermore shine down upon them.
GIUSEPPE VERDI

Great and wonderful are thy deeds,
O Lord God the Almighty!
Just and true are thy ways,
O King of the ages!
Who shall not fear and glorify thy name, O Lord?
For thou alone art holy.
All nations shall come and worship thee,
for thy judgements have been revealed.
REVELATION 15:3-4

When faith is firm, and conscience clear,
And words of peace the spirit cheer
And visioned glories half appear
'Tis joy, 'tis triumph then to die.
ANNA LAETITIA BARBAULD

✣

Bring us, O Lord our God, at our last awakening into the house and gate of heaven, to enter into that gate and dwell in that house, where there shall be no darkness or dazzling, but one equal light; no noise or silence, but one equal music; no fears or hopes, but one equal possession; no ends or beginnings, but one equal eternity; in the habitations of thy glory and dominion world without end.

~ JOHN DONNE

May the words of my mouth and the meditation of my heart be pleasing in your sight, O Lord, my Rock and my Redeemer.
PSALMS 19:14

Now it is you alone that I love,
you alone that I follow,
you alone that I seek,
you alone that I feel ready to serve,
because you alone rule justly.
It is to your authority alone that I want to submit.
Command me, I pray, to do whatever you will,
but heal and open my ears
that I may hear your voice.
Heal and open my eyes
that I may see your will.
Drive our from me
all fickleness,
That I may acknowledge you alone.
Tell me where to look
that I may see you,
and I will place my hope in doing your will. Amen.
ST. AUGUSTINE

Lord Jesus Christ, who returned form this world to the Father and loved those who were here in this world, make my mind turn from worldly pre-occupations to the contemplation of heaven, to despise everything transi-tory and to yearn only for celestial things, and to burn with the glowing fire of your love. And you, Lord, who deemed yourself worthy to wash the feet of your holy apostles with your sacred hands, cleanse also my heart by pouring in the radiance of the Holy Spirit, so that I may be able to love you, our Lord Jesus Christ, in all things and above all else.

~ LATIN PRAYER

Nevertheless, though I am sometimes afraid: yet put I my trust in thee.
PSALMS 56:3

Death, be not proud, though some have called thee
Mighty and dreadful, for thou art not so;
For those whom thou think'st thou dost overthrow,

Die not, poor Death, nor yet canst thou kill me.
From rest and sleep, which but thy pictures be,
Much pleasure; then from thee much more must flow,
And soonest our best men with thee do go,
Rest of their bones, and soul's delivery.
Thou art slave to fate, chance, kings, and desperate men,
And dost with poison, war, and sickness dwell;
And poppy or charms can make us sleep as well
And better than thy stroke; why swell'st thou then?
One short sleep past, we wake eternally,
And death shall be no more; Death, thou shalt die.
JOHN DONNE

But if Christ is in you, your body is dead because of sin,
yet your spirit is alive because of righteousness.
ROMANS 8:10

O Lord, who has ordained labour to be the lot of man, and seest the necessities of all thy creatures, bless my studies and endeavours; feed me with food convenient for me; and if it shall be thy good pleasure to entrust me with plenty, give me a compassionate heart, that I may be ready to relieve the wants of others; let neither poverty nor riches estrange my heart from thee, but assist me with thy grace so to live that I may die in thy favour, for the sake of Jesus Christ.

~ SAMUEL JOHNSON

The Lord preserveth the simple: I was in misery, and he helped me.
PSALMS 116:6

Blessed Lord, who was tempted in all things like as we are, have mercy upon our frailty. Out of weakness give us strength. Grant to us thy fear, that we may fear thee only. Support us in time of temptation. Embolden us in the time of danger. Help us to do thy work with good courage, and to continue thy faithful soldiers and servants unto our life's end; through Jesus Christ our Lord.

~ BISHOP BROOKE FOSS WESTCOTT

The people walking in darkness have seen a great light; on those living in
the land of the shadow of death a light has dawned.
ISAIAH 9:2

The Sea of Faith
Was once, too, at the full, and round earth's shore
Lay like the folds of a bright girdle furl'd.
But now I only hear Its melancholy, long, withdrawing roar,

Retreating, to the breath
Of the night-wind, down the vast edges drear
And naked shingles of the world.
MATTHEW ARNOLD

Here begins the open sea. Here begins the glorious adventure, the only one abreast with human curiosity, the only one that soars as high as its highest longing. Let us accustom ourselves to regard death as a form of life which we do not yet understand; let us learn to look upon it with the same eye that looks upon birth; and soon our mind will be accompanied to the steps of the tomb with the same glad expectation as greets a birth.

~ MAURICE MAETERLINCK

Heal me, O Lord, and I shall be healed;
Save me, and I shall be saved;
For thou art my praise.
JEREMIAH 17:14

Some there are who presume so far on their wits that they think themselves capable of measuring the whole nature of things by their intellect, in that they esteem all things true which they see, and false which they see not. Accordingly, in order that man's mind might be freed from this presumption, and seek the truth humbly, it was necessary that certain things far surpassing his intellect should be proposed to man by God.

~ THOMAS AQUINAS

Lord, now lettest thou thy servant depart in peace
LUKE 2:29

God's child in Christ adopted—Christ my all—
What that earth boasts were not lost cheaply, rather
Than forfeit that blest name, by which I call
The Holy One, the Almighty God, my Father?—
Father! in Christ we live, and Christ in Thee—
Eternal Thou and everlasting we.
The heir of heaven, henceforth I fear not death:
In Christ I live! in Christ I draw the breath
Of the true life!—let then earth, sea, and sky
Make war against me! On my front I show
Their mighty Master's seal. In vain they try
To end my life, that can but end its woe.
Is that a death-bed where a Christian lies?
Yes, but not his—'tis Death itself there dies.
SAMUEL TAYLOR COLERIDGE

And now, Lord, what is my hope: truly my hope is even in thee.
PSALMS 39:8

I beseech thee, good Jesus, that as thou hast graciously granted to me here on earth sweetly to partake of the words of thy wisdom and knowledge, so thou wilt vouchsafe that I may some time come to thee, the fountain of all wisdom, and always appear before thy face; who livest and reignest, world without end.

~ VENERABLE BEDE

For when he received honor and glory from God the Father and the voice was borne to him by the Majestic Glory, "This is my beloved Son, with whom I am well pleased," we heard this voice borne from heaven, for we were with him on the holy mountain. And we have the prophetic word made more sure. You will do well to pay attention to this as to a lamp shining in a dark place, until the day dawns and the morning star rises in your hearts.
PETER 1:17-19

Christ be with me,
Christ within me,
Christ behind me,
Christ before me,
Christ beside me,
Christ to win me,
Christ to comfort and restore me,
Christ beneath me,
Christ above me,
Christ in quiet,
Christ in danger,
Christ in hearts of all that love me,
Christ in mouth of friend and stranger.
ST. PATRICK

O God, who has brought us near to an unnumerable company of angels and to the spirits of just men made perfect; grant us, during our earthly pilgrimage, to abide in their fellowship, and in our heavenly country to be partakers of their joy; through Jesus Christ our Lord.

~ WILLIAM BRIGHT

And the world and its desire are passing away,
but those who do the will of God live forever.
1 JOHN 2:17

Sovereign Lord, as you have promised, you now dismiss your servant in peace. For my eyes have seen your salvation, which you have prepared in the sight of all people, a light for revelation to the Gentiles and for glory to your people Israel.
LUKE 2:29-32

No one who is fit to live need fear to die. Poor, timorous, faithless souls that we are! How we shall smile at our vain alarms, when the worst has happened! To us here, death is the most terrible word we know. But when we have tasted its reality, it will mean to us birth, deliverance, a new creation of ourselves. It will be what health is to the sick man. It will be what home is to the exile. It will be what the loved one given back is to the bereaved. As we draw near to it, a great solemn gladness should fill our hearts. It is God's great morning lighting up the sky.

~ GEORGE SPRING MERRIAM

At just the right time, when we were still powerless, Christ died for the ungodly. Very rarely will anyone die for a righteous man, though for a good man someone might possibly dare to die. But God demonstrates his own love for us in this: While we were still sinners, Christ died for us.
ROMANS 5:6-8

Death stands above me, whispering low
I know not what into my ear:
Of his strange language all I know
Is, there is not a word of fear.
WALTER SAVAGE LANDOR

To be grateful is to recognize the Love of God in everything He has given us—and He has given us everything.

~ THOMAS MERTON

Great peace have they who love your law,
and nothing can make them stumble.
PSALMS 119:165

You, O eternal Trinity, are a deep sea, into which the more I enter the more I find, and the more I find the more I seek. The soul cannot be satiated in your abyss, for she continually hungers after you, the eternal Trinity, desiring to see you with the light of your light. As the hart desires the springs of living water, so my soul desires to leave the prison of this dark body and see you in truth.

~ ST. CATHERINE OF SIENA

❧

*Then he called the crowd to him along with his disciples and said:
"If anyone would come after me, he must deny himself and take up his cross
and follow me. For whoever wants to save his life will lose it, but whoever
loses his life for me and for the gospel will save it. What good is it for a
man to gain the whole world, yet forfeit his soul?"*

MARK 8:34-36

---

*For if, when we were God's enemies, we were reconciled to him through the
death of his Son, how much more, having been reconciled,
shall we be saved through his life! Not only is this so, but we also rejoice in
God through our Lord Jesus Christ, through whom we have
now received reconciliation.*

ROMANS 5:10-11

---

*I have a sin of fear,
that when I've spun My last thread,
I shall perish on the shore;
But swear by Thyself that at my death Thy Son
Shall shine as He shines now and heretofore:
And having done that, Thou hast done;
I fear no more.*

JOHN DONNE

Religion is not ours till we live by it, till it is the Religion of our thoughts,
words, and actions, till it goes with us into every place, sits uppermost on
every occasion, and forms and governs our hopes and fears, our cares and
pleasures.

~ WILLIAM LAW

---

*Faithfulness will spring up from the ground,
and righteousness will look down from the sky.
The Lord will give what is good, and our land will yield its increase.*

PSALMS 85:12-13

---

*Now hath my life across a stormy sea
Like a frail bark reached that wide port where all
Are bidden, ere the final reckoning fall
Of good and evil for eternity.
Now know I well how that fond phantasy
Which made my soul the worshipper and thrall
Of earthly art, is vain; how criminal
Is that which all men seek unwillingly.
Those amorous thoughts which were so lightly dressed,
What are they when the double death is nigh?
The one I know for sure, the other dread.
Painting nor sculpture now can lull to rest*

My soul that turns to His great love on high,
Whose arms to clasp us on the cross were spread.
MICHELANGELO BUONARROTTI

Soon, for me, the light of day
Shall for ever pass away;
Then, from sin and sorrow free,
Take me, Lord, to dwell with Thee:
GEORGE WASHINGTON DOANE

Then Paul answered, "Why are you weeping and breaking my heart? I am ready not only to be bound, but also to die in Jerusalem for the name of the Lord Jesus." When he would not be dissuaded, we gave up and said, "The Lord's will be done."
ACTS 21:13-14

Mary rose up, as on in sleep might rise,
And went to meet her brother's Friend: and they
Who tarried with her said: "she goes to pray
And weep where her dead brother's body lies."
So, with their wringing of hands and with sighs,
They stood before Him in the public way.
"Had'st Thou been with him, Lord, upon that day,
He had not died," she said, drooping her eyes.
Mary and Martha with bowed faces kept
Holding His garments, one on each side. . . . "Where
Have ye laid him?" He asked. "Lord, come and see."—
The sound of grieving voices heavily
And universally was round Him there,
A sound that smote His spirit. Jesus wept.
WILLIAM MICHAEL ROSSETTI

O Lord, give us we beseech you in the name of Jesus Christ your Son our Lord, that love which can never cease, that will kindle our lamps but not extinguish them, that they may burn in us and enlighten others.

Do you, O Christ, our dearest Savior, yourself kindle our lamps that they may evermore shin in your temple and receive unquenchable light from you that will enlighten our darkness and lessen the darkness of the world.

~ ST. COLUMBA

But now that you have been set free from sin
and have become slaves to God,
the benefit you reap leads to holiness,
and the result is eternal life.
ROMANS 6:22

The world recedes; it disappears;
Heav'n opens on my eyes; my ears
With sounds seraphic ring:
Lend, lend your wings! I mount! I fly!
O Grave! where is thy Victory?
O Death! where is thy Sting?

ALEXANDER POPE

The God and Father of our Lord Jesus Christ open all our eyes, that we may see that blessed hope to which we are called; that we may altogether glorify the only true God and Jesus Christ; whom he has sent down to us from heaven; to whom with the Father and the Holy Spirit be rendered all honor and glory to all eternity.

~ BISHOP JEWELL

For from him and through him and to him are all things.
To him be the glory forever! Amen.

ROMANS 11:36

Grant, Lord God, that we may cleave to you without parting,
worship you without wearing,
serve you without failing, faithfully find you,
for ever possess you, the one only God,
blessed for all eternity. Amen.

ST. ANSELM

O God, by whom the meek are guided in judgment and light rises up in darkness for the godly; grant us, in all our doubts and uncertainties, the grace to ask what you would have us do; that the Spirit of Wisdom may save us from all false choices and that in your light we may see light and in your straight path may not stumble; through Jesus Christ our Lord.

~ WILLIAM BRIGHT

Whoever tries to keep his life will lose it,
and whoever loses his life will preserve it.

LUKE 17:33

Teach us, Lord,
to serve you as you deserve,
to give and not to count the cost,
to fight and not heed the wounds,
to toil and not to seek for rest,
to labor and not to seek for any reward
save that of knowing that we do you will.

ST. IGNATIUS LOYOLA

Lord God Almighty, shaper and ruler of all creatures, we pray for your great mercy to guide us to your will, to make our minds steadfast, to strengthen us against temptation, to put far from us all unrighteousness.

Shield us against our foes, seen and unseen, teach us so that we may inwardly love you before all things with a clean mind and clean body, for you are our maker and our redeemer, our trust and our hope.

~ KING ALFRED

A faith and knowledge resting on the hope of eternal life, which God, who does not lie, promised before the beginning of time . . .

TITUS 1:2

You said so gently,
So persistently
"Give me your weariness
And I'll give you my rest."
I did . . . finally.
You did immediately.
Then, Lord, I marveled
That I had waited so long.

RUTH HARMS CALKIN

Grant, O God, that amidst all the discouragements, difficulties, dangers, distress and darkness of this mortal life, I may depend upon your mercy and on this build my hopes, as on a sure foundation. Let your infinite mercy in Christ Jesus deliver me from despair, both now and at the hour of death.

~ THOMAS WILSON

Come to me, all you who are weary and burdened,
and I will give you rest.

MATTHEW 11:28

You have led me through my crowded travels of the day
to my evening's loneliness.
I wait for its meaning through the stillness of the night.

RABINDRANATH TAGORE

Renewal

I tell you the truth, if anyone keeps my word, he will never see death.
JOHN 8:51

To every thing there is a season,
and a time to every purpose under heaven:
A time to be born, and a time to die;
A time to plant, and a time to pluck up
That which is planted;
A time to kill, and a time to heal;
A time to break down, and a time to build up;
A time to weep, and a time to laugh;
A time to mourn, and a time to dance.
ECCLESIASTES 3:1-4

Glorious God, give me grace to amend my life and to have an eye to mine end without grudge of death, which to them that die in thee, good Lord, is the fate of a wealthy life . . .

Give me, good Lord, a full faith, a firm hope and a fervent charity, a love to thee incomparable above the love to myself.

Give me, good Lord, a longing to be with thee, not for the avoiding of the calamities of this world, nor so much for the attaining of the joys of heaven, as for very love of thee.

~ THOMAS MORE

It is the spirit that gives life; the flesh is useless.
The words that I have spoken to you are spirit and life.
JOHN 6:63

Lord, you have been our dwelling place
throughout all generations.
Before the mountains were born
or you brought forth the earth and the world,
from everlasting to everlasting you are God.
PSALMS 90:1-2

The search may begin with a restless feeling . . . One turns in all directions and sees nothing. Yet one senses that there is a source for this deep restlessness, and the path that leads there is not a path to a strange place, but the path home.

~ PETER MATTHEISSEN

Give us, O Lord, a steadfast heart, which no unworthy affection may drag downwards; give us an unconquered heart, which no tribulation can wear out; give us an upright heart, which no unworthy purpose may tempt aside. Bestow upon us also, O Lord our God, understanding to know you, diligence to seek you, wisdom to find you and a faithfulness that may finally embrace you; through Jesus Christ our Lord.

~ ST. THOMAS AQUINAS

Let everything that has breath praise the Lord.
Praise the Lord.
PSALMS 150:6

Whoever truly loves you, good Lord,
walks in safety down a royal road, far from the dangerous abyss;
and if he so much as stumbles, you, O Lord, stretch out your hand.
Not one fall, or many, will cause you to abandon him
if he loves you
and does not love the things of this world,
because he walks in the vale of humility.
ST. TERESA OF AVILA

If thou meet with the cross on thy journey, in what manner soever it be, be not daunted, and say, Alas, what shall I do now? But rather take courage, knowing that by the cross is the way to the kingdom.

~ JOHN BUNYAN

I am listening to what the God the Lord will say: He promises peace—
but let them not return to folly. Surely his salvation is near those who fear
him, that his glory may dwell in our land.
PSALMS 85:8-9

And when the earth shall claim your
limbs, then shall you truly dance.
KAHLIL GIBRAN

The door of death is made of gold,
That mortal eyes cannot behold;
But, when the mortal eyes are closed,
And cold and pale and limbs reposed,
The soul awakes; and wondering, sees
In her mild hand the golden keys . . .
WILLIAM BLAKE

Grant, O God, that amidst all the discouragements, difficulties, dangers, distress and darkness of this mortal life, I may depend upon your mercy

Renewal

and on this build my hopes, as on a sure foundation. Let your infinite
mercy in Christ Jesus Deliver me from despair

~ THOMAS WILSON

Who shall deliver me from the body of this death?
ROMANS 7:24

What lies behind us and what lies before us are tiny matters compared to
what lies within us.

~ RALPH WALDO EMERSON

The people living in darkness have seen a great light; on those living in the
land of the shadow of death a light has dawned.
MATTHEW 4:16

The dead shall live, their bodies shall rise.
O dwellers in the dust, awake and sing for joy!
For thy dew is a dew of light,
And on the land of the shades thou wilt let it fall.
ISAIAH 26:19

Out of the finite darkness, into the infinite light.

~ LOUISE CHANDLER MOULTON

In the bleak mid-winter
Frosty wind made moan,
Earth stood hard as iron,
Water like a stone;
Snow had fallen, snow on snow,
Snow on snow,
In the bleak mid-winter
Long ago.

Our God, Heaven cannot hold him,
Nor earth sustain;
Heaven and earth shall flee away
When he comes to reign:
In the bleak mid-winter
A table-place sufficed
The Lord God Almighty
Jesus Christ.

No, in all these things we are more than conquerors through him who loved us. For I am convinced that neither death nor life, neither angels nor demons, neither the present nor the future, nor any powers, neither height nor depth, nor anything else in all creation, will be able to separate us from the love of God that is in Christ Jesus our Lord.

ROMANS 8:37-39

Now it is you alone that I love,
you alone that I follow,
you alone that I seek,
you alone that I feel ready to serve,
because you alone rule justly.
It is to your authority alone that I want to submit.
Command me, I pray, to do whatever you will,
but heal and open my ears
that I may hear your voice.
Heal and open my eyes
that I may see your will.
Drive our from me
all fickleness,
That I may acknowledge you alone.
Tell me where to look
that I may see you,
and I will place my hope in doing your will. Amen.

ST. AUGUSTINE

I believe that man will not merely endure; he will prevail. He is immortal, not because he alone among creatures has an inexhaustible voice, but because he has a soul, a spirit capable of compassion and sacrifice and endurance.

~ WILLIAM FAULKNER

To him who overcomes and does my will to the end, I will give authority over the nations— He will rule them with an iron scepter; he will dash them to pieces like pottery, just as I have received authority from my Father. I will also give him the morning star.

REVELATION 2:26-28

We rest on Thee, our shield and our defender!
Thine is the battle, Thine shall be the praise;
When passing through the gates of pearly splendor,
Victors, we rest with Thee, through endless days.

EDITH GILLING CHERRY

Give rest, O Christ, to your servant with your saints: where sorrow and pain are no more; neither sighing, but life everlasting.

You alone are immortal, the creator and maker of man; and we are

❀

mortal, formed from the earth, and to the earth we shall return; for you so ordained when you created us, saying "Dust you are, and to dust you shall return"; we shall all go down to the dust; and, weeping over the grave, we sing alleluia, alleluia, alleluia.

Give rest, O Christ, to your servant with your saints: where sorrow and pain are no more; neither sighing, but life everlasting.

~ RUSSIAN LITURGY

For God so loved the world that he gave his one and only Son, that whoever believes in him shall not perish but have eternal life.

JOHN 3:15

Faithfulness will spring up from the ground, and righteousness will look down from the sky. The Lord will give what is good, and our land will yield its increase.

PSALMS 85:12-13

O God that art the only hope of the world,
The only refuge for unhappy men,
Abiding in the faithfulness of heaven,
Give me strong succour in this testing place.
O King, protect thy man from utter ruin
Lest the weak faith surrender to the tyrant,
Facing innumerable blows alone.
Remember I am dust, and wind, and shadow,
And life as fleeting as the flower of grass.
But may the eternal mercy which hath shone
From time of old
Rescue thy servant from the jaws of the lion.
Thou who didst come from on high in the cloak of flesh,
Strike down the dragon with that two-edged sword,
Whereby our mortal flesh can war with the winds
And beat down strongholds, with our Captain God.

VENERABLE BEDE

O Lord our God, grant us grace to desire Thee with our whole heart; that, so desiring, we may seek, and seeking find Thee; and so finding Thee may love Thee; and loving Thee, may hate those sins from which Thou hast redeemed us.

~ ST. ANSELM OF CANTERBURY

---

*But now that you have been set free from sin
and have become slaves to God,
the benefit you reap leads to holiness,
and the result is eternal life.*

ROMANS 6:22

Do not be afraid to throw yourself on the Lord!
He will not draw back and let you fall!
Put your worries aside and throw yourself on him;
he will welcome you and heal you.
ST. AUGUSTINE

O Lord Almighty, Father of our Lord Jesus Christ, grant us, we pray thee, to be grounded and settled in thy truth by the coming down of the Holy Spirit into our hearts. That which we know not do thou reveal, that which is wanting in us do thou fill up; that which we know do thou confirm, and keep us blameless in thy service, through the same Jesus Christ our Lord.

~ ST. CLEMENT OF ROME

Let us fix our eyes on Jesus, the author and perfecter of our faith, who for the joy set before him endured the cross, scorning its shame, and sat down at the right hand of the throne of God.
HEBREWS 12:2

Drop thy still dews of quietness,
Till all our strivings cease;
Take from our souls the strain and stress,
And let our ordered lives confess
The beauty of thy peace.
J. G. WHITTIER

When they had rowed three or three and a half miles,
they saw Jesus approaching the boat, walking on the water;
and they were terrified. But he said to them, "It is I; don't be afraid."
JOHN 6:19-20

Birth must seem to the new-born babe what death seems to us: the anni-hilation of all the conditions which had hitherto made life possible in the womb of its mother, but proved to be its emergence into a wider life
GUSTAVE FECHNER

We will have no other master but our caprice—that is to say, our evil self will have no God, and the foundation of our nature is seditious, impious, refractory, opposed to and contemptuous of all that tries to rule it, and

therefore contrary to order, ungovernable and negative. It is this foundation which Christianity calls the natural man. But the savage which is
within us, and constitutes the primitive stuff of us, must be disciplined
and civilized in order to produce a man. And the man must be patiently
cultivated to produce a wise man; and the wise man must be tested and
tried if he is to become righteous, and the righteous man must have sub-
stituted the will of God for his individual will, if he is to become a saint.

~ HENRI-FRÉDÉRIC AMIEL

---

*. . . A great voice from the throne said:
"Behold, the dwelling of God is with men . . . and they shall be his
people . . . he will wipe away every tear from their eyes, and death shall be
no more, neither shall there be mourning nor crying nor pain any more, for
the former things have passed away . . . Behold, I make all things new."*
REVELATION 1:17-18, 21:3-5

---

*He has come! the Christ of God;
Left for us His glad abode,
Stooping from His throne of bliss,
To this darksome wilderness.*

*He has come! the Prince of Peace;
Come to bid our sorrows cease;
Come to scatter with His light
All the darkness of our night.*

*He, the Mighty King, has come!
Making this poor world His home;
Come to bear our sin's sad load,—
Son of David, Son of God!*

*He has come whose name of grace
Speaks deliverance to our race;
Left for us His glad abode,—
Son of Mary, Son of God!*

HORATIUS BONAR

Let us go and wake up the universe . . . and sing His praises.

~ MARIAM BAOUARDY

---

*After he was raised from the dead, his disciples recalled what he had said.
Then they believed the Scripture and the words that Jesus had spoken.*
JOHN 2:22

Morning breaks upon the tomb,
Jesus scatters all its gloom.
Day of triumph through the skies—
See the glorious Savior rise.

Christians! Dry your flowing tears,
Chase those unbelieving fears;
Look on his deserted grave,
Doubt no more his power to save.

Ye who are of death afraid,
Triumph in the scattered shade:
Drive your anxious cares away,
See the place where Jesus lay.
WILLIAM BENGO COLLYER

Slowly, all through the universe, that temple of God is being built.
Wherever, in any world, a soul, by free-willed obedience, catches the fire of
God's likeness, it is set into the growing walls, a living stone. When, in
your hard fight, in your tiresome drudgery, or in your terrible temptation,
you catch the purpose of your being and give yourself to God, and so give
Him the chance to give Himself to you, your life—a living stone—is taken
up and set into that growing wall. Wherever souls are being tried and
ripened, in whatever commonplace and homely ways, there God is hewing
out the pillars for His temple. Oh, if the stone can only have some vision
of the temple of which it is to be a part forever, what patience must fill it
as it feels the blows of the hammer, and knows that success for it is simply to let itself be wrought into what shape the Master wills.

~ PHILLIPS BROOKS

Make every effort to live in peace
with all men and to be holy.
HEBREWS 12:14

O Lamb of god, who takest away the sin of the world,
look upon us and have mercy upon us;
thou who art thyself both victim and Priest,
thyself both Reward and Redeemer,
keep safe from all evil those whom thou has redeemed,
O Savior of the world.
ST. IRENAEUS

Lord, Lord almighty, Father of our Lord Jesus Christ, I am your servant;
come to my help. Send me your angel; take my soul and give it peace.
That will stop the foul dragon with his reek of blood from blocking my
way; no malice of his will then obstruct my soul, none of his stratagems
will deceive me.

Give me rest in the company of your martyrs; save your people, too,
Lord, from oppression by the godless. For it is fitting that you should have

honor, you and your only Son and the Holy Spirit, throughout the ages.

~ BONIFACE OF TARSUS

"God is spirit, and his worshipers must worship in spirit and in truth."
JOHN 4:24

For now my sight, clear and yet clearer grown,
Pierced through the ray of that exalted light,
Wherein, as in itself, the truth is known.

O light supreme, by mortal thought unscanned . . .

Make strong my tongue that in its words may burn
One single spark of all Thy glory's light
For future generations to discern.
DANTE ALIGHIERI

O to continue to drink deep of the streams of the great salvation, until I wholly lose the thirst for the passing things of earth; to live watching for my Lord, to be wide awake when he comes, to open to him quickly and enjoy his likeness to the full.

~ ANN GRIFFITHS

Jesus answered,
"The work of God is this: to believe in the one he has sent."
JOHN 6:29

O our Savior! Of ourselves we cannot love thee, cannot follow thee, cannot cleave to thee; but thou didst come down that we might love thee didst ascend that we might follow thee, didst bind us round thee as thy girdle that we might be held fast unto thee; Thou who hast loved us, make us to love thee, Thou who hast sought us, make us to seek thee, Thou who, when lost, didst find us be thou thyself the way, that we may find thee and be found in thee, our only hope, our everlasting joy.
E. B. PUSEY

High hearts are never long without hearing some new call, some distant clarion of God, even in their dreams; and soon they are observed to break up the camp of ease, and start on some fresh march of faithful service.

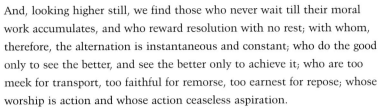

And, looking higher still, we find those who never wait till their moral work accumulates, and who reward resolution with no rest; with whom, therefore, the alternation is instantaneous and constant; who do the good only to see the better, and see the better only to achieve it; who are too meek for transport, too faithful for remorse, too earnest for repose; whose worship is action and whose action ceaseless aspiration.

~ J. MARTINEAU

I tell you the truth,
whoever hears my word and believes him who sent me
has eternal life and will not be condemned;
he has crossed over from death to life.

I tell you the truth,
a time is coming and has now come
when the dead will hear the voice of the Son of God
and those who hear will live.

JOHN 5:24-25

Fire of the Spirit, life of the lives of creatures,
spiral of sanctity, bond of all natures,
glow of charity, lights of clarity, taste
of sweetness to sinners, be with us and hear us . . .

Composer of all things, light of all the risen,
key of salvation, release from the dark prison,
hope of all unions, scop of chastities, joy
in the glory, strong honour, be with us and hear us.

ST. HILDEGARDE

God has plans which mortals don't understand. He rests in the womb when the new baby forms. Whispers the life dream to infinitesimal cells. It is God who lies under the thoughts of man. He is cartilage. Memory.

~ ELLEASE SOUTHERLAND

Mercy, peace and love be yours in abundance.
JUDE 1:2

O Lord, my God,
Grant us your peace; already, indeed, you have made us rich in all things!
Give us that peace of being at rest,
That sabbath peace,
The peace which knows no end.
ST. AUGUSTINE

As soon as Jesus was baptized, he went up out of the water. At that moment heaven was opened, and he saw the Spirit of God descending like a dove and lighting on him. And a voice from heaven said, "This is my Son, whom I love; with him I am well pleased."
MATTHEW 3:16-17

Beware in your prayer, above everything, of limiting God, not only by unbelief, but by fancying that you know what He can do.
ANDREW MURRAY

You, O eternal Trinity, are a deep sea, into which the more I enter the more I find, and the more I find the more I seek. The soul cannot be satiated in your abyss, for she continually hungers after you, the eternal Trinity, desiring to see you with the light of your light. As the hart desires the springs of living water, so my soul desires to leave the prison of this dark body and see you in truth.

~ ST. CATHERINE OF SIENNA

Therefore everyone who hears these words of mine and puts them into practice is like a wise man who built his house on the rock. The rain came down, the streams rose, and the winds blew and beat against that house; yet it did not fall, because it had its foundation on the rock.
MATTHEW 7:24-25

To see a World in a grain of sand,
And a Heaven in a wild flower,
Hold Infinity in the palm of your hand,
And Eternity in an hour.
WILLIAM BLAKE

God has set in the midst of you, as the ever present witness and figure of heaven, His holy House of Prayer. There it stands, built for no earthly purpose, different in shape, and in all things belonging to it, from earthly habitations; speaking only of heaven, and heavenly uses, and heavenly gifts, and heavenly blessings; the gate of heaven when we are brought into it as little children to Christ; the gate of heaven, if so God grant us, when we are brought to it, and pass through it the last time on our way to our grave beside it. And here we meet our God.

~ RICHARD WILLIAM CHURCH

To the Jews who had believed him, Jesus said,
"If you hold to my teaching, you are really my disciples.
Then you will know the truth, and the truth will set you free."
JOHN 8:31-32

"Thou shalt not" is the beginning of wisdom. But the end of wisdom, the new law, is, "Thou shalt." To be Christian is to be old? Not a bit of it. To be Christian is to be reborn, and free, and unafraid, and immortally young.

JOY DAVIDMAN

There can be nothing more terrible or wonderful than to be stricken with love for Christ so deeply that the whole being goes out in a pained adoration of His person, an adoration that disturbs and disconcerts while it purges and satisfies and relaxes the deep inner heart.

~ A.W. TOZER

. . . for I am honored in the eyes of the Lord, and my God has become my strength— he says: "It is too light a thing that you should be my servant to raise up the tribes of Jacob and to restore the preserved of Israel; I will give you as a light to the nations, that my salvation may reach to the end of the earth."

ISAIAH 49:5

It is not far to go
for you are near,
It is not far to go
for you are here.
And not by traveling, Lord,
we come to you,
but by the way of love,
and we love you.

AMY CARMICHAEL

He that is alive may know that he was born, though he know neither the place where nor the time when he was so; and so may he that is spiritually alive, and hath ground of evidence that he is so, that he was born again, though he know neither when, nor where, nor how. And this case is usual in persons of quiet natural tempers, who have had the advantage of education under means of light and grace. God ofttimes, in such persons, begins and carries on the work of his grace insensibly, so that they come to good growth and maturity before they know that they are alive.

~ JOHN OWEN

He told them, "This is what is written: The Christ will suffer and rise from the dead on the third day, and repentance and forgiveness of sins will be preached in his name to all nations, beginning at Jerusalem. You are witnesses of these things."

LUKE 24:46-48

We adore you, Lord Jesus Christ,
in all the churches of the whole world
and we bless you, for by means of your holy cross
you have redeemed the world.
ST. FRANCIS OF ASSISI

To you, O Son of God, Lord Jesus Christ, as you pray to the eternal Father, we pray, make us one in him. Lighten our personal distress and that of our society. Receive us into the fellowship of those who believe. Turn our hearts, O Christ, to everlasting truth and healing harmony.

~ PHILIP MELANCHTHON

Finally, my brothers, rejoice in the Lord!
PHILIPPIANS 3:1

Lord Jesus, think on me,
And purge away my sin;
From earthborn passions set me free,
And make me pure within.

Lord Jesus, think on me,
With care and woe oppressed;
Let me thy loving servant be,
And taste thy promised rest.

Lord Jesus, think on me,
Nor let me go astray;
Through darkness and perplexity
Point thou the heavenly way.

Lord Jesus, think on me,
That when the flood is past,
I may the eternal brightness see,
And share thy joy at last.
SYNESIUS

If thou believest that Christ was crucified for the sins of the world, thou must with Him be crucified . . . If thou refusest to comply with this order, thou canst not be a living member of Christ, nor be united with Him by faith.

~ JOHN ARNDT

Rejoice and be glad, because great is your reward in heaven, for in the same
way they persecuted the prophets who were before you.
MATTHEW 5:12

Give me a pure heart—that I may see you,
A humble heart—that I may hear you,
A heart of love—that I may serve you,
A heart of faith—that I may abide in you.
DAG HAMMARSKJÖLD

O Christ our God, who are yourself the fulfillment of the law and the prophets, and did fulfill all the ordered purpose of the Father, always fill our hearts with joy and gladness, now ad forever, world without end.

~ LITURGY OF ST. CHRYSOSTOM

As you go, preach this message: 'The Kingdom of heaven is near.'
MATTHEW 10:7

How great is your goodness, dear Lord!
Blessed are you for ever!
May all created things praise you, O God,
For loving us so much that we can truthfully speak
of your fellowship with mankind, even in this earthly exile;
and however virtuous we may be,
our virtue always depends on your great warmth
and generosity, dear Lord.
You bounty is infinite.
How wonderful are your works!
ST. TERESA OF AVILA

Yes, Lord Jesus Christ, whether we be far off or near, far away from you in the human swarm, in business, in earthly cares, in temporal joys, in merely human highness, or far from all this, forsaken, unappreciated in lowliness, and with this the nearer to you, do you draw us entirely to yourself.

~ SØREN KIERKEGAARD

When they heard this, they raised their voices together in prayer to God. "Sovereign Lord," they said, "you made the heaven and the earth and the sea, and everything in them."
ACTS 4:24

Words of Wisdom

Praise
&
Celebration

ॐ

The Lord is my strength and my song; he has become my salvation. He is my God, and I will praise him, my father's God, and I will exalt him. The Lord is a warrior; the Lord is his name.
EXODUS 15:2-3.

Praise God, from whom all blessings flow!
Praise Him, all creatures here below!
Praise Him above, ye heavenly host!
Praise Father, Son, and Holy Ghost!
T. KEN

"Listen, O heavens, and I will speak; hear, O earth, the words of my mouth Let my teaching fall like rain and my words descend like dew, like showers on new grass, like abundant rain on tender plants. I will proclaim the name of the Lord. Oh, praise the greatness of our God! He is the Rock, his works are perfect, and all his ways are just. A faithful God who does no wrong, upright and just is he."
DEUTERONOMY 32:1-4

You are wisdom, uncreated and eternal,
the supreme first cause, above all being,
sovereign Godhead, sovereign goodness,
watching unseen the God-inspired wisdom of Christian people.
Raise us, we pray, that we may totally respond
to the supreme, unknown, ultimate, and splendid height
of your words, mysterious and inspired.
There all God's secret matters lie covered and hidden
under darkness both profound and brilliant, silent and wise.
ST. DENIS

The Lord is my rock, my fortress and my deliverer; my God is my rock, in whom I take refuge, my shield and the horn of my salvation. He is my stronghold, my refuge and my savior—from violent men you save me. I call to the Lord, who is worthy of praise, and I am saved from my enemies.
2 SAMUEL 32:2-4.

Lord of the world, He reigned alone
While yet the universe was naught.
When by His will all things were wrought,
Then first His sovereign Name was known.

And when the All shall cease to be,
In dread lone splendor He shall reign,
He was, He is, He shall remain
In glorious eternity.
SOLOMON IBN-GABIROL

ॐ

How happy will be our shout of Alleluia, how carefree, how secure from any adversary, where there is no enemy, where no friend perishes. There praise is offered to God, and here, too, but here it is by men who are anxious, there by men who are free from care here by men who must die, there by men who will forever. Here praise is offered in hope, there by men who enjoy the reality, here by men who are pilgrims on the way, there by men who have reached their own country.

So, brethren, now let us sing Alleluia, not in the enjoyment of heavenly rest, but to sweeten our toil. Sing as travelers sing along the road: but keep on walking. Solace your toil by singing—do not yield to idleness. Sing by keep on walking. What do I mean by "walking"? I mean, press on from good to better. The apostle says there are some who go from bad to worse. But if you press on, you keep on walking. Go forward then in virtue, in true faith and right conduct. Sing up—and keep on walking.

~ ST. AUGUSTINE OF HIPPO

Life in my body pulsates only for Thee,
My heart beats in resignation to Thy will.
If on my dust a tuft of grass were to grow
Every blade would tremble with my devotion for Thee!
ANSARI

Receive my prayers, O Lord my God, and my desires of giving Thee infinite praise and unbounded benediction, which, according to the multitude of Thine unspeakable greatness, are most justly due Thee. These do I give Thee, and desire to give every day and very moment; and with beseechings affectionate desires I call upon all celestial spirits and all Thy faithful people to join with me in rendering Thee thanks and praises.

Let all peoples, nations, and tongues praise Thee, and magnify Thy holy and sweet-sounding Name, with highest jubilations and ardent devotion. And let all who reverently and devoutly celebrate Thymost high Sacrament, and receive it with full assurance of faith, be accounted worthy to find grace and with Thee.

~ THOMAS A. KEMPIS

The Lord lives! Praise be to my Rock! Exalted be God, the Rock, my Savior! He is the God who avenges me, who puts the nations under me, who sets me free from my enemies. You exalted me above my foes; from violent men you rescued me. Therefore I will praise you, O Lord, among the nations; I will sing praises to your name.
2 SAMUEL 22:47-50.

When I behold Thy Peerless face, beaming with love, O Lord,
What fear have I of earthly woe or of the frown of sorrow?
As the first ray of the dawning sun dispels the dark,
So too, Lord, when Thy blessed light bursts forth within the heart,
It too scatters all our grief and pain with sweetest balm.
When on Thy love and grace I ponder, in my heart's deepest depths,

ⓢ

Tears of joy stream down my cheeks beyond restraining.
Hail, Gracious Lord! Hail, Gracious One! I shall proclaim Thy love.
May me life-breath depart from me as I perform Thy works!
ANONYMOUS

God is especially present in the hearts of His people, by His Holy Spirit;
and indeed the hearts of holy men are temples in the truth of things, and
in type and shadow they are heaven itself. For God reigns in thehearts of
His servants; there is His Kingdom. The power of grace hath subdued all
His enemies; there is His power. They serve Him night and day, and give
Him thanks and praise; that is His glory. This is the religion and worship
of God in the temple.

~ JEREMY TAYLOR

Sing to the Lord, all the earth; proclaim his salvation day after day.
Declare his glory among the nations, his marvelous deeds among all peo-
ples. For great is the Lord and most worthy of praise; he is to be feared
above all gods.
1 CHRONICLES 16:23-25

From God above
Being sent, the Heavens me enflame:
To praise his Name
The stars do move!
The burning sun doth shew His love.
T. TRAHERNE

I give thanks to my God tirelessly, who kept me faithful in the day of trial,
so that today I offer sacrifice to him confidently, the living sacrifice of my
life to Christ, my Lord, who preserved me in all my troubles. I can say
therefore: Who am I, Lord, and what is my calling that you should cooper-
ate with me with such divine power? Today, among heathen peoples, I
praise and proclaim your name in all places, not only when things go well
but also in times of stress. Whether I receive good or ill, I return thanks
equally to God, who taught me always to trust him unreservedly. His
answer to my prayer inspired me in these latter days to undertake this
holy and wonderful work in spite of my ignorance, and to imitate in some
way those who, as the Lord foretold, would preach in his Good News as a
witness to all nations before the end of the world.

~ ST. PATRICK

I will praise you, O Lord, with all my heart;
I will tell of all your wonders. I will be glad and rejoice in you;
I will sing praise to your name, O Most High.
PSALMS 9:1-2.

꩜

The prayers I make will then be sweet indeed,
If Thou the spirit give by which I pray;
My unassisted heart is barren clay,
That of its native self can nothing feed;
Of good and pious works Thou art the seed
That quickens only where Thou say'st it may,
No man can find it: Father! Thou must lead;
Do Thou then breathe those thoughts into my mind
By which such virtue may in me be bred
That in Thy holy footsteps I may tread;
The fetters may have the power to sing to Thee,
And sound Thy praises everlastingly!

MICHELANGELO

Because the divine goodness could not be adequately represented by one creature alone, God produced many and diverse creatures, that what was wanting in one in the representation of the divine goodness might be supplied by another. For goodness, which in God is simple and uniform, in creatures is manifold and divided. Thus the whole universe together participates in the divine goodness more perfectly and represents it better than any single creature.

~ ST. THOMAS AQUINAS

Sing joyfully to the Lord, you righteous; it is fitting for the upright to praise him. Praise the Lord with the harp; make music to him on the ten-stringed lyre. Sing to him a new song; play skillfully, and shout for joy.

1 PSALMS 33:1-3

See, this kingdom of God is now found within us. The grace of the Holy Spirit shines forth and warms us, and, overflowing with many and varied scents into the air around us, regales our senses with heavenly delight, as it fills our hearts with joy inexpressible.

~ ST. SERAPHIM OF SAROV

Lord, when the sense of thy sweet grace
Send up my soul to seek thy face.
Thy blessed eyes breed such desire,
I die in love's delicious Fire.
O love, I am thy Sacrifice.
Be till triumphant, blessed eyes.
Still shine on me, fair suns! that I
Still may behold, though still I die.

R. CRASHAW

I will exalt you, O Lord for you lifted me out of the depths and did not let my enemies gloat over me. O Lord my God, I called to you for help and you healed me. O Lord, you brought me up from the grave; you spared me

꩜

from going down into the pit.
Sing to the Lord, you saints of his; praise his holy name.

PSALMS 30:1-4

From heaven my strains begin; from heaven descends
The flame of genius to the human breast,
And love, and beauty, and poetic joy,
And inspiration.

M. AKENSIDE

Even as bright and shining bodies, once touched by a ray of light falling on them, become even more glorious and themselves case another light, so too souls that carry the Spirit, and are enlightened by the Spirit, become spiritual themselves and send forth grace upon others.

This grace enables them to foresee the future, to understand mysteries, to grasp hidden things, to receive spiritual blessings, to have their thoughts fixed on heavenly things, and to dance with the angels. So is their joy unending, so is their perseverance in God unfailing, so do they acquire likeness to God, so—most sublime of all—do they themselves become divine.

~ ST. BASIL THE GREAT

Those who know your name will trust in you, for you, Lord,
have never forsaken those who seek you.

PSALMS 9:10

Thou, so far, we grope to grasp thee—
Thou, so near, we cannot clasp thee—
Thou, so wise, our prayers grow heedless—
Thou, so loving, they are needless!
In each human soul thou shinest,
Human-best is thy divinest,
In each deed of love thou warmest;
Evil into good transformest.
Soul of all, and moving centre
Of each moment's life we enter.
Breath of breathing—light of gladness—
Infinite antidote of sadness;—
All-preserving ether flowing
Through the worlds, yet past our knowing.
Never past our trust and loving,
Nor from thine our life removing.

C. P. CRANCH

৯

The world is charged with the grandeur of God.
It will flame out, like shining from shook foil;
It gathers to a greatness, like the ooze of oil
Crushed. Why do men then now not wreck his rod?
Generations have trod, have trod, have trod,
And all is seared with trade; bleared, smeared with toil;
And wears man's smudge and shares man's smell: the soil
Is bare now, nor can foot feel being shod.
And for all this, nature is never spent;
There lives the dearest freshness deep down things;
And though the last lights off the black West went
Oh, morning, at the brown brink eastward, springs—
Because the Holy Ghost over the bent
World broods with warm breast and with ah! bright wings.
GERARD MANLEY HOPKINS

The cross is called the glory of Christ, and his exaltation; it is the chalice for which he longed, the consummation of his sufferings on our behalf. It is the glory of Christ—listen to his words: "Now is the Son of man glorified, and God is glorified in him, and God will glorifyhim at once." And again: "Glorify me, Father, with the glory that I had with you before the world was made." And again: "Father, glorify your name." So there came a voice from the heavens: "I have glorified it, and I will glorify it again." By this he means the glory that Christ received on the cross. The cross is also Christ's exaltation—listen again to his own words: "When I am lifted up, I will draw all men to myself." You see then that the cross is the glory and the exaltation of Christ.

~ ST. ANDREW OF CRETE

In the same way, let your light shine before men, that they may see your good deeds and praise your Father in heaven.
MATTHEW 5:16

Come down, O love divine,
Seek thou this soul of mine,
And visit it with thine own ardor glowing;
O Comforter draw near,
Within my heart appear,
And kindle it, thy holy flame bestowing.
BIANCO DA SIENA

May the God who gives endurance and encouragement give you a spirit of unity among yourselves as you follow Christ Jesus, so that with one heart and mouth you may glorify the God and Father of our Lord Jesus Christ. Accept one another, then, just as Christ accepted you, in order to bring praise to God.
ROMANS 15:5-7

૭

O for a thousand tongues to sing
Glory to God, and praise and love
be ever, ever given,
by saints below and saints above,
the church in earth and heaven.

On this glad day the glorious Sun
of Righteousness arose;
on my benighted soul he shone
and filled it with repose.

O for a thousand tongues to sing
my great Redeemer's praise!
The glories of my God and King,
the triumphs of his grace.

My gracious Master and my God,
assist me to proclaim,
to spread through all the earth abroad
the honors of thy name.
CHARLES WESLEY

The great thing, and the only thing, is to adore and praise God.

~ THOMAS MERTON

Grace and peace to you from God our Father and the Lord Jesus Christ. Praise be to the God and Father of our Lord Jesus Christ, who has blessed us in the heavenly realms with every spiritual blessing in Christ. For he chose us in him before the creation of the world to be holy and blameless in his sight.
EPHESIANS 1:2-4

To the Trinity be praise!
God is music, God is life
that nurtures every creature in its kind.
Our God is the song of the angel throng
and the splendor of the secret ways
hid from all humankind,
But God our life is the life of all.
ST. HILDEGARD OF BINGEN

The most devout king David danced with all his might before the Ark of God, calling to mind the benefits granted to his forefathers in days past; he fashioned musical instruments of various sorts, put forth Psalms, and appointed them to be sung with joy, played also himself ofttimes on the harp, being inspired with the grace of the Holy Ghost; he taught the people of Israel to praise God with the whole heart, and with unity of voice to bless and praise Him every day. If so great devotion was then exercised, and celebration of divine praise was carried on before the Ark of the

૨

Testimony, how great reverence and devotion ought now to be shown by me and all Christian people at the ministering of the Sacrament, at receiving the most precious Body and Blood of Christ.

~ THOMAS A. KEMPIS

What pleasure were to walk and see,
Endlong a river clear,
The perfect form of every tree
Within the deep appear.
O then it were a seemly thing,
While all is still and calm,
The praise of God to play and sing
With cornet and with shalm!
All labourers draw home at even,
And can to other say,
Thanks to the gracious God of heaven,
Which sent this summer day.
ALEXANDER HUME

I will praise you, O Lord, with all my heart; I will tell of all your wonders. I will be glad and rejoice in you; I will sing praise to your name, O Most High. The Lord is a refuge for the oppressed, a stronghold in times of trouble. Those who know your name will trust in you, for you, Lord, have never forsaken those who seek you.
PSALMS 9:1-2, 9-10

Joy to the world! the Lord is come:
Let earth receive her King;
Let every heart prepare Him room,
And heaven and nature sing.

Joy to the world! The Savior reigns:
Let men their songs employ,
While fields and floods, rocks, hills, and plains,
Repeat the sounding joy.

No more let sins and sorrow grow,
Nor thorns infest the ground;
He comes to make His blessings flow
Far as the curse is found.

He rules the world with turth and grace,
And makes the nations prove
The glories of His righteousness,
And wonders of His love.
ISAAC WATTS

ʕ

Meet every rising sun with such sentiments of God's goodness, as if you had seen it, and all things, new-created upon your account: and under the sense of so great a blessing, let your joyful heart praise and magnify so good and glorious a Creator.

~ WILLIAM LAW

But let all those rejoice who put their trust in You; let them ever shout for joy, because You defend them; let those also who love Your name be joyful in You.

PSALMS 5:11

Still creating, still inspiring,
Never of thy creatures tiring;
Artist of thy solar spaces;
And thy humblehuman face;
Mighty glooms and splendors voicing;
In thy plastic work rejoicing;
Through benignant law connecting
Best with best—and all perfecting,
Though all human races claim to thee,
Thought and language fail to name thee,
Mortal lips be dumb before thee,
Silence only may adore thee!

CHRISTOPHER PEARSE CRANCH

I will give thanks to the Lord because of his righteousness and will sing praise to the name of the Lord Most High.

PSALMS 7:17

Of all great Nature's tones that sweep
Earth's resonant bosom, far or near,
Low-breathed or loudest, shrill or deep,
How few are grasped by mortal ear.

Ten octaves close our scale of sound:
Its myriad grades, distinct or twined,
Transcend our hearing's petty bound,
To us as colors to the blind.

AUBREY DE VERE

Great is the Lord and most worthy of praise; his greatness no one can fathom. One generation will commend your works to another; they will tell of your mighty acts. They will speak of the glorious splendor of your majesty, and I will meditate on your wonderful works. They will tell of the power of your awesome works, and I will proclaim your great deeds. They will celebrate your abundant goodness and joyfully sing of your righteousness. The Lord is gracious and compassionate, slow to anger and rich in love.

ॐ

The Lord is good to all; he has compassion on all he has made. All you have made will praise you, O Lord; your saints will extol you.
PSALMS 145:3-10

The Holy Spirit is life that gives, life,
Moving in all things.
It is the root in every creature
And purifies things,
Wiping away sins,
Anointing wounds.
It is radiant life, worthy of praise,
Awakening and enlivening
All things.
ST HILDEGARD OF BINGEN

What is Christ's joy in us, but that He deigns to rejoice on our account? And what is our Joy, which He says shall be full, but to have fellowship with Him? He had perfect joy on our account, when He rejoiced in foreknowing and redestinating us; but that joy was not in us, because we did not then exist; it began to be in us, when He called us. And this joy we rightly call our own, this joy wherewith we shall be blessed; which is begun in the faith of them who are born again, and shall be fulfilled in the reward of them who rise again.

~ ST. AUGUSTINE.

O Lord, you are my God; I will exalt you and praise your name, for in perfect faithfulness you have done marvelous things,
things planned long ago.
ISAIAH 25:1

No coward soul is mine,
No trembler in the world's storm-troubled sphere:
I see heaven's glories shine,
And faith shines equal, arming me from fear.

O God within my breast,
Almighty, ever-present Deity!
Life—that in me has rest,
As I—undying Life—have power in Thee!
EMILY BRONTE

Most High, all-powerful, good Lord, yours are the praises, the glory, the honor and all blessing. To You alone, Most High, do they belong, and no man is worthy to mention Your name. Praised be You, my Lord, with all your creatures, especially Sir Brother Sun, Who is the day and through whom You give us light. And he is beautiful and radiant with great splendor; and bears a likeness of You, Most High One. Praised be You, my Lord,

৩

through Sister Moon and the stars, in heaven You formed them clear and precious and beautiful. Praised be You, my Lord, through Brother Wind, and through the air, cloudy and serene, and every kind of weather through which You give sustenance to Your creatures.

~ ST. FRANCES OF ASSISI

Praise him in his Temple and in the heavens he made with mighty power. Praise him for his mighty work. Praise his unequaled greatness. Praise him with the trumpet and with lute and harp. Praise him with the drums and dancing. Praise him with the cymbals, yes, loud clanging cymbals. Let everything alive give praises to the Lord! You praise him! Hallelujah!

PSALMS 150

He who is in you and outside you,
Who works through all hands,
Who walks on all feet,
Whose body are all ye,
Him worship, and break all other idols!
He who is at once the high and low,
The sinner and the saint,
Both God and worm,
Him worship—visible, knowable, real, omnipresent,
Break all other idols!
In whom is neither past life
Nor future birth nor death,
In whom we always have been
And always shall be one,
Him worship. Break all other idols!

VIVEKANADA

Now the great thing is this: we are consecrated and dedicated to God in order that we may thereafter think, speak, meditate, and do, nothing except to his glory. For a sacred thing may not be applied to profane uses without marked injury to him

~ JOHN CALVIN

Glory to God in the highest,
And on earth peace, goodwill towards men!

Then, as He was now drawing near the descent of the Mount of Olives, the whole multitude of the disciples began to rejoice and praise God with a loud voice for all the mighty works they had seen, saying.

Blessed is the King who comes in the name of the Lord!
Peace in heaven and glory in the highest!

LUKE 2:8-9, 13-14; 19:37-38

෧

GOD is the One everlasting,
perpetual, eternal, unending.
From endless time hath He been,
and shall be henceforth and for ever.
GOD is hidden,
and no man His form hath perceived nor His likeness.
Unknown of gods and of men,
mysterious, incomprehensible.
GOD is Truth,
and on truth doth He live;
King of truth divine is He.
GOD is life;
and man liven through Him,
the Primeval Alone.
PRE-4TH CENTURY EGYPTIAN

Make an effort, then, to meet more frequently to celebrate God's Eucharist and to offer praise. For, when you meet frequently in the same place, the forces of Satan are overthrown, and his baneful influence is neutralized by the unanimity of your faith.

~ ST. IGNATIUS

Though you have not seen him, you love him; and even though you do not
see him now, you believe in him and are filled with an inexpressible and
glorious joy, for you are receiving the goal of your faith,
the salvation of your souls.
1 PETER 1:8-9

You make what is ultimate and beyond brightness
secretly to shine in all that is most dark.
In your way, ever unseen and intangible,
you fill to the full with most beautiful splendor
those souls who close their eyes that they may see.
And I, please, with love that goes on beyond mind
to all that is beyond mind,
seek to gain such for myself through this prayer.
ST. DENIS

O Lord, thou greatest and most true light, whence this light of the day and of the sun doth spring! O Light, which does lighten every man that cometh into the world! O Light, which knowest no night nor evening, but art always a mid-day most clear and fair, without whom all is most dark darkness, by whom all be most resplendent! O thou Wisdom of the eternal "Father of mercies"! lighten my mind that so soon as you behold the daylight pray: that I may only see those things that please thee, and may be blinded to all other things. Grant that I may walk in thy ways, and that nothing else may be light and pleasant unto me. Lighten mine eyes, O Lord, that I sleep not in death . . .

~ JOHN BRADFORD

ॐ

*I wash my hands in innocence, and go about your altar,
O Lord, proclaiming aloud your praise and telling of
all your wonderful deeds. I love the house where you live,
O Lord, the place where your glory dwells.*

PSALM 26:6-8

---

*The soul that sees him or receives sublimed
New faculties, or learns at least to employ
More worthily the powers she owned before;
Discerns in all things what, with stupid gaze
Of ignorance, till then she overlooked,
A ray of heavenly light, gilding all forms
Terrestrial in the vast and the minute—
The unambiguous footsteps of the God
Who gives its lustre to an insect's wing,
And wheels his throne upon the rolling worlds.*

WILLIAM COWPER

---

*My heart is steadfast, O God, my heart is steadfast;
I will sing andmake music. Awake, my soul!
Awake, harp and lyre! I will awaken the dawn.
I will praise you, O Lord, among the nations;
I will sing of you among the peoples.
For great is your love, reaching to the heavens;
your faithfulness reaches to the skies.
Be exalted, O God, above the heavens;
let your glory be over all the earth.*

PSALMS 57:7-11

---

*That we should make the skies
More glorious far before Thine eyes
Than Thou didst make them, and even Thee
Far more Thy works to prize,
As used they be
Than as they're made, is a stupendous work,
Wherein Thy wisdom mightily doth lurk.*

*Thy greatness, and Thy love,
Thy power, in this, my joy doth move;
Thy goodness, and felicity
In this expressed above
All praise I see:
While Thy great Godhead over all doth reign,
And such an end in such a sort attain.*

THOMAS TRAHERNE

༅

O gracious light, pure brightness of the everliving Father in heaven,
O Jesus Christ, holy and blessed! Now as we come to the setting of the
sun, and our eyes behold the vesper light, we sing your praised, O God:
Father, Son, and Holy Spirit. You are worthy at all times to be praised by
happy voices, O Son of God, O Giver of Life, and to be glorified through
all the worlds

~ THE BOOK OF COMMON PRAYER

Ah, have you seen Aoranghi rise,
His white cloud-robes unrolled,
And lift his prayer to sapphire skies
Gleamed through with pearl and gold,
And Tasman's river, strong and fleet,
Through timeless nights and days,
Chanting for ever at his feet
The thunder of his praise?
Oh, in the splendour and the light,
The strength, the grace, the gleam,
Heaven's gate seems lifting clear in sight,
And God's face not a dream

J. LAURENCE RENTOUL

Blessed are you, O Lord, the God of our fathers, creator of the changes
of day and night, giving rest to the weary, renewing the strength of those
who are spent, bestowing upon us occasions of song in the evening. As
you have protected us in the day that is past, so be with us in the coming
night; keep us from every sin, every evil, and every fear; for you are our
light and salvation, and the strength of our life. To you be glory for endless
ages. Amen.

~ THE BOOK OF COMMON PRAYER

Sing for joy, O heavens, for the Lord has done this;
shout aloud, O earth beneath. Burst into song, you mountains,
you forests and all your trees
ISAIAH 44:23

Acquaint thyself with God, if thou wouldst taste
His works. Admitted once to his embrace,
Thou shalt perceive that thou wast blind before:
Thine eye shall be instucted; and thine heart
Made pure shall relish, with divine delight,
Till then unfelt, what hands divine have wrought. . . .
The soul that sees him or receives sublimed
New faculties, or learns at least to employ
More worthily the powers she owned before;
Discerns in all things what, with stupid gaze
Of ignorance, till then she overlooked,
A ray of heavenly light, gilding all forms
Terrestrial in the vast and the minute—

꒱

The unambiguous footsteps of the God
Who gives its lustre to an insect's wing,
And wheels his throne upon the rolling worlds.
WILLIAM COWPER

Holy spirit, life that gives life,
moving all things,
rooted in all beings;
you cleanse all things of impurity,
wiping away sins,
and anointing wounds,
this is radiant, laudable life,
awakening and re-awakening
every thing.
HILDEGARD OF BINGEN

For the kingdom of God is not a matter of eating and drinking, but of
righteousness, peace and joy in the Holy Spirit.
ROMANS 14:17

Great God, within whose simple essence we
Nothing but that which is thyself can find;
When on thyself thou didst reflect thy mind,
Thy thought was God, and took the form of thee:
And when this God, thus born, thou lov'st, and he
Loved thee again, with passion of like kind
(As lovers sighs which meet become one wind),
Both breathed one sprite of equal deity,
Eternal Father, whence these two do come
And with the title of my father have,
And heavenly knowledge in my mind engrave,
That it thy son's true Image may become:
And cleanse my heart with sighs of holy love,
That it the temple of the Sprite may prove.
HENRY CONSTABLE

Receive my prayers, O Lord my God, and my desires of giving Thee infinite praise and unbounded benediction, which, according to the multitude of Thine unspeakable greatness, are most justly due unto. These do I give Thee, and desire to give every day and very moment; and with beseechings and affectionate desires I call upon all celestial spirits and all Thy faithful people to join with me in rendering Thee thanks and praises.

~ THOMAS A. KEMPIS

My mouth will speak in praise of the Lord.
Let every creature praise his holy name for ever and ever.
PSALMS 145:21

ॐ

Make me, O Lord, thy Spinning Wheel complete,
Thy Holy Word my Distaff make for me,
Make mine Affections thy Swift Flyers neat
And make my Soul thy holy Spool to be.
My Conversation make to be thy Reel
And reel the yarn thereon spun of they Wheel.

Make me thy Loome then, knit therein this Twine:
And make the Holy Spirit, Lord, wind quills:
Then weave the Web theyself. The yarn is fine.
Thine Ordinances make my Fulling Mills.
Then mine apparel shall display before ye
That I am Cloathed in Holy robes for glory.

EDWARD TAYLOR

Through Jesus, therefore, let us continually offer to God a sacrifice of praise—the fruit of lips that confess his name.
HEBREWS 13:14

Proclaim the Glory of God's name as long as life remains in you;
The dazzling splendour of His radiance floods the universe!
Like nectar streams His boundless love, filling the hearts of men with joy:
The very thought of His compassion sends a thrill through every limb!
How can one fittingly describe Him? Through His abounding grace The bit-
ter sorrows of this life are all forgotten instantly. On every side—on land
below, in sky above, beneath the seas: In every region of this earth—men
seek Him tirelessly, And as they seek Him, ever ask: Where is His limit,
where His end? True Wisdom's Dwelling-place is He, the Elixir of Eternal
Life, The Sleepless, Every-wakeful Eye, the Pure and Stainless One:
The vision of His face removes all trace of sorrow from our hearts.

RAMAKRISHNA

Because there is no other God, nor ever was, nor will be, than God the Father unbegotten, without beginning, from whom is all beginning, the Lord of the universe, as we have been taught; and His son Jesus Christ, whom we declare to have always been with the Father, spiritually and inef- fably begotten by the Father before the beginning of the world, before all beginning; and by Him are made all things visible and invisible. He was made man, and, having defeated death, was received into heaven by the Father; and He hath given Him all power over all names in heaven, on earth, and under the earth, and every tongue shall confess to Him that Jesus Christ is Lord and God, in whom we believe, and whose advent we expect soon to be, judge of the living and of the dead, who will render to every man according to his deeds; and He has poured forth upon us abun- dantly the Holy Spirit, the gift and pledge of immortality, who makes those who believe and obey sons of God and joint heirs with Christ; and Him do we confess and adore, one God in the Trinity of the Holy Name.

~ ST. PATRICK

Index

Index